S M I T H S O N I A N

The New
Children's
Encyclopedia

Packed with thousands of facts, stats, and illustrations

    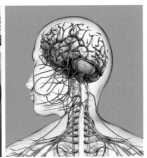

FOURTH EDITION

DK DELHI
Senior editor Sreshtha Bhattacharya
Project art editor Mansi Agrawal **Picture researcher** Rituraj Singh
Managing editor Kingshuk Ghoshal **Managing art editor** Govind Mittal
Senior DTP designer Shanker Prasad **DTP designers** Ashok Kumar, Rakesh Kumar
Jacket designer Vidushi Chaudhry **Senior Jackets coordinator** Priyanka Sharma Saddi

DK LONDON
Senior art editor Jacqui Swan
US editor Heather Wilcox
US executive editor Lori Cates Hand
Managing editor Rachel Fox
Managing art editor Owen Peyton Jones
Production editor Jacqueline Street-Elkayam
Senior production controller Meskerem Berhane
Jacket design development manager Sophia MTT
Publisher Andrew Macintyre
Associate publishing director Liz Wheeler
Art director Karen Self
Publishing director Jonathan Metcalf

Consultants Dr. Jacqueline Mitton, Dr. Douglas Palmer, Philip Parker,
Dr. Kristina Routh, Chris Woodford, John Woodward
Authenticity reader Chimaoge Itabor
Fact checkers Michelle Harris, Steve Hoffman, Priyanka Lamichhane

FIRST EDITION
Senior editors Carrie Love, Caroline Stamps, Deborah Lock, Ben Morgan
Senior designers Rachael Smith, Tory Gordon-Harris
Editors Fleur Star, Joe Harris, Wendy Horobin, Lorrie Mack
Designers Clemence Monot, Mary Sandberg, Sadie Thomas, Lauren Rosier,
Gemma Fletcher, Sonia Moore
Packaging services supplied by **Bookwork**

Publishing manager Bridget Giles **Art director** Rachael Foster
Production controller Claire Pearson **Production editor** Siu Chan
Jacket designer Natalie Godwin **Jacket editor** Mariza O'Keeffe
Picture researcher Liz Moore

This American Edition, 2022
First American Edition, 2009
Published in the United States by DK Publishing
1745 Broadway, 20th Floor, New York, NY 10019

Copyright © 2009, 2013, 2019, 2022 Dorling Kindersley Limited
DK, a Division of Penguin Random House LLC
22 23 24 25 26 10 9 8 7 6 5 4 3 2
003–324986–Nov/2022

A catalog record for this book is available from the Library of Congress.
ISBN 978-0-7440-5621-1 (Paperback)
ISBN 978-0-7440-5622-8 (Hardcover)

DK books are available at special discounts when purchased in bulk
for sales promotions, premiums, fund-raising, or educational use.
For details, contact: DK Publishing Special Markets,
1745 Broadway, 20th Floor, New York, NY 10019
SpecialSales@dk.com

Printed and bound in UAE

For the curious
www.dk.com

Smithsonian

Established in 1846, the Smithsonian is the world's largest museum and research
complex, dedicated to public education, national service, and scholarship in the arts,
sciences, and history. It includes 21 museums and galleries and the National
Zoological Park. The total number of artifacts, works of art, and specimens in the
Smithsonian's collection is estimated at 155.5 million.

MIX
Paper | Supporting
responsible forestry
FSC™ C018179

This book was made with Forest Stewardship
Council™ certified paper – one small step
in DK's commitment to a sustainable future.
For more information go to
www.dk.com/our-green-pledge

Contents

Introduction

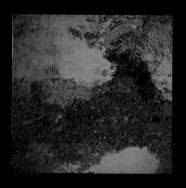 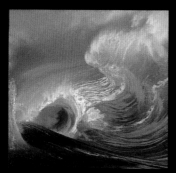  

Every child needs a book that answers their questions about the world: how it was made, what makes plants grow, why the sun shines, how the human body works, what happened in the past, and why other countries are different than their own. Properly stimulated, this early thirst for knowledge can become a lifelong process of discovery and understanding. This encyclopedia aims to encourage young readers to make these discoveries for themselves by presenting clear and concise information in an exciting visual manner that draws them in and entices them to read on.

This brand-new *Children's Encyclopedia* is divided into thematic chapters. All the major topics are represented: space, earth science, the environment, animals and plants, countries of the world, culture, history, science and technology, and the human body. Stunning photographs and illustrations accompany the text, which is packed with fascinating facts, timelines, and special features. Cross references lead the reader to related topics that help cover the subject in more depth and from new angles. Unique features focus on items of special interest, such as an orchestra, time zones, or collections of bugs or minerals. With so much to look at and find out about, this book will prove to be a valuable reference that young readers will treasure for years to come.

(👁 pp110–111) When you see this symbol in the book, turn to the pages listed to find out more about a subject.

KEY TO SYMBOLS

The following symbols are used in this chapter:
Habitat The type of place where the animal is typically found in the wild.
Lifespan The average maximum age of the species in the wild, which might be different than specimens kept in captivity. A question mark is used when there are no data available.

Status These triangles show whether the animal is endangered, as listed on the IUCN Red List (👁 p85 for more information). A purple triangle shows there are not enough data to assess the animal.

 See how large (or small) an animal is compared to an adult human.

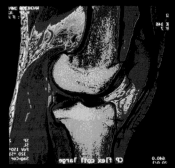

 Tropical forest and rainforest

 Temperate forest, including woodland

 Coniferous forest, including woodland

 Grassland habitats: moor, savanna, fields, scrubland

 Desert and semi-desert

 Seas and oceans

 Coastal areas, including beaches and cliffs

 Coral reefs and waters immediately around them

 Rivers, streams, and all flowing water

 Wetlands and still water: lakes, ponds, marshes, bogs, and swamps

 Polar regions and tundra

 Mountains, highlands, scree slopes

 Caves

 Urban

 Parasite

 Animal lifespan in the wild

 Animal not endangered

 Animal numbers are declining

 Animal endangered

 Animal status unknown

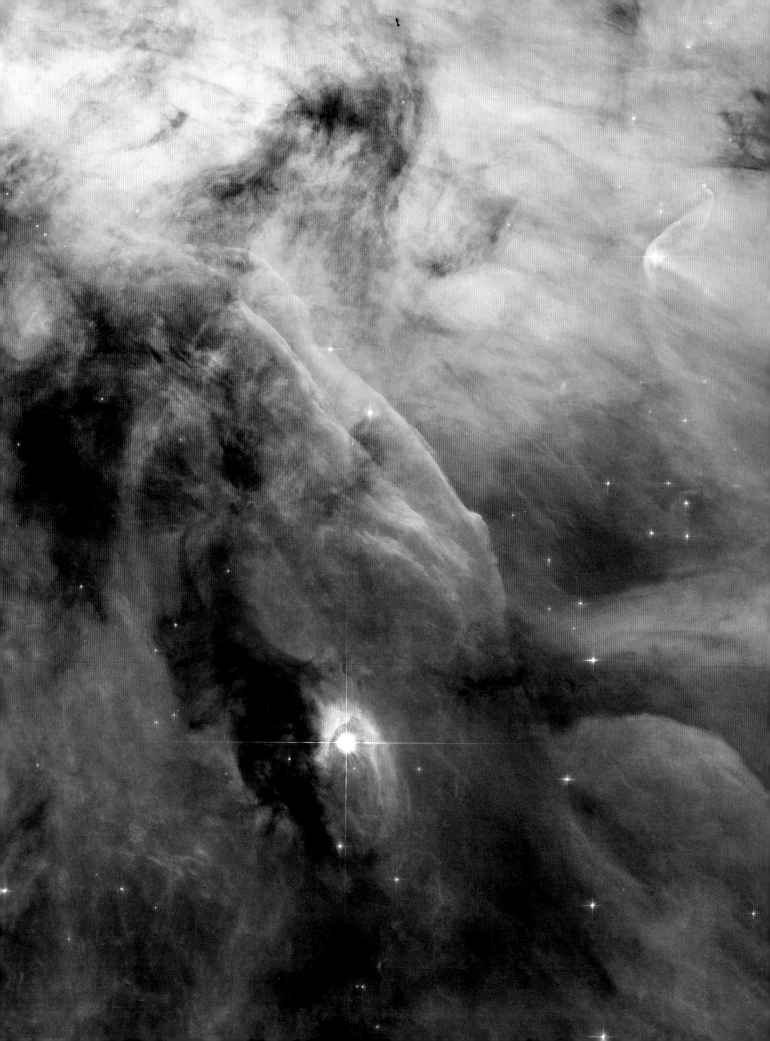

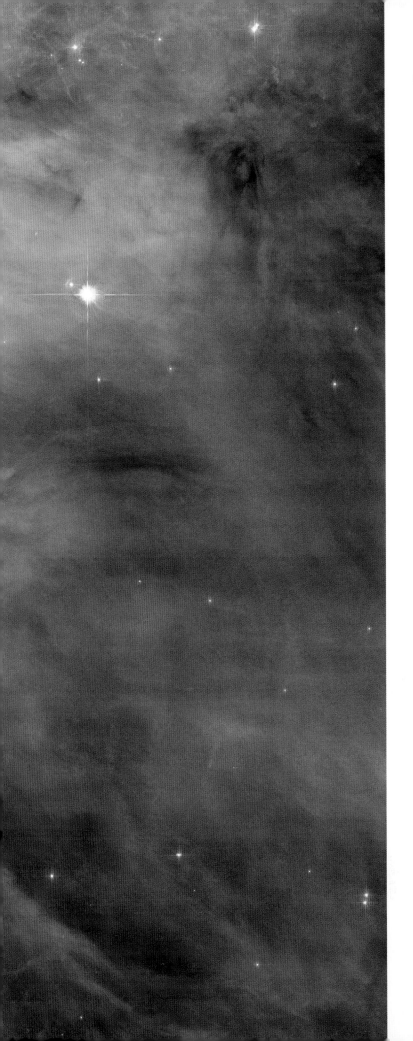

SPACE

Space is the universe beyond Earth's atmosphere—including planets, moons, stars, and galaxies. Since its beginning, space has been expanding outward continuously.

The Universe

The universe is unbelievably huge. It is everything we can touch, feel, sense, measure, or detect, and much that we cannot. It includes people, planets, stars, galaxies, dust clouds, light, and even time. Scientists believe our universe has existed for almost 14 billion years.

FACT
Across the visible universe, galaxies are found to be moving away from each other—sort of like spots on an inflating balloon. However, it is actually space that is expanding. The farther away from us galaxies are, the faster they seem to be moving.

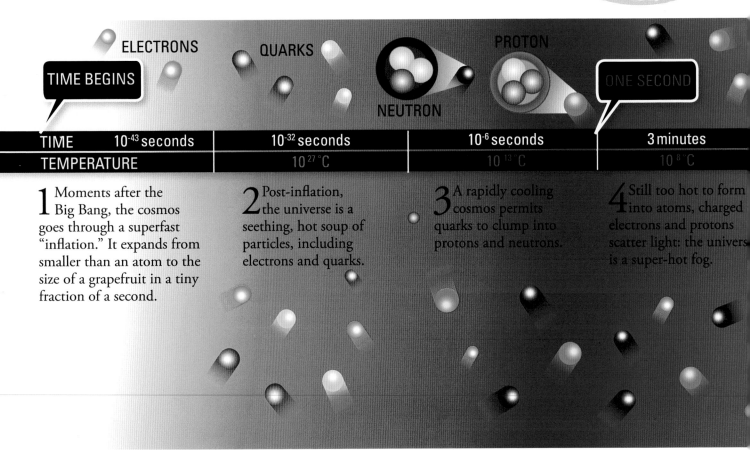

ELECTRONS   QUARKS   PROTON

TIME BEGINS

NEUTRON

ONE SECOND

TIME	10^{-43} seconds	10^{-32} seconds	10^{-6} seconds	3 minutes
TEMPERATURE		10^{27} °C	10^{13} °C	10^{8} °C

1 Moments after the Big Bang, the cosmos goes through a superfast "inflation." It expands from smaller than an atom to the size of a grapefruit in a tiny fraction of a second.

2 Post-inflation, the universe is a seething, hot soup of particles, including electrons and quarks.

3 A rapidly cooling cosmos permits quarks to clump into protons and neutrons.

4 Still too hot to form into atoms, charged electrons and protons scatter light: the universe is a super-hot fog.

FAST FACTS

- Light from distant galaxies has taken more than 12 billion years to arrive—so we see them as they were before Earth formed.
- There are more stars in the universe than there are grains of sand on all of Earth's beaches.
- In its first second, the universe grew from smaller than an atom to about 1,000 times the size of our solar system today.

Astronomers measure distance in light-years. One light-year is the distance light travels in one year. Light travels at 186,000 miles/second (300,000 km/second) in space. It takes a long time for light to reach us from distant stars and planets. Telescopes are like time machines, allowing us to see what things looked like in the past.

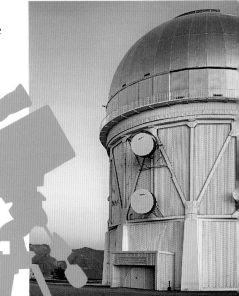

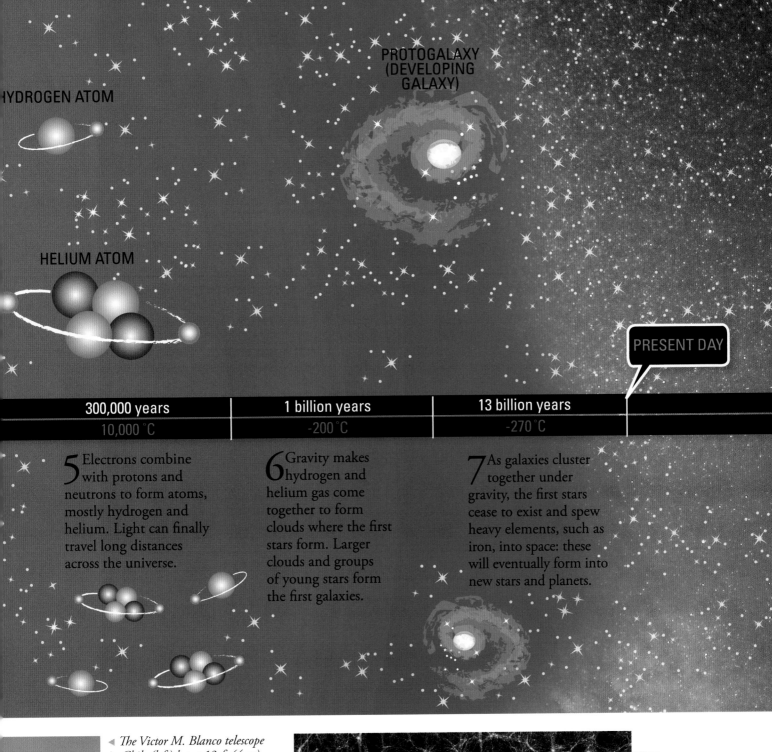

HYDROGEN ATOM

HELIUM ATOM

PROTOGALAXY
(DEVELOPING
GALAXY)

PRESENT DAY

300,000 years	1 billion years	13 billion years
10,000 °C	-200 °C	-270 °C

5 Electrons combine with protons and neutrons to form atoms, mostly hydrogen and helium. Light can finally travel long distances across the universe.

6 Gravity makes hydrogen and helium gas come together to form clouds where the first stars form. Larger clouds and groups of young stars form the first galaxies.

7 As galaxies cluster together under gravity, the first stars cease to exist and spew heavy elements, such as iron, into space: these will eventually form into new stars and planets.

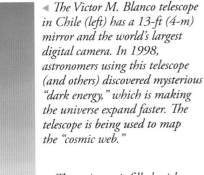

◄ *The Victor M. Blanco telescope in Chile (left) has a 13-ft (4-m) mirror and the world's largest digital camera. In 1998, astronomers using this telescope (and others) discovered mysterious "dark energy," which is making the universe expand faster. The telescope is being used to map the "cosmic web."*

► *The universe is filled with galaxies in clumps and strings, around vast bubbles of empty space. This "cosmic web" is held in place by the gravity of invisible "dark matter."*

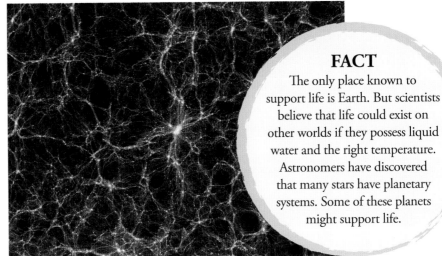

FACT
The only place known to support life is Earth. But scientists believe that life could exist on other worlds if they possess liquid water and the right temperature. Astronomers have discovered that many stars have planetary systems. Some of these planets might support life.

Galaxies

Scattered across the universe are billions of galaxies, each containing millions or even billions of stars. They come in many different shapes and sizes. Modern telescopes can now see very young galaxies that formed not long after the universe began.

SHAPES AND SIZES

Some galaxies are "elliptical" or almost round, like huge eggs. Some are spirals, with long, curved arms. Many small galaxies are "irregular," with no special shape. Small galaxies may contain a few million stars and measure less than 3,000 light=years across. The galactic supergiants contain billions of stars and are more than 1,000,000 light-years across.

GALAXY SHAPES

■ **Spiral galaxy** Spiral galaxies have long, curved arms. Young stars, pink nebulas, and dust are found in the arms.

■ **Barred spiral** In barred spirals, the spiral arms wind out from the ends of a central bar of stars that extends from the central bulge.

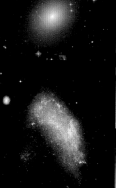

■ **Elliptical galaxy** These galaxies are oval and made up of older stars. Ellipticals range in size from the largest known giant galaxies down to small dwarfs.

■ **Irregular galaxy** Galaxies with no recognizable shape are irregular. Most are small with lots of young stars and bright nebulas.

◀ THE WHIRLPOOL GALAXY
This is a huge, well-defined spiral galaxy, 31 million light-years away. Its smaller satellite galaxy can be seen to the right. Its gravity has caused bursts of star formation in the Whirlpool Galaxy.

ANTENNAE GALAXIES *A well-known collision involves the two Antennae galaxies. They are 45 million light-years from Earth and were lit up by bursts of star formation as they collided.*

Colliding galaxies

Most galaxies are separated by vast distances, but sometimes galaxies collide. In fact, the very common elliptical galaxies are thought to have grown through collisions with other galaxies long ago. During collisions, the clouds of gas between the stars are forced together, triggering the formation of new stars. One of the best-known examples is the Antennae galaxies.

FACTFILE

▲ SATELLITE GALAXIES *Most large galaxies have smaller satellite galaxies orbiting them. The Andromeda Galaxy has many satellite galaxies—two appear as bright spots in this photo. Our own galaxy, the Milky Way, has several dozen.*

▲ GALAXY CLUSTER *Galaxies are held together in clusters by gravity. In dense clusters, galaxies often collide with each other.*

▲ BLACK HOLE *Most galaxies have supermassive black holes at their center. Their gravity is so strong that not even light can escape. We can see only the hot gas, dust, and stars being pulled in.*

Balls of gas

A star is a huge, glowing ball of hydrogen gas that shines because of nuclear reactions in its core that turn this fuel (hydrogen) into helium, releasing a lot of energy. The hottest stars last up to a few million years. Red dwarf stars are the coolest and last the longest.

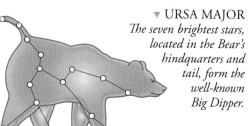
Ultraviolet light from the massive stars at the center of the nebula makes the gas cloud glow.

There are four young, massive stars at the centre of the Orion Nebula.

This image has been color-coded to show where there are different gases.

Center of the Orion Nebula
New stars are being formed in this cloud of glowing gas, which is around 15,000 light-years away.

STAR BIRCH

STAR BIRTH

GHOST HEAD NEBULA
An extremely hot, new star lights up the nearby gas and dust.

■ **Stars are born** inside giant clouds of dust and gas. Parts of these clouds collapse and as they shrink, the gas and, dust get hotter and form a star. When nuclear reactions begin in its core, radiation makes the surrounding material glow. Eventually, the surrounding dust clears away to reveal the star.

◄ *The Ghost Head Nebula is a star-forming region in the Large Magellanic Cloud, a satellite galaxy of the Milky Way (our own galaxy). The "eyes of the ghost" are two very hot, glowing blobs of gas that are heated by massive stars within them.*

The Sun

- **Diameter** 864,000 miles (1,390,000 km)
- **Mass (Earth=1)** 330,000
- **Core temperature** 27,000,000 °F (15,000,000 °C)
- **Average Distance from Earth** 93,000,000 miles (150,000,000 km)

The sun is our nearest star. Without the sun, Earth would be frozen and lifeless. The sun formed in a cloud of gas and dust about 4.6 billion years ago and has another 5 billion years to go.

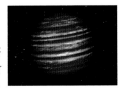
THE SUN

The sun is a yellow dwarf, a fairly ordinary star made mainly of hydrogen. Hydrogen is changed to helium at its center (the core). When this happens, huge amounts of radiation are released.

Huge plumes of hot gas sometimes stream away from the sun. They are called prominences.

STAR DEATH

- **Planetary nebulas** Small stars expand to become red giants. When they run out of fuel, they collapse. Their outer layers are puffed out in rings called planetary nebulas. Each star creates a different shape, such as a cat's eye (below), a butterfly, or a ring. The central star shrinks to a tiny, hot white dwarf.

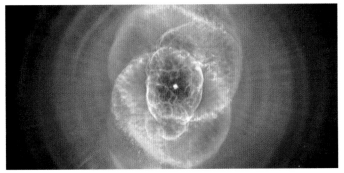

▲ *The Cat's Eye Nebula is made up of many gas clouds ejected by a dying star.*

Before

After

- **Supernovas** Larger stars collapse in a different way when they run out of fuel. Their outer layers explode into space in a supernova (right). These can briefly outshine an entire galaxy, but are rare events. The photograph on the left shows the same star 10 days before a supernova. Medium-sized stars become neutron stars. Massive stars create black holes.

The Solar System

The solar system is our local area of space. At its center is the sun, our nearest star, which accounts for almost all (99.9 percent) of the solar system's mass. The sun's gravity keeps the planets in their orbits.

MERCURY   EARTH

THE SUN   VENUS   MARS

DISTANCE FROM THE SUN

The red line to the right shows the distance of each planet from the sun in millions of miles. Mercury is closest and Neptune is farthest away. Earth is about 93 million miles (150 million kilometers) from the sun. (The planets are not shown to scale.)

All of the planets and asteroids go around the sun in near-circular orbits in the same direction (west to east).

SUN Mercury Venus Earth Mars

0   250

INNER PLANETS

The four planets closest to the sun are called the inner planets. They are also known as the rocky planets because they are balls of rock and metal. They are dense and have central cores made of iron.

LUNAR AND SOLAR ECLIPSES

In any calendar year, there are between four and seven eclipses, when Earth, the moon, and the sun line up. Solar eclipses are more common, but are seen only in a narrow area. Lunar eclipses can be seen anywhere on Earth where the moon is shining in the sky.

People at the center of the moon's shadow experience a total solar eclipse

The sun

The moon

SOLAR ECLIPSE   *Earth*

A "diamond ring effect" appears just before or just after an eclipse of the sun. During totality the sun's corona (atmosphere) can be seen around the moon.

■ A lunar eclipse happens when Earth passes between the sun and the moon, so that Earth casts a shadow on the moon.

■ A solar eclipse happens when the moon passes between Earth and the sun, casting a shadow on Earth. A total eclipse lasts for up to seven and a half minutes.

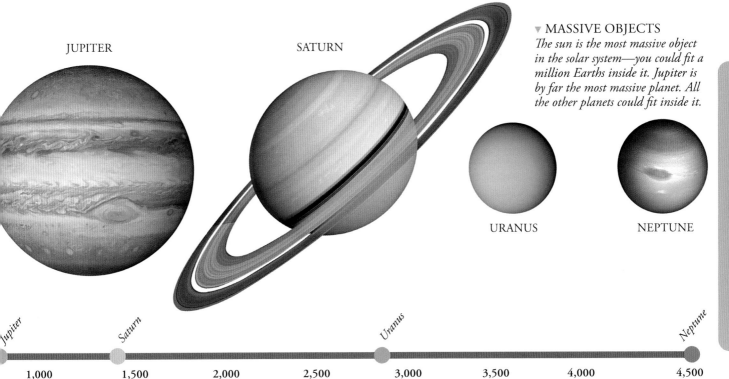

JUPITER

SATURN

▼ MASSIVE OBJECTS
The sun is the most massive object in the solar system—you could fit a million Earths inside it. Jupiter is by far the most massive planet. All the other planets could fit inside it.

URANUS

NEPTUNE

SPACE

Jupiter	Saturn			Uranus			Neptune
1,000	1,500	2,000	2,500	3,000	3,500	4,000	4,500

OUTER PLANETS

The four outer planets are huge balls of liquid surrounded by gas. Jupiter and Saturn, called gas giants, are mainly hydrogen and helium. Uranus and Neptune contain heavier materials, such as oxygen and carbon. They are called "ice" giants, although they are mostly hot liquid inside.

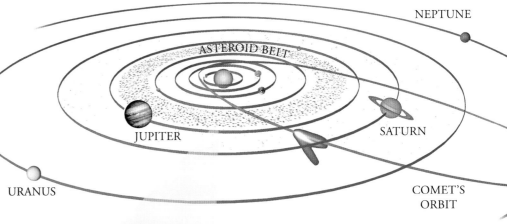

NEPTUNE

ASTEROID BELT

JUPITER

SATURN

URANUS

COMET'S ORBIT

FAST FACTS

■ Only five planets are visible to the naked eye. The first planet to be discovered using a telescope was Uranus, in 1781.
■ The planets formed in a huge cloud of gas and dust about 4.5 billion years ago.
■ About 4 billion years ago the sun was 25 percent dimmer than it is today.
■ Halley's comet orbits the sun in the opposite direction of the planets. It travels from beyond Neptune to inside the orbit of Venus as it circles the sun.
■ Excluding the sun, Jupiter and Saturn contain 90 percent of the solar system's mass.

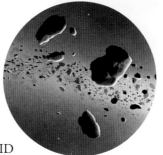

▶ ASTEROID BELT *Between Mars and Jupiter is the asteroid belt. It separates the inner planets from the outer planets. More than a million asteroids have been discovered, although most do not have names. They are thought to be rocks that never clumped together to form planets.*

ORBITING THE SUN

The solar system includes eight planets, at least five dwarf planets, at least 219 moons, and millions of comets and asteroids. These bodies are all orbiting the sun.

15

Mercury
Messenger of the Roman gods

- **Earth days to orbit sun** 88
- **Discovery date** Unknown (but known since ancient times)
- **Number of moons** 0
- **Location** First planet from the sun

The solar system's smallest planet, and the densest, temperatures on Mercury range from a freezing 279°F (−173°C) to a blistering 801°F (427°C). Unlike Earth, Mercury has no atmosphere, so the planet cannot retain heat.

Venus
Roman goddess of love

- **Earth days to orbit sun** 224.7
- **Discovery date** Unknown (but known since ancient times)
- **Number of moons** 0
- **Location** Second planet from the sun

Venus is almost the same size as Earth, but you wouldn't want to visit Venus. Its atmosphere is incredibly dense, and the temperature is so high you would be fried to a crisp. The planet is covered in acid clouds that trap heat.

Earth
Terra

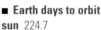

- **Earth days to orbit sun** 365.2
- **Number of moons** 1
- **Location** Third planet from the sun

Earth is the only planet known to support life. It has plenty of liquid water and the right temperature. This is because it's neither too close to the sun nor too far from it. The air helps keep our planet warm, acting like a greenhouse. It also protects life from harmful radiation.

Mars
Roman god of war

- **Earth days to orbit sun** 687
- **Discovery date** Unknown (but known since ancient times)
- **Number of moons** 2
- **Location** Fourth planet from the sun

Mars is one of the closest planets to us in space. It is barren and mainly covered with dust and rocks. Two ice caps cover the poles. It is about half the size of Earth, but has no flowing water, and, as yet, no signs of life.

Jupiter
King of the Roman gods

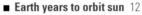

- **Earth years to orbit sun** 12
- **Discovery date** Unknown (but known since ancient times)
- **Number of moons** At least 79
- **Location** Fifth planet from the sun

The solar system's largest planet, Jupiter is a gas giant made mainly of hydrogen. It has many storms in its deep, cloudy atmosphere. The largest of these, which has been blowing for at least 300 years, is called the Great Red Spot. Jupiter's moon Ganymede is larger than Mercury.

Saturn
Roman god of agriculture

- **Earth years to orbit sun** 29½
- **Discovery date** Unknown (but known since ancient times)
- **Number of moons** 82
- **Location** Sixth planet from the sun

Saturn is an enormous gas giant, made mainly of hydrogen gas. It is so light that it would float—if you could find a big enough ocean! Clouds of icy crystals form hazy bands blowing around the planet at high speed. Its rings are made of billions of small chunks of nearly pure water ice.

Uranus
Greek god of the sky

- **Earth years to orbit sun** Just over 84
- **Discovery date** 1781
- **Number of moons** 27
- **Location** Seventh planet from the sun

Uranus was discovered in 1781 by astronomer William Herschel. Much of the planet is thought to be a hot liquid mix of water, ammonia, and methane. It has 13 thin, dark rings. The planet spins on its side, like a top that has fallen over. This is probably the result of a huge impact long ago.

Neptune
Roman god of the sea

- **Earth years to orbit sun** 165
- **Discovery date** 1846
- **Number of moons** 14
- **Location** Eighth planet from the sun

Neptune is quite similar to Uranus. Both are very cold because of their great distances from the sun. A day on Neptune lasts 16 hours and 7 minutes. Neptune has huge storms and strong winds. It also has five dark, thin rings.

Moon
Luna

- **Days to orbit Earth** 27.3
- **Discovery date** Unknown (but known since ancient times)
- **Location** Only moon of Earth

The moon orbits Earth at an average distance of 238,855 miles (384,400 km)—a journey of three days by spacecraft. It formed when a huge Mars-sized object crashed into young Earth. The dark patches on its surface are old seas of lava. The moon has no atmosphere.

PHASES OF THE MOON

As the moon orbits Earth, it seems to change shape night after night. We say it goes through phases. This is because we see different amounts of the moon's sunlit side. At new moon it is dark and cannot be seen (except during a solar eclipse). At full moon the entire Earth-facing side is lit up by the sun. (👁 p31)

▶ PHASES *The period from full moon to full moon lasts 29½ days.*

◀ FACE OF THE MOON
The moon always keeps the same side pointing towards Earth. We never see the "far side."

THE OCEAN PLANET

Earth is the only planet with oceans of water on its surface. This water turns to gas, then forms clouds and rain (or snow). It is also the only planet we know with lots of oxygen—the gas that keeps us alive. Our planet's powerful magnetic field shields it from harmful particles from the sun.

FACT
Earth and Mars have had many ice ages in the past. When they get colder, ice sheets spread out from the poles and cover large areas. Most of Earth may have been covered in ice 600 million years ago. Ice ages happen because of changes in the orbits and tilt of the planets.

▶ LIFE ON EARTH *Life is thought to have existed on Earth for almost four billion years.*

FAST FACTS

- The orbits of the planets around the sun are elliptical (oval).
- Our nearest neighbor, Venus, is only 23½ million miles (38 million km) away during close approaches.
- Use this simple sentence to remember the order of the planets: **M**y **V**ery **E**ducated **M**other **J**ust **S**erved **U**s **N**oodles (My = Mercury, Mother = Mars).
- Even today, comets and small asteroids crash into the planets (including Earth). One impact 66 million years ago may have wiped out most of the dinosaurs.

Flying rocks

There are billions of chunks of rock and ice orbiting the sun between the planets. Sometimes they crash into each other or onto planets and moons. A large impact could be devastating. Small bits burn up in Earth's air and create streaks of light.

ASTEROIDS

Asteroids are small, rocky bodies that orbit the sun. Most of them are found between the orbits of Mars and Jupiter. They are left-overs from the formation of the planets 4.5 billion years ago. The main asteroid belt contains millions of asteroids. The first asteroid to be discovered was Ceres, in 1801.

PLUTO

The Roman god of the underworld

- **Diameter** 1,476 miles (2,376 km)
- **Mass (Earth=1)** 0.002
- **Earth years to orbit sun** 248
- **Number of moons** 5

Pluto was discovered in 1930. In 2006, astronomers decided it should be classed as a dwarf planet. It is smaller than the moon. Its stretched-out, elliptical orbit crosses Neptune's orbit and is tilted to the orbits of the major planets. Pluto is very cold because it is so far away from the sun.

DWARF PLANETS

Pluto, Haumea, Eris, Makemake, and Ceres are the only confirmed dwarf planets. Ceres is the only asteroid big enough to be classed as a dwarf planet. The other dwarf planets are much like Pluto and are found in the outer solar system beyond the orbit of Neptune.

FACT

Most meteorites are too small to cause much damage. However, 66 million years ago, a 6-mile (10-km) wide asteroid hit Earth, causing massive earthquakes and tidal waves. A cloud of dust from the impact entered the atmosphere and blocked sunlight, causing plants and animals to die. This impact may have ended the age of the dinosaurs.

▶ COMETS *sometimes arrive near Earth from the outer solar system. A huge cloud of gas and dust surrounds a solid nucleus of ice and rock and stretches out into two tails. Comet Hale-Bopp, seen in 1997, was one of the brightest comets of the 20th century.*

METEORS

Look up at the sky on a cloudless night and you will eventually see a meteor, or "shooting star." Meteors are particles of dust and rock that burn up as they enter Earth's atmosphere.

Meteor showers occur at the same time each year, when Earth passes through trails of dust left by passing comets. Very rarely, a shower may produce thousands of shooting stars that light up the sky.

The Willamette Meteorite (above), which can be found in a museum in New York City, was once a brilliant fireball shooting towards Earth. It's made of iron and nickel.

METEORITES

Meteorites are chunks of rock that have come from space and landed on Earth's surface. Most of them are pieces that have broken off asteroids. A few have come from the moon and Mars.

▶ METEOR CRATER
One of the youngest and best-preserved impact craters on Earth is in Arizona. It is 50,000 years old and more than 550 ft (168 m) deep. The meteorite that made it was originally about 160 ft (50 m) across, but nearly all of it was destroyed by heat as it came down.

The crater is 4,000 ft (1,200 m) wide.

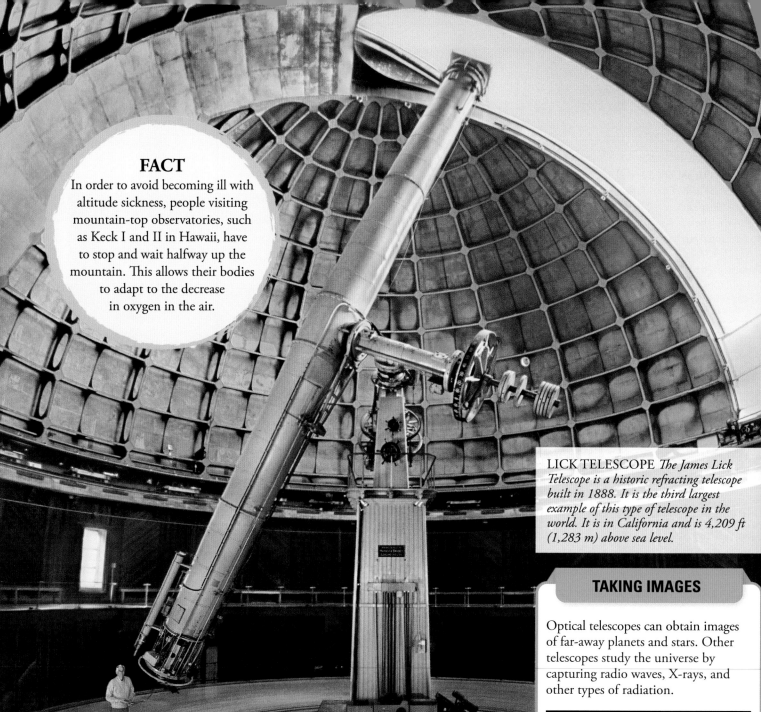

FACT

In order to avoid becoming ill with altitude sickness, people visiting mountain-top observatories, such as Keck I and II in Hawaii, have to stop and wait halfway up the mountain. This allows their bodies to adapt to the decrease in oxygen in the air.

LICK TELESCOPE *The James Lick Telescope is a historic refracting telescope built in 1888. It is the third largest example of this type of telescope in the world. It is in California and is 4,209 ft (1,283 m) above sea level.*

TAKING IMAGES

Optical telescopes can obtain images of far-away planets and stars. Other telescopes study the universe by capturing radio waves, X-rays, and other types of radiation.

▲ MARS FROM HUBBLE *This picture of Mars was taken with the Hubble Space Telescope. It shows the southern polar cap, the orange deserts, and sheets of ice cloud.*

Eye spy space

People have been staring at the heavens since prehistoric times. They watched the movement of the sun, moon, and planets across the sky and measured the positions of the stars. But there was a limit to what could be learned with the naked eye.

Gran Telescopio Canarias
Largest optical telescope

- **Diameter of main mirror** 34.1 ft (10.4 m)
- **Weight of main mirror** 19 tons (17 metric tons)
- **Altitude** 7,456 ft (2,300 m) above sea level
- **Location** La Palma, Canary Islands, Spain

The world's largest optical telescope with one main mirror is the Gran Telescopio Canarias, built on the peak of an extinct volcano on La Palma. The main mirror is made up of 36 hexagonal segments each 6¼ ft (1.9 m) across. The metal segments are coated with aluminum, which is a very good reflector of light. Observations began in 2009.

James Webb Space Telescope
Largest space telescope

- **Length** 72 ft (22 m)
- **Weight** 14,300 lb (6,500 kg)
- **Mission length** 10 years
- **Location** 1 million miles (1.5 million km) from Earth

The James Webb Space Telescope is an infrared telescope launched on December 25, 2021. Its mirror is made of 18 segments and is 21 ft (6.5 m) across— nearly three times bigger than Hubble's mirror.

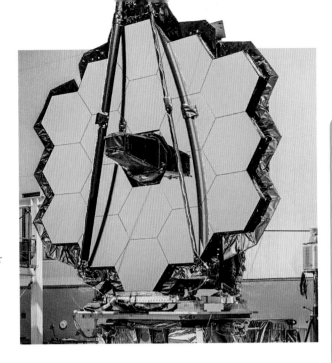

Kepler Space Telescope
Discovered planetary systems around other stars

- **Length** 15 ft (4.7 m)
- **Weight** 2,300 lb (1,050 kg)
- **Mission length** 9 years (2009–2018)
- **Location** In orbit around the sun

The Kepler Space Telescope had a mirror 4 ft 6 in (1.4 m) across. It was built specially to search for planets orbiting stars other than the sun (extrasolar planets) and found over 2,000, more than any other telescope.

Hubble Space Telescope
Famous NASA-ESA observatory

- **Height** 43½ ft (13.2 m)
- **Weight** around 24,000 lb (10,886 kg)
- **Date of launch** 1990
- **Location** Earth orbit

Launched in 1990, the world's most famous space observatory has a 8-ft (2.4-m) mirror. It is named after American astronomer Edwin Hubble, who showed that the universe is expanding.

ALMA
66-dish radio telescope

- **Size** 66 dishes; 54 with a 39-ft (12-m) diameter, 12 with a 23-ft (7-m) diameter
- **Altitude** 3 miles (5 km) above sea level
- **Location** Atacama Desert, northern Chile

The Atacama Large Millimeter/submillimeter Array (ALMA) is the world's largest radio telescope array. Its 66 dishes work together to gather information about newly forming stars and planets.

Square Kilometre Array
World's most powerful radio telescope

- **Construction** 2021–2030
- **Location** Australia and southern Africa

Fifteen countries have joined together to build the most powerful radio telescope ever. The signals from thousands of separate dishes and radio aerials spread out over huge areas will be combined by computer.

Giant Magellan Telescope
7-mirror optical giant

- **Main mirrors** Seven 28-ft (8.4-m) mirrors
- **Total moving weight** More than 1102 tons (1,000 metric tons)
- **Location** Cerro Las Campanas, Chile

Due to be operational in 2029, the Giant Magellan Telescope will produce images ten times sharper than the Hubble Space Telescope.

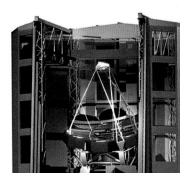

The Apollo program

In the early 1960s, the Soviet Union was ahead in the space race, so President John F. Kennedy announced that American astronauts would land on the moon before 1970. In July 1969, after spending around $25 billion on the Apollo program, they did.

GETTING THERE

■ The astronauts' journey to the moon would not have been possible without the *Saturn V*, the most powerful rocket ever built. The huge, three-stage rocket towered 363 ft (111 m) above the Florida launch pad. After the first two stages ran out of fuel, they were released and the third stage was used to boost the *Apollo* spacecraft and its crew toward the moon.

First man on the moon *Apollo 11* was the first crewed mission to land on the moon. On July 20, 1969, Neil Armstrong made the first lunar footprint. He was joined on the moon's surface by Buzz Aldrin.

APOLLO TIMELINE

1966	1967	1968		1969
February 26 First uncrewed test flight of *Saturn* 1B rocket. It eventually carried the first crewed *Apollo* test flight to orbit Earth.	**January** 27 Gus Grissom, Edward White, and Roger Chaffee were killed on the launch pad by a fire in their *Apollo* spacecraft during a launch test.	**October** 11 First crewed *Apollo* flight tested the Command Module in Earth's orbit.	**December 21** *Apollo 8* was the first crewed spacecraft to leave Earth's orbit and orbit the moon.	**July** 20 *Apollo 11* made the first crewed landing on the moon.

APOLLO SPACECRAFT

For the three-day trip between Earth and the Moon, the *Apollo* crew spent most of their time in the cone-shaped Command Module (CM). The crew also returned to Earth in the Command Module and landed by parachuting into the ocean.

MOON ROCK

Scientists wanted to learn more about the moon, so astronauts on the six crewed missions that landed on the lunar surface collected lots of soil and rock samples.

▶ *Altogether, 842 lb (382 kg) of rocks were brought to Earth and stored in a special laboratory.*

▼ COMMAND MODULE
One astronaut stayed in the CM in orbit around the moon. The other two went down to the moon's surface.

◀ LUNAR MODULE *The moon lander was officially called the lunar module. The crew lived in the upper of the two sections. It was this section that blasted off from the moon and carried them back to the CM for the trip home.*

Dish antenna for communications with Earth.

A camera took pictures and sent them back to Earth.

Lunar Roving Vehicle
Walking and carrying samples was hard work, even in the moon's low gravity (everything weighs one-sixth of what it does on Earth). So NASA gave the last three *Apollo* crews a lunar rover to drive. Crews traveled farther and could carry more.

The lightweight wheels were made of wire mesh.

1970	1971	1972	1975
April 13 An oxygen tank exploded on *Apollo 13,* canceling its moon landing.	**July** 26 Launch of *Apollo 15,* the first mission with a rover. 	**December 19** Splashdown of *Apollo 17,* the last crewed mission to the moon. 	**July 17** *Apollo-Soyuz* docking: first joint US-Soviet crewed mission.

Exploring space

The Space Age began in 1957, with the launch of *Sputnik 1*, the world's first artificial satellite, by the Soviet Union. In 1961, Soviet astronaut Yuri Gagarin became the first person to fly in space.

The International Space Station is the most expensive and ambitious object ever flown. The 462-ton (420-metric ton) station was built in Earth orbit by the U.S., Russia, Japan, Canada, and 11 European countries.

▶ LARGEST OBJECT *The International Space Station is the largest object ever built to orbit Earth.*

International Space Station (ISS)

FAST FACTS

- Valeri Polyakov holds the record for the longest space mission—437 days.
- The Russian space station Mir was home to 125 people (1986–2001).
- Mir flew more than 1⁹⁄₁₀ billion miles (3 billion km) in its lifetime.
- In 1986, the shuttle *Challenger* and its crew perished during ascent, just 71 seconds after launch.
- The shuttle *Columbia* broke apart during its return to Earth in 2003.
- More than 90 percent of the world's population can see the International Space Station when it flies overhead.
- The International Space Station orbits Earth every 90 minutes.

THE FIRST SPACE STATIONS

Space stations are places where people can live and work in space for long periods of time. The first space station, *Salyut (Salute) 1*, was launched by the Soviet Union on April 19, 1971. Six more *Salyuts* were launched until 1986 —two of them mainly for taking spy photographs.

▶ SALYUT 7 SPACE STATION *The 22-ton (20-metric ton) Salyut 7 space station was launched in 1982 and burned up during reentry in 1991.*

FOOTBALL FIELD ▲ *The ISS is about the size of a football field.*

TIMELINE OF HUMAN SPACEFLIGHT

1950s	1960s				1970s
1957 First artificial satellite, *Sputnik 1*, in space.	**1961** First human in space, Yuri Gagarin.	**1963** First woman in space, Valentina Tereshkova.	**1965** Alexei Leonov made the first spacewalk.	**1969** First human to walk on the moon, Neil Armstrong.	**1971** First orbiting space station, *Salyut 1*.

Space shuttle In 1981, a new space age began when the first reusable spacecraft lifted off from Cape Canaveral, Florida. Five space shuttle orbiters flew a total of 135 missions. The final flight was in 2011.

▼ SPACE SHUTTLE LANDING
The shuttle came back to Earth like a giant glider. It landed on a runway at a speed of around 215 mph (346 kmph). A tail parachute helped it slow down.

SPACE

REUSABLE LAUNCHERS

Most space launchers can only be used once. After their fuel is used up, the rockets fall away and burn up in the air. But the Falcon Heavy, built by SpaceX, is a powerful reusable launcher system based on the earlier Falcon 9 rocket. Its first stage has three reusable "cores"—each a separate Falcon 9 that can land back on Earth.

▶ THE FALCON 9 *rocket's first stage has one "core", with nine identical engines, that returns to Earth after launching a payload (satellite or spacecraft).*

Space tourism Almost all of the astronaut flights have been funded by governments. However, space tourism is becoming increasingly popular. The first real space tourist was millionaire businessman Dennis Tito, who paid $20 million for a week on board the ISS.

Dennis Tito

FACT
Just 12 astronauts have walked on the moon. They are the only people ever to have set foot on another world. More than 600 people have flown in space since Gagarin's historic flight. Most have come from the Soviet Union/ Russia or the U.S.

▶NEW SHEPARD
In July 2021, Blue Origin's New Shepard craft made its first crewed suborbital flight. By 2022, this reusable craft had ferried more than 20 passengers to space.

1980s		**1990s**	**2000s**		**2021**
1981 First orbital flight of the space shuttle.		**1986** First section of *Mir* space station launched.	**1998** First part of the ISS launched.	**2003** First human spaceflight in Chinese space program, on *Shenzhou 5.*	**2021** First orbital flight by all private citizens, on SpaceX's *Inspiration4.*

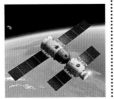

The red planet

Even though Mars is the planet most like Earth, it is a hostile place for humans. In the past, it was much more like Earth than it is today. It looks red because iron minerals in its surface rocks have rusted.

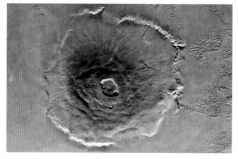

Volcanoes Mars has the largest volcanoes in the solar system. The most impressive is Olympus Mons, which is 375 miles (600 km) across and more than 16 miles (26 km) high. The volcano hasn't erupted for millions of years.

GIANT CANYONS

The Valles Marineris is more than 2,500 miles (4,000 km) long—10 times the length of the Grand Canyon—and extends a fifth of the way around Mars. The canyon is about 5 miles (7 km) deep and more than 375 miles (600 km) wide in the center.

These dark circles are volcanoes.

VALLES MARINERIS
The canyon system was discovered by the Mariner 9 *orbiter (after which it was named).*

POLAR ICE CAPS

There are ice caps at both Martian poles, but they are much smaller than Earth's. Each pole is different. The northern sheet is about 2 miles (3 km) thick and mainly water ice. The southern polar cap is colder and thicker and made of water ice with a coating of carbon dioxide ice. The polar caps melt and shrink in summer, then grow in winter when the temperature drops.

North polar ice cap

TIMELINE OF MARS EXPLORATION

1960s	1970s		1990s	2000s
1965 *Mariner 4* (U.S.), the first success, returned 21 images of the red planet.	**1971** *Mariner 9* (U.S.) became the first successful Mars orbiter.	**1976** *Viking 1* (U.S.) made the first successful landing on Mars. 	**1997** *Mars Pathfinder* (U.S.) delivered the first successful rover to Mars.	**2003** Europe's *Mars Express* orbiter began taking detailed pictures of Mars.

WHERE IS THE WATER?

Today, Mars is very cold, and the air is too thin for liquid water to exist on the surface. However, huge, winding channels suggest that large rivers flowed over the surface long ago. The water was probably released in sudden floods, possibly when underground ice melted. These river channels have been dry for billions of years.

Northern plains

Southern highlands

FACT
Mars has two small moons, Phobos and Deimos. They could be asteroids that were captured by Mars long ago. Phobos is no more than 17 miles (27 km) across with large craters on its surface. Deimos is just 7 miles (12 km) across and has a smoother surface.

Phobos

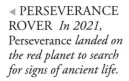

◄ PERSEVERANCE ROVER *In 2021, Perseverance landed on the red planet to search for signs of ancient life.*

A drill on the rover can extract samples from rocks for study.

A small helicopter called Ingenuity *became the first machine to fly on another planet.*

Mars Explorers Many of the early attempts to send spacecraft to Mars failed. The successful *Viking* missions in the 1970s included two orbiters and two landers. The first rover was part of the *Mars Pathfinder* mission of 1997. In 2021, there were eleven working spacecraft studying Mars from five different space agencies. Three of them were rovers. Missions carrying humans to Mars are planned for the 2030s.

2004	**2008**	**2012**	**2014**	**2018**	**2021**
NASA's twin rovers, *Spirit* and *Opportunity*, landed on the red planet.	*Phoenix* (U.S.) landed in the Martian Arctic and operated for more than five months.	Mars Science Laboratory landed on Mars with the *Curiosity* rover.	The first Indian planetary mission, *Mangalyaan,* reached Mars orbit.	The *InSight* lander started to investigate the interior of Mars.	*Hope* (UAE), China's *Tianwen-1* and Zhurong rover (right), and *Perseverance* (U.S.) were missons that reached Mars.

27

EARTH

Earth is the planet on which we live.
Unlike other planets in our solar system,
it is covered with liquid water, which
makes it look blue.

Our unique world

Among all the planets in the solar system, Earth is the only one known to support life. It is a perfect distance from the sun, has a breathable atmosphere, and is bathed in life-giving water.

EARTH'S STRUCTURE

Earth may look like a solid ball of rock, but if you slice through it, you can see it is made up of different layers. At the center is a hot metallic core. It is surrounded by the stony mantle, part of which is like sticky caramel. On top is a thin crust that forms the continents and ocean floor.

The atmosphere gives us our weather, provides us with oxygen, and protects us from harmful solar energy.

The crust shapes the continents and sea floor.

The outer mantle is fused to the crust.

The inner mantle has a temperature of about 5,400°F (3,000°C).

The outer core is made of molten metal.

The temperature of the inner core is about 10,800°F (6,000°C).

▲ EARTH'S CORE
The core is a mixture of iron and nickel mixed with lighter elements. The pressure at the center is so high that the inner core remains solid.

TIMELINE OF LIFE ON EARTH

EARLY EARTH		FIRST LIFE		EXPLOSION OF LIFE	
4.5 billion years ago: Earth formed, gradually turning into a red-hot ball of liquid rock.	4.4 billion years ago: Earth developed a crust, and oceans form.	3.7 billion years ago: first living cells.	630 million years ago: complex (multicellular) animals evolved.	540 million years ago: the Cambrian explosion—sudden appearance of many new species with teeth, feet, intestines, spines, and hard shells.	425 million years ago: first land animals appeared. 500 million years ago: Earth's atmosphere became breathable.

Magnetic field Our Earth acts like a huge bar magnet, which is why it has north and south magnetic poles. The magnetic field is thought to be produced by movement in the liquid outer core. The molten metal carries an electrical charge, which generates an electromagnetic field as it swirls around.

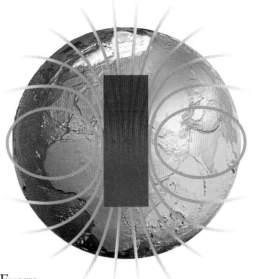

DAY AND NIGHT

Our planet doesn't stand still. Every 24 hours it rotates once around its axis, so that half the planet is in sunlight and the other half is in darkness. If it didn't rotate, one side would have permanent day and the other, permanent night.

📷 TAKE A PICTURE

Auroras are created when high-energy particles from the sun are drawn in at the poles by Earth's magnetic field. This energizes atoms in the atmosphere, which show as curtains of light.

Phases of the Moon If you look at the night sky you will see that the appearance of the moon changes over the course of a month. As the moon orbits Earth, the angle between it and the sun shifts, so that the amount of the moon's face that is lit by the sun changes. It is difficult to see a new moon as the light is shining on the side we cannot see. A slender crescent then appears and gradually increases (waxes) until the full face is lit. It then starts to decrease (wane) back into darkness.

WAXING GIBBOUS

FIRST QUARTER

FULL MOON

WANING GIBBOUS

WAXING CRESCENT

EARTH

LAST QUARTER

NEW MOON

SUN

We only ever see the same face of the moon because for every orbit it makes around Earth, it spins once on its axis.

WANING CRESCENT

PANGAEA	**AGE OF THE DINOSAURS**		**HUMANKIND**
299–273 million years ago: all land joined into one continent, Pangaea.	145 million years ago: the modern continents began to take shape. 241 million years ago: the age of the dinosaurs began.	66 million years ago: mass extinction of species, including all non-avian dinosaurs.	300,000 years ago, modern humans appeared.

Today

Dynamic planet

Earth's surface is constantly changing. The rocks it is made from have been recycled many times. Even though we rarely feel it moving, the signs that our planet is active are all around us.

▲ MAGMA
erupting onto the surface cracks as it cools. The whole of the planet once looked like this.

RISING HEAT

Below the surface, the mantle moves very slowly. Currents of heat rise from the lower mantle, cool as they near the surface, and then sink back down again. This has a dragging effect on the surface layers, carrying them along like a conveyor belt.

Earth's metal core provides the heat. It contains radioactive elements that give out heat as they become more stable. Even though the inner core is very hot, the huge pressure keeps it solid. The slightly cooler outer core is liquid.

EARTH'S CRUST

Our planet's surface rocks form a cool and brittle crust. It has two layers: a light top layer and a slightly thinner but denser bottom layer. The crust is broken into pieces that fit together like a jigsaw. These plates float on the mantle. As the mantle moves, the plates go with it.

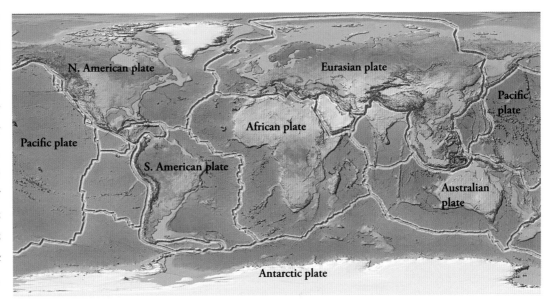

N. American plate

Eurasian plate

Pacific plate

African plate

Pacific plate

S. American plate

Australian plate

Antarctic plate

Divergent boundaries At the points where the mantle currents rise upward, the plates above them rise and part (diverge). Some of the mantle melts to form magma and fills the gap between the plates. Each time this happens the plates move apart. Sometimes the plates simply slide past each other without any volcanic activity. These are called transform boundaries.

Plates moving in opposite directions.

Plates slide past each other at transform boundaries.

Magma rises up from the mantle.

Oceanic crust forms as the magma cools and solidifies.

Ridge forms along divergent boundary.

Volcanoes form where the magma erupts on the surface.

Direction of continental plate.

The mantle starts to melt and rises to the surface as magma.

The oceanic plate is pulled under the continental plate.

Direction of oceanic plate.

Convergent boundaries When two plates meet (converge), one of the plates pushes under the other. If a continental plate meets an oceanic plate, the denser oceanic plate gives way. If two oceanic plates meet, the cooler, older plate is dragged under. Should two continental plates collide, the rocks on both sides bend and fold to form mountains.

PLATE MOVEMENTS

The continents have not always been where they are today. Since Earth's crust cooled they have split, collided, rotated, and reformed many times. They are still moving about 6 in (15 cm) a year.

N. America

▲ *About 225 million years ago all the continents were joined together.*

N. America

▲ *Over time, new oceans opened up, separating the continents.*

N. America

▲ *Today, the continents look like this, but they are still on the move.*

Volcanoes and earthquakes

People have always been terrified by the fiery power of volcanoes and earthquakes shaking the ground. Although these are just the natural movements of our planet, they can be highly destructive.

VOLCANOES

Volcanoes form when hot molten rock rises through Earth's crust. When molten rock is underground it is called magma, but when it flows onto the surface it is called lava. Some volcanoes erupt gently but others can be explosive, blasting gas, ash, and rock into the air. Volcanoes may erupt at regular intervals, while others lie dormant for centuries.

◄ MOLTEN LAVA *Lava that does not contain much gas flows over longer distances.*

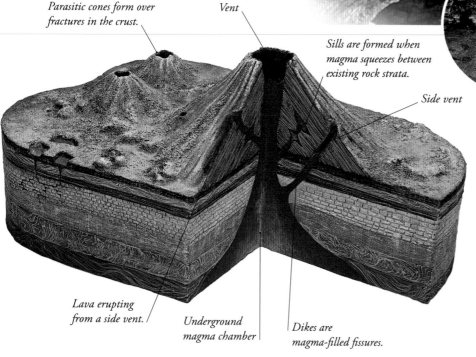

Parasitic cones form over fractures in the crust.

Vent

Sills are formed when magma squeezes between existing rock strata.

Side vent

Lava erupting from a side vent.

Underground magma chamber

Dikes are magma-filled fissures.

▲ SHIELD VOLCANO *These are broad, low-profile cones. They are formed when runny lava flows over a long distance before it cools and hardens.*

▲ CINDER CONE *Most volcanoes are cinder cones. They are made of ash and lava blown into fragments by escaping gas.*

Ash clouds blast fine particles high up into Earth's atmosphere where they can affect the world's weather for months.

EARTHQUAKES

Earthquakes occur when two blocks of Earth's crust slip past each other. The place where this happens is called a fault. Because the blocks do not slide easily, a large amount of energy is released when they move. This ripples away like waves on a pond, shaking the ground above.

Energy wave / *The epicentre is the source of the earthquake.* / *Fault line*

◄ ON SHAKY GROUND
When the ground shakes, buildings and other structures may collapse. The strength of an earthquake is measured using the Richter scale. This earthquake in Kobe, Japan, measured 7.3. It lasted for 20 seconds and made 200,000 buildings fall down. An even bigger earthquake hit Japan in 2011.

RING OF FIRE

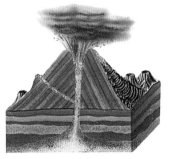

■ The "ring of fire" lies around the rim of the Pacific Ocean. It is an area where a number of crustal plates meet, resulting in frequent volcanic and earthquake activity. There are 452 volcanoes in the ring, and 80 percent of the world's largest earthquakes occur in this area.

▲ COMPOSITE VOLCANO *These cones rise steeply towards the summit. They are the most deadly type because they usually erupt explosively.*

TSUNAMI

■ **Tsunamis** are giant ocean waves caused by a sudden movement of the ocean floor. Sometimes colliding plates get stuck. When they finally release, it can trigger an earthquake, which gives the overlying water a huge shove. The waves grow larger when they reach shallow water and cause devastation when they hit land.

Bangladesh 2.5 hours

India 2 hours

Sri Lanka 1.5 hours

Malaysia 30 minutes

Epicentre

Indonesia 15 minutes

▲ WORLD-WIDE WAVE *The tsunami of 2004 began with an earthquake off the coast of Indonesia. The wave was eventually felt as far away as Iceland and Chile.*

▲ BEFORE *Banda Aceh in Indonesia was close to the epicentre of the 2004 earthquake and was the first place the tsunami struck.*

▲ AFTER *Most of the northern shore was submerged by the tsunami. An estimated 230,000 people in eleven countries died when the waves hit land.*

Making mountains

Mountain ranges cover about a fifth of Earth's land surface. They have built up over many millions of years, as massive tectonic plates crash into one another. Many ranges, such as the Himalayas, are still being pushed upward.

LIFT AND FOLD

Most mountains on land are fold mountains, which have been created by the movement of tectonic plates across Earth's surface. When two tectonic plates push against each other, the rock of Earth's crust crumples into folds and faults, which get bigger with continuing pressure.

Shifting sand This experiment below uses layers of sand on a sheet of paper to show how rock strata buckle and double over as a mountain forms. Each layer of sand represents a layer of rock strata. The paper is pulled along slowly, at a rate of ½ inch (1 cm) per 100 seconds. As the paper moves, it drags the sand with it. This is similar to the way Earth's slowly flowing upper mantle pulls along the crust.

▲ MOUNTAIN MACHINE *The paper and sand are held between fixed wooden blocks inside a tank.*

▼ SEDIMENTS *Layers of sediment are laid down evenly on top of the paper.*

▲ CROSS SECTION *This cliff face in Dorset, England shows how rock strata twisted and folded over as the African and European plates collided millions of years ago. This same collision gave birth to the Alps.*

▼ ZIG-ZAGS *The moving paper makes wrinkles in the bottom layer of sand. These are magnified into z-shaped folds in higher layers.*

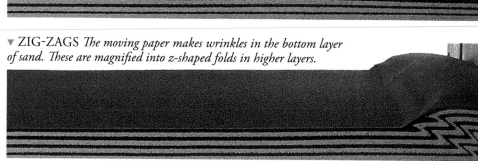

▼ HIGHER AND HIGHER *The sand folds build up on top of each other, making large loops.*

TYPES OF MOUNTAIN

Not all mountains are fold mountains. Some are formed by eruptions from volcanoes, and others are made of faulted blocks of rock pushed up as Earth's crust cracks. Mountains are given their jagged appearance by heavy erosion, which strips the rock away from their sides.

Going up The higher you climb, the air becomes thinner and the temperature gets colder. The tree line marks the cut-off point beyond which it is too cold for trees to grow.

TAKE A PICTURE

The Matterhorn is an easily recognizable peak in the Alps. It was first climbed in 1865 by an English mountaineer, Edward Whymper.

**MT. EVEREST
(SAGARMATHA)**
Nepal–China
29,029 ft (8,848 m)

**K2
(MT. GODWIN AUSTEN)**
Pakistan–China
28,251 ft (8,611 m)

ACONCAGUA
Argentina
22,831 ft (6,959 m)

DENALI
United States
20,310 ft (6,190 m)

KILIMANJARO
Tanzania
19,340 ft (5,895 m)

MELTING ICE-CAP
It is estimated that the ice-caps on Mount Kilimanjaro will have melted by 2060.

MT. FUJI
Japan
12,388 ft (3,776 m)

MONT BLANC
France–Italy
15,774 ft (4,808 m)

**MATTERHORN
(CERVINO)**
Italy–Switzerland
14,692 ft (4,478 m)

AN ACTIVE VOLCANO
The last eruption of Mount Fuji was in 1707–1708, when it erupted for 16 days. Some scientists believe that it may erupt again soon.

**MT. COOK
(AORAKI)**
New Zealand
12,218 ft (3,724 m)

OTHER NAMES *Mountains often have different names in different languages. The Matterhorn is so-called in English and German, but in Italian it is called Cervino, and in French, Mont Cervin.*

NAMED FOR AN EXPLORER
Mount Cook was named for the explorer Captain James Cook. Its original Māori name is Aoraki.

VESUVIUS
Italy
4,203 ft (1,281m)

Rocks

Our planet is mostly a big ball of rock. Rock is what gives Earth its features—mountains, canyons, and plains. Rocks can be massive, or as small as a grain of sand. Many of them started life deep inside the mantle.

WHAT IS A ROCK?

Rocks are usually made up of several different minerals. Looking closely at a rock can tell you a lot about its history. The shapes of crystals or grains in the rock and how they fit together reveal whether the rock is one of three types: igneous, metamorphic, or sedimentary.

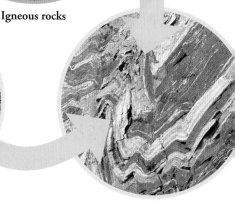
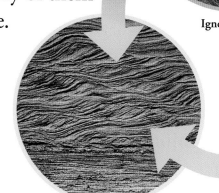

▼ STONE CYCLE
Earth's rocks are endlessly recycled, but it takes millions of years for rocks to form and change.

Igneous rocks

Sedimentary rocks

Metamorphic rocks

Igneous rocks began as molten rock deep inside Earth. They are the commonest rocks in Earth's crust. Some were erupted onto the surface as lava, others solidified underground. The speed at which they cooled is shown by the crystals they contain—big crystals indicate slow cooling.

Metamorphic rocks These began as other types of rock but have been altered by great heat, pressure, or both, deep inside Earth's crust. Most of the minerals in the original rock have changed. These rocks often show folded or squashed bands.

Most sedimentary rocks are made of small particles of other rocks, transported by water, wind, or ice. The particles may all be the same size or a jumble of sizes. These build up in layers, and pressure from new layers above squashes them into hard rock.

Minerals

When Earth first formed, it inherited many different chemical elements. Over billions of years, these elements combined to form thousands of different chemical compounds.

WHAT IS A MINERAL?

Minerals are the building blocks of rocks. They consist of either a single chemical element or a compound of mixed elements. There are about 4,000 different minerals, but only 100 occur in any great quantity.

How minerals form Most minerals form when molten rock or a hot solution cools and forms crystals. The crystals that form are affected by pressure and temperature, so a mineral can look different depending on how it crystallizes. However, some minerals, such as coal and chalk, start off as living organisms.

Types of minerals The common minerals that make up Earth's crust are called "rock-forming minerals." They are mostly compounds of the elements silicon and oxygen. Other useful minerals include carbonates common in limestones and ore minerals containing metallic elements.

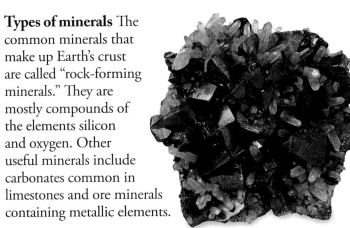

◀ DIAMOND *is made of pure carbon. It is the hardest mineral on Earth.*

◀ CHALCOPYRITE *is a copper and iron sulphide ore seen here mixed with clear quartz crystals.*

CRYSTALS

Most minerals are crystals. The atoms in the minerals are arranged in regular patterns, which give crystals their simple geometrical shapes. The crystal structure affects many of the mineral's physical properties, such as hardness, and how the crystal fractures.

▲ CINNABAR *is a sulphide of mercury that forms hexagonal crystals.*

▲ GALENA *is the name given to lead sulphide. Its crystals are cubic in shape. If it is hit with a hammer, the crystals break off into smaller cubes.*

MINERAL USES

Minerals have a huge range of practical uses...

■ They can be mined to extract metals (for example, gold, silver, copper, or iron, which is used to make bridges).
■ Minerals such as sylvite and apatite can be used as plant fertilizers.
■ Crystals can be cut and polished into gemstones (diamond, ruby, emerald).
■ Colored minerals are used as pigments.
■ Some minerals are used in bath or beauty products.

Rock and mineral guide

Collecting rocks and minerals can be a rewarding hobby. Rocks are identified by features such as color, texture, and mineral content. Minerals are classified by crystal structure, hardness, and how they break.

KEY

Rocks are graded by the size of their grains, as either fine, medium, or coarse. The size limits for each category vary depending on whether rocks are igneous, metamorphic, or sedimentary (👁 p38).

F = fine

M = medium

C = coarse

EARTH

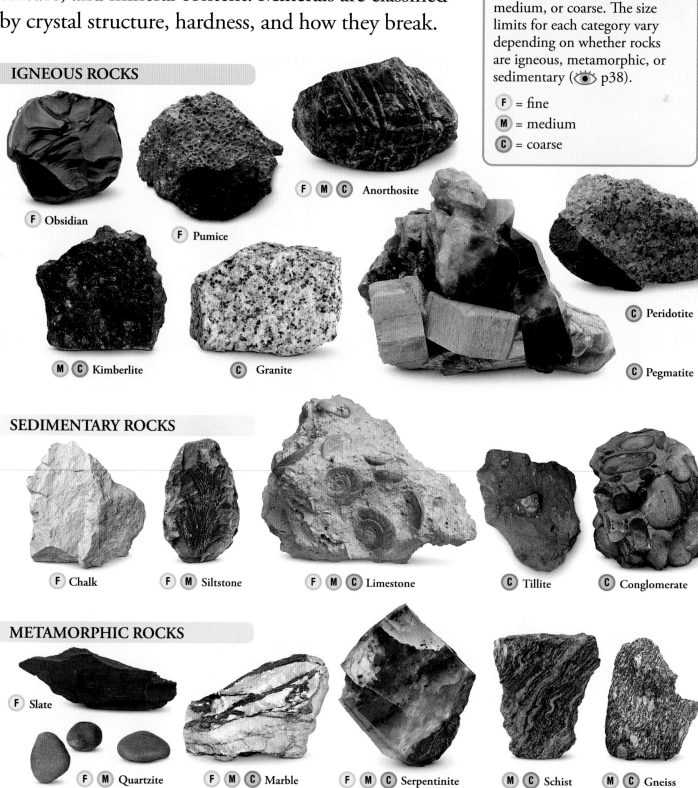

IGNEOUS ROCKS

F Obsidian

F Pumice

F M C Anorthosite

M C Kimberlite

C Granite

C Peridotite

C Pegmatite

SEDIMENTARY ROCKS

F Chalk

F M Siltstone

F M C Limestone

C Tillite

C Conglomerate

METAMORPHIC ROCKS

F Slate

F M Quartzite

F M C Marble

F M C Serpentinite

M C Schist

M C Gneiss

MOHS SCALE

One way of telling the difference between similar-looking minerals is to test their hardness. This is measured by scratching minerals against each other. A hard mineral can always scratch a softer one. The hardest mineral is diamond.

1. Talc 2. Gypsum 3. Calcite 4. Fluorite 5. Apatite 6. Feldspar 7. Quartz 8. Topaz 9. Corundum 10. Diamond

Softest → *Hardest*

ORES

Sulphur: 1.5–2.5 on Mohs scale

Gold: 2.5–3

Silver: 2.5–3

Malachite *(contains copper)*: 3.5–4

Ilmenite *(contains titanium)*: 5–6

Magnetite *(contains iron)*: 5–6

Cobaltite *(contains cobalt)*: 5.5

Rhodonite *(contains manganese)*: 5.5–6.5

SEMI-PRECIOUS STONES

Lapis lazuli: 3–5.5

Jade: 6–7

Olivine: 6.5–7

Agate: 7

Amethyst: 7

Tourmaline: 7

Zircon: 7.5

PRECIOUS STONES

■ Gemstones are divided into precious and semi-precious stones based on value. The four that qualify as precious are diamond, emerald, sapphire, and ruby.

Diamond

Emerald

Sapphire

Ruby

Riches from Earth

Many useful materials are hidden below Earth's surface. Some of them, such as metals and gemstones, have been used since ancient times. Exploitation of others, such as fossil fuels, is more recent, but their use has left its mark on the environment.

FAST FACTS

- South Africa is one of the world's leading mining nations, holding large reserves of gold, diamonds, and other valuable mineral resources.
- By 2026, the world demand for oil will be about 104 million barrels a day.
- The U.S. is the world's leading oil producer.
- Mining kills and injures more workers than any other industry.

MINING

People need to dig up the resources from Earth's crust before they can use them. This is called mining. There are two main techniques, depending on the types of mineral being extracted. They are surface mining, or quarrying, and underground mining.

▼ IRON MINE *Iron ore mines in Brazil are some of the most productive in the world.*

◄ HEMATITE, *the mineral form of iron oxide, is identified by its rusty red streaks.*

▲ DRILLING FOR GOLD *A miner drills for deposits of gold at a mine in South Africa. The rock face lies deep underground, and the work is physically demanding and very dangerous.*

Underground mining Any minerals buried deep beneath Earth's surface must be extracted using underground mining techniques. Miners use heavy machinery to drill deep shafts under the ground. They lay rails to carry the minerals, drilling gear, waste material, and the miners themselves to and from the rock face. Underground mining is dangerous work and much more expensive than surface mining.

Surface mining The largest mines are open-cast mines, which extract minerals on or near Earth's surface. Miners use explosives, diggers, and heavy machinery to dig huge holes in the ground. Most of the world's mining output comes from surface mining, which is environmentally destructive, but is much safer than underground mining.

FOSSIL FUELS

Coal, oil, and natural gas are fossil fuels. These vital resources formed from the remains of animals and plants that lived millions of years ago. Over time, the vast pressure and temperature under the ground changed the remains into coal, oil, and natural gas. Fossil fuels now provide most of the world's power.

ENVIRONMENTAL CONCERNS

- **Oil spills** from tankers spread over vast distances in ocean currents. These environmental disasters devastate marine wildlife such as fish and seabirds.

- **Burning fossil fuels** in car engines and power plants pumps huge volumes of carbon dioxide into the air, which is leading to global warming ( p78).

- **Oil exploration** destroys habitats in wilderness areas, decimating local populations of animals and plants.

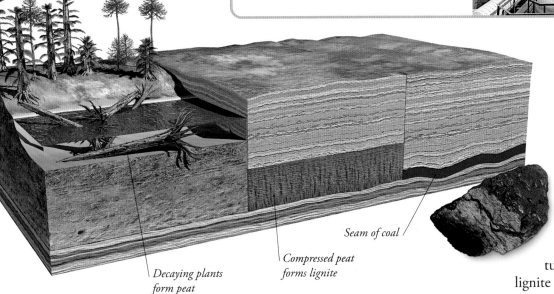

Seam of coal

Compressed peat forms lignite

Decaying plants form peat

Coal This hard black solid forms when peat deposits become buried underground. Peat is a rich type of soil formed from plants and their decaying remains. Over millions of years, the weight of the top layers of peat pushes down on the lower levels. This squeezes the peat, which first turns into a mineral called lignite and eventually into coal.

Oil This thick black liquid forms from the remains of marine animals and plants that lived millions of years ago. The dead bodies were buried under the sea floor and then slowly transformed into crude oil, which became trapped in layers of rock.

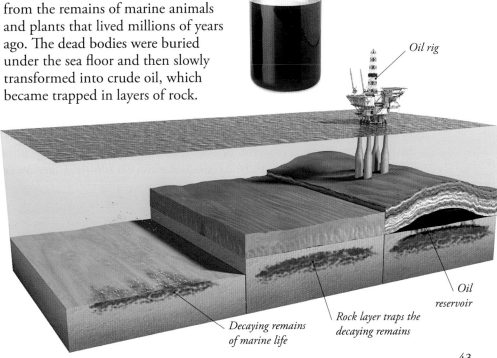

Oil rig

Oil reservoir

Rock layer traps the decaying remains

Decaying remains of marine life

▲ STRIKE IT LUCKY *An oil worker guides a giant hydraulic pump into position to extract the crude oil from an oil well.*

Erosion

Earth's landscape is constantly changing, as rock and soil are worn away by the destructive effects of water, wind, ice, and gravity. Erosion can be sudden, such as when a landslide happens. But gradual erosion can be just as dramatic, for example as rivers carve deep valleys into Earth's surface.

WIND EROSION

As wind flows across the land, it lifts up and carries countless grains of sand and other tiny particles. These particles, called sediment, may be blown against rocks at high speeds, grinding away at their surfaces. Over many years wind erosion along with water and ice has the effect of wearing rock into new shapes. Wind erosion happens most in dry, desert regions.

TELL ME MORE...

What happens to the sediment transported by erosion? Much of it mixes with organic remains and becomes soil. Rivers drop sediment as they lose speed. In time, sediment may become buried and harden into new sedimentary rock strata.

LANDSLIDE!

Heavy rains cause huge amounts of rock and mud to suddenly slip down hillsides. Landslides are more frequent where there is tree-felling. Trees' roots hold soil in place, so when forests are cut down, landslides become more likely.

▼ WIND SCULPTURES
Wind erosion wears down soft rock faster than hard rock. As the soft rock disappears, strange shapes are revealed.

The caprock at the top of this pillar is harder than the mudstone underneath.

Wind erosion will eventually wear away the mudstone to the point where the caprock falls off.

WATER EROSION

As rainwater flows downhill, it picks up small fragments of rock. These fragments and the force of moving water wear channels into the earth, carving out the beds of rivers. In the same way, ocean waves and tides grind down the rocks of the shoreline, creating bays, headlands, cliffs, and rock pillars called stacks.

THE POWER OF WATER

Rivers constantly erode their riverbeds and dump the eroded material downstream. This gradually changes river courses and can form features such as oxbow lakes.

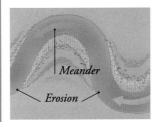

Meander

Erosion

▲ STEP 1 *As a river flows round a meander, it erodes the outside of each bend.*

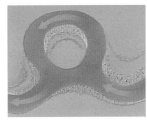

▲ STEP 2 *The bends gradually change shape, until a shortcut is created.*

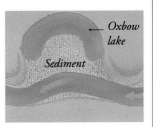

Oxbow lake

Sediment

▲ STEP 3 *Sediment deposited by the river cuts off the meander.*

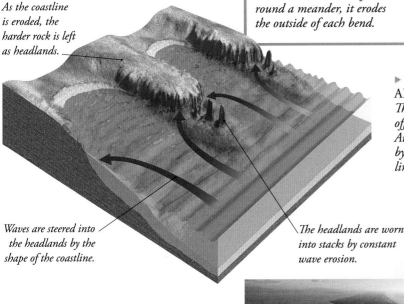

As the coastline is eroded, the harder rock is left as headlands.

Waves are steered into the headlands by the shape of the coastline.

The headlands are worn into stacks by constant wave erosion.

▶ TWELVE APOSTLES
These rock formations off the coast of Victoria, Australia, were created by the sea eroding limestone headlands.

ICE EROSION

Glaciers are slow-moving masses of ice. With global warming, they now cover less than 10 percent of land. As glaciers move, rocks trapped in the ice scour the land, wearing it smooth. Water can also split rocks as it freezes, since water in cracks expands as it turns to ice.

▲ DEPOSITION *The sediments transported by rivers and by ocean tides can be deposited in large quantities, creating new land features such as this spit.*

A look at time

What time is it right now? The answer depends on where you are. If it's midday in Santiago, Chile, it will be midnight in Perth, Australia. To make sense of this, the world is divided into 24 time zones, and clocks in each zone are set to the same time.

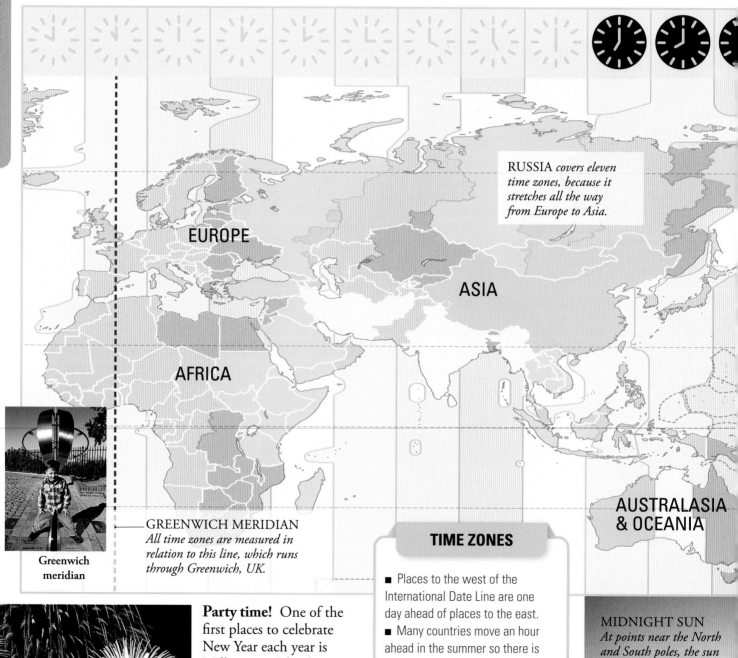

RUSSIA *covers eleven time zones, because it stretches all the way from Europe to Asia.*

EUROPE

ASIA

AFRICA

AUSTRALASIA & OCEANIA

Greenwich meridian

GREENWICH MERIDIAN
All time zones are measured in relation to this line, which runs through Greenwich, UK.

TIME ZONES

■ Places to the west of the International Date Line are one day ahead of places to the east.
■ Many countries move an hour ahead in the summer so there is more light in the evenings. This is called daylight saving time. However the practice isn't always popular with farmers, who need light in the early morning.

Party time! One of the first places to celebrate New Year each year is Millennium Island in Kiribati. Hawaii, which is to the east of the International Date Line, is one of the last places to join the party.

MIDNIGHT SUN
At points near the North and South poles, the sun doesn't set at all at certain times of the year.

THE TIME BELOW IS...

Some countries are split into several time zones, whereas others lie in just one. If you fly from one side of the U.S. to the other, you will go through four time zones. In contrast, China has just one official time across the whole country, despite its size.

FACT
Your internal body clock tells you when to wake and sleep. Plane passengers who cross several time zones may experience jet lag, which makes them tired during the day, but restless at night.

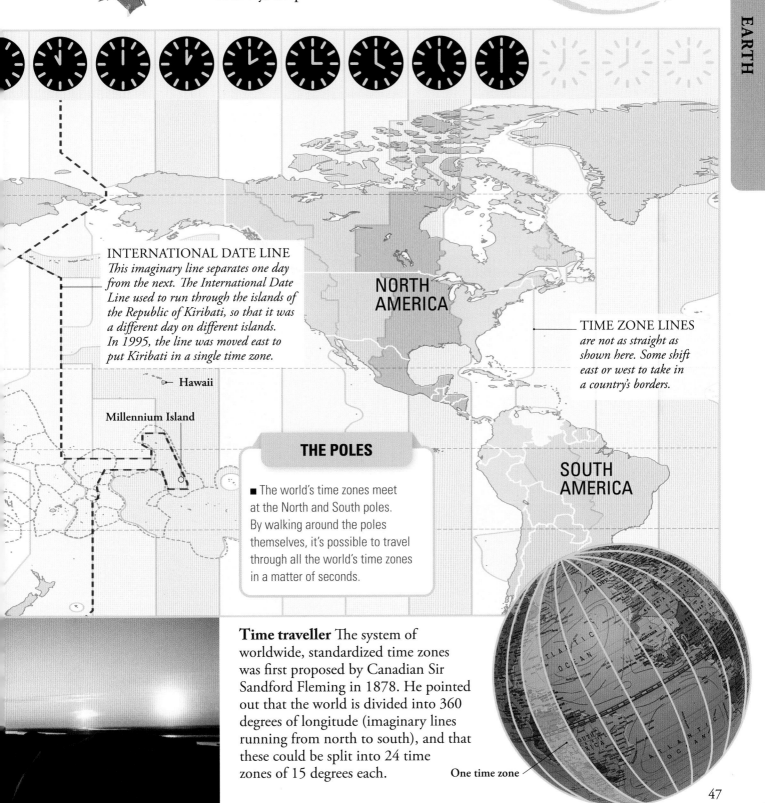

INTERNATIONAL DATE LINE
This imaginary line separates one day from the next. The International Date Line used to run through the islands of the Republic of Kiribati, so that it was a different day on different islands. In 1995, the line was moved east to put Kiribati in a single time zone.

Hawaii

Millennium Island

NORTH AMERICA

SOUTH AMERICA

TIME ZONE LINES
are not as straight as shown here. Some shift east or west to take in a country's borders.

THE POLES

■ The world's time zones meet at the North and South poles. By walking around the poles themselves, it's possible to travel through all the world's time zones in a matter of seconds.

Time traveller The system of worldwide, standardized time zones was first proposed by Canadian Sir Sandford Fleming in 1878. He pointed out that the world is divided into 360 degrees of longitude (imaginary lines running from north to south), and that these could be split into 24 time zones of 15 degrees each.

One time zone

Precious water

Without water, life on Earth could not exist. This precious resource fills the world's oceans, lakes, and rivers or soaks into the earth to form ground water. A small fraction of the world's water exists as ice or water vapor in the air, or is held inside the bodies of animals and plants.

FAST FACTS

- The Caspian Sea is the largest inland body of water in the world.
- Lake Baikal in Siberia is the deepest freshwater lake in the world, holding 23 percent of Earth's fresh water.
- Lake Superior in North America has the largest surface area of any lake in the world.
- The Dead Sea on the border of Israel and Jordan is the world's lowest lake and also one of the saltiest.

FRESH WATER

The salty seas and oceans make up 97 percent of the world's water. The rest is fresh water, and most of it is locked away in the polar ice caps and glaciers. The fresh water we drink comes from rainwater, which fills wells, rivers, and lakes and accounts for just 0.6 percent of the world's water supply.

Water cycle Water moves through a continuous cycle between the oceans, the atmosphere, and the land. The water cycle provides fresh water, which is essential to life on Earth.

FACT
Earth's oceans contain 324 million cubic miles (1.36 billion cubic kilometers) of water.

Only 3 percent of Earth's water is fresh water.

Water runs down the slopes to form streams and rivers.

The clouds release water as precipitation (rain or snow).

As the air rises and cools over land, the water condenses in clouds.

Plants release water into the air by a process called transpiration.

The sun warms the ocean, and fresh water evaporates into the air.

Some water soaks through the soil to form ground water.

The reservoir that forms behind a dam supplies people with water.

Most of the world's water is held in the oceans.

Rivers channel the water back toward the ocean.

A dam interrupts the water cycle by delaying the return of water to the ocean.

WORLD'S LONGEST RIVERS

▲ *The Nile River was the lifeblood of the ancient Egyptians, providing the water to grow their crops.*

The world's longest rivers (by continent) are:

- **Nile:** Africa's longest river, at 4,145 miles (6,671 km).

- **Amazon:** At 4,000 miles (6,437 km), the longest river in South America.

- **Yangtze:** Asia's longest river, at 3,915 miles (6,300 km).

- **Mississippi:** At 3,710 miles (5,970 km), the longest river in North America.

- **Volga:** Europe's longest river, at 2,292 miles (3,688 km).

- **Murray–Darling:** At 2,330 miles (3,750 km), the longest river in Australia.

Underground water Some of the water that falls as rain seeps into the soil and into the rocks below to become ground water. Some rocks soak up water and form a saturated layer, the top of which is called the water table. But water can also leak through cracks in rocks and form pools in underground caves.

▶ BLIND CAVE FISH *These fish live in deep caves and rely on touch, rather than sight, to sense their surroundings.*

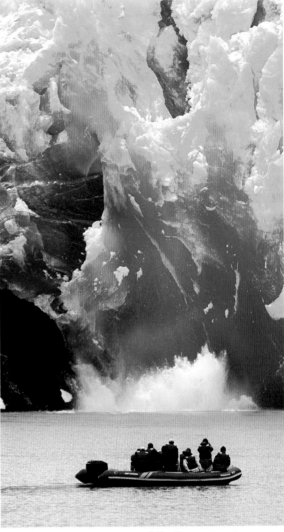

Solid water Some water falls from clouds as snow. In the polar regions, and high in the mountains, the snow builds up in layers that push down to form an icy mass called a glacier. The glacier flows to the sea and breaks up into icebergs, which gradually melt, and the water cycle starts all over again.

WATER

- There are more than 90,000 dams in the U.S. alone.
- Las Vegas, Nevada, gets 85 percent of its water from Lake Mead—the vast reservoir behind the Hoover Dam.
- At 1,001 ft (305 m) tall, Jinping-1 Dam in China is currently the world's tallest dam.

▲ WATER SUPPLY *Lucky Peak Dam traps water from the Boise River in Idaho.*

FRESH WATER

- Access to clean water is vital for human health.
- With climate change, there is a growing shortage of fresh water across the world.
- People suffering from water shortage may be forced to move from their homes. Human migration puts pressure on other places and countries, which may themselves be in need.

The world's oceans

Earth is known as the "blue planet", after the oceans that cover two-thirds of its surface. Much of the ocean remains mysterious because the dark, cold conditions make its deep waters difficult to explore.

MIGHTY OCEANS

Our oceans are in constant motion. They are driven by flowing currents that mix warm and cold water, which, in turn, affect our climate. There are five great oceans. In order of size, these are the Pacific, Atlantic, Indian, Southern, and Arctic oceans. Smaller bodies of salt water are called seas.

▼ WAVE POWER *Waves contain a huge amount of energy. This energy can be captured and turned into electricity.*

TELL ME MORE...

Twice a day the sea level rises and falls. This movement is called a tide. It is caused by the gravitational effects of the moon and the sun. When these combine, a bulge of water forms on either side of Earth causing a high tide. When it passes, the tide goes out.

North Sea
Average depth 308 ft (94 m)

Arctic Ocean
Average depth 3,248 ft (990 m)

Mediterranean Sea
Average depth 4,921 ft (1,500 m)

World oceans

The depth of the ocean varies enormously. On average, the Southern Ocean is the deepest, but many oceans have submarine canyons running through them. The deepest of these is the Mariana Trench in the Pacific. At 35,829 ft (10,920 m) deep, you could fit in Mount Everest with room to spare.

Caribbean Sea
Average depth 8,684 ft (2,647 m)

Atlantic Ocean
Average depth 10,925 ft (3,330 m)

Indian Ocean
Average depth 12,762 ft (3,890 m)

Pacific Ocean
Average depth 14,041 ft (4,280 m)

Southern Ocean
Average depth 14,763 ft (4,500 m)

Ocean circulation The circulation of the ocean partly controls climate, because warm or cold air masses move with ocean currents. The Gulf Stream takes warm, salty water from the Caribbean to the Nordic seas, and brings mild weather to northern Europe. Without the Gulf Stream, winters in Lisbon, Portugal, would be more like winters in New York City, which is a similar distance from the North Pole. Around Iceland, the Gulf Stream's salty water gets cold and heavy, and sinks down, sucking more warm water from further south to replace it. That deep cold water flows from the Arctic to the Southern Ocean, where it meets an even deeper cold current flowing eastwards around Antarctica. Similar processes take place in the Indian and Pacific Oceans.

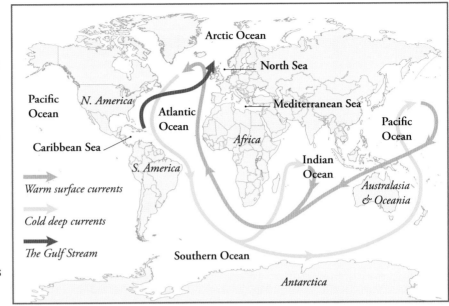

Arctic Ocean
North Sea
Pacific Ocean
N. America
Atlantic Ocean
Mediterranean Sea
Pacific Ocean
Caribbean Sea
Africa
Indian Ocean
S. America
Australasia & Oceania

→ *Warm surface currents*
→ *Cold deep currents*
→ *The Gulf Stream*

Southern Ocean
Antarctica

Beach — Continental shelf — Submarine canyon — Continental slope — Continental rise — Deep-sea trench — Sea mount — Abyssal plain — Mid-ocean ridge

Continental margins The land does not stop when it meets the sea. The continental shelf slopes down to 660 ft (200 m) and then drops sharply down to the ocean floor. Although large areas of the floor, or abyssal plain, are flat, it is not featureless. There are deep canyons and trenches, volcanic sea mounts, and spreading ocean ridges.

Breaking wave crashes onto beach.

Waves pile up as they near land.

Ocean swell

Waves Waves are caused by winds blowing over the sea. These produce smooth, large waves called swells. As they get closer to shore they begin to pile up. The depth between the wave and the sea floor becomes shallower, causing the wave to break into a foamy crest that crashes onto the beach.

▼ BUOYED UP *Some "seas" are actually salty lakes. The Dead Sea is so salty, you can float without making any effort.*

DEEP, BLUE SEA

Life at the bottom of the deep ocean is hard. The weight of water above is so heavy it would crush any organism not adapted to life at these depths. It is very dark because light cannot reach very far, which also makes it very cold. Animals that live here need special adaptations to help them survive.

Salt water As everyone knows, sea water tastes salty, and will make you thirsty if you try to drink it. Not only is common salt (sodium chloride) found in sea water, but many other minerals as well. There is even a little dissolved gold. Scientists estimate there could be as much as 55 million billion tons of dissolved salts in the sea. If this were spread on the land, it would measure 500 ft (150 m) deep.

Atmosphere

Life on Earth could not exist without the thick blanket of gases that surrounds the planet. This "atmosphere" is a complex, dynamic system that interacts with the oceans, land, and the sun to create our weather and climate.

PROTECTING EARTH

The atmosphere plays a vital role in protecting life on Earth. It absorbs much of the sun's harmful rays but allows enough through to warm up the planet. It protects the planet from meteor showers. The atmosphere also holds oxygen and water, which are essential for life.

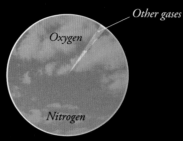

Other gases

Oxygen

Nitrogen

▲ WHAT'S IN THE AIR? *Around 21 percent of the atmosphere consists of oxygen, which we need to breathe. Most of the rest is nitrogen, but a tiny fraction is made up of other gases, such as carbon dioxide and methane.*

FACT

A satellite orbiting Earth at an altitude of roughly 12,500 miles (20,000 km) will be traveling at an amazing 8,500 mph (14,000 kmph).

ATMOSPHERE LAYERS

The atmosphere consists of five layers—the troposphere, stratosphere, mesosphere, thermosphere, and exosphere.

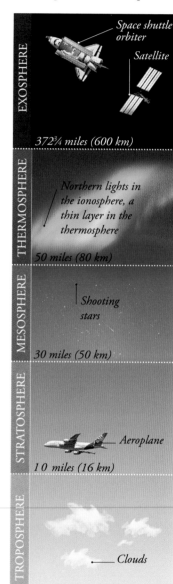

EXOSPHERE

Space shuttle orbiter

Satellite

372¾ miles (600 km)

THERMOSPHERE

Northern lights in the ionosphere, a thin layer in the thermosphere

50 miles (80 km)

MESOSPHERE

Shooting stars

30 miles (50 km)

STRATOSPHERE

Aeroplane

10 miles (16 km)

TROPOSPHERE

Clouds

◀ TIGHT SQUEEZE *Gravity squeezes 99 percent of the gases in the atmosphere into the first 25 miles (40 km) above Earth's surface. The rest extends 600 miles (1,000 km) out into space.*

OZONE LAYER

◀ HOLE
A satellite image reveals the ozone hole (purple).

■ **Ozone forms** a thin layer around Earth, about 15 miles (25 km) above the surface.

■ **Harmful gases** in aerosols and other systems destroy ozone, creating holes in the ozone layer over the polar regions.

■ **The ozone layer** protects life from the harmful ultraviolet (UV) radiation in sunlight.

Climate

The climate of a particular area is the different patterns of weather and temperature over time. Factors that influence climate include distance from the equator and the sea, height above sea level, and the surrounding landscape.

SEASONS

The seasons are annual changes in climate that occur in the northern and southern hemispheres. There are four seasons in temperate regions—spring, summer, autumn, and winter. They are due to the differences in day length and the strength of the sunlight as Earth orbits the sun. In many tropical and subtropical areas, there are two seasons—dry and wet.

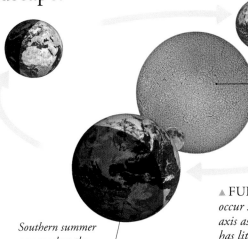

Northern summer occurs when the North Pole is tilted toward the sun.

Sun

Southern summer occurs when the North Pole is tilted away from the sun.

▲ FULL TILT *The seasons occur since Earth is tilted on its axis as it orbits the sun. This has little effect at the equator, which has warm weather for most of the year.*

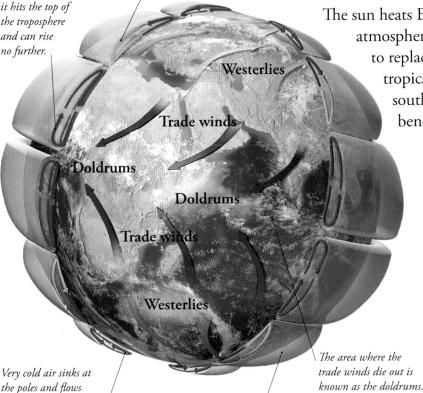

Warm air rises at the equator until it hits the top of the troposphere and can rise no further.

Dry air sinks over the world's deserts.

Westerlies

Trade winds

Doldrums

Doldrums

Trade winds

Westerlies

Very cold air sinks at the poles and flows outward, creating winds called easterlies.

The circulating air patterns are called "cells."

The area where the trade winds die out is known as the doldrums. Sailing ships may become stranded here.

WEATHER MACHINE

The sun heats Earth's surface, which warms the atmosphere. Warm air rises, and cool air moves in to replace it, causing winds. Warm air rises in the tropics. Cool air moves in from the north and south. Since Earth rotates on its axis, the winds bend, creating huge swirling weather patterns.

◀ TEMPERATE *This zone experiences changes in temperature and rainfall during the year, but none are too extreme.*

◀ POLAR *The Arctic and Antarctic polar regions have freezing conditions and little rainfall.*

◀ TROPICAL *This zone lies north and south of the equator and is generally hot and humid.*

Extreme weather

These days, we can watch the weather from space and even forecast it, but the one thing we cannot do is control it. Weather is one of the great powers on our Earth and in its extreme form is an awesome, deadly natural force.

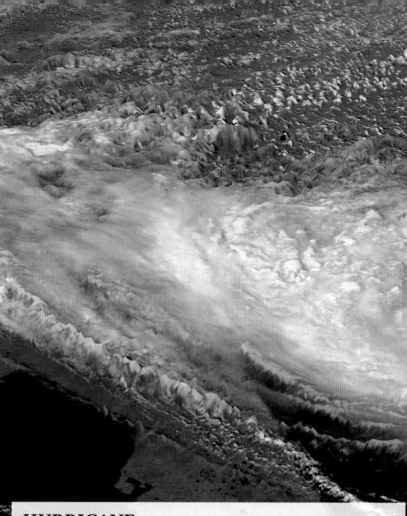

FAST FACTS

- There are about 2,000 thunderstorms happening in the world right now.
- Lightning kills some 24,000 people every year.
- Australia suffered its worst recorded bushfire season in 2019–2020.
- Arica, Chile, is one of the driest places on Earth. From 1903 to 1918 it had no rain.
- A tidal wave, or tsunami, hit Indian Ocean shorelines in 2004. It killed an estimated 230,000 people (p35).

HURRICANE

Also known as cyclones and typhoons, these enormous swirling storms rip away buildings, and wash away roads. In 2017, the winds of Hurricane Maria—at more than 175 mph (280 kmph)—caused catastrophic flooding and destruction in Dominica and Puerto Rico, killing more than 3,000 people.

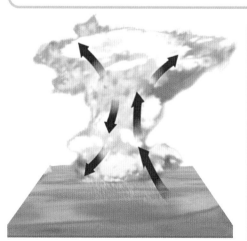

▲ THUNDERSTORMS *Huge storms form when warm air rises and cools causing huge clouds to grow higher and higher. As the water vapor cools, it falls down as heavy rain.*

▲ LIGHTNING *High up in a thundercloud, icy raindrops collide and create an electric charge. The bottom of the cloud is negatively charged, and the top is positive. Electricity jumps between them, and that's lightning.*

▲ FLOODS *cause more damage and kill more people than any other catastrophe caused by extreme weather. In 2018, more than 1,200 people lost their lives during flooding in India and Bangladesh.*

PREDICTING WEATHER

Weather can be very unpredictable, but most of the time, forecasts warn us of extreme weather and can help save lives. Orbiting weather satellites continuously image Earth's atmosphere. There are thousands of weather stations all over the world, on land and at sea, gathering data on clouds, temperature, air pressure, wind direction and speed, and so on. They pass the information to computers allowing meteorologists to predict how the weather will change.

▲ FIRE *All it takes is dry, parched earth and a bolt of lightning for a devastating forest fire to rage across miles and miles of land. If a fire hits urban areas it can destroy homes and claim many lives. Wildfires in California in 2021 alone have burned down more than 3 million acres (1 million ha) of land.*

▲ SNOW *A snowstorm can be deadly. A blizzard can bury cars and even houses. In 1999, a heavy snowfall caused an avalanche and buried the town of Galtür, Austria, under 33 ft (10 m) of snow.*

▶ HAILSTONES
Hail forms inside huge cumulonimbus clouds and often falls during a storm. Most of the time, hailstones are no bigger than marbles, but in June 2003, a hailstone measuring 7 in (17.8 cm) wide fell in the U.S. That's the size of a football!

◀ TORNADO
A tornado is a whirling funnel of air that moves across the ground and destroys everything in its way. The U.S. suffers from more tornadoes than any other country.

55

ENVIRONMENT AND ECOLOGY

Environment is the natural surroundings or conditions in which a plant, organism, or animal is found. Ecology is the study of species in their environment.

WHAT IS ECOLOGY?

Ecology is the study of the relationships between animals and plants and the environment they live in. Ecologists divide the world up into a series of environmental regions called biomes, which are based on climate and inhabited by similar types of animals and plants. Within these biomes are smaller areas called ecosystems, which have their own groups of animals and plants that interact with each other and have adapted to the particular conditions found there.

A shared planet

Humans are not the only species on the planet. We share it with many types of plants and animals—nearly two million have been identified. The way that living things interact is highly complex, but vital for their survival.

LIVING WORLD

There are very few places on Earth where life does not exist. Even extreme places, such as the icy poles or hot volcanoes, are populated by organisms. Scientists describe the whole of the living world as the biosphere.

JUST THE JOB

Animals and plants have adopted different strategies to survive in their environment. Some have specialized to live in one particular habitat, others can survive in many. Often, they have changed physically or adapted their lifestyle to suit the conditions.

Habitat Thorny devils change the color of their skin when they are cold or alarmed.

Migration Some birds and animals travel great distances every year to find food or to breed.

Population Lemming numbers change based on food availability among other things.

FOOD CHAINS

All living things need energy to survive. Energy from sunlight is used by plants and phytoplankton. Animals eat other living things, including plants, to get the nutrients they need for energy and to build their bodies. A food chain is a "chain" of living things—from plants to a series of bigger and more predatory animals—through which energy is transferred.

▼ SUN *The energy that shines down from the sun is absorbed by phytoplankton.*

▼ KRILL *Billions of these shrimplike creatures feed on plankton in the cold polar seas.*

▼ COD *Fish eat krill and plankton in the upper layers of the ocean.*

▼ SEAL *Hungry seals chase schools of fish, such as herring and young cod.*

▼ KILLER WHALE *These large predatory mammals eat seals.*

 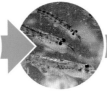   

▲ THE CRABS *of Christmas Island will cross roads, tennis courts, and golf courses to get to the sea during the breeding season.*

THE CARBON CYCLE

Carbon is a vital element to all life on Earth. Its atoms move in a natural cycle between land, water, and the atmosphere. Animals and plants are part of that cycle. Many systems on Earth work in a similar way, recycling vital ingredients such as nutrients, water, and oxygen.

Plants take in CO_2 during the day and emit it at night.

Burning gas from oil deposits releases CO_2.

Animals give off CO_2 and methane.

Volcanoes emit CO_2

Marine algae and phytoplankton absorb and release CO_2

CO_2 in rain washes carbonates out of rock.

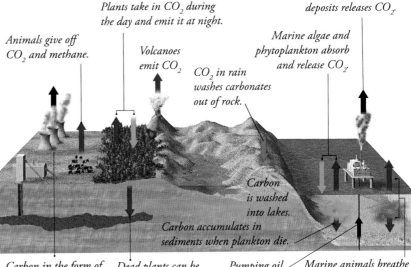

Carbon is washed into lakes.

Carbon accumulates in sediments when plankton die.

Carbon in the form of oil and coal gives off CO_2 when it is burned.

Dead plants can be slowly compressed under rock and turn into coal.

Pumping oil and gas releases stored carbon.

Marine animals breathe out CO_2 and release carbon when they die.

Lifestyle Pandas are only found in the wild in small areas of China where their main food, bamboo, grows.

Numbers Small plants grow quickly and produce lots of seeds so they have more chance of survival.

Cooperation Many plants need insects to pollinate them. In turn, the insect benefits from their nectar.

Dominance Trees put more effort into growing tall so they can get more light and nutrients than other plants.

Habitats

All living things need a place where they can live and breed successfully. This place is called a habitat. Habitats can be as big as a prairie or as small as a puddle. There can be many different habitats in a single area of land or sea.

Mountains Near cold and rocky mountain tops animals need a warm coat and nimble feet to survive.

Forests These are home to a wide variety of plants and animals that live at different levels among the trees.

Coasts Animals that live here have to cope with the tide coming in and out twice a day and constant battering by waves.

Mangroves The roots of mangrove trees are surrounded by salty water, and they make good hiding places for fish.

Coral reefs Reefs provide homes for hundreds of species. They are created by the skeletons of marine animals.

A home of their own Every animal and plant needs particular conditions for it to thrive. Plants need the right temperature, rainfall, and soil to grow in. Animals need shelter, food, and space to roam around. An organism will often adapt its lifestyle or even how it looks and behaves to suit its surroundings. This process is called adaptation.

FRAGMENTATION OF HABITAT

Fragmentation happens when land is cleared for farming, roads, or other uses, so the original habitat is broken up. The creatures that live there are left with small islands of habitat, leaving them vulnerable to predators because there is less cover when they search for food. Plants may also suffer as light, water, or wind levels can change significantly.

BIOMES OF THE WORLD

Ecologists group similar types of ecosystems into areas called biomes. Each type of biome, such as a tropical rainforest, has the same sort of climate and habitat as other rainforests around the world, but the species it contains may be different. Hot, wet, tropical biomes have many more species than cold or dry ones.

Evolution Every part of the world has species that do not live anywhere else. These are called native species and have evolved to suit the local conditions. This species of tree fern only grows wild in New Zealand.

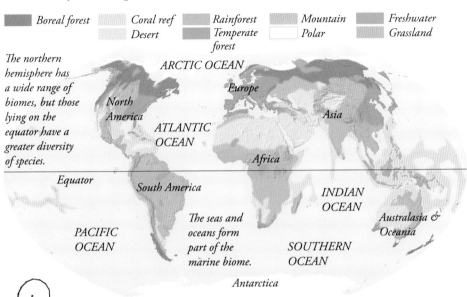

Boreal forest	Coral reef	Rainforest	Mountain	Freshwater
	Desert	Temperate forest	Polar	Grassland

The northern hemisphere has a wide range of biomes, but those lying on the equator have a greater diversity of species.

ARCTIC OCEAN

Europe

North America

Asia

ATLANTIC OCEAN

Africa

Equator

South America

INDIAN OCEAN

The seas and oceans form part of the marine biome.

Australasia & Oceania

PACIFIC OCEAN

SOUTHERN OCEAN

Antarctica

Invaders When new species are introduced to an area they can have a devastating effect on the ecosystem. Cane toads (right) were brought in to eat beetles in Australian sugar fields, but have become a pest because they also eat other animals.

BIODIVERSITY

Biodiversity is a measure of the variety of species in an ecosystem. All species have a role to play in the ecosystem. To understand an ecosystem properly, scientists have to identify all the organisms living there and find out how they interact. These researchers are collecting moths. Then they can protect any species or groups of species that are important to that ecosystem.

FAST FACTS

- More than 1.7 million species of different plants and animals have been identified.
- More than 1 million of these species are insects, and more than 390,000 are plants.
- As many as 18,000 new species are discovered each year, mostly plants and insects.
- More than 40 percent of amphibian species are threatened with extinction.
- Rainforests are the most biodiverse regions on Earth.

Many species face extinction. These groups are the most threatened. Approximate percentages are given here.

Birds 13%
Mammals 26%
Warm reef-forming corals 33%
Conifers 34%
Amphibians 41%

Percentages of threatened species

Deserts

We think of deserts as being hot, but some of them are very cold. What deserts *are* is dry. Any place that gets less than 10 in (25 cm) of rain or snow per year (such as the Antarctic ice sheet) is a desert.

This is the Sonoran Desert in the southwestern United States.

WARM DESERTS

Hot deserts are hot all the time during the day—cold deserts can be frosty in winter and moderately warm in summer. There is not much moisture in desert air, so there are very few clouds. At night, with little cloud cover, the temperature can plummet in a hot desert.

Golden barrel cactus

DESERT IN BLOOM

Once in a while, there is a rare and precious shower of rain, and the desert bursts into bloom (see above, Anza-Borrego Desert State Park, California). This is because seeds lie dormant—sometimes for years. When water falls, they germinate, flower, and create new seeds.

FIT FOR PURPOSE

A cactus is a type of plant called a succulent. Its "body" is actually a swollen, water-storing stem. The "prickles" are a kind of leaf that allows very little water to evaporate. In some other succulents, it's the leaves that swell and store water.

■ Deserts have formed in many different landscapes, wherever water is in short supply. Because there aren't many plants on the surface, deserts are vulnerable to weathering and erosion. Also, the huge variation in temperature can cause massive rocks to crack.

▲ DUNES *form large "sand seas" called ergs. The wind sculpts their graceful shapes.*

▲ ARCHES *Erosion by wind and water over time can puncture a rocky ridge to form an arch.*

▲ EARTH *Natural salts can cement rocks together into "desert pavement."*

▲ BUTTES *form when a plateau has been eroded to leave a rocky tower with steep sides.*

COLD DESERTS

The coldest and most northern of all the world's non-polar deserts, the Gobi Desert (shown here) stretches across China and Mongolia. Like many cold deserts, it sits on a high plateau, where the temperature is naturally lower than at sea level.

SANDSTORMS

Strong, dry winds blow across the desert, carrying clouds of sand and dust that reduce visibility to almost zero. Roads and wells are often covered completely, and a violent storm can dehydrate—or even suffocate—animals and people. Sandstorms last for hours, and some can even go on for days.

DESERT ANIMALS

From insects and reptiles to huge mammals, most desert animals have highly specialized characteristics that are precisely suited to their extreme conditions. Some get their water from the food they eat, for example, while others sleep during the hot days.

▲ FENNEC FOXES *use their huge ears to help them locate prey. The large surface area also allows heat to escape.*

▲ JERBOAS *keep cool by staying in an underground burrow.*

▶ THORNY DEVILS *have skin that absorbs water like blotting paper.*

Grasslands

Grasslands spring up in places that are too dry for forests to grow but get enough water to stop them becoming deserts. Almost 40 percent of Earth's land surface is covered by grasslands. They support a wide variety of animals, but the wide open spaces offer little protection from predators for larger animals.

TROPICAL GRASSLANDS

Also called savannas, tropical grasslands have distinct wet and dry seasons. Although it is warm all year round, rain only falls for six to eight months of the year. During a drought the grass can catch fire, but this is good for regenerating the savanna.

SAVANNA TREES
The leaves and small branches of savanna trees provide important food for browsing animals such as giraffes.

CHEETAHS *are perfectly camouflaged against the savanna grass.*

TEMPERATE GRASSLANDS

Temperate grasslands (called prairies in the U.S.) have hot summers and cold winters. Although they get rain throughout the year, there is too little for trees or shrubs to survive. However, the rich soil is good for the hundreds of wild flower species that grow among the grasses.

WILD BISON *are native to the prairies of the U.S. and were once hunted almost to extinction. Thanks to decades of conservation efforts, they are making a comeback.*

LIFE ON THE PLAIN

The huge quantities of grass out on the prairie support some of the world's biggest herbivores, such as elephants, rhinos, and giraffes. It also offers a hiding place for smaller animals and cover for predators to stalk their victims.

Burrowers Many small animals live in burrows. These protect them from the hot sun and cold nights, and help them escape from predators. Some animals live in burrows dug by other species.

Meerkat   Aardvark   Prairie dogs

Grazers Most grazing animals live in herds that offer protection from predators. They have long legs for running and strong teeth for chewing. Many have to migrate to find fresh grass in the dry season.

Kangaroos   Bison   Zebra

Predators These rely on stealth to obtain food. They frequently hunt in packs to isolate an animal from a herd or to scare other predators from a kill.

Hyena   Wolf   Jackal   Lion

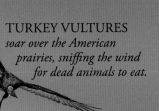

TURKEY VULTURES *soar over the American prairies, sniffing the wind for dead animals to eat.*

AMAZING GRASS

■ Grasses are one of the biggest families of flowering plants. They are well suited to dry conditions as they can store food in their deep roots, which absorb a lot of water. Because their leaves grow from below ground, grasses can survive being nibbled by animals as long as their roots are not disturbed. Their flowers are pollinated by the wind.

▲ FOXTAILS *These grasses have spiky seeds that attach to passing animals for dispersal.*

▲ BUFFALO GRASS *This short, hardy grass is found on the plains of North America.*

▲ SPINIFEX *Properly known as* Triodia, *this hummock grass covers the Australian bush.*

▲ WHEAT *Cereal crops were originally wild grasses cultivated for food by humans.*

Forests

Trees are the biggest plants on the planet. Forests of them cover large areas of land and provide shelter for other plants and animals. They will flourish anywhere that is warm and wet enough during their growing season.

TELL ME MORE...

The Amazon rainforest in South America covers an area almost as big as Australia. A mere 2.5 acres (1 hectare) may contain more than 750 types of tree and 1,500 other plants. Almost 50,000 plant species and one-seventh of all bird species live there. The trees keep their leaves all year long.

RAINFOREST

There are two types of rainforest—temperate and tropical. Both are found in areas of very high rainfall, which helps the trees grow tall and fast. Rainforests are full of animals and plants. In fact, about half of all land plant and animal species live in rainforests. Despite all the plant material, the soils in these regions are thin and poor in nutrients.

BOREAL FOREST

Boreal forests are found in northern countries that have long, snowy winters. Most of the trees that grow here are conifers, such as pine, spruce, and larch. Instead of flat leaves they have thin needles with a waxy coating, which keeps water from evaporating. Their branches slope downwards so that snow slides off.

▼ DYING LEAVES *turn brown in autumn.*

▲ LEAVES *fall from deciduous trees in autumn when light levels and the temperature drop. This allows trees to save energy and conserve water over the winter.*

TEMPERATE FOREST

Mixed, mainly broadleaf woodlands grow in regions that have long, warm summers and cool, frosty winters. They drop their leaves in winter, which allows flowering plants such as bluebells and aconites to grow in early spring before it gets too shady. The leaves break down to form a deep, rich soil. Many of these forests have been cleared for farming.

▼ BUTTERFLIES *are important pollinators of rainforest flowers high up in the canopy. The caterpillars of this postman butterfly feed on passion flower vine leaves.*

UNDER THREAT: DEFORESTATION

■ Forests face a number of threats. Large areas of the Amazon rainforest are being cleared to provide land for cattle ranching and soybean production. Other forests are logged for their valuable timber or for fuel. This can have a devastating effect on the forest ecosystem. Animals lose their homes and food supply, and the changing conditions affect plant growth. Some forests are planted to produce wood, but these lack much of the native wildlife of natural forest.

RAINFOREST LAYERS

■ EMERGENTS—the tallest trees are home to butterflies, eagles, and bats.

■ CANOPY—this layer is full of animals, birds, climbing plants, and orchids.

■ UNDERSTORY—provides homes for snakes and lizards and cover for predators.

■ SHRUB LAYER—consists of saplings and broad-leaved shrubs.

■ FOREST FLOOR—receives little light and is covered in decaying plant material.

▼ CONIFERS *protect their seeds in cones.*

Cone

Seeds

▲ SQUIRRELS *are experts at breaking open cones. Their sharp teeth can gnaw through the woody casing to expose the seeds.*

◄ FUNGI *are vital parts of forests. They break down rotting trees and leaves and provide food for animals.*

67

Mountains

No other places on Earth show such dramatic variations of habitat as the slopes of mountain ranges. The warm, sheltered valleys abound with animal and plant life, but only the hardiest of species can survive the windswept, often freezing environment of the exposed peaks.

RICH RESOURCES

Almost 25 percent of Earth's land surface area is covered by mountains. They feed most of the world's river systems and are rich in mineral resources. Few people live high up in the mountains, but many use them for activities such as climbing and skiing.

MOUNTAIN HIGHS AND LOWS

- Standing at a height of 29,032 ft (8,849 m), Mount Everest is the highest mountain on the land. It is part of the enormous range called the Himalayas in Asia.
- Mauna Kea, in Hawaii, is the world's tallest mountain, rising up 33,497 ft (10,210 m) from the ocean floor. Only 13,796 ft (4,205 m) is visible above sea level.
- Oxygen levels drop sharply with increasing altitude. Many animals produce more red blood cells, or have larger hearts, to carry more oxygen around their bodies.
- A "dead zone" occurs above 19,600 ft (6,000 m). Few animals can survive in the dead zone due to the high winds and freezing temperatures.
- The yellow-rumped leaf-eared mouse has been found at an altitude of 22,110 ft (6,739 m)—the highest of any known mammal in the world.

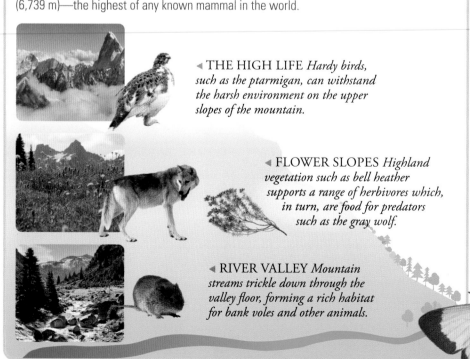

◀ THE HIGH LIFE *Hardy birds, such as the ptarmigan, can withstand the harsh environment on the upper slopes of the mountain.*

◀ FLOWER SLOPES *Highland vegetation such as bell heather supports a range of herbivores which, in turn, are food for predators such as the gray wolf.*

◀ RIVER VALLEY *Mountain streams trickle down through the valley floor, forming a rich habitat for bank voles and other animals.*

TELL ME MORE...

Mountains contain a rich range of habitats. Lush alpine meadows give way to conifer forests, while the snow-capped peaks dominate above. The main reason for the variation is the sharp drop in temperature with altitude—about 11°F (6°C) for every ⅗ mile (1 km) in winter.

MOUNTAIN MAMMALS

Despite the rugged terrain and cold air, many mammals make their home in the mountains. They must adapt to survive, so many grow thick winter coats to keep warm. Others migrate up and down the slopes through the year to avoid the worst weather.

▲ MOUNTAIN GOAT *Thick winter coats protect these agile, muscular herbivores as they scramble up steep mountain slopes.*

▲ SNOW LEOPARD *The predatory snow leopard has thick fur and small, rounded ears to conserve body heat.*

BUILDING MOUNTAINS

Mountains form when vast sheets of rock, called tectonic plates, collide beneath Earth's surface. Depending on which plates collide, the land is either pushed up to form mountains or molten rock rises to the surface to form volcanoes (👁 p32–33, p34–35). Volcanoes are more regularly shaped than mountains that have been folded and bent. Mountains tend to have poor, rocky soils and little grows near their peaks. Despite the danger of volcanoes, their ash turns into fertile soil for growing crops.

Polar regions

Imagine living in a place where the Sun doesn't rise during the winter months, then doesn't set in the summer. Add to this freezing temperatures, and you have two of the most inhospitable places on Earth—the North and South polar regions. Yet even here, life manages to survive.

NORTH POLE

THE ARCTIC

The Arctic is an ocean that is mostly frozen. At the North Pole the ice remains frozen all year, but farther south, the ice breaks up in summer and melts. In the future, climate change may melt all the Arctic sea ice in summer.

FAST FACTS

- The Arctic Ocean is the smallest and shallowest of the five major oceans.
- Ninety percent of Earth's ice is found in Antarctica. At its thickest point, the ice is 3 miles (4.7 km) deep.
- There are hundreds of lakes under the Antarctic ice sheet.
- The coldest recorded polar temperatures are −93.3°F (−69.6°C) in the Arctic and −128.6°F (−89.2°C) in the Antarctic.

▼ ICE *looks blue because it absorbs red light and reflects back the blue.*

Walking on top of the world

More animals live in the Arctic than Antarctica. This is because the winter ice provides a bridge to Russia and North America and more varied food sources. Land predators, including polar bears, also take advantage of the seals and fish that live beneath the ice.

HUMAN INFLUENCES

People have lived in the Arctic for thousands of years. Indigenous peoples, such as the Inuit and Yupik, have learned to survive the cold and live on mainly fish and meat. However, there is oil beneath the surface of the Arctic and Antarctica, which makes them a target for prospectors. Antarctica is protected from exploitation by treaty, but the shrinking ice of the Arctic is opening it up for exploration. Oil and gas pipelines already cross Alaska and Siberia, which has led to oil spills and environmental damage.

THE ANTARCTIC

The Antarctic differs from the Arctic because there is land beneath the ice. Nothing lives in the interior, and it is classed as a cold desert because it is so dry. Freezing winds help make it the coldest place on Earth.

THE TUNDRA

Tundra is the name given to cold, windy regions where the soil is frozen most of the year. The plants that grow here are low and stunted, but mosses, lichens, and small shrubs can survive the freezing conditions.

A safe refuge
There are no predatory land mammals on Antarctica, which makes it an ideal place for colonies of seals, penguins, and seabirds to breed. Despite it being so cold, the water is full of plankton, krill, and fish to feed their young.

▼ CARIBOU *scrape away snow in search of lichen and moss.*

Migration Every summer, huge herds of caribou cross the tundra in search of food. Arctic foxes and hares stay all year.

Winter coats Some animals that live on the tundra change their coat from brown to white to hide them when it snows.

71

Fresh water

Fresh water covers about three percent of Earth's surface. Falling rain flows back to the ocean in streams and rivers, or gathers to form ponds, lakes, and wetlands.

FRESHWATER HABITATS

Lakes and rivers contain water with a low salt content compared to seawater. Most sea creatures cannot survive in fresh water, and most freshwater animals cannot live at sea. But salmon (right) spend part of their lives at sea and have special adaptations that allow them to change from fresh to salt water and back again when they return to their home river to breed.

FOOD CHAINS

Food chains in rivers depend on inputs from the land around. This can be nutrients from farm land or fallen leaves, which provide food for algae and bacteria. These are eaten by insect larvae and snails, which are then eaten by fish and frogs.

Water snail

▲ POND LIFE
A sample of water from a pond shows a sample of species living there, such as insects, snails, tadpoles, and pond weed.

FISH HAVENS

Around 50 percent of fish species live in fresh water. Many fresh waters contain unique species, such as this African cichlid, because rivers and lakes rarely connect for species to colonize new areas.

LIFE OF A RIVER

▲ SOURCE *Rivers start out as fast-flowing streams.*

▲ MOUTH *When they reach the sea, rivers are slow and wide.*

The ecology of a river changes as it runs from the hills to the sea. At its source, the water is too fast for plants to take root, but invertebrates and fish thrive in the well-oxygenated conditions. As it slows, a wider variety of plants take root in mud brought down from the hills. Animals make homes and hunt along its banks.

Wetlands

Wetlands are among the richest habitats on Earth. They include permanently wet swamps and marshes, and bogs and fens that have waterlogged soils. The water can be fresh or salty.

WATERY ROOTS

Wetland plants have adapted to cope with the wet conditions. Many can float, or have waxy leaves that resist water. Their leaves also transport oxygen to submerged roots to keep them alive. Some roots can survive being exposed to the air, or changes from fresh to salt water.

▶ HERONS *stalk wetlands for fish, including those hiding among plant roots.*

SWIMMERS

Capybaras are rodents that live in the Pantanal, a large wetland in South America. Like most semi-aquatic mammals their ears, eyes, and nostrils are on top of their heads so they can stay alert while swimming.

FACT

Archerfish (below) live in mangrove swamps around Indonesia. They prey on insects that land on the leaves and roots of mangrove trees. After selecting a target from under the water, the fish sticks its snout out and blasts the insect with a jet of water. The insect falls into the water and is gobbled up by the fish.

LIFE IN THE WETLANDS

Wetlands are home to many species of insects, amphibians, and reptiles that need water to feed or reproduce in. This, in turn, attracts hungry birds and larger animals that prey on them. Many mammals have also adapted to wetland life, including beavers, hippos, and water buffalo.

▲ PITCHER PLANTS *These trap insects to obtain nutrients they can't get from the soil.*

▲ MAMMALS *The Okavango Delta in Africa is an ideal home for water-loving hippos.*

▲ REPTILES *Caimans and alligators are the chief predators in many swamps.*

▲ BIRDS *Still, wetland waters make ideal fishing grounds for waterbirds.*

Oceans and sea life

Not only do oceans cover more than 70 percent of Earth's surface, but they're also incredibly deep—easily the biggest habitat on the planet. What's more, they offer their residents a fairly stable temperature—and plenty of water!

FACT

The biggest fish in the ocean is the whale shark. It can grow up to 60 ft (18 m) long—bigger than a bus!

INGENIOUS FEEDERS

Earth's oceans accommodate a wide variety of exotic creatures. Many of these have developed unique adaptations that allow them to search for food and devour prey in their watery environment.

▲ SQUID *grab prey using the suckers at the end of their two long tentacles.*

OCEAN ZONES AND HABITATS

The ocean is not just one habitat, but many. The first 3 ft (1 m) from the top—the surface layer—is the richest in both nutrients and vital gases from the atmosphere. But the surface layer is also vulnerable to pollution and floating litter, which can damage ocean life. Below this lie five more layers:

THE SUNLIT ZONE *gets enough sunlight for photosynthesis to fuel the growth of plankton—the basis of the food chain. This layer may extend down to 660 ft (200 m).*

THE TWILIGHT ZONE *gets just enough light so that ocean creatures can hunt, but not enough for photosynthesis.*

THE DARK ZONE *gets virtually no light, and a lot of the food is fallout or "snow" from above. Temperatures are low (39°F), and pressure is high.*

THE ABYSSAL ZONE *contains the vast, muddy, seabed plains (abyssal plains) after which it's named, but animals are scarce.*

THE HADAL ZONE *extends below the abyssal zone over less than two per cent of the ocean floor. Only a few human beings have ever been there, and we know little about it.*

HARMING THE OCEAN

Modern fishing techniques often take too many of one fish, or scoop up endangered species by accident.

▶ FISHING *is difficult to control because no one owns the open sea, and its vast waters are hard to police.*

▲ SEA ANEMONES *cling to rocks and kill their prey with venomous barbs.*

▲ SEA SLUGS *scrape algae off hard surfaces using sharp, toothlike scales called denticles.*

▲ ANGLER FISH *use a lure on the end of a spine to attract prey.*

COASTS

Coastlines provide many different habitats. High up on rocky shores, tough creatures such as barnacles survive crashing waves and exposure at low tide. In coastal mud, buried bivalves such as clams filter food from the water.

▲ ROCKPOOL *ecosystems contain small algae and seaweeds. Limpets feed on the algae, and starfish feed on limpets, mussels, and other shellfish.*

BLACK SMOKERS

At hydrothermal vents, water heated under the sea dissolves minerals from the rocks. When the water erupts through the ocean floor, it forms crusty "chimneys" that can reach several yards (meters) in height.

Coral reefs

Sometimes called "rainforests of the sea," coral reefs are spectacular marine ecosystems that thrive in warm, clear, shallow waters. Ecotourists love to visit the reefs to see the colorful and amazing variety of animals that live and hunt here.

RICH PICKINGS
Ocean predators such as dolphins (left) and sharks (right) lurk in coral reefs. They feed on the fish that live there.

FAST FACTS

- Corals are actually simple animals with tiny algae cells living inside them.
- The Great Barrier Reef, off northeastern Australia, is about 1,430 miles (2,300 km) long.
- Excess CO_2 in the atmosphere is making the ocean more acidic, which could damage coral.
- Coral fossils have been discovered dating from more than 500 million years ago.

THREATS TO CORAL

A reef can be damaged by anchors scraping its surface, and explosives thrown into the water to kill fish. Coastal developments release harmful sediment into the water, and higher temperature can cause coral to expel the algae in their body, so they turn white. This is called coral bleaching.

STONY CORALS

Coral reefs are made by reef-forming polyps (stony corals). These small organisms (right) secrete calcium carbonate from their gut cavity, which builds up on the rock underneath, forming coral reefs. Some corals exist as single, large polyps, but most live in colonies.

ALL SHAPES AND SIZES

Coral reefs come in different forms. The most common is the fringing reef (such as this one in the Indo-Pacific Ocean), which grows off many tropical coasts. Corals can't grow above water, so the reef's flat top usually lies just below the surface. Barrier reefs are separated from a coastline by a lagoon, while atolls (see right) form coral rings in the middle of the sea.

BIRTH OF AN ATOLL

An atoll starts life as a fringing reef around a volcanic island. As the volcano weakens and sinks (or sea levels rise), the coral grows and turns into a barrier reef. Eventually, the volcano disappears, leaving an atoll—a ring of established coral reef around a central lagoon.

◄ FRINGING REEF *forms around volcanic island.*

◄ BARRIER REEF *grows around the sinking volcano.*

◄ VOLCANO DISAPPEARS *leaving atoll with central lagoon.*

CROWN OF THORNS

One of the world's largest starfish (it has a leg span of 12–16 in/30–40 cm), the crown of thorns feeds mainly on corals. When there are too many, it can cause serious harm to coral reefs. The Great Barrier Reef off the coast of Australia, for example, has been severely damaged by hungry crown of thorns. These prickly creatures hurt people too—their spines are poisonous, so stepping on one can cause severe pain and sickness.

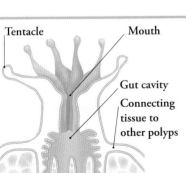

Tentacle Mouth

Gut cavity

Connecting tissue to other polyps

Calcium carbonate exoskeleton

▲ BRAIN CORAL *is arranged in wiggly lines that look like the surface of a brain.*

▲ FAN CORAL *feathers into delicate shapes and provides a home for tiny animals.*

▲ STAGHORN *coral grows in the shape of branches, which look like tiny antlers.*

▲ SOFT CORALS *have tiny, individual polyps and can look like branching bushes.*

Climate change

The biggest problem facing our planet is climate change. Although Earth has swung between extreme heat and cold throughout its existence, human activity, especially the burning of fossil fuels, is interfering with the natural cycle and heating up the atmosphere.

IMPACT OF CLIMATE CHANGE

Trying to predict what will happen as our planet warms up is not easy. We know that ice at the poles is melting and this is making sea levels rise. Warmer temperatures are likely to change other aspects of the weather. Some countries, such as those in North Africa, may become hotter and drier, while other areas, such as Northern Europe, may become colder and wetter. There will probably be more intense storms, droughts, and flooding.

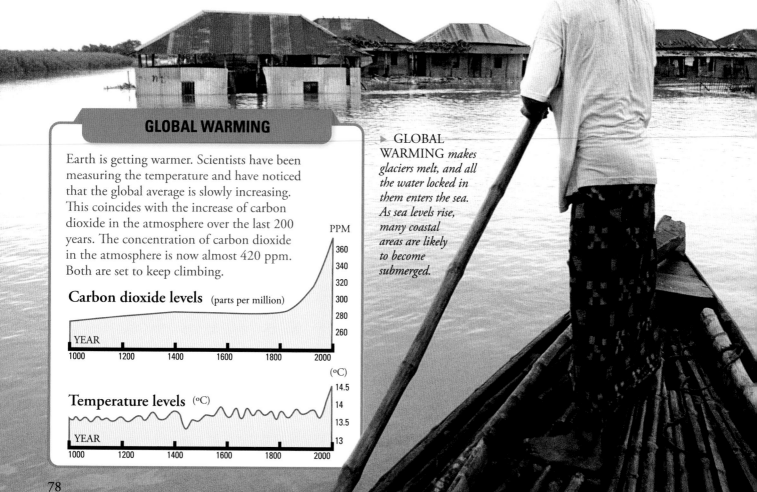

▶ GLOBAL WARMING *makes glaciers melt, and all the water locked in them enters the sea. As sea levels rise, many coastal areas are likely to become submerged.*

GLOBAL WARMING

Earth is getting warmer. Scientists have been measuring the temperature and have noticed that the global average is slowly increasing. This coincides with the increase of carbon dioxide in the atmosphere over the last 200 years. The concentration of carbon dioxide in the atmosphere is now almost 420 ppm. Both are set to keep climbing.

Carbon dioxide levels (parts per million)

PPM
360
340
320
300
280
260

YEAR
1000   1200   1400   1600   1800   2000

(°C)
14.5
14
13.5
13

Temperature levels (°C)

YEAR
1000   1200   1400   1600   1800   2000

GREENHOUSE GASES

■ The atmosphere helps keep Earth warm. Gases such as water vapour, carbon dioxide, and methane trap heat from the sun and keep the surface warm enough to support life. However, if these gases increase, Earth gets warmer and warmer.

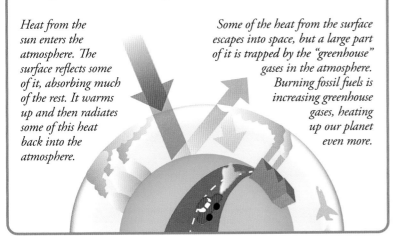

Heat from the sun enters the atmosphere. The surface reflects some of it, absorbing much of the rest. It warms up and then radiates some of this heat back into the atmosphere.

Some of the heat from the surface escapes into space, but a large part of it is trapped by the "greenhouse" gases in the atmosphere. Burning fossil fuels is increasing greenhouse gases, heating up our planet even more.

Beware of the burps!
One of the most worrying greenhouse gases is methane. Huge quantities of it are produced in rice paddies and also by cows, which belch it out as a by-product of eating grass. Methane is better able to trap heat in the atmosphere than carbon dioxide. One cow can produce up to 53 gallons (200 liters) of methane a day—that's a lot of gas.

UNDER THREAT

Climate change is not just a threat to humans. Many animals and plants will also suffer through changes to their environment. For example, reduced rainfall can be serious for trees or wetland habitats. The most vulnerable species are those that live only in one small area, or are unable to move quickly. This includes some of the world's rarest species.

▶ THE COSTA RICAN *golden toad is thought to have been driven to extinction by climate change.*

SAVING ENERGY

Almost everything humans do in everyday life requires energy. Most of our energy comes from burning coal, gas, or oil, but these produce greenhouse gases. To prevent this happening, scientists are looking at new ways to save energy and cleaner ways of making it.

Preventative measures We can all do our bit to prevent global warming by using energy-saving devices, switching off lights, and turning the heating down a few degrees.

▼ WIND-UP *radios save on batteries and electricity.*

▼ LED *lights use far less energy than old-style light bulbs.*

Alternative fuels Transport is one of the biggest sources of greenhouse gases. Scientists are trying to develop new vehicles that use hydrogen, biofuels, and electricity instead of polluting petrol.

◀ THIS CAR *runs on batteries that have been charged by electricity.*

Eco living Houses can be built that need less energy to run them. This one is kept warm by the soil around it, and is lit by special tubes that reflect and magnify sunlight. Solar panels and windmills, which are used to harness renewable energy, can be used to provide electricity, too.

Looking to the future

Humans are the dominant species on the planet. We make use of all Earth's resources, but there is a limit to how long these will last if we carry on using them up at our current rate. It is in our own best interests to find ways of living that do not harm the environment, and protect the animals and plants that live here too.

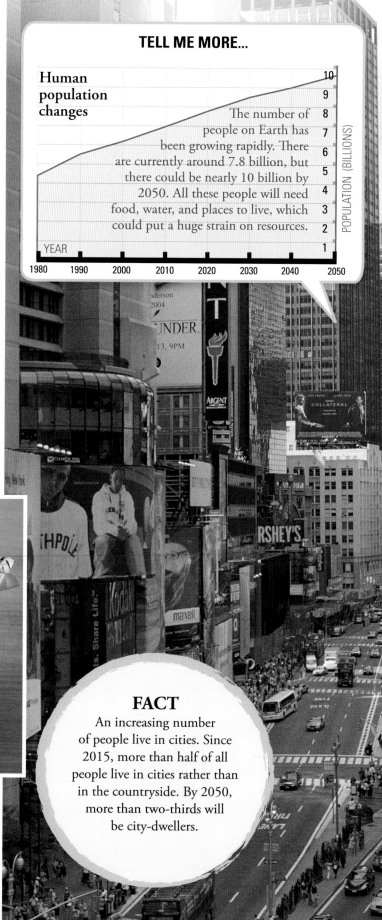

TELL ME MORE...

Human population changes

The number of people on Earth has been growing rapidly. There are currently around 7.8 billion, but there could be nearly 10 billion by 2050. All these people will need food, water, and places to live, which could put a huge strain on resources.

YEAR

POPULATION (BILLIONS)

1980 1990 2000 2010 2020 2030 2040 2050

POLLUTION PREVENTION

For years, humans have been dumping the waste products of industrial processes on the ground, in bodies of water, or into the air. By using new and cleaner technologies we can reduce the amount of toxic substances produced and find ways to make them less damaging to the environment.

FACT
An increasing number of people live in cities. Since 2015, more than half of all people live in cities rather than in the countryside. By 2050, more than two-thirds will be city-dwellers.

Recycling Humans use and waste an enormous amount of Earth's resources. Most trash is put in large holes in the ground or piles on the ground, but we are rapidly running out of space. A better way to save resources is recycling. Paper, plastics, metal, glass, and textiles can all be recycled and used again.

PROTECTING SEEDS

More than one-third of all flowering plants are vulnerable to extinction. Many of these species could be valuable to humans, but are being wiped out before their uses can be discovered. Scientists are now going around the world looking for plants and taking their seeds for storage in seed banks. This way, they can grow new plants if their original habitat is destroyed.

CONSERVATION

Wild areas are important, but many are being destroyed or raided for their resources. Organizations around the world are trying to protect wildlife and habitats by building sanctuaries for endangered species, such as the orangutan, and preserving key areas, including wetlands and forests.

Ecotourism Traveling to a new place is fun, but tourism has an impact on the people, animals, and plants that live there. Ecotourism helps protect the future of national parks and other protected areas by encouraging operators to plan resorts in a way that looks after the local wildlife and environment.

📷 **TAKE A PICTURE**

Tourists bring wealth to an area. When wildlife itself is a tourist attraction, local businesses are likely to look after the habitat.

Reforestation Many of the world's original forests have been cut down. Forests are a vital ecosystem, so in some areas new woodlands are being developed using native trees. If managed sustainably, they will provide an income for local people and a safe home for wildlife.

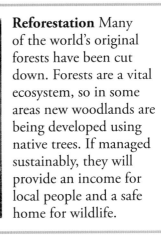

LIVING WORLD

Animals, plants, fungi, protists, bacteria, and archaea are the six main groups—or kingdoms—of life on Earth. They make up the living world.

Life on Earth

Life on Earth is hugely varied. Sunflowers and sharks look like they have nothing in common, but all living things share certain features: they are made up of cells; they need energy to survive; they have a life cycle; and they can reproduce.

THE SIX KINGDOMS

Scientists organize all life forms using a classification system. At the top of the system used in this book are six broad groups called kingdoms. Every living thing fits into a kingdom based on its cell structure and the way it gets energy. Kingdoms are divided into smaller and smaller groups, based on shared characteristics. The smallest grouping is species.

Animals are living things that are made up of many cells (multicelled). They get energy by eating food.

Plants are also multicelled. The cell walls are made of cellulose. Plants make their own food through a process called photosynthesis.

Fungi are organisms that do not need sunlight to grow. Many fungi live underground—all that can be seen above ground are the parts that make spores for reproduction, which are called mushrooms.

PHYLUM: *Chordates*—*Animals with some form of spine.*

CLASS: *Mammals*—*These are chordates that nurse their young with milk. Most give birth to live young.*

ORDER: *Carnivores*—*These mammals have powerful jaws and specialized teeth for killing and eating meat.*

FAMILY: *Felids*—*These are carnivores that have extending claws. The common name for Felids is "cat."*

GENUS: **Panthera**—*These are large cats that can roar as well as purr.*

SPECIES: **Panthera pardus**—*This name identifies the roaring cat as a leopard.*

LIFE CYCLE

All living things have a time when they grow and a time when they die. They also reproduce, which ensures the survival of the species. Animals lay eggs or give birth to live young, plants and fungi produce seeds or spores, and bacteria and protists usually divide in two to reproduce.

DUCKLING

EGG

ADULT DUCK

FOOD CHAINS

Desert shrub
Fagonia sp.

Gerbil
Meriones sp.

Fennec fox
Vulpes zerda

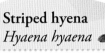

Striped hyena
Hyaena hyaena

▲ PRODUCERS *such as plants are the first stage in a food chain. Plants need energy from sunlight, nutrients from the soil, and water to grow.*

▲ PRIMARY CONSUMERS, *such as gerbils, are the first animals in a chain. They are herbivores —animals that eat only plants.*

▲ SECONDARY CONSUMERS *are carnivores—animals that eat meat.*

▲ SCAVENGERS AND DECOMPOSERS *Scavengers eat dead animals, helping to break down organic matter. Maggots, fungi, and bacteria are major decomposers.*

Protists are basic life forms. Most protists are single-celled and are microscopic, but some group together and are more easily seen, such as algae on a pond.

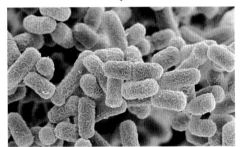

Bacteria are among the simplest forms of life. They are single-celled and too small to see without a microscope. Bacteria can live in the air, in water, and even inside bodies.

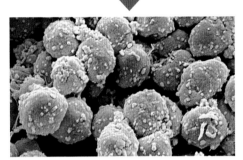

Archaea Although similar to bacteria in both size and structure, archaea have different ways of gathering energy. Some are able to live in extreme habitats, such as hot springs.

THREATENED SPECIES

In every kingdom, there are species that are under threat of extinction.
There are many reasons why a species fails to continue, from habitat loss to disease to poaching (👁 p80–81).

The International Union for the Conservation of Animals (IUCN) has researched more than 142,500 animal and plant species to create their Red List of Threatened Species. They found that:

■ In 2016, at least 780 animals and plants became extinct or extinct in the wild.

■ More than 40,000 species are under threat of extinction.

◁ More than one out of every four mammal species are threatened with extinction, including the Père David's deer.

◁ Plants are also at risk, with more than 22,000 species under threat, including the lady's slipper orchid.

◁ More than 41 percent of amphibians are under threat. Poison dart frogs are being wiped out along with their forest habitat.

Which species are at risk?

⚠ Most of the animals in this chapter appear on the IUCN Red List. Those with red triangles are at risk of extinction, and may already be extinct in the wild. Yellow triangles show species that are vulnerable— they risk becoming endangered in the near future. Green triangles mean there is little or no risk of them becoming endangered at present.

Plant life

There are more than 390,900 identified species of plants in the world. From the tallest redwood tree to the smallest duckweed, and the plainest moss to the most exotic orchid, plants all play a vital role in sustaining life on Earth.

WHAT IS A PLANT?

A plant is an organism made up of many cells that is able to manufacture its own food. Most plants do this using sunlight, carbon dioxide, and water to make carbohydrates.

■ The world's largest plant is the **giant redwood** tree, at more than 275 ft (84 m) tall with a trunk 36 ft (11 m) in diameter. The largest flower head is that of the titan arum from Sumatra, which grows to about 10 ft (3 m) tall.

■ Some plants are too small to see clearly without a magnifying lens. The tiniest flowering plant is a duckweed known as **watermeal**. A whole plant is about 1⁄32 in (1 mm) long.

*The **flower** contains the reproductive parts of flowering plants.*

Leaves collect sunlight and contain the tiny structures that make food for the plant.

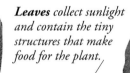

*The **stem** provides support for the leaves and flower head and carries water, minerals, and food to all parts of the plant.*

*Some plants, such as daisies have **simple leaves**: a leaf that has just one flat blade.*

*The main **root**, or taproot, anchors the plant in the ground. Together with the side roots, it absorbs water and minerals from the soil.*

*Other plants have **compound leaves**, made up of smaller leaflets.*

PLANTS ARE ESSENTIAL FOR LIFE...

■ Without plants there would be very little oxygen in the air for us to breathe. Plants help reduce the Greenhouse Effect (👁 p78–79) by using up some of the extra carbon dioxide we produce.

■ Plants and algae form the base of most food chains. Nearly everything we eat comes from plants, or from animals that eat plants. Animals that eat only plants are called herbivores.

■ Plants have many other uses. Without them there would be no timber for building or burning, and no cotton, coal, paper, or rubber. Many medicines, toiletries, and dyes also come from plants.

Photosynthesis

All living things need food for energy but, unlike animals, plants make their own food. The plant's leaves absorb sunlight and a gas called carbon dioxide from the air, while the roots take up water. Inside the leaf, energy from the sunlight is used to turn the carbon dioxide and water into sugary food for the plant. The process is called photosynthesis, which means "making things with light." The plant also creates oxygen as a by-product of photosynthesis, which it releases through its leaves.

*At night the plant takes some of the **oxygen** back in to help it burn its own sugars for energy.*

*The plant's leaves absorb **carbon dioxide** from the air and use it in photosynthesis.*

CARBON DIOXIDE

OXYGEN

▲ INSIDE A LEAF
Photosynthesis takes place within tiny structures called chloroplasts, inside leaf cells. Chloroplasts are green because they contain a pigment called chlorophyll.

*Plants need **water** to stay strong and healthy. Water is carried round a tree in minute tubes called xylem.*

*Tree **roots** can take up even more space underground as branches do above it. They give the tree stability and take up water and minerals.*

WATER

TRANSPIRATION

The surface of a leaf is covered in microscopic pores called stomata. When a stoma opens it allows carbon dioxide into the leaf for photosynthesis, and also water vapor to escape in a process called transpiration. The lost moisture is replaced by water drawn up through the roots. Water from the soil contains many of the minerals that the plant needs.

Guard cell   *Stoma*

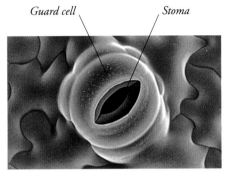

▲ OPEN STOMA *Each stoma or pore is flanked by a pair of guard cells, which open and close to control the amount of gas and water vapor passing in and out of the leaf.*

Leaf colors

Leaves contain a variety of pigments. In spring and summer the green pigment chlorophyll masks the colors of the others. In winter, lack of sunlight forces deciduous trees to stop photosynthesis. The chlorophyll in their leaves is broken down, allowing other colors—yellow, red, and brown—to show.

Types of plants

There are two main groups of plants: those that make seeds in order to reproduce and those that are seedless. Seedless plants reproduce from spores.

SPORES

Spores are tiny cells that can divide to form a many-celled body. This body contains sex cells that can be fertilized and grow into a new plant.

Ferns store spores in capsules on the underside of their leaves.

SEEDLESS PLANTS

■ **Mosses** *around 10,000 species* Mosses do not have roots. Instead, they take in water through their leaves, which means they can grow without soil. They attach to bare ground, trees, and rock using rootlike hairs called rhizoids.

■ **Liverworts** *around 7,500 species* Liverworts are the earliest known form of plant life. They are generally small, leafy-looking plants that grow in damp places, and sometimes in water. The umbrella-like structures are reproductive bodies.

■ **Horsetails** *about 20 species* We can tell from fossils that today's horsetails look very similar to those living 300 million years ago. Modern horsetails are smaller than the ancient ones, which grew up to 150 ft (45 m) high and formed great forests.

■ **Ferns** *around 12,000 species* Ferns are typically found in damp, shaded places. They come in a great variety of shapes and sizes, from dainty miniatures to great tree ferns with fronds (leaves) up to 16 ft (5 m) long.

PLANT EVOLUTION

Seedless plants are the oldest plants on the planet, first appearing about 475 million years ago. Flowering plants are the youngest, a mere 130 million years old.

I'M A SURVIVOR

Ginkgo biloba is the sole surviving species of a group of plants that once grew all over the world, but today grows wild only in China. Ginkgo fossils have been found that are 200 million years old—and they show that the plant has not changed in all that time.

TIMELINE OF PLANT EVOLUTION

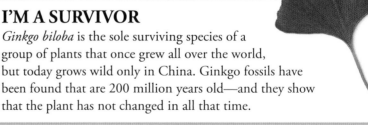

475 Million Years Ago	390–360 mya	360–290 mya	130 mya
Liverworts and mosses—the first seedless plants	Ferns	Conifers—the first seeded plants	Flowering plants

CONIFERS

The group of trees known as conifers produce seeds on cones rather than in flowers. Most conifers are "evergreen" plants, which don't drop their leaves in the winter. There are about 600 species of conifer, including cypresses, firs, pines, larches, and the tallest trees in the world, coastal redwoods. Yew trees are unusual, coneless conifers.

Monterey cypress
Cupressus macrocarpa

Korean fir
Abies koreana

Norway spruce
Picea abies

English yew
Taxus baccata

BROADLEAF TREES

Trees that produce their seeds in flowers rather than cones tend to have broad leaves. Many broadleaf trees are "deciduous"—they lose their leaves in winter to save energy.

FLOWERING PLANTS

About 80 percent of all known plant species are flowering plants, also known as angiosperms. This group includes a huge range of plants, from trees and grasses to garden flowers, and from cacti to carnivorous plants.

TOUGH FLOWERING PLANTS

Some flowering plants have extraordinary abilities to survive in harsh environments.

■ **No soil**
Parasitic plants such as mistletoe can grow without soil, because they tap into a host plant and steal its nutrients instead. Epiphytes such as bromeliads also grow on other plants, usually to help them reach sunlight, but do not damage their hosts.

■ **Poor soil**
Carnivorous plants cannot get all their nutrients from the soil, so they supplement their diet with meat. When a fly lands on a Venus flytrap, the leaves close up and the plant releases juices that help it digest the fly's body.

■ **No water**
Cacti grow in very dry places. After rain, the cactus absorbs and stores enough water in its thick stem to survive the next dry spell.

Types of flower

Flowers contain the organs that a plant uses to make seeds and pollen.

▶ SIMPLE *Tulips have simple flowers. They are built around a circle, and all the petals look the same.*

▶ COMPLEX *Orchid flowers are complex. They have the same parts as simple flowers, but they develop into all kinds of unusual forms to attract the right kind of pollinating insect.*

▶ COMPOSITE *Gerberas produce composite flowers. The head is not one flower, but made up of hundreds of little florets.*

▶ SPIRE *Gladioli flowers grow in tall spires or inflorescences. The flowers open one at a time, starting from the bottom.*

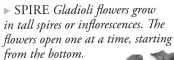

Plant reproduction

Flowering plants and cone-bearing plants (such as conifers) are seed-producers. Most flowering plants reproduce through seeds, although some have vegetative reproduction too. In order to produce seeds, a flower must first be pollinated.

FACT
Pollinators such as insects and bats may be attracted to flowers by their scent—but that doesn't mean the flower smells nice to us. Rafflesia flowers fill the air with the smell of rotting meat to attract flies. Yuck!

WHAT IS A FLOWER?
Flowers contain a plant's sexual organs. Flowers are often brightly colored or scented to attract pollinators.

*In a simple plant, **petals** grow in a circle, or whorl.*

*The **filaments** and **anthers** together are called **stamens**. They are the male parts of the plant.*

*The **anther** is where pollen is produced.*

***Sepals** grow on the outer whorl. In some flowers, they look the same as the petals.*

*The **filament** supports the anther.*

*The stigma, style, and ovary together are called the **carpel**. They are the female parts of the plant.*

*The **stigma** receives pollen.*

*The **ovary** is where seeds are produced.*

*The **style** connects the stigma to the ovary.*

GERMINATION

■ Seeds contain everything a plant needs to grow: an embryo and a food supply, which are protected inside a hard coat called a testa.

■ In the right conditions—usually a dark, damp, and warm place, such as in soil—the seed will germinate. First, the seed absorbs water. Then the embryo starts to grow, using its food store. A root appears, followed by a shoot. Seed leaves are attached to this shoot; the first true leaves don't appear until later.

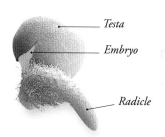

Testa
Embryo
Radicle

▲ ROOT *As the embryo starts to grow, the testa splits and the first root, called a radicle, grows downwards.*

Plumule

▲ SHOOT *The first shoot, called the plumule, grows upwards. The plumule reaches above ground, and becomes the plant stem.*

Seed leaf

▲ SEED LEAF *Some plants have just one seed leaf, but others have two. They contain the remains of the seed's food store.*

PLANT REPRODUCTION

■ Flowers attract insects, birds, and mammals, which come to feed on nectar. Bees also collect pollen. Once a plant is fertilized, the flower is no longer needed. The petals die and fall off.

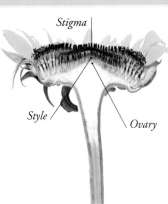

Stigma

Style

Ovary

▲ POLLINATION *When a bee visits a flower to drink nectar, it picks up pollen from the flower's anthers.*

▲ FERTILIZATION *The bee visits a second sunflower and transfers the pollen to the stigmas. This fertilizes the plant.*

▲ SEEDS *The pollen grows down the style to the ovary, where it fertilizes an egg cell. A new plant starts to form. This is the seed.*

▲ DISPERSAL *In order to grow, seeds need to leave the plant. Birds eat some of them and scatter others, which sprout and grow.*

SEED DISPERSAL

■ Many plants produce fruit that encourage animals to eat and disperse their seeds, but not all...

▲ HITCHING A RIDE *Burrs become hooked onto animal fur. Their host carries them away, then they fall off to the ground.*

▲ FORCE *When the seeds are ready, Himalayan balsam flowers burst open. The force sends the seeds flying out.*

▲ WATER *Coconut palms use the sea to disperse their seeds. Coconuts have been known to drift for huge distances.*

▲ WIND *Dandelion seeds are light and fluffy. Like tiny parachutes, they catch the wind to disperse far and wide.*

VEGETATIVE REPRODUCTION

■ Some flowering plants don't only reproduce through seeds. Instead, they form plantlets that are genetically identical to the parent plant.

▲ STOLONS *Strawberries have stolons—stems that grow along the ground. New plants grow from leaf nodes along the stolon.*

▲ TUBERS *such as Jerusalem artichokes are food stores for the parent plant, but they can also sprout and grow into new plants.*

▲ RHIZOMES *Irises spread through underground stems called rhizomes. The rhizome divides and forms new plants.*

▲ BULB *Onions and tulips grow from bulbs, which are buds that are surrounded by very swollen leaves.*

Animal life

There are nearly 1.4 million identified species of animal, making this the largest kingdom of living things.

WHO'S WHO?

Most animals are invertebrates: they have no backbone. Animals with backbones are known as vertebrates, and they can be divided up into different classes.

▲ THOSE ARE ANIMALS?
It's usually easy to tell an animal from a plant—animals are the ones that move about. But this isn't always the case. Corals look like plants and have limited movement. However, they take in food to get energy and they have nerves that control their reactions (such as shrinking away from danger). These things are what make them animals.

Vertebrates

Invertebrate

▲ MAMMALS
There are about 6,300 species of mammals. What makes this class unique is that the young feed on milk from their mother. Mammals are warm-blooded, most have a hairy body, and most give birth to live young.

▲ BIRDS *There are more than 10,700 species of birds. They are warm-blooded, have wings and a bill, and a body covered in feathers. All birds lay eggs and most can fly.*

▲ REPTILES
There are more than 11,000 species of reptiles. Most of these scaly, cold-blooded animals lay eggs to reproduce.

Leopard tortoise

▲ AMPHIBIANS
There are more than 8,400 species of amphibians. Most of them live part of their life in water and part on land. They are cold-blooded.

▲ FISH *This is an informal group of three different classes, which together have nearly 34,000 species. All fish are cold-blooded and live in water.*

▲ INVERTEBRAT
An informal grouping of more than 30 maj groups (phyla), the invertebrates include all those animals that do not have a backbo Worms, insects, shrin jellyfish, and octopuse are all invertebra

Rhinoceros beetle

RECORD BREAKERS

BIGGEST, HEAVIEST, LOUDEST
At up to 98 ft (30 m) long, the blue whale is easily the biggest animal on Earth. It's also the heaviest, weighing 132 tons (120 metric tons), and the loudest. At 188 decibels, its calls are louder than a jet engine. A blue whale's heart is the size of a small car, and its largest blood vessel is wide enough for a small person to crawl inside. Blue whales are threatened with extinction due to overhunting in the past.

▲ SMALLEST VERTEBRATE
Australia's infantfish is less than ½ in (1 cm) long.

▲ STRONGEST
The rhinoceros beetle can lift 850 times its own weight. If the beetle weighed as much as a human it could lift at least two fully laden buses.

TELL ME MORE...

Animals need oxygen to survive. Many species that live on land have lungs to breathe air; those that live underwater, such as fish, have gills to filter oxygen from the water. Aquatic birds and mammals have lungs and must surface to breathe air.

THE INSIDE STORY

Animals come in an enormous variety of forms. Yet on the inside, most of them share certain features. Apart from the simplest creatures, all animals have a body made up of many cells. These cells are organized into tissues. In complex animals, these tissues form organs that perform particular jobs that help keep the whole body functioning.

ON THE OUTSIDE

Animals have different body coverings that protect them from heat and cold, from waterlogging or drying out, and from all kinds of attack. Birds are the only animals to have feathers; reptiles and most fish have scales; and mammals are the only animals to have hair on their body.

Bright colors and patterns can be used to attract mates...

... as a warning that the animal is foul-tasting or poisonous...

... or as camouflage so the animal blends in with its surroundings.

▲ SOCIAL *Elephants live in large herds.*

▶ SOLITARY *Pandas live alone.*

Solitary or social?

Some animals are solitary: they hunt, eat, sleep, and live alone and only seek out other members of their species to mate and produce offspring. Other animals live in pairs or groups, which increases their chance of survival. Members of a group may work together to find food, defend a territory, rear young, or keep watch for predators.

Body heat

Mammals and birds are warm-blooded, or endothermic—they generate their own body heat using energy from food, and can control their body temperature. Most other animals are ectothermic, which means they cannot control their temperature naturally. When they want to warm up they sunbathe, and if they are too hot, they seek shade to cool down.

Ectothermic animals such as lizards can be seen basking in the morning sunlight in order to warm their body.

◀ FASTEST *The peregrine falcon can swoop at a breathtaking 200 mph (320 kmph) in unpowered flight. The fastest creature on land is the cheetah, and in water is the sailfish. Both can reach 68 mph (110 kmph).*

▲ MOST DEADLY *A single sea wasp jellyfish has enough venom to kill 60 people. The venom of cone snails and some fish is even more toxic.*

▲ BIGGEST KILLER *Female Anopheles mosquitoes kill up to 400,000 people a year by infecting them with malaria.*

▲ LONGEST LIFESPAN *A Madagascan radiated tortoise like this one is known to have lived at least 188 years. Bowhead whales may survive even longer, maybe as long as 200 years.*

Mammals

Mammals are vertebrates that feed their young on milk produced by the mother The milk is made in her mammary glands, which is why the group is called "mammals." Most mammals give birth to live young.

WHAT IS A MAMMAL?

All mammals have a lower jaw made up of just one bone. This is how scientists identify mammal fossils, long after mammary glands and hair have disappeared.

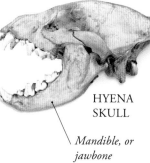

HYENA SKULL

Mandible, or jawbone

▲ ALL EARS *Grazing impala must live in the open where their food grows. They are wary animals with large eyes and mobile ears tuned to signs of danger.*

Browsers and grazers

Nearly all hoofed mammals are herbivores—they eat only plants. Some are browsers, which means they nibble leaves and shoots from trees and shrubs; others are grazers that eat mainly grass. Plant matter, especially grass, is hard to digest, so many of these animals ruminate, or chew the cud. After swallowing a meal, they lie down to rest while bacteria in their stomach weaken the tough plant cell walls. Then the animal regurgitates its food (now called cud) and chews it again to help release nutrients.

HAIR

Mammals are the only animals to have hair. Hair is made from keratin, the same material found in fingernails and bird feathers. A dense coat of hair is called fur; its main purpose is to keep the animal warm. Hair also appears in other forms, such as protective spines (as in hedgehogs and echidnas) and the sensitive facial whiskers of other mammals.

Short-beaked echidna
Tachyglossus aculeatus

MANY ORDERS

There are about 6,300 species of mammals, arranged into 28 orders. The members of an order tend to be descended from a shared ancestor, and are united by similar anatomy or lifestyle. For example, camels, deer, hippopotamuses, giraffes, cattle, whales, and dolphins are all families within the order Cetartiodactyla.

BATS

Bats are the only mammals that can truly fly (not just glide). All bats have wings, which are in fact delicate webbed hands. Hearing is very important to bats: they can find prey and avoid obstacles in total darkness by listening to the way their calls echo off nearby objects.

POUCHED MAMMALS

There are more than 350 species of pouched mammals in seven orders, including kangaroos, opossums, and the koala. Commonly called marsupials, these mammals give birth to very tiny young. The newborns crawl inside their mother's pouch, where they feed on milk and continue to grow.

▶ SAFE INSIDE
A joey in its mother's pouch.

MONOTREMES

There are five species of mammals that don't give birth to live young, but instead lay eggs. They are called monotremes, and include the duck-billed platypus. Once hatched, young monotremes feed on their mother's milk, just like other mammals.

PRIMATES

Monkeys, lemurs, apes, and humans are all primates. Primates have grasping hands and forward-facing eyes. The great apes (including chimpanzees, gorillas, and the orangutan) are humans' closest relatives.

CARNIVORES

◀ LESSON TIME
Polar bear cubs learn to hunt by watching their mother.

There are 16 families of meat-eating mammals grouped into one order called carnivores. They have bodies that are adapted to hunting and eating flesh.

Some leopards have a black coat.

Leopard
Panthera pardus

Mammal record breakers

Mammals come in a staggering variety of forms and have mastered almost every habitat on Earth. They walk, run, swim, burrow, and fly, and one species, our own, has even been to the moon.

Human beings

Humans (species *Homo sapiens*) are mammals from the great ape family. We can live to more than 120 years, but the worldwide average is 73.4 years. We inhabit every continent except Antarctica, making us the most widespread mammals.

Hog-nosed bat
Craseonycteris thonglongyai
- **Length** 1¼ in (30 mm)

The world's **smallest mammal** is also known as the bumblebee bat. It weighs about half as much as a cube of sugar.

The **biggest mammal on land** reaches full size at about 20 years of age, but its tusks keep on growing.

African savanna elephant
Loxodonta africana
- **Weight** 6½ tons (6 metric tons)

Giraffe
Giraffa sp.
- **Height** 18 ft (5.5 m)

The **tallest** mammal's long legs and neck allow it to reac[h] leaves on high branches.

Blue whale
Balaenoptera musculus
- **Length** 98 ft (30 m)

Eastern gorilla
Gorilla beringei
- **Weight** 440 lb (200 kg)

Compared to the size of its body, a male gorilla has one of the **longest arms** of any mammal.

With a body that is 50 percent fat after feeding on its mother's fatty milk, a ringed seal pup is the **fattest** wild mammal.

Ringed seal
Phoca hispida
- **Length** 4¼ ft (1.3 m)

Sea otter
Enhydra lutris
- **Length** 4¼ ft (1.3 m)

With 800,000 hairs per square inch (125,000 hairs per cm²), sea otter fur is waterproof, warm, and the **densest fur** of any mammal.

Striped skunk
Mephitis mephitis
- **Length** 2¼ ft (68 cm)

The stinking spray from a skunk is used as a defense against predators—and makes it the **smelliest** mammal.

Brown-throated sloth
Bradypus variegatus
- **Length** 2 ft (60 cm)

Sloths are the **slowest** mammals, averaging 0.1 mph (0.16 kmph) when moving among trees. They often remain motionless for long periods of time.

Cheetah
Acinonyx jubatus
- **Length** 4½ ft (1.35 m)

Over short distances, a cheetah can sprint at up to 62 mph (100 kmph) in pursuit of prey, making it the **fastest** mammal.

Camels are the **biggest drinkers**. Bactrians can drink 30 gal (113 liters) in one session.

Bactrian camel
Camelus bactrianus
- **Height** 7½ ft (2.3 m)

FACT
The blue whale is the **largest living animal** on Earth. Its voice carries up to 500 miles (800 km) through the ocean.

Scimitar-horned oryx
Oryx dammah
- **Length** 5½ ft (1.7 m)

These antelope have been hunted to extinction in the wild, making them among the **rarest** mammals.

Grey whale
Eschrichtius robustus
- **Length** Up to 49 ft (15 m)

Grey whales make one of the **longest migrations**: an annual round-trip of 12,500 miles (20,000 km) from the Arctic to breeding grounds off Mexico.

White rhinoceros
Ceratotherium simum
- **Length** 14 ft (4 m)

Rhinos have **very thick skin**, which acts as armor. In vulnerable places such as the shoulders, it can be almost 2 in (5 cm) thick.

Killer carnivores

Many animals are described as carnivorous: it means that they eat meat. But there is also an order of mammals called carnivores, which have unique features such as sharp cheek teeth. Many can kill prey bigger than themselves.

BUILT TO HUNT

A typical carnivore has a body that is adapted to hunting. It has good eyesight, hearing, and sense of smell to locate prey, and can run fast or for long distances to give chase. Cats have sharp claws to grab prey and bring it down, while powerful jaws and teeth bite to kill.

Scavengers Not all carnivores are predators. Hyenas are very good at hunting, but they also scavenge—eat an animal that is already dead, killed by others or by natural causes.

JAWS AND CLAWS

Killer carnivores have four sharp cheek teeth, called carnassial teeth, which can cut through hide, meat, and bone. A huge muscle called the temporalis muscle gives enough power for the teeth to break bones or suffocate prey. Sharp claws are equally important for some carnivores. Lions and other cats use their claws to hold onto prey, in defense, for climbing, and for grip when running.

Lion's sharp claws

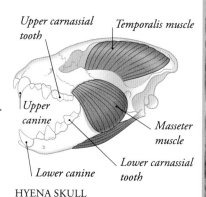

Upper carnassial tooth

Temporalis muscle

Upper canine

Masseter muscle

Lower canine

Lower carnassial tooth

HYENA SKULL

Snow leopard
Panthera uncia

 11

- **Length** 3¼–4¼ ft (1–1.3 m)
- **Weight** 60–120 lb (27–54 kg)
- **Location** Central, southern, and eastern Asia

The snow leopard has a thick tail that's around the same length as its body. This gives the cat balance when climbing mountain slopes and hunting for prey such as wild sheep.

Red panda
Ailurus fulgens

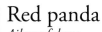

 14

- **Length** 20–25 in (51–64 cm)
- **Weight** 8–17 lb (3.6–7.7 kg)
- **Location** Southern and southeastern Asia

Red pandas are not pandas, nor any other type of bear. They are more closely related to raccoons. However, like giant pandas, they mostly eat bamboo. Red pandas are rare and solitary (they live alone). They are known for being shy, and spend most of the time hidden up in trees, where they find food, hide from predators, and even sunbathe in the winter. It can get very cold in the pandas' natural habitat—temperate mountain forests.

Least weasel
Mustela nivalis

 1

- **Length** 9½ in (24 cm)
- **Weight** 1 oz (25 g)
- **Location** North America, Europe, and northern, central, and eastern Asia

Weasels eat mostly mice and voles. They can track their prey through thick grass and under snow, and are small enough to squeeze into mouse burrows. Weasels are usually brown and white, but those that live in the far north turn completely white in the winter, so they are camouflaged in snow.

Lion
Panthera leo

15

- **Length** 5½–8¼ ft (1.7–2.5 m)
- **Weight** 270–550 lb (120–250 kg)
- **Location** Sub-Saharan Africa and southern Asia

Lions are the only big cats to live in groups, called prides. There may be up to 40 members in a pride, including lionesses, their cubs, and two or three male lions. Lionesses often work together to hunt and kill prey for the pride.

Eurasian badger
Meles meles

 14

- **Length** 35 in (90 cm)
- **Weight** 17½–26½ lb (8–12 kg)
- **Location** Europe and eastern Asia

Badgers live in groups in setts—underground dens and tunnels they dig out with their strong claws. Badgers are nocturnal (active at night), but have poor eyesight, so hunt mainly by smell. Their main diet is earthworms.

Giant panda
Ailuropoda melanoleuca

26

- **Length** 4–6 ft (1.2–1.8 m)
- **Weight** 155–275 lb (70–125 kg)
- **Location** Central China

Giant pandas are easily recognized, but rarely seen: there are thought to be about 1,800 left in the wild. They are also known as bamboo bears, after their main source of food.

Gray wolf
Canis lupus

 16

- **Length** 4¼–6¾ ft (130–205 cm)
- **Weight** 50–175 lb (23–80 kg)
- **Location** North America, eastern Europe, and Asia

All domestic dogs have evolved from the gray wolf, the largest member of the dog family. Gray wolves hunt in packs to kill large animals. Each pack has a territory where it lives and hunts, and wolves will howl to stop other packs straying into their patch.

Tiger
Panthera tigris

 26

- **Length** 9¼ ft (2.8 m)
- **Weight** upto 660 lb (300 kg)
- **Location** Southern and eastern Asia

Tigers ambush their prey, which includes deer and cattle. They silently prowl in tall grasses, camouflaged by their stripes. With a sudden pounce, the tiger leaps onto its prey, bringing it down and killing it by breaking its neck or biting its throat, suffocating it.

Brown bear
Ursus arctos

 47

- **Height** 10 ft (3 m)
- **Weight** 215–1500 lb (97–680 kg)
- **Location** Northern North America, northern and eastern Europe, and northern Asia

Brown bears feed on forest fodder: nuts, berries, and small animals, such as river salmon. The bears can become aggressive when protecting their cubs.

Amphibians

Most amphibians begin life in water breathing with gills, and then venture onto land as adults, where they breathe using lungs and through their skin. They live in damp places, and most return to the water to breed. There are three groups of amphibians: frogs and toads, newts and salamanders, and caecilians.

▲ SEE-THROUGH SKIN *Frogs have delicate skin. A glass frog's skin lacks strong pigment and is almost transparent.*

Gills, lungs, and skin

Some salamanders spend their whole life in water, and may keep their tadpole gills even as adults (although they do have lungs as well). Others live entirely on land, where some manage without lungs. They absorb oxygen directly into their bloodstream through their thin skin. Keeping the skin moist helps the oxygen pass through.

FAST FACTS

■ There are more than 8,400 amphibian species.

■ Amphibians are cold-blooded, and have no hair or scales.

■ Most adult amphibians are carnivorous, eating insects, worms, and even birds and snakes. Tadpoles start life as vegetarians.

■ All amphibians lay eggs. Some lay just one or two eggs at a time, but others can lay up to 50,000.

FROM EGG TO ADULT

Young amphibians such as this frog hatch as larvae (tadpoles) that look nothing like their parents. The series of changes that take place as a larva grows into an adult is called metamorphosis.

▶ 1. SPAWN
Frog and toad eggs are laid in clusters or strings, protected by a special jelly.

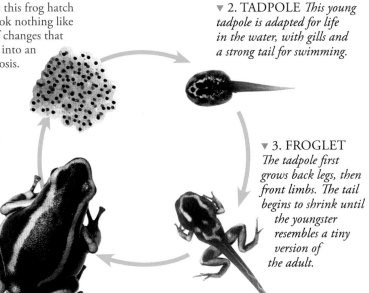

▼ 2. TADPOLE *This young tadpole is adapted for life in the water, with gills and a strong tail for swimming.*

▼ 3. FROGLET
The tadpole first grows back legs, then front limbs. The tail begins to shrink until the youngster resembles a tiny version of the adult.

▶ 4. FROG
The adult lives mostly on land but is also happy in water. It breathes using lungs and through its skin.

Bright colors warn predators

▲ POISON! *Some amphibians have skin glands that ooze toxins. Tree frog toxins have even been used to make deadly poison-tipped darts. Other frogs secrete chemicals that leave a foul taste to deter predators.*

Golden poison dart frog
Phyllobates terribilis

| 2–5 | ⚠ | 🖐 |

- **Length** 1⅘–2⅖ in (4.7–5.5 cm)
- **Weight** ⅒–⅕ oz (3–5 g)
- **Location** Colombia, South America

This frog's striking colors carry a serious warning. The toxin that secretes from glands in its skin is the most deadly poison produced by any vertebrate animal, and predators will avoid contact with the frog at all costs. There are three varieties of this frog— gold (like this one), green, and orange.

European common frog
Rana temporaria

| | | | | 5–8 | ⚠ | 🖐 | |

- **Length** 2⅖–3½ in (6–9 cm)
- **Weight** ⁹⁄₁₀–1⅕ oz (25–35 g)
- **Location** Europe

A familiar animal in Europe, the common frog lives and breeds in pools and damp places. In climates with harsh winters it may hibernate for several months in a moist burrow or in mud at the bottom of a pool. Prey, including slugs, worms, and insects, are whipped into the frog's large mouth with its sticky tongue.

Tiger salamander
Ambystoma tigrinum

| | | | | 16 | ⚠ | 🖐 | |

- **Length** 6–12 in (15–30 cm)
- **Weight** 4–6 oz (100–150 g)
- **Location** Most of North America

Like most amphibians, this large salamander begins life in water. Most metamorphose into land-living adults but some manage to mature and breed without ever leaving the water. On land, tiger salamanders live in grasslands or woodland edges, where they hunt insects, worms, and even mice and frogs.

Oriental fire-bellied toad
Bombina orientalis

| | | 20 | ⚠ | 🖐 | |

- **Length** 1⅗–3⅕ in (4–8 cm)
- **Weight** 1–2 oz (28–57 g)
- **Location** China, Russia, North Korea, and South Korea

The magnificent colors of the fire-bellied frog give this species its name—and warns predators about the poison glands in its skin. The frogs live in habitats such as broad-leaved forests, swamps, and meadows, and spend time in shallow water. Their vision is limited to detecting movement, so potential prey that does not move may get away.

Emperor newt
Tylototriton shanjing

| | | | 10 | ⚠ | 🖐 | |

- **Length** 7 in (17 cm)
- **Weight** Exact weight unknown
- **Location** Yunnan Province, China

This handsome newt is at risk in its native China where it is collected for food, the pet trade, and for use in traditional medicine. Adults live on land most of the year, but return to the shallow pool where they were born to find a mate and lay eggs, which are deposited carefully on water weeds. The name shanjing means "mountain spirit" in Mandarin.

Caecilian
Gymnopis multiplicata

| | 13 | ⚠ | 🖐 | |

- **Length** 20 in (50 cm)
- **Weight** Exact weight unknown
- **Location** Tropical forests

This strange legless creature belongs to the smallest group of amphibians, the caecilians. They spend their lives burrowing through the warm, damp leaf litter or soil of tropical forests. Earthworms happen to be the caecilian's favorite prey, which they hunt by smell, using short tentacles to pick up the earthworm's faint chemical signals. Rather than spawning eggs, this species gives birth to live young that look like miniature adults.

FROG FEET

Amphibians usually live in damp, humid, or sheltered places, which helps them keep their skin moist. Their ability to swim, walk, hop, climb, and even glide means they are able to live a wide variety of lifestyles. The frogs shown here have feet adapted to very different habitats.

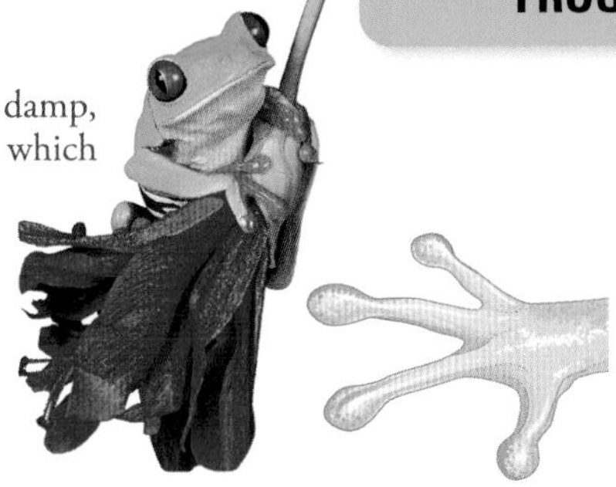

▲ STICKY FEET *Tree frogs have sticky toe pads to provide extra grip.*

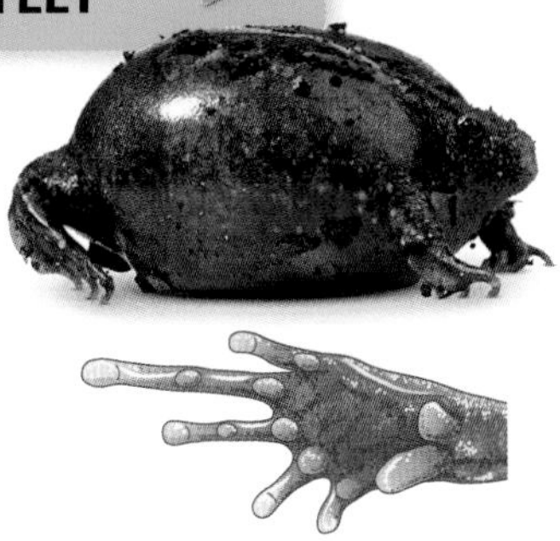

▲ DIRTY FEET *Burrowing frogs have strong feet for loosening and shovelling soil.*

▲ WEBBED FEET *Common frogs have webbed, flipperlike hind feet to help them swim.*

Reptiles

Reptiles are cold-blooded vertebrates that have tough skin covered in scales. The scales are made of keratin—the same material as mammal hair and bird feathers. There are more than 11,000 species of reptiles, grouped in four orders. The biggest order is snakes and lizards.

Panther chameleon
Furcifer pardalis

FEARSOME FANGS

Some snakes have venom glands just behind their fangs. Venom is used to kill prey, and sometimes in defense. Baring fangs is a warning to attackers to back off.

Western diamondback rattlesnake
Crotalus atrox

TAKE A PICTURE

A dione rat snake (*Elaphe dione*) begins "sloughing" its skin. Snakes shed their skin up to eight times a year.

Emerald tree boa (juvenile)
Corallus caninus

BENDY BACKBONE

A snake's backbone is incredibly flexible. Tree boas coil around branches to rest and to spot prey. Desert vipers squeeze under rocks for shade. Sidewinding snakes zip across the ground in S-shape waves.

Thorny devil
Moloch horridus

REPTILE EGGS

Although some snakes and lizards give birth to live young, most reptiles reproduce by laying eggs. Some look like birds' eggs —they have hard, rounded shells—but most eggs have softer, leathery shells. The hatchlings break through their shells using a sharp "egg tooth," which then falls out.

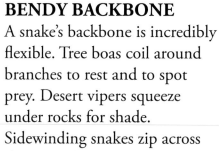

◄ SNAKE *Young snakes coil up tightly inside a shell. Some can be up to seven times longer than their egg.*

▲ LIZARD *Leopard geckos lay a clutch of two long, sticky eggs.*

◄ TORTOISE *Large tortoises and turtles, such as leopard tortoises, lay almost perfectly round eggs.*

TAKING A STAND

A reptile's legs stick out at right angles to its body (unlike mammals' and birds', which do not). This gives them a very sturdy frame for walking on uneven land.

SNAKES

Despite having no limbs, snakes are incredible predators. There are nearly 3,790 species of snakes, and more than 300 of these are venomous. Other snakes are constrictors: they coil around their prey and squeeze until it suffocates.

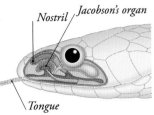

Nostril   Jacobson's organ

Tongue

▲ JACOBSON'S ORGAN
A snake often hunts by smell and by tasting the air—picking up scents with its tongue. It uses its Jacobson's organ to analyze the scent for signs of prey.

◀ DEADLY GRIP *A rock python kills a gazelle.*

LIZARDS

There are more than 6,680 species of lizards, from the enormous Komodo dragon to the tiny pygmy chameleon. Most of them have long tails. Some lizards, mostly skinks, have an interesting defense technique: if a predator catches their tail, it can break off so the lizard can run free. Eventually the tail will grow back.

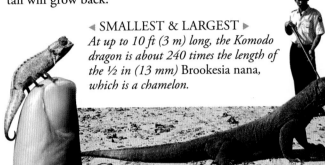

◀ SMALLEST & LARGEST ▶
At up to 10 ft (3 m) long, the Komodo dragon is about 240 times the length of the ½ in (13 mm) Brookesia nana, which is a chamelon.

CROCODILES AND ALLIGATORS

There are 25 species of crocodilians, which have flat, wide bodies, powerful tails, and menacing jaws. They have eyes on the tops of their heads and nostrils on the tops of their noses so they can see and breathe while lying submerged in water, which is where they wait to ambush prey. Fish, and mammals that come down to a lake or river to drink, are the main targets: caught in the crocodile's immense jaws, mammals are dragged into the water and drowned. The crocodile can safely open its mouth underwater: it has a flap of skin that it closes across the back of its throat.

▲ CAUGHT *Crocodiles that live in the Grumeti River, Africa, take advantage of the wildebeest migration that crosses the river.*

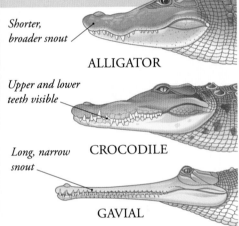

Shorter, broader snout

ALLIGATOR

Upper and lower teeth visible

CROCODILE

Long, narrow snout

GAVIAL

▲ SNOUTS *Alligators have shorter, wider snouts than crocodiles; gavial snouts are the narrowest. Only the alligator's top teeth can be seen when its mouth is shut.*

TORTOISES AND TURTLES

The 353 species of tortoises, turtles, and terrapins are easily recognized by their hard shells. They move slowly, and so most are herbivorous (eat plants) and are too slow to catch prey. Turtles are more likely to be carnivorous (eat meat): they lie in wait for fish to swim past, then snap their jaws around the prey.

▲ LAND AND SEA *Tortoises live on land, but turtles are water-based.*

◀ LONG NECK *The common snake-necked turtle uses its long neck to lunge at prey.*

TUATARAS

There is just one species of tuatara. They look a lot like iguanas (which are lizards), but tuataras are found only on islands off the coast of New Zealand, coming out of their burrows at night to hunt prey, including insects. Tuataras have changed little in the 100 million years since their prehistoric ancestors died out.

Tuatara
Sphenodon punctatus

Birds

There are more than 10,700 species of birds. Like mammals, they are warm-blooded vertebrates, but unlike most mammals, they lay eggs, their bodies are covered in feathers, and most can fly.

FEATHERS FOR FLIGHT

A bird's feathers not only help to keep the bird warm, but also play an essential role in flight by giving the wings and tail the correct shape. Feathers are made of a substance called keratin—the same protein found in your hair and fingernails.

*Long, stiff **flight feathers** give wings the shape needed to create lift.*

*Smaller than flight feathers, **contour feathers** give the bird its streamlined body shape in flight.*

*Under the contour feathers on the bird's body, a layer of short, fluffy **down feathers** keeps the bird warm.*

Most birds have excel[lent] eyesight. Hawks such [as] this one can spy prey [at] great distances.

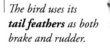

Chisel-shaped bill

Woodpecker

Conical bill

Barbet

Sharp, slim bill

Puffbird

Bill shapes

Birds have no teeth or jaws. Instead they have a bill made of tough, horny keratin. The bill serves many purposes: it can be a deadly weapon for stabbing and tearing, a tool for probing, crushing, or drilling, and a delicate filter. Most birds also use their bill for grooming.

*The bird uses its **tail feathers** as both brake and rudder.*

Red-tailed hawk
Buteo jamaicensis

*Birds use their **talons** as weapons and to help them grip perches. Water birds have webbed toes to help them swim efficiently.*

Bird bones

Most animal bones are filled with squishy marrow, but bird bones are hollow, which makes them light. They are also strong, thanks to the supporting struts inside.

FLIGHTLESS BIRDS

Not all birds fly. Flightlessness can be a feature of birds that have few natural predators, such as the New Zealand kiwi. Flying would use a vast amount of energy in very large birds such as ostriches, rheas, emus, and cassowaries. Instead, they invest their energy in running fast. They also grow too large for most predators to tackle.

Male common ostriches
Struthio camelus

FACT

All birds lay eggs. One reason why is that the female would struggle to fly with a brood of heavy chicks developing inside her. Most birds incubate their eggs by sitting on them. Mother birds usually lay a single egg at a sitting.

Ruby-throated hummingbird
Archilochus colubris

- **Length** 2¾–3½ in (7–9 cm)
- **Wingspan** 3–4 in (8–11 cm)
- **Weight** ⅟₁₅–⅕ oz (2–6 g)
- **Location** North and Central America

This tiny jewel of a bird uses its specially adapted bill to sip nectar from tube-shaped flowers, while it hovers on wings that beat about 50 times per second. Hummingbirds are among the smallest warm-blooded animals on Earth.

Hyacinth macaw
Anodorhynchus hyacinthinus

- **Length** 3¼ ft (100 cm)
- **Wingspan** 4 ft (130 cm)
- **Weight** 3⅓–4⅖ lb (1.5–2 kg)
- **Location** Central and South America

This is the world's largest parrot, though the flightless kakapo from New Zealand is heavier.
Sadly it is also one of the rarest of its kind, as it suffered greatly from over-collection for the pet trade. Its habitat has shrunk as loggers and farmers fell its native forests.

Lesser rhea
Pterocnemia pennata

- **Height** Up to 39½ in (100 cm)
- **Weight** 44 lb (20 kg)
- **Location** South America

Rheas are South America's version of the ostrich. They favor open habitats where they can see trouble coming. A male will mate with several females and care for all the resulting eggs himself, in one large nest.

Atlantic puffin
Fratercula arctica

- **Length** 12 in (30 cm)
- **Wingspan** 24 in (60 cm)
- **Weight** 16 oz (450 g)
- **Location** High Arctic to the Mediterranean

Puffins are not the best flyers, and are awkward on land too—but they are expert swimmers, hunting fish under water. Outside the breeding season they spend all their time at sea.

Common peafowl
Pavo cristatus

- **Length** Male 6–7½ ft (1.8–2.3 m), Female 3¼ ft (1 m)
- **Wingspan** 4½–5¼ ft (1.4–1.6 m)
- **Weight** 8¾–13 lb (4–6 kg)
- **Location** India and Pakistan

The male peafowl (a peacock) is famous for his magnificent tail, which he displays to show off his health and vigor. The female (peahen) has dowdy brown plumage and a short tail. Peafowl eat a varied diet of seeds, flowers, and insects.

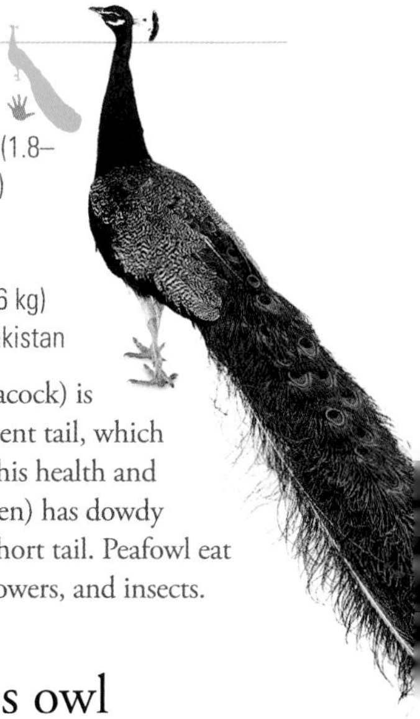

Lesser flamingo
Phoenicopterus minor

- **Height** 31½–35⅖ in (80–90 cm)
- **Wingspan** 3¼ ft (100 cm)
- **Weight** 4½ lb (2 kg)
- **Location** Africa, Yemen, Pakistan, and India

Colonies of lesser flamingos form a spectacle when they gather in their thousands to breed in the alkaline lakes of the Rift Valley. Each pair produce one egg in a nest of baked mud. Lesser flamingos feed on blue-green algae, which they filter from the water using a specially adapted bill.

Plumed whistling duck
Dendrocygna eytoni

- **Length** 16–20 in (40–50 cm)
- **Weight** 1–3¼ lb (0.5–1.5 kg)
- **Location** Australia, Indonesia, and Papua New Guinea

The plumed whistling duck is named for the ornate plumage on its flanks (sides), and its distinctive call, which resembles the noise created by blowing air past a blade of grass trapped between two thumbs. It eats grass and weeds.

Webbed foot

Sokoke Scops owl
Otus ireneae

- **Height** 6⅓–7 in (16–18 cm)
- **Weight** 1¾ oz (50 g)
- **Location** Kenya and Tanzania

One of the world's smallest owls, the Sokoke Scops owl specializes in catching beetles and other insects. It hunts by night and hides by day in thickets of scrub. Loss of this habitat means the owl is threatened with extinction.

Penguins

Agile and speedy in the water, penguins more than make up for their inability to fly. These birds hunt fish, krill, and squid in the waters of the southern hemisphere. Most species come onto land in the warmer months to breed in large colonies.

SWIMMING

Emperor penguins have sleek, streamlined bodies and flattened wings, or flippers, to cut through the water. Dense feathers and a thick layer of blubber keep them warm in the icy Antarctic waters.

HUDDLING

When they are seven weeks old, emperor penguin chicks huddle together in a "crèche" to keep warm. The fluffy gray down feathers of the chicks also trap body heat, insulating them from the cold Antarctic winds.

Adélie penguin
Pygoscelis adeliae

 16

- **Height** 16–30 in (40–75 cm)
- **Weight** 6½–13 lb (3–6 kg)
- **Location** Antarctica

One of the smallest and most abundant of all penguins, the Adélie spends most of the winter at sea but then comes ashore in the summer to breed. Mating pairs build nests in large colonies, which offers protection from egg thieves such as skuas (seabirds).

Yellow-eyed penguin
Megadyptes antipodes

 23

- **Height** 26–28 in (66–70 cm)
- **Weight** 12 lb (5.5 kg)
- **Location** New Zealand

About 3,000 of these rare penguins live on the islands of southern New Zealand. The striking yellow eye-stripe gives them their common name.

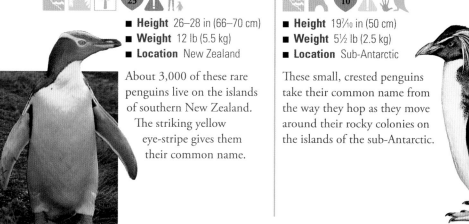

Southern rockhopper
Eudyptes chrysocome

 10

- **Height** 19⁷⁄₁₀ in (50 cm)
- **Weight** 5½ lb (2.5 kg)
- **Location** Sub-Antarctic

These small, crested penguins take their common name from the way they hop as they move around their rocky colonies on the islands of the sub-Antarctic.

Emperor penguin
Aptenodytes forsteri

  20

- **Height** 43 in (110 cm)
- **Weight** 77–88 lb (35–40 kg)
- **Location** Antarctica

Emperor penguins breed in the winter. The female lays a single egg and leaves it with the male. The male rests the egg on his feet, under his belly, and incubates it for about 2½ months.

Birds of prey

These spectacular birds are some of the most efficient predators of the animal world. Most of them have acute vision and excellent hearing, which they put to use when hunting. The smallest species hunt insects, but large raptors, such as eagles, can kill a young deer.

MASTER FISHER
The osprey is a skilled hunter, perfectly adapted for catching fish.

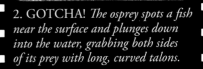

1. EYE IN THE SKY *The osprey patrols a stretch of water in search of fish, hovering and gliding 120 ft (37 m) or more above the surface.*

2. GOTCHA! *The osprey spots a fish near the surface and plunges down into the water, grabbing both sides of its prey with long, curved talons.*

3. DINNER TIME *The osprey returns to the nest to feed its young. The male is the main provider of food for the female and her chicks.*

Osprey
Pandion haliaetus

- **Height** 19⁷⁄₁₀–23⁶⁄₁₀ in (50–60 cm)
- **Weight** 3¾ lb (1.5 kg)
- **Diet** Mainly fish
- **Location** Worldwide (except Antarctica)

This magnificent bird of prey lives near freshwater rivers and lakes and coastal waters, where it has a plentiful supply of its favorite food: fish.

Peregrine falcon
Falco peregrinus

- **Length** 13–20 in (34–50 cm)
- **Weight** 1–3¼ lb (0.5–1.5 kg)
- **Diet** Small birds
- **Location** Worldwide (except Antarctica)

The fastest bird of prey hunts at high speed, reaching a dizzying 220 mph (360 kmph) in a "stoop" (dive).

Griffon vulture
Gyps fulvus

- **Length** 37–43 in (94–109 cm)
- **Weight** 13¼–22 lb (6–10 kg)
- **Diet** Carrion
- **Location** North Africa, southern Europe, and Asia

The Griffon vulture does not kill. It is a scavenger, feeding on carrion (dead animals)— often the leftovers of predatory animals.

Bald eagle
Haliaeetus leucocephalus

- **Length** 28–38 in (71–96 cm)
- **Weight** 6½–14 lb (3–6.5 kg)
- **Diet** Fish, small mammals, birds, and carrion
- **Location** North America

Bald eagles are expert fishers, swooping down to grab fish from the water. They may also steal the catch of another eagle.

Fish

Fish are the biggest and oldest group of vertebrates. They were the first animals to have backbones, evolving over 500 million years ago. There are nearly 34,000 species of fish, all of which are cold-blooded and have bodies that are adapted to living in water.

FISH CLASSES

Fish are grouped into three main groups:
- **Jawless fish**, such as lampreys, have a suckerlike mouth and no scales. Their body is supported by a notochord—a basic kind of spine that is like a flexible rod.
- **Cartilaginous fish** include sharks, skates, and rays. Their skeleton is made of cartilage, and their scales resemble tiny teeth.
- **Bony fish** are the biggest class of fish. They have skeletons made of bone.

Also called the tail fin, the **caudal fin** acts as a paddle, providing "thrust" to propel the fish forward.

Dorsal fins give the fish stability, helping it to make sudden changes in direction and stopping it rolling from side to side. This fish has two dorsal fins, but other fish might have three separate dorsal fins or just one.

The **trunk**, or back end, of the fish is packed with swimming muscles.

The gas-filled **swim bladder** helps the fish control its buoyancy. By inflating or deflating its swim bladder, a fish can rise up or sink in the water.

The **skeleton** of a bony fish comprises a backbone made up of vertebrae, fine rays to support the fins, and a skull.

Horny **scales** grow from the skin, providing a flexible protective covering.

The **anal fin** provides stability as the fish swims.

The **gills** contain a great many blood vessels. Oxygen and other gases are exchanged here.

There are two sets of paired fins. The **pelvic fins** (shown) help "steer" the fish up and down in the water, while the pectoral fins (not shown) may be used for steering and propulsion or even for "walking" along the sea bed.

REPRODUCTION

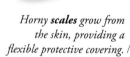

◄ MALE MOM *Seahorses are unusual in that the female lays her eggs in the male's pouch and he carries the young until they hatch.*

While some fish mate and give birth to live young, most reproduce by releasing eggs into the water. This is called spawning. Often fish will gather at special spawning sites where their young will have the best chance of survival.

▲ LARVAE *Some species hatch as small, fully formed fish, but others hatch as larvae and will change as they grow.*

▲ SPAWNING *Many species release vast amounts of eggs at a time to increase the chances of some surviving.*

GILLS

Fish obtain oxygen using their gills. Water is taken in through the mouth, flows over the gills, and out under the gill covers on the sides of the head. Most cartilaginous fish do not have gill covers.

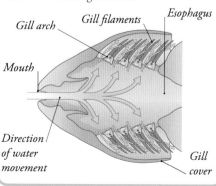

Gill arch

Gill filaments

Esophagus

Mouth

Direction of water movement

Gill cover

Blue spotted ribbontail ray

Taeniura lymma

- **Length** 28 in (70 cm); up to 6½ ft (2 m) incl. tail
- **Weight** Up to 65 lb (30 kg)
- **Depth** Shallow water to 65 ft (20 m)
- **Location** Indian Ocean, western Pacific, Red Sea

This relatively common fish lives around tropical coasts and reefs, where it feeds on mollusks and crustaceans hidden on the sandy sea floor. Like most rays, it "flies" through the water using wavelike movements of its large pectoral fins, which give the body its disc shape. The long tail bears a stinger, used in self-defense.

Clown anemonefish

Amphiprion ocellaris

- **Length** 3–4 in (8–11 cm)
- **Depth** Up to 50 ft (15 m)
- **Location** Seas around southeast Asia and northern Australia

These brightly colored little fish live in the shallow sheltered lagoons created by coral reefs. They gain protection from predators by hiding among the tentacles of anemones, which other fish avoid because of their deadly stings. Anemonefish begin life as males and change into females once they have reached a certain size.

West African lungfish

Protopterus annectens

- **Length** Up to 3¼ ft (1 m)
- **Weight** Up to 8¾ lb (4 kg)
- **Location** West and Central Africa

Lungfish live in the swamps and backwaters of sluggish rivers, which often dry up completely in the dry season. When this happens, the fish survives up to a year in a cocoon of mud, breathing air with primitive lungs and waiting to emerge with the next rains.

Common fangtooth

Anoplogaster cornuta

- **Length** 6–7 in (15–18 cm)
- **Weight** Unknown
- **Depth** 1,600–16,000 ft (500–5,000 m)
- **Location** Oceans worldwide

Also known as the ogrefish, this fish usually lives at great depths. It detects prey, mainly other fish, using its lateral line organs—lines of pressure-sensitive cells on the sides of its body that pick up vibrations in the water.

Puffer fish

Diodon sp.

- **Length** 36 in (90 cm)
- **Weight** Exact weight unknown
- **Depth** 6–160 ft (2–50 m)
- **Location** Tropical and subtropical Atlantic, Pacific, and Indian Oceans

Inflated

Deflated

When threatened, the puffer fish inflates its body into a spiky ball, making it impossible for all but the largest predators to swallow. But even large predators may avoid eating puffer fish: they not only have an unpleasant taste, but some are also poisonous.

Red-bellied piranha

Pygocentrus nattereri

- **Length** 13 in (33 cm)
- **Weight** 2 lb (1 kg)
- **Location** South America

Famed for their powerful bite and wickedly sharp teeth, these ferocious freshwater fish live in large schools. Their usual prey includes other fish and aquatic invertebrates, though they will attack other animals. Their sensitive hearing and lateral line organ allow them to hone in on disturbances caused by struggling prey. Piranhas, in turn, are hunted and eaten by people.

Giant sea bass

Stereolepis gigas

- **Length** 8¼ ft (2.5 m)
- **Weight** Up to 563 lb (255.6 kg)
- **Depth** 16–148 ft (5–45 m)
- **Location** Eastern Pacific, from California to Mexico and Japan

These huge fish lurk close to kelp-fringed drop offs on the rocky coasts of California, Mexico, and Japan. An individual may live to the great age of 100 years, but the species breed so slowly that losses due to over-fishing take decades to make up.

Banded moray eel

Gymnothorax rueppelliae

- **Length** 31½ in (80 cm)
- **Weight** Exact weight unknown
- **Depth** 3–130 ft (1–40 m)
- **Location** Tropical Indian and Pacific Oceans

Like other morays, this species is an aggressive ambush hunter. By day it hides in dark crevices on shallow reefs and at night lurks in the entrance to its lair, waiting to strike at passing fish or shrimp.

Great white shark

Carcharodon carcharias

- **Length** Up to 23 ft (7 m)
- **Weight** Can be more than 6,600 lb (3,000 kg)
- **Depth** 0–4,300 ft (0–1,300 m)
- **Location** Oceans worldwide

Probably the most formidable fish in the seas, the great white is a predator of large fish, squid, and seals. Great white sharks are protected in many places. They were over-fished in the past.

Invertebrates

Of the nearly 1.4 million species of animals roaming the planet, the majority are invertebrates. They are the world's most successful animals and can be found on land, in the sea, in the air, and even inside your body!

There is a huge variety of invertebrates.
The differences lie not just in the way they look, but also in their behavior and even the way they move.

INVERTEBRATES

As well as no backbone, invertebrates also have no true jaws.

Earthworm

Garden snail

Tenebrionid beetle

WHAT IS AN INVERTEBRATE?
Animals without a backbone are called invertebrates. They have no internal skeleton; instead, some have an exoskeleton (a hard outer cover, like a crab or a beetle), some live inside a shell (such as snails and clams), and some are divided into soft segments (such as worms).

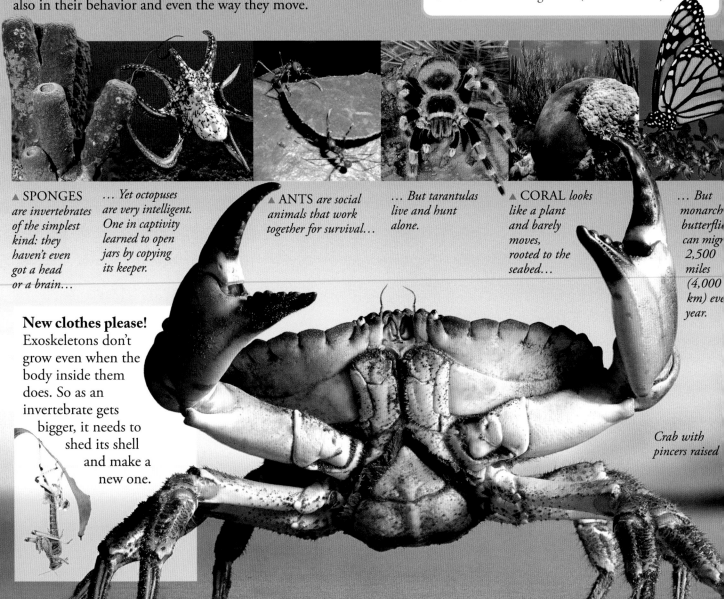

▲ SPONGES are invertebrates of the simplest kind: they haven't even got a head or a brain…

… Yet octopuses are very intelligent. One in captivity learned to open jars by copying its keeper.

▲ ANTS are social animals that work together for survival…

… But tarantulas live and hunt alone.

▲ CORAL looks like a plant and barely moves, rooted to the seabed…

… But monarch butterflies can migrate 2,500 miles (4,000 km) every year.

New clothes please!
Exoskeletons don't grow even when the body inside them does. So as an invertebrate gets bigger, it needs to shed its shell and make a new one.

Crab with pincers raised

INVERTEBRATE GROUPS

In a classification tree of the animal kingdom (👁 p84–85), there is no group called invertebrates. There is one called vertebrates (it is part of the chordates phylum, and is split into mammals, birds, etc.)—but there are more than 30 different main groups of invertebrates, including:

◄ MOLLUSKS—*squid, snails, bivalves* (nearly 72,000 known species) *Squid, slugs, and oysters are all mollusks. Most mollusks have a shell, and a radula—a ribbonlike "tongue" covered in scaly denticles.*

◄ ECHINODERMS—*starfish, sea urchins, sea cucumbers* (more than 7,400 known species) *Nearly all echinoderms live on the sea floor. They have spiny bodies, which are usually divided into five equal parts.*

◄ ANNELIDS—*earthworms, leeches, polychaetes* (about 18,000 species) *Annelid worms have bodies that are divided into segments.*

◄ CNIDARIANS—*jellyfish, corals, hydras* (nearly 12,000 species) *All cnidarians have basic bodies with stinging tentacles, a very simple nervous system, and just one opening: the mouth.*

◄ ARTHROPODS—*insects, arachnids, crustaceans* (about 1.2 million species) *Arthropods, such as this beetle, have an exoskeleton—a hard outer cover. The exoskeleton is divided into parts connected by flexible joints.*

◄ SPONGES (more than 9,000 species) *It was once thought that sponges were plants, but they are simple animals. They are fixed to the seabed and filter food from the water as it washes over them.*

Making sense

Simple invertebrates, such as sea anemones, have simple senses: they can detect food and reach towards it, and they can sense danger and shrink from it. More advanced invertebrates have superior senses. Flies have big multi-lens compound eyes that are sensitive to the slightest movement. Grasshoppers have eardrums in their abdomen.

WITHOUT INVERTEBRATES, other life could not survive. Krill (a type of crustacean) form the basis of the food chain in polar seas. Insects such as ants and beetles, and their larvae, help clean up the planet. Other insects, such as bees, are essential for pollination (👁 p90–91).

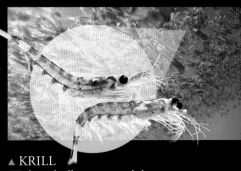

▲ KRILL
Without krill, many much bigger marine animals would disappear. These tiny creatures form the main part of their diets, including the whale shark, the world's biggest fish.

► ANTS
Insects such as these ants outnumber and outweigh all other land animals. They are a vital source of food for all kinds of bird, reptile, and even some mammals.

▼ DUNG BEETLE
Without dung beetles rolling away animal poo, all sorts of places from African savannas to Australian farmland would be knee-deep in dung. Less dung means fewer places for flies to breed, so there are fewer fly-borne diseases.

▼ BUTTERFLIES *can taste with their feet. Chemical sensors on the insect's feet "taste" what it lands on, so it knows if it's standing on something it can drink, such as nectar.*

Amazing arthropods

With more than 1.2 million species, arthropods make up the largest phylum (main group) in the animal kingdom. They were the first creatures to walk on land, more than 500 million years ago.

INSECTS

Insects have three pairs of legs, and a body made up of three parts: a head, a thorax, and an abdomen. This is the biggest group of arthropods; in fact, 80 percent of *all* animal species are insects. Bugs, butterflies, bees, and beetles are all insects.

► WING PATTERNS *help some species to hide and evade predators.*

ARACHNIDS

Arachnid bodies are made up of two parts. They have four pairs of legs, and two pairs of mouthparts: one set look like legs or claws for grabbing prey, while the other set form pincers or fangs for stabbing and killing. They have no antennae. Spiders, scorpions, ticks, and mites are all arachnids.

▲ THE IMPERIAL SCORPION *uses its sting in defense, and its claws to catch prey.*

CENTIPEDES AND MILLIPEDES

These arthropods have a long body divided into many segments. Centipedes have one pair of legs per segment and millipedes have two pairs per segment. *Centipede* means "100 feet" and *millipede* means "1,000 feet," but different species can have between a dozen and 750 legs.

◄ THE GIANT DESERT *centipede has a painful, venomous bite.*

CRUSTACEANS

Most crustaceans live in water—including crabs, lobsters, shrimps, and barnacles—although woodlice live on land. The species can look very different: acorn barnacles are a tiny ½ in (15 mm) across, but a blue lobster grows up to 2¼ ft (65 cm) long.

► LIVE LOBSTERS *range in color, but most are bluish-brown. They turn orangey-red when they are cooked.*

HORSESHOE CRABS

While they look like crustaceans, horseshoe crabs are actually related to arachnids: they have five pairs of legs, two pairs of mouthparts, and no antennae. These animals have scarcely changed in the millions of years they have existed.

▲ HORSESHOE CRABS *are close relatives to extinct trilobites.*

SEA SPIDERS

Sea spiders are not spiders at all, although they do have long, spiderlike legs. Most have four pairs of legs, but some have five or six pairs. They have two pairs of eyes.

► SEA SPIDERS *live deep below the waves.*

SPIDER ATTACK

There are more than 45,000 species of spiders, and almost all of them are venomous. Most are harmless to people—their venom is deadly only to their prey.

BEWARE OF THE SPIDER

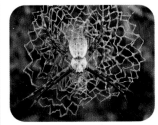

Trapped! Many spiders do not hunt but wait for prey to come to them. Using sticky silk spun from a gland in its abdomen, the orb weaver spider creates a web to trap passing insects. The victim is then killed with a deadly bite.

Do not disturb Spiders don't usually attack people, but some are dangerous if they are disturbed and bite in self-defense. Mediterranean black widow spiders are highly venomous. Females usually have the deadliest bite.

Mexican red-knee tarantula
Brachypelma smithi

- **Length** 2–3 in (5–7.5 cm)
- **Legspan** 4–5 in (10–15 cm)
- **Prey** Insects, small mammals, and lizards
- **Location** western central Mexico

The red-knee tarantula hunts at night. It can sense smells, tastes, and vibrations through the ends of its legs. Females live to 30 years, whereas males live up to 6 years.

▲ FATAL FANGS *Tarantulas bite into their prey with hollow fangs, injecting potent venom to paralyze their victim.*

Four-spot orb weaver
Araneus quadratus

- **Length** ¼–¾ in (8–17 mm)
- **Legspan** Up to 2¾ in (7 cm)
- **Prey** Small flying insects
- **Location** Europe and Asia

Orb weavers spin webs in grasses or scrub. Females can change color over several days to camouflage themselves.

Peacock parachute spider
Poecilotheria metallica

- **Length** 2½ in (6 cm)
- **Legspan** 7 in (18 cm)
- **Prey** Insects, baby birds, lizards
- **Location** Southern India

This spider is also known as the Gooty sapphire because of its blue coloring. While females live to 12 years, males live only 3–4 years. It is critically endangered and faces extinction because of habitat loss.

Fen raft spider
Dolomedes plantarius

- **Length** Females ⁶⁄₁₀–⁹⁄₁₀ in (17–22 mm) Males ½–⁷⁄₁₀ in (13–18 mm)
- **Legspan** Up to 2¾ in (7 cm)
- **Location** Europe

This spider uses its feet to sense the movement of prey in pools of water—then it runs across the water to catch it.

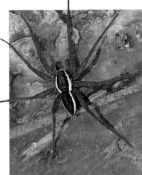

Incredible insects

Insects are the most successful animals on Earth. There are about 1.1 million known species, but scientists think there may be millions more still to be discovered. Many other life forms rely on insects: most plants use them as pollinators, and lots of animals are insect-eaters.

TELL ME MORE...

An insect's body is made up of three parts: the head, thorax, and abdomen. These parts are linked by the exoskeleton, the circulatory system, soft tissue, and ner which control the insect's body functions.

The **thorax** is packed with muscle to power the legs and wings.

Head

Thorax

The **head** conta sense organs such eyes and antenn.

The **abdomen** contains most of the digestive system and the reproductive system.

Abdomen

Insects have one pair of **antennae**, or feelers, which they use to explore their environment. Insects use their feelers in many different ways: to touch, smell, taste, and even hear (by picking up vibrations in the air).

Most insects have two pairs of **wings**. In this wasp the front and hind wings are linked. In beetles and many bugs the front wings form hard cases called elytra, which protect the softer hind wings below.

Adult insects respire (breathe) by taking in air through **spiracles**— openings along the thorax and abdomen.

INSECT MOUTHS

Different types of insects eat very different foods, and so the mouthparts of each species are suited to different styles of feeding. Some insects have jaws shaped into pincers to kill their prey, or tiny clippers for cutting plant leaves. In many other insects the jaws are replaced by other specialized mouthparts.

Labium

Spongelike labellum

▲ SPONGER *Houseflies soak up liquid foods using a sponge-ended tube.*

Proboscis

▲ SUCKER *Butterflies uncurl their long, thin proboscis to use as a straw for sucking up nectar.*

Piercing stylet

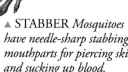

▲ STABBER *Mosquitoes have needle-sharp stabbing mouthparts for piercing skin and sucking up blood.*

LADYBUG LIFE CYCLE

1. EGG LAYING *Insects reproduce by laying eggs. After mating, a female ladybug lays her eggs on a leaf. About a week later, the larvae emerge.*

2. HATCHING *The larvae look nothing like their parents! They have a soft body covering, called a cuticle, which soon hardens and turns dark.*

3. GROWING *The larva must eat lots of food to grow. Over about four weeks it will kill and eat hundreds of sap-sucking aphids.*

4. PUPATING *When the larva is ready to pupate, it fixes itself to the underside of a leaf and sheds its skin, revealing a soft cuticle underneath. This "pupal cuticle" takes about a week to turn hard and dark. The pupa does not move during this time.*

5. EMERGENCE *A week later, the pupal cuticle splits open and a new adult ladybug crawls out. To begin with, its body and wing cases are soft and lack the typical bright color and spots.*

6. ADULT *The new adult's wing cases expand and harden into a protective shield. The color darkens and the distinctive ladybug spots appear. The cycle can now begin again.*

Warning colors

Many insects protect themselves from predators by storing toxins in their body. They then warn predators by displaying bright colors, usually red, orange, or yellow. Monarch and viceroy butterflies, which look similar, both benefit from a color and pattern that say "I taste *really* bad!"

Monarch
Danaus plexippus

Viceroy
Limenitis archippus

Rustic sphinx moth *Manduca rustica*

Insect camouflage

Another great way of avoiding being eaten is to make yourself invisible. Many insects are masters of disguise, able to hide in full view of predators by blending in perfectly with their background. Can you spot this moth?

IS IT A BEE OR WASP?

There are many differences between these similar-looking insects.

- There are about 20,000 bee species.
- Social bees live in colonies in nests made of beeswax.
- Bees feed on nectar and pollen from plants.
- Bees have hairier bodies than wasps.
- A bee can sting only once—the stinger is ripped out of the bee's abdomen and left behind in the victim. Some bees will die soon after.

- There are around 75,000 species of wasp.
- Social wasps live in nests made out of paper, which they make by chewing wood.
- Wasps eat other insects.
- Wasps are more brightly colored than bees.
- A wasp's sting can be used many times. Like bees, only females have a stinger. It is adapted from her ovipositor—the tube through which she lays her eggs.

Bees feed on nectar...

... but wasps eat other insects.

Bugs *and* Beetles

The word "bug" is often used to mean any creepy-crawly, but it is actually an order of a particular kind of insect. This order is called *Hemiptera*, and it has 82,000 species. Beetles are not the same as bugs: they have their own order, *Coleoptera*. There are at least 350,000 beetle species—over one-third of all known insect species.

Lantern bug
Phrictus quinquepartitus

BUGS

Cotton stainer bug
Dysdercus decussatus

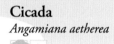

Cicada
Angamiana aetherea

FACT
All the insects you see here are life-size. The giant water bug has the longest body, but it's dwarfed by the Hercules beetle.

Assassin bug
Eulyes illustris

Water scorpion
Nepa sp.

Squash bug
Coreus marginatus

Giant water bug
Lethocerus grandis

Bed bug (magnified x 2)
Cimex lectularius

Leaf hopper
Cicadella viridis

HOW CAN YOU TELL IF IT'S A BUG?

Bugs have two pairs of wings and a beaklike mouth for piercing and sucking up food.

◄ *A predatory bug preys on a caterpillar.*

Shield bug nymph

Adult shield bug

Bugs have incomple[te] metamorphosis: they start life as nymphs that look similar to the adult form, but without wings or reproductive organs.

BEETLES

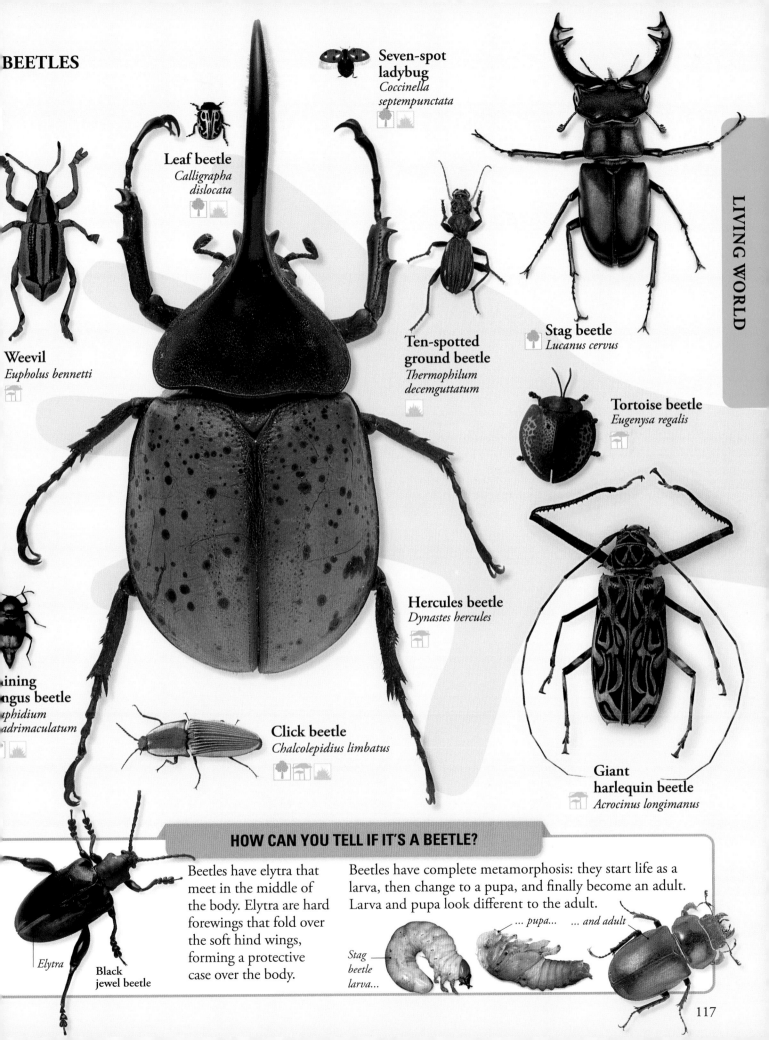

Leaf beetle
Calligrapha dislocata

Seven-spot ladybug
Coccinella septempunctata

Weevil
Eupholus bennetti

Ten-spotted ground beetle
Thermophilum decemguttatum

Stag beetle
Lucanus cervus

Tortoise beetle
Eugenysa regalis

Hercules beetle
Dynastes hercules

ining ngus beetle
phidium adrimaculatum

Click beetle
Chalcolepidius limbatus

Giant harlequin beetle
Acrocinus longimanus

HOW CAN YOU TELL IF IT'S A BEETLE?

Beetles have elytra that meet in the middle of the body. Elytra are hard forewings that fold over the soft hind wings, forming a protective case over the body.

Beetles have complete metamorphosis: they start life as a larva, then change to a pupa, and finally become an adult. Larva and pupa look different to the adult.

Stag beetle larva...

... pupa...

... and adult

Elytra

Black jewel beetle

Marine invertebrates

Huge numbers of invertebrates live in the sea. Some, such as corals and sponges, live fixed to the spot, but others, including jellyfish and squid, drift in mid-water. Starfish and crabs creep and scuttle on the seabed everywhere from sunlit shallows to pitch-black depths.

OCTOPUS ANATOMY

Octopuses belong to a group of mollusks called cephalopods, thought to be the smartest of all invertebrates. Some cephalopods have an external shell, but an octopus has no shell. Most of an octopus's organs are inside its head, including its digestive system and gills.

Day octopus
Octopus cyanea

- **Size** Body: 6¼ in (16 cm); arms 32 in (80 cm)
- **Location** Indo-Pacific region

Unlike most other octopuses, this animal hunts by day, using changing body patterns to disguise itself. Its preferred foods include clams, shrimps, crabs, and fish.

The octopus's eight arms bear rows of suckers that grip onto rocks—and also onto prey.

▶ OCTOPUSES *generally crawl on the seabed, but also use arm movements and a form of jet propulsion to swim in open water.*

COLORFUL CHARACTERS

Octopuses can change color rapidly, adopting different patterns to communicate emotions and to camouflage themselves on the sea floor to avoid predators. If the camouflage doesn't work, they squirt out a jet of ink. Hidden in the cloud, they can escape from danger.

▲ ESCAPE *An octopus releases ink over a potential threat.*

▲ MOUTH *The octopus's mouth is a stretchy circular opening. Inside is a sharp beak made of horn, used for tearing up prey.*

Red knob starfish
Protoreaster linckii

- **Diameter** Up to 12 in (30 cm)
- **Location** Indian Ocean

Like most starfish, the red general is a slow-moving predator. It creeps over reefs and rocks on hundreds of tiny, suckered, tube feet, hunting small clams, tube worms, sponges, and other fixed invertebrates. It feeds by covering the prey with its body and pushing its stomach out through its mouth (in the middle of the star).

Sea slug
Chromodoris kuniei

- **Length** 2 in (5 cm)
- **Location** Western Pacific Ocean

Sea slugs, also known as nudibranchs, are shell-less relatives of snails. They are carnivorous, and hunt by gliding through coral reefs in search of prey that cannot escape, such as sponges, barnacles, and corals.

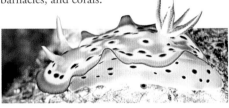

Dahlia anemone
Urticina felina

- **Width** 10–14 in (25–35 cm)
- **Location** Northern hemisphere coastal waters

The dahlia anemone's colorful, flowerlike body grows attached to a rock or other hard surface. The tentacles bear tiny stinging cells that paralyze small animals. Food caught this way is passed to the mouth.

Horned ghost crab
Ocypode ceratophthalmus

- **Width** 2½–3 in (6–8 cm)
- **Location** Indian and Pacific Oceans

Ghost crabs live on sandy beaches, where they feed on organic matter washed up by the tide. They scuttle and burrow at such speed that they sometimes seem to disappear.

European lobster
Homarus gammarus

- **Length** 24–40 in (60–100 cm)
- **Location** European coasts

This powerful cousin of shrimps and crabs lurks in rocky lairs by day, emerging at night to hunt smaller invertebrates and fish using its sensitive antennae and large claws. Like other crustaceans, lobsters must shed their rigid body armor in order to grow.

Lion's mane jellyfish
Cyanea capillata

- **Width** Up to 8 ft (2.4 m)
- **Location** Cool northern seas

Named for the mass of brown frills on its central arms, the lion's mane jellyfish is common in northern seas and is often washed ashore in storms. Jellyfish lack any kind of brain, but their simple design has been successful for 500 million years.

Yellow tube sponge
Aplysina fistularis

- **Height** Up to 24 in (61 cm)
- **Location** Tropical seas

Sponges are among the simplest of animals. Yellow tube sponges have a chimney-shaped body supported by a flexible skeleton made of protein. Some other species may have more rigid skeletal parts. Water is drawn in through pores in the tube.

Elkhorn coral
Acropora palmata

- **Size** Up to 12 ft (3.6 m) across
- **Location** Caribbean Sea

This brittle structure is not a single animal, but a colony of thousands, all growing on a stony base which they build themselves. Each tiny coral animal, or polyp, has a simple bag shape, with a mouth at the top surrounded by tiny tentacles.

What are you doing here?

Birds that can't fly and reptiles that appear to; snakes that live in the sea and fish out of water... sometimes animals just don't seem to behave how you might expect them to!

AIR

Only birds, bats, and insects are capable of true flight, but several other kinds of animal have developed the ability to control long glides through the air.

▼ FLYING GECKO
Flaps of skin, webbed feet, and a flat tail help the gecko control glides from tree to tree.

▲ GOLDEN TREE SNAKE
By spreading its ribcage this amazing snake turns its whole body into a ribbonlike glider.

LAND

Sometimes life on land is the best option even for animals you would normally expect to see in the air or under water.

◄ EMU
The Australian emu has huge, powerful legs, but no wings.

SURFACE OF WATER

The surface of water is an important barrier for most animals, but some species use it to their advantage to escape predators or to surprise unwary prey.

▲ FLYING FISH
Flying fish skim over the waves at up to 37 mph (60 kmph) to escape underwater predators.

◄ BASILISK LIZARD
Big feet and an amazing turn of speed allow this reptile to sprint over still water.

UNDERWATER

Many air-breathing animals visit the underwater realm, which is a great place to find food. Some, such as penguins, must return to land to breed, but others manage this in water too.

▼ PENGUINS
Penguins gave up flight but have perfected the art of swimming underwater.

A DIFFERENT APPROACH

We're used to seeing certain animals in particular places, but in the struggle for life, many animals find that they can gain an advantage by exploiting a completely different environment. They may have developed their extraordinary behavior as a way of finding food, of escaping predators, or simply to stay alive.

◄ FLYING SQUIRREL
A flap of skin along the squirrel's flanks acts as a controllable parachute.

◄ FLYING FROG
Long, strong toes support webs of skin on the flying frog's umbrella-like feet.

◄ CASSOWARY
The forest-dwelling cassowary uses its big feet for running and fighting.

◄ MUDSKIPPER
The mudskipper crosses mud flats using its fins to drag its body over the sand.

UNDERGROUND

Many animals spend at least part of their lives underground, where there are few predators. Some animals survive unfavorable conditions, such as droughts, by hibernating underground.

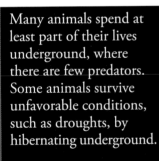

◄ PERIODICAL CICADA
Periodical cicada larvae spend their early lives underground before emerging all together after 13 or 17 years.

► AFRICAN LUNGFISH
When tropical rivers dry up, these fish burrow and survive by breathing air in small, damp chambers in the mud.

◄ WATER SPIDER
Hairs on the water spider's body trap air, which the spider breathes while under water. It's just like diving with an air tank.

► MANATEE
These gentle vegetarians live and breed in shallow tropical seas.

◄ SEA SNAKE
Sea snakes spend their whole life in water, and are often seen hundreds of miles from land.

Microlife

Some living things, such as elephants and oak trees, are difficult to miss if you're standing next to one, but others are much harder to see. There are thousands of species of microscopic organisms living in the air, on land, and in water all around you, and on your body too!

WHAT'S IN THE WATER?

As well as fish and other marine creatures, our oceans, rivers, and lakes are teeming with plankton—microscopic life that drifts with the current. Plankton includes tiny animals (zooplankton) and plantlike life forms (phytoplankton). Many creatures eat plankton, and in this way whole aquatic ecosystems depend on it.

◄ KRILL *are tiny crustaceans that eat plankton. Large marine animals, including whales, feed on the krill, making them a vital link in many food chains.*

◄ ALGAE *Most phytoplankton is made up of algae. Many algae, such as these diatoms, are made up of just one cell.*

ALGAE

Single-celled algae belong to a group of organisms known as protists. Like plants, these algae make food from sunlight, using a process called photosynthesis (👁 p87).

◄ BLOOMING
Algal blooms are a sign of nature out of balance. The bloom blocks sunlight, uses up nutrients, and starves or poisons other plants and animals.

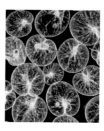

◄ GLOWING
Several algae are bioluminescent: they give out light when they are disturbed. This alga, Noctiluca, can make the sea glow an eerie green.

BRILLIANT BACTERIA

Bacteria are an essential part of life on Earth. Some types live in soil and release nitrates, without which plants would not grow and food chains would collapse. Other types live in your gut, helping you digest your food. But bacteria can also be harmful, causing dangerous diseases in all kinds of plants and animals, including people.

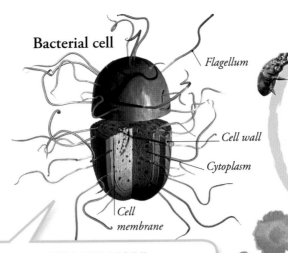

Bacterial cell

Flagellum

Cell wall

Cytoplasm

Cell membrane

TELL ME MORE...

In 1862, French scientist Louis Pasteur created a way of killing bacteria with heat. This process, called pasteurization, is still used today.

FACT

There are around 30,000 species of ticks and mites, most of which are less than 1/32 in (1 mm) long. They can be found in stored food such as flour and cheese; in animal dung; and skin, hair, and fur. They feed on plants, and on the skin and blood of host animals.

Penicillin colony

▶ POWERFUL PENICILLIN
If you have an illness, your doctor might give you penicillin. This is an antibiotic—a medicine that kills bacteria. In 1928, scientist Alexander Fleming found a dish of bacteria with a type of mold growing on it. Where the mold grew, the bacteria had died. From this discovery, Fleming developed penicillin.

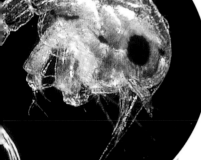

▼ CRAB LARVA *Many animals start life as microscopic larvae. Crab larvae find places to settle as tiny crabs where they can then grow to be adults.*

MINI MONSTERS

Ticks and mites belong to the same class of invertebrate as spiders, the arachnids. They are parasites, living and feeding on plants or other animals, known as hosts. Some species destroy crops, while others pass on diseases.

▶ MEAL MITE
Many of the foods you eat probably contain the remains of mites like this one, which feeds on stored cereal products such as flour and oatmeal.

◀ GROWING
Noctiluca algae are also responsible for "red tides." These are usually caused, for example, by sewage or fertilizer. Algae growing in this way can kill other life forms.

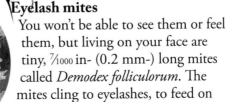

Eyelash mites
You won't be able to see them or feel them, but living on your face are tiny, 7/1000 in- (0.2 mm-) long mites called *Demodex folliculorum*. The mites cling to eyelashes, to feed on dead skin cells at the eyelash roots—but don't worry, they are harmless.

▼ A DUST MITE *can fit on the tip of a needle. This tiny creature eats fragments of dead skin and hair found in house dust.*

Animals of the past

The most famous prehistoric animals have got to be the dinosaurs—but they lived many millions of years after the first life forms appeared on Earth. It is thought that life first appeared on Earth around 3.8 billion years ago. They were small, single-celled organisms called prokaryotes. These organisms survive today in the form of archaea and bacteria.

WHAT WAS A DINOSAUR?

The word "dinosaur" means "terrible lizard." These reptiles ruled the Earth for more than 160 million years until most of them were wiped out 66 million years ago. But they were not all terrible: many were timid plant eaters, and while some were huge and ferocious, others were no bigger than a modern chicken.

▶ DINKY DINOSAUR
The plant-eating Lesothosaurus *was one of the smaller dinosaurs.*

TIMELINE OF PREHISTORIC LIFE

PRECAMBRIAN 4,600–541 MYA	CAMBRIAN 541–485 MYA	ORDOVICIAN 485–443 MYA	SILURIAN 443–419 MYA	DEVONIAN 419–358 MYA	CARBONIFERO 358–298 MYA
The first forms of life appeared on Earth: simple, single-celled prokaryotes.	The first multicelled and hard-bodied life developed, including mollusks and arthropods such as trilobites.	The first crustaceans and jawless fish evolved.	Evolution of the first fish with jaws, and giant sea scorpion—the ancestors of modern arachnids.	The "Age of Fishes," when fish diversified rapidly. The first amphibians evolved from fish, becoming the first vertebrates to live on land.	Flying insects and amphibians lived in swampy forests during this warm period, but reptiles ruled the land.

HIP, HIP

There were two types of dinosaurs, classified by the shape of their hip bones: bird-hipped (ornithischians), and lizard-hipped (saurischians). Birds actually evolved from the lizard-hipped dinosaurs (👁 p244).

Bird-hipped
Iguanodon

Lizard-hipped
T. rex

👁 p244

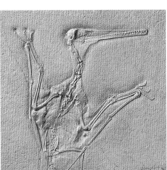

Fossil of a *Pterodactylus*

What is a fossil?

Palaeontologists use fossils to work out what early life forms would have looked like. Most fossils form when the remains of an animal or plant get buried in sediment (sand or mud). Over time, the remains are replaced by minerals in the sediment, which keep the shape of the animal or plant.

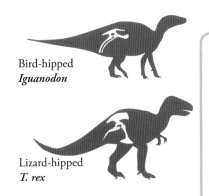

Tyrannosaurus rex
"King of the tyrant lizards"

- **Length** 39 ft (12 m)
- **Time** Late Cretaceous
- **Fossil location** North America

Like all life forms, dinosaur species have scientific names, which are often Latin or Greek. The name may reflect what the species looks like, or one of its characteristics—as with *T. rex*, one of the largest and fiercest meat-eating dinosaurs.

Dimorphodon
"Two-form tooth"

- **Wingspan** 4–8 ft (1.2–2.5 m)
- **Time** Early Jurassic
- **Fossil location** Europe and North America

Dimorphodon was not a dinosaur, but a pterosaur—a flying reptile. It had an enormous skull and differently sized teeth in its bill—large, pointy teeth at the front, and small teeth at the back. It ate fish, insects, and small animals, but no one knows if it caught its prey while flying or standing on all fours.

Dimetrodon
"Two types of teeth"

- **Length** up to 11.5 ft (3.5 m)
- **Time** Early Permian
- **Fossil location** Europe and North America

Dimetrodon was a sail-backed synapsid. The sail probably helped it warm up and cool down. Synapsids were cold-blooded and scaly like reptiles, but they are actually the ancestors of mammals.

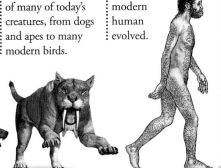

PERMIAN 298–252 MYA	TRIASSIC 252–201 MYA	JURASSIC 201–145 MYA	CRETACEOUS 145–66 MYA	PALEOGENE 66–23 MYA	NEOGENE 23–2 MYA	QUATERNARY 2 MYA to present
Sail-back synapsids appeared.	The first dinosaurs, early mammals, turtles, and frogs appeared.	The first bird, *Archaeopteryx*, evolved from the dinosaurs.	Giant dinosaurs died out, but birds and mammals survived.	Mammals evolved many bigger forms and spread out.	The first appearance of many of today's creatures, from dogs and apes to many modern birds.	The first modern human evolved.

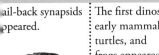

CONTINENTS of the WORLD

The continents are Earth's major landmasses. There are seven continents: North America, South America, Africa, Europe, Asia, Australasia & Oceania, and Antarctica.

Our world

Just one-third of Earth's surface is land; the rest is covered by water. The land is divided into seven vast landmasses (continents): North America, South America, Europe, Asia, Africa, Australasia & Oceania, and Antarctica.

▲ EARTH *A night map shows those parts of the world with plentiful electricity supplies.*

EUROPE

ASIA

AFRICA

ATLANTIC

OCEAN

INDIAN

OCEAN

SOUTHERN OCEAN

ANTARCTICA

Arctic Circle
60°N
30°N
Tropic of Cancer
Equator
Tropic of Capricorn
30°S
60°S
Antarctic Circle

30°W   0°   30°E   60°E   90°E   120°E

FAST FACTS

- World population **7.9 billion** (June 2022)
- Independent countries 196
- Dependent territories 58
- Continents 7
- Oceans 5
- Largest continent Asia
- Smallest continent (by land area) Australasia & Oceania

KEY TO MAPS

- ■ Capital city
- ○ State capital city
- State border
- International border
- — Coastline
- ---- River
- △ Mountain

N North compass

Scale

Note: Only main languages are given.

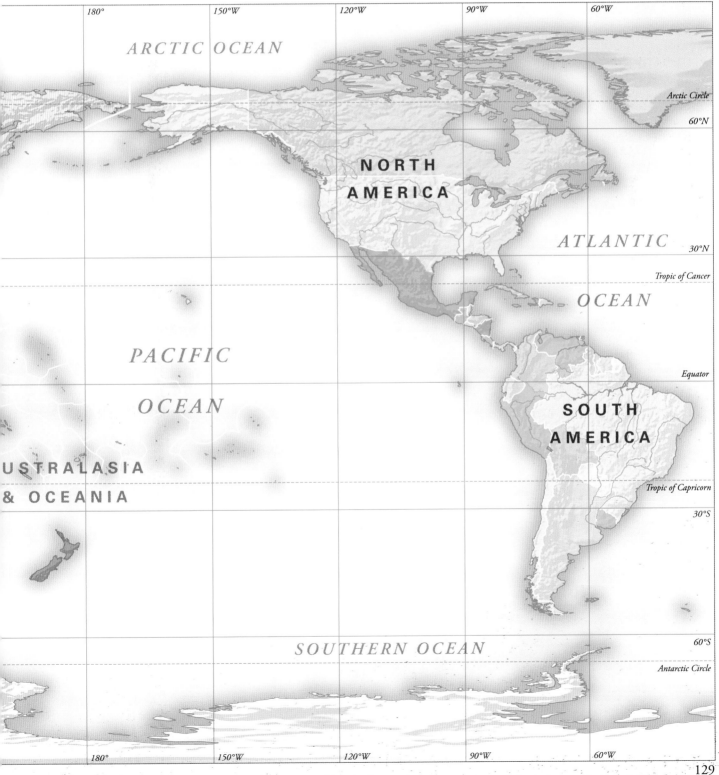

ARCTIC OCEAN

NORTH AMERICA

ATLANTIC

OCEAN

PACIFIC

OCEAN

AUSTRALASIA & OCEANIA

SOUTH AMERICA

SOUTHERN OCEAN

Arctic Circle
60°N
30°N
Tropic of Cancer
Equator
Tropic of Capricorn
30°S
60°S
Antarctic Circle

180°   150°W   120°W   90°W   60°W

North America

Stretching from the Arctic Circle to the tropics, North America is the third-largest continent. It is made up of multiple nations of varying sizes, including Canada, the U.S., Mexico, seven Central American countries, and the Caribbean Islands.

NORTH AMERICAN FACTS

- **Covers** approximately 16.5 percent of Earth's land area
- **Number of countries** 23
- **Biggest country** Canada
- **Smallest country** St. Kitts and Nevis
- **Most common languages** English, Spanish, and French
- **Population of continent** About 597 million
- **Largest North American city** Mexico City, Mexico
- **Highest point** Denali (Mount McKinley) in Alaska at 20,310 ft (6,190 m)
- **Longest river** The Mississippi-Missouri in the U.S. is 3,710 miles (5,970 km) long.
- **Biggest lake** Lake Superior, situated between the U.S. and Canada, is the world's largest freshwater lake by surface area.

How many people?
About 597 million people live in North America, more than half of them in the U.S. Barbados is the most densely populated country, with 1,730 per sq mile (668 people per sq kilometer).

▼ HAWAII *The Hawaiian Islands lie in the mid-Pacific Ocean but are part of the U.S.*

UNITED STATES
OF AMERICA
HAWAII

0 km   200
0 miles   200

Population density
People per 0.39 sq mile (1 sq km)

below 50	150-199
50-90	200-299
100-149	above 300

THE POLAR REGION

The climate in the Arctic is harsh. The average winter temperatures here can be as low as –40°F (–40°C), but the climate is changing. The permanent covering of ice is decreasing, making life increasingly difficult for animals such as polar bears and seals.

EXTENT OF THE ARCTIC
The Arctic region includes Greenland, northern Canada, and Alaska, as well as the northernmost parts of Europe and Asia, and a huge area of frozen ocean around the North Pole.

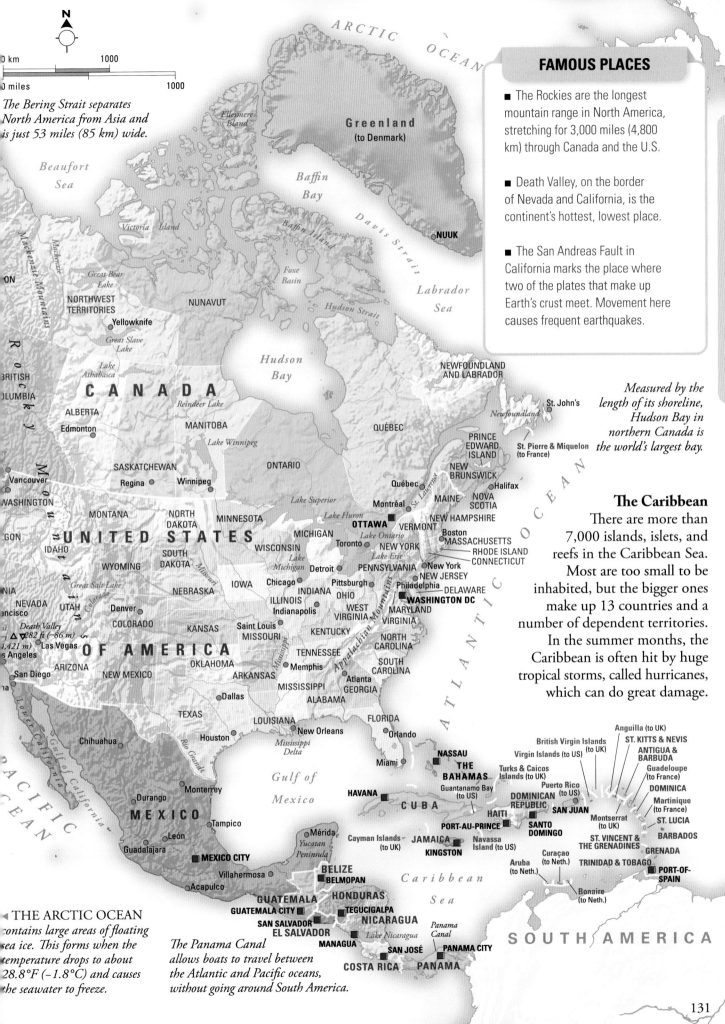

FAMOUS PLACES

■ The Rockies are the longest mountain range in North America, stretching for 3,000 miles (4,800 km) through Canada and the U.S.

■ Death Valley, on the border of Nevada and California, is the continent's hottest, lowest place.

■ The San Andreas Fault in California marks the place where two of the plates that make up Earth's crust meet. Movement here causes frequent earthquakes.

Measured by the length of its shoreline, Hudson Bay in northern Canada is the world's largest bay.

The Caribbean
There are more than 7,000 islands, islets, and reefs in the Caribbean Sea. Most are too small to be inhabited, but the bigger ones make up 13 countries and a number of dependent territories. In the summer months, the Caribbean is often hit by huge tropical storms, called hurricanes, which can do great damage.

The Bering Strait separates North America from Asia and is just 53 miles (85 km) wide.

◄ THE ARCTIC OCEAN
contains large areas of floating sea ice. This forms when the temperature drops to about 28.8°F (−1.8°C) and causes the seawater to freeze.

The Panama Canal allows boats to travel between the Atlantic and Pacific oceans, without going around South America.

Map labels

Oceans and seas: ARCTIC OCEAN, Beaufort Sea, Baffin Bay, Davis Strait, Labrador Sea, Hudson Bay, Hudson Strait, Foxe Basin, ATLANTIC OCEAN, Gulf of Mexico, Caribbean Sea, PACIFIC OCEAN, Gulf of California

Greenland (to Denmark), Ellesmere Island, Victoria Island, Baffin Island, NUUK

CANADA — NORTHWEST TERRITORIES, NUNAVUT, Yellowknife, Great Bear Lake, Great Slave Lake, Lake Athabasca, Mackenzie Mountains, BRITISH COLUMBIA, ALBERTA, Edmonton, Vancouver, SASKATCHEWAN, Regina, MANITOBA, Winnipeg, Reindeer Lake, Lake Winnipeg, ONTARIO, QUÉBEC, Québec, Montréal, OTTAWA, Toronto, NEWFOUNDLAND AND LABRADOR, Newfoundland, St. John's, St. Pierre & Miquelon (to France), PRINCE EDWARD ISLAND, NEW BRUNSWICK, NOVA SCOTIA, Halifax

UNITED STATES OF AMERICA — WASHINGTON, OREGON, IDAHO, MONTANA, WYOMING, NEVADA, CALIFORNIA, UTAH, COLORADO, ARIZONA, NEW MEXICO, NORTH DAKOTA, SOUTH DAKOTA, NEBRASKA, KANSAS, OKLAHOMA, TEXAS, MINNESOTA, IOWA, MISSOURI, ARKANSAS, LOUISIANA, WISCONSIN, ILLINOIS, MICHIGAN, INDIANA, OHIO, KENTUCKY, TENNESSEE, MISSISSIPPI, ALABAMA, GEORGIA, FLORIDA, SOUTH CAROLINA, NORTH CAROLINA, VIRGINIA, WEST VIRGINIA, PENNSYLVANIA, NEW YORK, VERMONT, NEW HAMPSHIRE, MAINE, MASSACHUSETTS, RHODE ISLAND, CONNECTICUT, NEW JERSEY, DELAWARE, MARYLAND

Cities: Las Vegas, Los Angeles, San Diego, Denver, Saint Louis, Chicago, Indianapolis, Detroit, Pittsburgh, Philadelphia, New York, Boston, WASHINGTON DC, Memphis, Atlanta, Dallas, Houston, New Orleans, Orlando, Miami

Physical: Rocky Mountains, Great Salt Lake, Death Valley △282 ft (−86 m), (4,421 m), Colorado, Missouri, Mississippi, Rio Grande, Lake Superior, Lake Michigan, Lake Huron, Lake Erie, Lake Ontario, Appalachian Mountains, Mississippi Delta, Lower California, Yucatan Peninsula

MEXICO — Chihuahua, Durango, Monterrey, Tampico, León, Guadalajara, MEXICO CITY, Mérida, Villahermosa, Acapulco

Central America — BELIZE, BELMOPAN, GUATEMALA, GUATEMALA CITY, HONDURAS, TEGUCIGALPA, EL SALVADOR, SAN SALVADOR, NICARAGUA, MANAGUA, Lake Nicaragua, COSTA RICA, SAN JOSÉ, PANAMA, PANAMA CITY, Panama Canal

THE BAHAMAS — NASSAU, CUBA, HAVANA, Guantanamo Bay (to US), Cayman Islands (to UK), JAMAICA, KINGSTON, HAITI, PORT-AU-PRINCE, DOMINICAN REPUBLIC, SANTO DOMINGO, SAN JUAN, Puerto Rico (to US), Turks & Caicos Islands (to UK), Navassa Island (to US), British Virgin Islands (to UK), Virgin Islands (to US), Anguilla (to UK), ST. KITTS & NEVIS, ANTIGUA & BARBUDA, Guadeloupe (to France), DOMINICA, Martinique (to France), ST. LUCIA, Montserrat (to UK), ST. VINCENT & THE GRENADINES, BARBADOS, GRENADA, Curaçao (to Neth.), Aruba (to Neth.), Bonaire (to Neth.), TRINIDAD & TOBAGO, PORT-OF-SPAIN

SOUTH AMERICA

Life in North America

People from many cultures live in North America today. They include the descendants of Indigenous peoples, European settlers, and enslaved Africans.

Cattle ranching

The cowboys made famous in films were farmhands employed to round up and drive the large herds of cattle that once roamed free in the American West and Mexico. Cattle are still raised for their meat in many parts of the continent.

▲ RANCH *Cattle are raised on farms, called ranches, such as this one in Alberta, Canada.*

Dance

A diverse range of dance styles evolved in North America, many of which come from Indigenous communities.

◀ IN MEXICO *Traditional dances common in Mexico include* concheros.

INDUSTRY

North American companies have been responsible for the invention of the silicon chip, the microprocessor, the iPhone, and many other advances in computer technology.

LANDSCAPE

North America contains a huge variety of landscapes. Many areas are popular tourist destinations.

📷 TAKE A PICTURE

The Grand Canyon is a steep-sided gorge in Arizona. It has been cut out of the rock by the Colorado River.

FAMOUS NORTH AMERICANS

■ **Sir Frederick Banting** (1891–1941) and **Charles Best** (1899–1978) Canadian scientists who discovered insulin, since used to treat millions of people who have diabetes.
■ **Amelia Earhart** (1897–1937) American pioneer of flying and the first woman to fly solo across the Atlantic (in 1932).
■ **Frida Kahlo** (1907–1954) Mexican artist who is famous for her self-portraits, painted in vibrant colors.
■ **Barack Obama** (born 1961) The first Black president of the U.S., he was elected in 2008 and served two terms, until 2017.

📷 TAKE A PICTURE

Each year, more than 13 million people visit Niagara Falls, a massive group of waterfall on the U.S.-Canada border.

▼ MANHATTAN *New York is the biggest city in the U.S.*

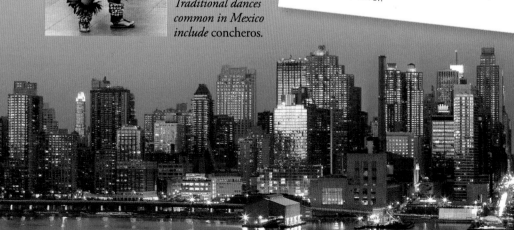

MUSIC

The U.S. is the birthplace of some of the world's most popular styles of music, including jazz, rock and roll, blues, hip-hop, and country music. Jazz, blues, and rock all evolved from the blending of African, Indigenous, and European musical styles that started in communities in the American South.

Many sports popular in the U.S. have their origins in the sports of the Indigenous peoples.

SPORT

The most popular spectator sports in North America are basketball, baseball, football, and ice hockey. Football follows different rules than European football (soccer) and is popular in the U.S., while Mexico favors the European game. Canadian football is similar to the American version.

Football is a contact sport in which tackling is essential, so players wear helmets and pads to protect themselves from injury.

CAR CULTURE

People in the U.S. and Canada own a lot of cars—record car sales were recorded in 2016, when 1.95 million cars were sold in Canada and 17.54 million in the U.S. Many of these vehicles were built in Detroit, Michigan, where carmakers saw sales double between 2008 and 2015, despite losing ground to foreign competitors in recent years.

American towns are designed around the car, with streets laid out in a grid pattern.

INDIGENOUS PEOPLE

The Indigenous people of the U.S. and Canada are the original inhabitants of the continent. They are survivors of war, disease, and forced migration by Europeans.

Like many other Indigenous communities, these children of the Oglala Lakota Nation live on a reservation—land administered by Indigenous people.

DID YOU KNOW?

1 Canada's 151,000-mile (243,000-km) coastline is the longest of any country in the world.

2 The Indigenous communities of Alaska are the original owners of the land. Russia colonized it in the 1700s. The U.S. bought it from the Russians in 1867 for a bargain price of just two cents per acre (0.4 hectares).

1 cent
1 cent

3 Many Indigenous Nations have different names for North America, the land where they live. These include Turtle Island.

4 The five Great Lakes, on the U.S.-Canadian border, are the largest group of freshwater lakes in the world. They cover an area of 95,000 sq miles (246,000 sq km).

5 Cacao plants were first cultivated by Indigenous peoples in Mexico and Central America. Chocolate comes from the plant's seeds.

South America

South America is the fourth-largest continent. It contains the world's longest mountain range, biggest rainforest, driest desert, and highest waterfall. It is also home to a vast range of plants and animals, and to 435.5 million people.

Population density
People per 0.39 sq mile (1 sq km)

- below 50
- 50-90
- 100-149
- 150-199
- 200-299
- above 300

SOUTH AMERICAN FACTS

- **Covers** approximately 12 percent of Earth's land area
- **Number of countries** 12
- **Biggest country** Brazil
- **Smallest independent country** Suriname
- **Most common languages** Spanish, Portuguese, French, Dutch, and Indigenous languages such as Quechua and Guarani
- **Population of continent** About 435.5 million
- **Largest South American city** São Paulo, Brazil
- **Highest point** Cerro Aconcagua in Argentina at 22,831 ft (6,959 m)
- **Longest river** The Amazon is approximately 4,000 miles (6,437 km) long.
- **Biggest lake** Lake Titicaca, situated between Peru and Bolivia

THE AMAZON

The Amazon is the world's second-longest river and the largest by volume. It pours enough fresh water into the Atlantic to fill 88 Olympic-size swimming pools every second.

How many people?

About 6 percent of the total world population live in South America. Brazil is the largest country and has the biggest population, while Colombia and Ecuador are the most densely populated countries.

▲ FOREST *The Amazon River is surrounded by the biggest tropical rainforest on Earth, home to a huge variety of wildlife and groups of Indigenous peoples.*

▲ CATTLE RANCHING
Vast areas of forest are being cut down each year to clear land for cattle ranches, threatening the area's delicate ecosystem.

SHRINKING AMAZON

Cutting down trees for human activities has shrunk the Amazon Rainforest by 15 percent since the 1970s.

▶ HABITAT *The weather in the rainforest is hot and humid all year round.*

ANIMALS IN THE AMAZON

One in 10 of the world's known species of plants and animals lives in the Amazon rainforest, including:

- 40,000 species of plants
- 3,000 species of fish
- 1,300 species of birds
- more than 425 mammal species
- more than 425 amphibian species
- more than 400 reptile species

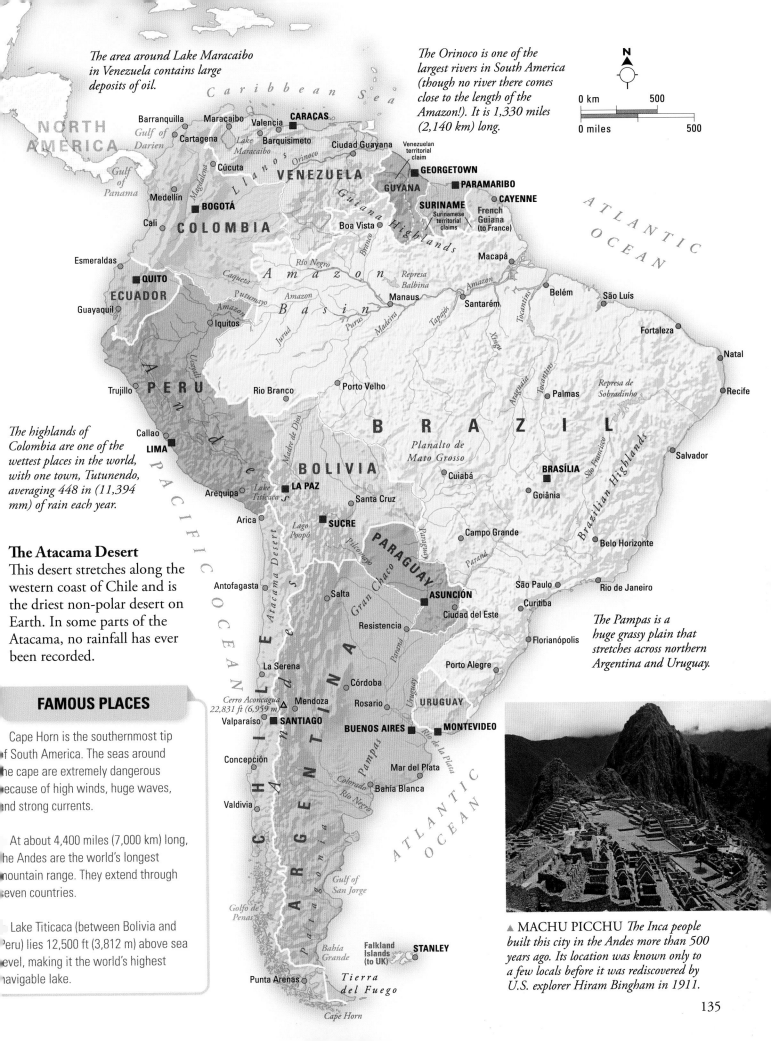

The area around Lake Maracaibo in Venezuela contains large deposits of oil.

The Orinoco is one of the largest rivers in South America (though no river there comes close to the length of the Amazon!). It is 1,330 miles (2,140 km) long.

N

0 km — 500
0 miles — 500

Caribbean Sea

NORTH AMERICA

Gulf of Darien
Gulf of Panama

Barranquilla
Maracaibo
Valencia
CARACAS
Cartagena
Lake Maracaibo
Barquisimeto
Ciudad Guayana
Cúcuta
Llanos
Orinoco
Venezuelan territorial claim
GEORGETOWN
GUYANA
PARAMARIBO
CAYENNE
SURINAME
Surinamese territorial claims
French Guiana (to France)
Medellín
BOGOTÁ
VENEZUELA
Boa Vista
Cali
COLOMBIA
Guiana Highlands
Macapá

ATLANTIC OCEAN

Esmeraldas
Caquetá
Río Negro
Amazon
Represa Balbina
Belém
São Luís
QUITO
Putumayo
Amazon
Branco
Manaus
Santarém
ECUADOR
Amazon Basin
Amazon
Guayaquil
Iquitos
Jurúa
Purus
Madeira
Tapajós
Xingu
Tocantins
Fortaleza
Natal

The highlands of Colombia are one of the wettest places in the world, with one town, Tutunendo, averaging 448 in (11,394 mm) of rain each year.

Trujillo
PERU
Andes
Rio Branco
Porto Velho
Madre de Dios
Araguaia
Tocantins
Represa de Sobradinho
Palmas
Recife

Callao
LIMA
B R A Z I L
Planalto de Mato Grosso
Cuiabá
BRASÍLIA
São Francisco
Brazilian Highlands
Salvador

PACIFIC OCEAN

BOLIVIA
LA PAZ
Santa Cruz
Goiânia

Arequipa
Lake Titicaca
Lago Poopó
SUCRE
Campo Grande
Belo Horizonte

The Atacama Desert

This desert stretches along the western coast of Chile and is the driest non-polar desert on Earth. In some parts of the Atacama, no rainfall has ever been recorded.

Arica
Atacama Desert
Pilcomayo
PARAGUAY
Paraguay
Paraná
São Paulo
Rio de Janeiro
Curitiba

Antofagasta
Salta
Gran Chaco
ASUNCIÓN
Campo Grande
Ciudad del Este
Florianópolis
Resistencia

FAMOUS PLACES

Cape Horn is the southernmost tip of South America. The seas around the cape are extremely dangerous because of high winds, huge waves, and strong currents.

At about 4,400 miles (7,000 km) long, the Andes are the world's longest mountain range. They extend through seven countries.

Lake Titicaca (between Bolivia and Peru) lies 12,500 ft (3,812 m) above sea level, making it the world's highest navigable lake.

La Serena
Andes
Córdoba
Paraná
Porto Alegre
URUGUAY

The Pampas is a huge grassy plain that stretches across northern Argentina and Uruguay.

Cerro Aconcagua 22,831 ft (6,959 m)
Mendoza
Rosario
Uruguay
Valparaíso
SANTIAGO
BUENOS AIRES
MONTEVIDEO
A R G E N T I N A
C H I L E
Pampas
Río de la Plata

Concepción
Mar del Plata
Colorado
Bahía Blanca
Río Negro

Valdivia

ATLANTIC OCEAN

Gulf of San Jorge

Golfo de Penas

Patagonia

Bahía Grande
Falkland Islands (to UK)
STANLEY

Punta Arenas
Tierra del Fuego

Cape Horn

▲ MACHU PICCHU *The Inca people built this city in the Andes more than 500 years ago. Its location was known only to a few locals before it was rediscovered by U.S. explorer Hiram Bingham in 1911.*

135

Life in South America

Dramatic landscapes including the Andes mountains and the Amazon Rainforest, lively cities, music, dancing, carnivals, and passionate soccer crowds are just some of the things to see in South America.

▼ ANDEAN CONDOR *This bird has the largest wings of any bird of prey.*

LANDSCAPE

South America contains almost every kind of landscape, including rainforest, grassland, desert, and mountain.

WILDLIFE

This continent is home to a huge variety of animals: tropical parrots and snakes in the rainforest, bears and condors in the Andes, and anteaters and cavies on the Pampas grasslands.

▲ LLAMA *People who live in the Andes keep llamas for their wool and use them to carry heavy loads.*

TAKE A PICTURE

At 3,212 ft (979 m), Angel Falls in Venezuela is the world's highest waterfall. It was named after an American pilot, Jimmy Angel, in 1933.

FAMOUS SOUTH AMERICANS

- **Simón Bolívar** (1783–1830), born in Venezuela, was a key leader in the successful struggle for independence of much of South America, including Peru, Venezuela, Colombia, Ecuador, and Bolivia.
- **Eva Perón** (1919–1952), often known as Evita, was married to the Argentinian president and dictator Juan Perón. She tried to help poor people and campaigned for better conditions for workers.
- **Gabriel Garcia Márquez** (1927–2014) Colombian novel writer who was awarded the Nobel Prize for literature in 1982.
- **Pelé** (born 1940) Brazilian former soccer player, considered by many to be the greatest player of all time.

▲ FAVELA *Rio is not all beaches and skyscrapers. Some of its inhabitants live in poverty in shantytowns called favelas.*

◄ RIO DE JANEIRO *Famous for its dramatic setting on the Atlantic coast, Brazil's second-largest city is overlooked by a giant statue of Christ the Redeemer.*

FOOD

Potatoes originally come from the Andes, where there are thousands of varieties. Only a few are grown around the world. Meat-based dishes are a common part of the diet in South America. A traditional dish in Paraguay, Uruguay, and Argentina is a barbecue of sausages, steaks, and chicken, known as *asado*.

TOURISM

Many people visit Rio to see the famous carnival or to relax on its beaches or surf in its coastal waters. Other popular tourist attractions include Iguazú Falls and the Inca city of Machu Picchu in Peru.

PANAMA HAT

Despite their name, these brimmed straw hats do not actually come from Panama— they are made in Ecuador.

SOCCER

Soccer is a passion for people in many South American countries— from children playing soccer in the streets up to fanatical support for the big teams. Brazilian soccer is famous for its fast-flowing and attacking style of play. The national team has won the men's soccer World Cup a record five times.

FARMING

Almost a third of all the world's coffee is grown in Brazil. Other important South American crops include bananas, cocoa, and sugarcane, as well as soya bean, which is widely cultivated in Brazil, Argentina, and Paraguay.

MUSIC

The samba, tango, and bossa nova are just some of the famous dances that come from South America. This couple is dancing the tango, a dramatic dance that originated in the slums of Buenos Aires in Argentina. Tango music is played on a type of concertina called a bandoneon, accompanied by a piano and violin.

INDUSTRY

Venezuela has some of the world's largest oil and gas reserves. In Brazil, many cars run on ethanol, which is a fuel made from sugar cane. Mining is also a big industry. Some of the largest copper mines in the world are in Chile and Peru.

DID YOU KNOW?

1 Chile is the longest and thinnest country in the world. It is 2,610 miles (4,200 km) long but only 215 miles (346 km) at its widest point.

2 The city of Ushuaia is the southernmost city in the world. It is situated on the island of Tierra del Fuego at the southern tip of Argentina.

3 There are around 132 million Roman Catholics in Brazil—more than in any other country in the world.

4 La Paz in Bolivia is the world's highest capital city at 11,942 ft (3,640 m) above sea level.

5 More than 2.5 million Indigenous people, belonging to hundreds of groups, call the Amazon Rainforest their home. Some of these Indigenous groups have no contact with the outside world.

137

Africa

Africa is often called the "birthplace of humankind." That's because human beings originated in Africa several million years ago, although humans as we would recognize them only emerged about 300,000 years ago. Today, about 1 in 6 of the world's population live in Africa.

AFRICAN FACTS

- **Covers** approximately 20 percent of Earth's land area
- **Number of countries** 54 + dependencies
- **Biggest country** Algeria
- **Smallest country** The Seychelles
- **Most common languages** Swahili, Yoruba, Igbo, and Fula
- **Population of continent** About 1.4 billion
- **Largest African city** Egypt's capital, Cairo
- **Highest point** Kilimanjaro in Tanzania at 19,340 ft (5,895 m)
- **Longest river** Nile, running through Uganda, Sudan, South Sudan, and Egypt into the Mediterranean Sea, at 4,145 miles (6,671 km)
- **Biggest lake** Lake Victoria, bordering Tanzania, Uganda, and Kenya. The lake contains more than 3,000 islands, many inhabited.

How many people?

The population of Africa is thought to be around 17 percent of the total world population. Nigeria is the most populated African country.

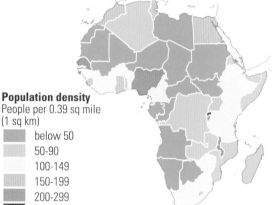

Population density
People per 0.39 sq mile (1 sq km)

- below 50
- 50-90
- 100-149
- 150-199
- 200-299
- above 300

Madei (to Portu

Canary Isla (to Spain

LAÂYOUN

WESTE SAHAR (dispute

Nouâdhibo

MAURITA

CAPE VERDE   NOUAKC

PRAIA   DAKAR   SENEGAL

BANJUL   THE GAMBI

BISSAU

GUINEA-   GU
BISSAU

CONAKRY   SIE

FREETOWN   LEO

MONROVIA

N

0 km   1000

0 miles

◄ OASIS *There are about 90 big oases scattered across the Sahara. These are places where underground water comes to the surface, allowing plants to grow.*

▲ DESERT MAMMAL *This fennec fox keeps cool by losing heat through its huge ears.*

THE SAHARA

"Sahara" comes from the Arabic word *sahra'*, meaning "desert." The Sahara stretches across North Africa and covers parts of 11 countries. Much of it consists of vast seas of sand, with dunes up to 600 ft (180 m) high.

A VARIED LANDSCAPE

Africa's varied landscapes include deserts such as the Sahara (Earth's largest non-polar desert) in North Africa, and the Kalahari and Namib in the south. There are also large areas of forest and grassland.

*Red areas indicate the extent of the named deserts.

SAHARA

Kalahari
Namib

- Desert*
- Dry grassland
- Tropical grassland
- Tropical forest
- Mediterranean
- Mountain

EUROPE

Mediterranean Sea

(to Spain)
Tanger
Melilla (to Spain)
ALGIERS
TUNIS
Constantine
AT
nca

MOROCCO
Atlas Mountains

TUNISIA
Malta
Gulf of Sirte
TRIPOLI
Benghazi

Alexandria
Port Said
Nile Delta
Suez Canal
CAIRO
Sinai

The Red Sea divides Africa from Asia. At the northernmost end, the Suez Canal allows ships to travel between the Red Sea and the Mediterranean.

ALGERIA

Ahaggar

LIBYA

EGYPT

Qattara Depression
Western Desert
Nile
Eastern Desert

Aswan
Lake Nasser

Red Sea

Libyan Desert

Nubian Desert

ERITREA
ASMERA

The easternmost part of the continent is known as the "Horn of Africa" because it is shaped like an animal's horn.

S
MALI

Sahara
NIGER
Ténéré
Tibesti
CHAD

Sahel

NIAMEY
Zinder

BURKINA FASO
OUAGADOUGOU

Lake Chad
NDJAMENA

SUDAN
KHARTOUM
El Obeid

White Nile
Blue Nile

DJIBOUTI
DJIBOUTI
SOMALILAND (not internationally recognized)
Hargeysa

Gulf of Aden

Horn of Africa

Black Volta

GHANA
TOGO
BENIN

NIGERIA
ABUJA

Niger

Moundou

Massif des Bongo

Ethiopian Highlands

ADDIS ABABA

ETHIOPIA

Sheheli

Raas Xaafuun

IRE
OAST)
SOUKRO
ACCRA

LOMÉ
PORTO-NOVO
COTONOU
Lagos

Adamawa Highlands
CAMEROON

CENTRAL AFRICAN REPUBLIC
BANGUI
Ubangi

Sudd
SOUTH SUDAN

JUBA

Lake Turkana (Lake Rudolf)

SOMALIA

MOGADISHU

SÃO TOMÉ & PRÍNCIPE
MALABO
YAOUNDÉ
EQUATORIAL GUINEA

Congo

Kisangani

UGANDA
KAMPALA

Lake Victoria

Ngorongoro Crater

KENYA

NAIROBI

Kismaayo

SÃO TOMÉ
LIBREVILLE

GABON

Congo

Basin
DEM. REP. CONGO

KIGALI RWANDA
BUJUMBURA
GITEGA
BURUNDI

Kilimanjaro
△ 19,340 ft (5,895 m)

Mombasa

INDIAN OCEAN

The Great Rift Valley

This huge valley cuts right through eastern Africa, from Ethiopia to Mozambique. It contains a chain of volcanoes and vast lakes, including Tanganyika, Victoria, and Nyasa—some of the deepest lakes in the world.

BRAZZAVILLE
KINSHASA
Cabinda (to Angola)
Matadi

Kasai

Ilebo

Kananga

Kalemie

DODOMA

Masai Steppe

TANZANIA

Lake Tanganyika

Great Rift Valley

Pemba
Zanzibar
Dar es Salaam

SEYCHELLES

Aldabra Group

LUANDA

Cuanza

Congo
Cuango

ANGOLA

Lubumbashi

Kitwe

Lake Mweru

Lake Rukwa

MALAWI

LILONGWE

Lake Nyasa

Ruvuma

COMOROS
MORONI

Mayotte (to France)

FAMOUS PLACES

■ Hottest place: the highest ever temperature of 136°F (57.8°C) recorded at Al' Aziziyah in Libya in 1922 has now been disqualified.

■ The Ngorongoro Crater in Tanzania is a circular valley, enclosed by mountain walls. It is the remains of an ancient volcano. The crater is home to a huge variety of animals.

■ The Okavango River does not flow into the sea. Instead it ends in a large inland swamp, known as the Okavango Delta, in Botswana.

Huambo

Bié Plateau

Lubango

Zambezi

Cuando

ZAMBIA

LUSAKA

Zambezi

Victoria Falls

HARARE

ZIMBABWE

Bulawayo

Beira

MOZAMBIQUE

Mozambique Channel

Nacala

MADAGASCAR

ANTANANARIVO

Cunene
Etosha Pan

Cubango

Okavango Delta

Kalahari Desert

NAMIBIA

WINDHOEK

Namib Desert

Nosob

BOTSWANA

GABORONE

Limpopo

ATLANTIC OCEAN

Orange River

SOUTH AFRICA

Johannesburg

PRETORIA
MAPUTO
MBABANE
LOBAMBA
ESWATINI (formerly SWAZILAND)

MASERU
LESOTHO

Toliara

Madagascar is the world's fourth-largest island. It is home to many unique animals, such as lemurs and fossas, which are not found anywhere else in the world.

BLOEMFONTEIN

Great Karoo
Drakensberg

Durban

CAPE TOWN
Cape of Good Hope

East London
Port Elizabeth

Life in Africa

Home to the world's longest river and the biggest non-polar desert, to one of the oldest tourist attractions, and to some of the most dramatic wildlife on the planet, Africa is a hugely diverse continent.

LANDSCAPE

Africa contains a huge variety of landscapes, from snow-capped mountains to baking deserts. Northern Africa is mostly desert, while farther south are grassy plains, called savanna, and dense rainforest.

TAKE A PICTURE

Africa's highest mountain is Mount Kilimanjaro in Tanzania at 19,340 ft (5,895 m). Its peak is always covered in snow.

TAKE A PICTURE

Nalubaale, or Lake Victoria, in East Africa is the largest lake in Africa and the second largest freshwater lake in the world.

Traditional African villages

Many Africans live in rural areas or outside of cities, often in small villages. Many homes, such as these in a Shona village, are made from mud.

▼ NAIROBI

Around two out of every five Africans now live in cities like Nairobi, the capital of Kenya.

FARMING

About 60 percent of African workers are subsistence farmers, farming their own land and growing such crops as barley, cassava, corn, sorghum, and sweet potatoes to feed their families. Many also produce "cash crops," such as coffee, which are sold to make money. Larger farms usually grow cotton, cocoa, or rubber as cash crops.

In Kenya, coffee grows in the rich volcanic soil of the country's highlands. Seen here are coffee seedlings being sprayed with water at a farm north of the capital city of Nairobi.

FOOD

The main ingredients of most African dishes are the staple crops grown on local farms—maize, cassava, yams, rice, and beans—along with various green vegetables. One popular dish eaten across West Africa is jollof rice. It is made from rice with tomatoes, onions, spices, and chilies, all cooked in one pot, and is often served with cooked meat or fish.

WILDLIFE

Africa is famous for its zebra, giraffes, lions, and other large animals. But it is also home to many other creatures, from the different species of fish that live in Lake Malawi to colonies of penguins in South Africa.

INDUSTRY

The main African industries are mining for gold, diamonds, and copper, as well as oil production. The biggest oil producers are Angola and Nigeria.

TOURISM

Each year, the ancient pyramids at Giza in Egypt pull in millions of visitors, making them Africa's number one tourist attraction. Many people also travel to Africa to see the continent's spectacular wildlife.

FACT

Diamonds About half of all diamonds come from southern Africa, especially South Africa and Botswana. The largest diamond ever found, the Cullinan, was mined in South Africa in 1905.

MUSIC

Most African music features complex rhythms, created through patterns of drumbeats. African musicians also play flutes, xylophones, and stringed instruments.

▶ MBIRA *This African instrument is made of metal keys set on a wooden soundboard. The musician plucks the keys with their fingers.*

DID YOU KNOW?

1 One of the toughest races on Earth is the *Marathon des Sables* (Marathon of the Sands), which takes place each year in Morocco. Entrants run 156 miles (254 km) across the Sahara in six days.

2 About 1.5 million wildebeest migrate through northern Tanzania's Serengeti grasslands each year.

3 Ellen Johnson Sirleaf was the first female head of state of an African country, a feat yet to be achieved by the U.S. or many other nations in the West.

4 At 4,184 miles (6,695 km), the Nile is the longest river in the world. It flows north through 11 African countries.

5 The world's five fastest land animals are the cheetah, pronghorn antelope, wildebeest, lion, and Thomson's gazelle. Four are found in Africa. The pronghorn is native to North America.

Europe

Unlike some of the other continents, Europe is not a separate landmass—it is connected to Asia. Europe's eastern boundary is formed by the Ural mountains and the Caspian Sea. Russia falls into both Europe and Asia.

EUROPEAN FACTS

- **Covers** approximately 7 percent of Earth's land area
- **Number of countries** 50
- **Biggest country** Russia (note that part of Russia also lies in Asia)
- **Smallest country** Vatican City
- **Most common languages** English, German, and Russian
- **Population of continent** about 748 million
- **Largest European city** Moscow
- **Highest point** Mount Elbrus in Russia at 18,510 ft (5,642 m) high
- **Longest river** The Volga in Russia is 2,292 miles (3,688 km) long.
- **Biggest lake** Lake Ladoga in Russia

How many people?

The 748 million Europeans make up about 10 percent of the total world population. Russia has the largest population, while the most densely populated country among the larger European nations is the Netherlands.

Population density
People per 0.39 sq mile (1 sq km)

	below 50
	50-90
	100-149
	150-199
	200-299
	above 300

▲ ST. BASIL'S CATHEDRAL
This beautiful cathedral, with its onion-shaped domes, stands in Red Square in Moscow, Russia.

THE ALPS

Extending through eight countries, the Alps are the largest and geologically youngest mountain range in Europe. They are a popular vacation destination in both winter and summer for skiing, mountaineering, and walking.

▼ ALPS *Mont Blanc is the highest peak in the Alps at 15,774 ft (4,808 m).*

RESCUE DOG
Specially trained German Shepherd dogs are used in the Alps to find missing people. They can smell a person buried under snow.

FAMOUS PLACES

■ Surtsey, a small island off Iceland, was formed by the eruption of an underwater volcano. It rose above sea level in 1963–1968, making it one of the world's youngest islands.

■ The Low Countries—Belgium and the Netherlands—are so low that some of the land actually lies below sea level and has to be protected by huge dikes (sea walls).

The northeastern part of Europe, known as Scandinavia, includes the countries of Norway, Sweden, Denmark, and Finland.

The island of Iceland is extremely active volcanically. It is home to several volcanoes and many geysers.

Svalbard
(to Norway)

Novaya Zemlya

Kara Sea

Denmark Strait

REYKJAVÍK
ICELAND

Faroe Islands
(to Denmark)

Norwegian Sea

Shetland Islands

ATLANTIC OCEAN

Outer Hebrides

SCOTLAND
Glasgow
Edinburgh
NORTHERN IRELAND
Belfast

Isle of Man

UNITED
Manchester

WALES
KINGDOM
Birmingham
Cardiff
ENGLAND

LONDON

Channel Islands

English Channel

Lille
le Havre
BELGIUM
Nantes
BRUSSELS
LUXEMBOURG
PARIS
LUXEMBOURG

Seine

FRANCE

Clermont-Ferrand
Lyon

Bordeaux

Toulouse
Marseille

Loire

MONACO

ANDORRA
LA VELLA
ANDORRA
Barcelona

Zaragoza

Pyrenees

Mallorca
Menorca
Ibiza
Palma
Balearic Islands

Mediterranean

AFRICA

NORWAY
Bergen
Stavanger
OSLO

SWEDEN

Trondheim

Gulf of Bothnia

FINLAND
Tampere

Murmansk

Barents Sea

White Sea
Arkhangel'sk

Northern Dvina

RUSSIA

Lake Onega

Lake Ladoga
St. Petersburg

HELSINKI

STOCKHOLM

Åland

TALLINN
ESTONIA

Gotland

Vänern
Gothenburg
Vättern
Aalborg

DENMARK
COPENHAGEN

North Sea

Hamburg

NETHERLANDS
AMSTERDAM
THE HAGUE

BERLIN

GERMANY

Frankfurt
am Main

Strasbourg

Munich

SWITZERLAND
BERN VADUZ LIECHTENSTEIN
Mont Blanc 15,774 ft (4,808 m)

Alps

Milan
Turin
Venice

Po

ITALY

SAN MARINO

Corsica

VATICAN CITY
ROME

Naples

Sardinia

Tyrrhenian Sea

Palermo
Sicily
Mount Etna
10,922 ft (3,329 m)

Cagliari

MALTA
VALLETTA

Ionian Sea

Mediterranean Sea

Elbe
Oder

Gdansk
Poznan
Vistula

POLAND
WARSAW
Wroclaw
Krakow

PRAGUE
CZECHIA
(CZECH REPUBLIC)

SLOVAKIA

VIENNA
AUSTRIA
BRATISLAVA
BUDAPEST

LJUBLJANA
SLOVENIA
ZAGREB
CROATIA

HUNGARY

BOSNIA
& HERZEGOVINA
SARAJEVO

MONTENEGRO
PODGORICA

BELGRADE
SERBIA

KOSOVO
(disputed)
PRISTINA

SKOPJE
NORTH MACEDONIA
TIRANA
ALBANIA

Danube

RIGA
LATVIA

LITHUANIA
VILNIUS

Kaliningrad
RUSSIA
(Kaliningrad)

MINSK
BELARUS

Vitsyebsk

KYIV

L'viv

UKRAINE

Kharkiv

Dnipro
Dnieper

MOLDOVA
CHISINAU

Odessa

ROMANIA

BUCHAREST

SOFIA
BULGARIA

GREECE
ATHENS

Aegean Sea

Salonica
Lárisa

Istanbul

TURKEY

ASIA

Crete
Irákleio

Nizhniy Novgorod

MOSCOW

Voronezh

Kazan'
Ufa

Samara
Orenburg

Saratov

Volgograd

Volga

Astrakhan'

Rostov-na-Donu

Donets'k

Sea of Azov
Crimea
(Annexed by Russia, 2014)
Simferopol'

Black Sea

Caucasus
Elbrus 18,510 ft (5,642 m)

Groznyy

Caspian Sea

Ural Mountains

ASIA

Mount Etna, on the island of Sicily, is the largest active volcano in Europe. Etna erupts almost continuously, making it one of the world's most active volcanoes.

Istanbul, the largest city in Turkey, is the only city to span two continents. Part is in Europe, and part in Asia.

The Mediterranean Sea
The Mediterranean Sea divides Europe from Africa and is almost completely surrounded by land. The only ways out are through the Strait of Gibraltar, which is just 9 miles (14 km) wide, and the Suez Canal.

143

Life in Europe

Europe is only slightly bigger than the U.S. but has more than twice the U.S. population. It is also crowded with countries—50 are crammed into the densely populated continent.

EUROPEAN UNION

The European Union (EU) is a political and economic union of 27 countries that operate as a single market. This means that people, goods, and money can move freely between the various countries. Nineteen of the member states share a common currency, the euro. The EU has its own parliament, court of justice, and central bank.

▲ EU FLAG *The circle of stars on this flag represents unity among EU members.*

📷 **TAKE A PICTURE**

Chambord is one of more than 300 beautiful châteaux (castles) in the Loire Valley in France.

📷 **TAKE A PICTURE**

Stonehenge is a circle of standing stones, erected in prehistoric times, that stands on Salisbury Plain in Britain.

▼ ROME'S *mix of old and newer buildings shows how the city has evolved over centuries.*

FOOD

Pizza, croissants, moussaka, goulash, and profiteroles are just some of the foods that originated in Europe and are now popular worldwide.

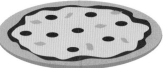

Tapas from Spain

Pizza from Italy

WEALTH

All the European countries have high standards of living. Europe's poorest country is Moldova, with wealth per person around one-eighth that of Singapore. According to World Bank and IMF statistics, 15 of the 25 richest countries in the world are in Europe, with Ireland and Norway both in the top 10.

CROWDED CONTINENT

Europe is densely populated. Overall, there are about 87 people per square mile (33 people per square kilometer), compared to just 51 people per square mile (20 people per square kilometer) in North America. About three-quarters of its population live in towns and cities.

London, UK

SPORTS

Soccer, tennis, cricket, golf, and rugby are played around the world but were all invented in Europe. Rugby, for example, was a variant of soccer invented at a school in the UK in the early 19th century.

▲ MOZART *(1756–1791)*

MUSIC

Europe is the birthplace of classical music, opera, and the modern orchestra. These styles of music were performed in concert halls or opera houses, many of them extremely grand buildings, with audiences paying to attend. Europe's famous composers include Mozart, Bach, Beethoven, Verdi, Tchaikovsky, and Dvořák.

TOURISM

Around 750 million tourists arrived in Europe in 2019. They visited sites such as the Eiffel Tower in France, the Colosseum in Italy, the Acropolis in Greece, and the Hermitage Museum in Russia.

Eiffel Tower, Paris, France

DID YOU KNOW?

1 The Danube River flows through 10 European countries and four European capital cities (Vienna, Bratislava, Budapest, and Belgrade).

2 Europe's population is shrinking. The average number of births per woman is just 1.53. Experts estimate that by 2050, Europeans will make up just over 7 percent of the world's population (currently 10 percent).

3 Europe is named after Europa, a character in Greek myth. She was a princess, abducted by the god Zeus, who had disguised himself as a white bull.

4 Swiss people eat more chocolate than any other nation. Each of them munches through an average of 25½ lb (11.6 kg) of chocolate in a year.

5 The three smallest states in Europe are San Marino (34,000 residents), Vatican City (800 residents), and Monaco (39,000 residents). Vatican City is just 0.17 mile² (0.44 km²).

Asia

Asia is the biggest continent, covering about a third of Earth's land area. It is the most populated continent and contains the world's largest country, highest mountain, and largest lake.

- Mount Pinatubo is an active volcano in the Philippines. It exploded in 1991 in one of the biggest eruptions ever recorded.

- The Dead Sea is actually an extremely salty lake on the border of Israel and Jordan. It is the lowest place on Earth, at 1,312 ft (430 m) below sea level.

- K2 is the second-highest mountain on Earth at 28,251 ft (8,611 m), after Mount Everest. It is located on the China-Pakistan border.

ASIAN FACTS

- **Covers** approximately 30 percent of Earth's land area
- **Number of countries** about 49
- **Biggest country** Russia (though part of Russia also lies in Europe)
- **Smallest country** the Maldives
- **Most common languages** Mandarin, Hindi, and Russian
- **Population of continent** 4.7 billion (60 percent of the world's population)
- **Largest Asian city** Tokyo, Japan
- **Highest point** Mount Everest, on the border of Nepal and China, at 29,029 ft (8,848 m)
- **Longest river** The Yangtze River (Chang Jiang) in China is 3,915 miles (6,300 km) long.
- **Biggest lake** The Caspian Sea is the world's largest lake.

How many people?

Around 4.7 billion people live in Asia—that's about two out of every three people in the world. China has the biggest population, with 1.4 billion people.

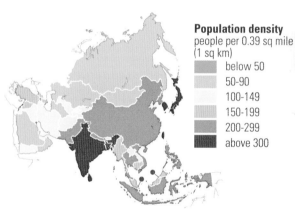

Population density
people per 0.39 sq mile (1 sq km)

- below 50
- 50-90
- 100-149
- 150-199
- 200-299
- above 300

Caspian Sea

Black Sea

Istanbul
GEORGIA
T'BILISI
ANKARA
ARMENIA
AZER
YEREVAN
TURKEY
Mosul
CYPRUS
NICOSIA
SYRIA
TEHRAN
BEIRUT
DAMASCUS
LEBANON
BAGHDAD
ISRAEL
AMMAN
IRAQ
JERUSALEM
JORDAN
KUWAIT CITY
Sh
KUWAIT
The Gulf
SAUDI
ARABIA
BAHRAIN
MANAMA
RIYADH
DOHA
AFRICA
Red Sea
Jeddah
Arabian Peninsula
SANAA
YEMEN
Aden
Gulf of Aden

THE GANGES

The Ganges or Ganga is the longest river in the Indian subcontinent and a sacred river for Hindus. Each year, thousands of pilgrims visit Varanasi and other holy cities along its banks.

▼ BATHING *in the Ganges is said to wash away sins.*

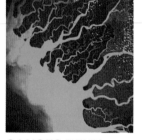

GANGES DELTA

This satellite picture shows the Ganges delta in Bangladesh. This area is very low-lying and often floods.

ARCTIC OCEAN

Laptev Sea

East Siberian Sea

The Ural Mountains in Russia form the boundary between Asia and Europe.

The northern and central part of Russia is known as Siberia. This region is bitterly cold in winter.

Noril'sk

Central Siberian Plateau

Anabar

Yenisey

Lena

Kolyma

Kolyma Range

RUSSIA

S i b e r i a

○ Yakutsk

Magadan

West Siberian Plain

Irtysh

Ob'

Angara

Viliui

Aldan

Amur

Sea of Okhotsk

Sakhalin

Kamchatka

○ Yekaterinburg

○ Omsk ○ Novosibirsk

Lake Baikal

○ Irkutsk

○ Khabarovsk

Pacific Islands

PACIFIC OCEAN

■ **NUR-SULTAN**

Karagandy ○

KAZAKHSTAN

Lake Balkhash

MONGOLIA

■ **ULAANBAATAR**

Gobi

Harbin ○

Kuril Islands

○ Kyzylorda

Altai Mountains

Jilin ○

Vladivostok ○

Hokkaido

Sapporo ○

■ **BISHKEK**

Almaty ○ Urumqi ○

Tien Shan

Inner Mongolia

NORTH KOREA

Sea of Japan (East Sea)

■ **TASHKENT**

KYRGYZSTAN

■ **DUSHANBE**

TAJIKISTAN

Takla Makan Desert

BEIJING ■ Dalian ○

Qingdao ○

■ **PYONGYANG**

■ **SEOUL**

SOUTH KOREA

Honshu

JAPAN

■ **TOKYO**

K2 28,251 ft △
(8,611 m)

Kunlun Mountains

Lanzhou ○

Yellow River

Xi'an ○

■ **SEJONG CITY**

Busan ○

Hiroshima ○

○ Osaka

■ **KABUL**

AFGHANISTAN

■ **ISLAMABAD**

(administered by China, claimed by India)

Plateau of Tibet

CHINA

Yellow Sea

○ Kandahar

○ Lahore

Himalayas

Salween

Brahmaputra | Mount Everest 29,032 ft
(8,849 m)

Chengdu ○

Chongqing ○

○ Nanjing

○ Shanghai

East China Sea

Ryukyu Islands

PAKISTAN

Thar Desert

Indus

■ **NEW DELHI**

NEPAL

■ **KATHMANDU**

Ganges

△

BHUTAN

■ **THIMPHU**

○ Wuhan

Guiyang ○

Mekong

Yangtze

○ Fuzhou

■ **TAIPEI**

TAIWAN

Karachi ○

Varanasi ○

BANGLADESH

Kunming ○

Guangzhou ○

Kaohsiung ○

Ahmadabad ○

Bhopal ○

INDIA

■ **DHAKA**

MYANMAR (BURMA)

Hong Kong ○

Nagpur ○

Kolkata (Calcutta) ○

■ **NAY PYI TAW**

■ **HANOI**

○ Mumbai (Bombay)

Godavari

Bay of Bengal

Yangon (Rangoon) ○

LAOS

■ **VIENTIANE**

VIETNAM

Hainan Dao

Philippine Sea

Luzon

Hyderabad ○

THAILAND

■ **BANGKOK**

Mekong

○ Bengaluru (Bangalore)

Chennai (Madras) ○

Andaman Islands (to India)

CAMBODIA

■ **MANILA**

PHILIPPINES

Legazpi City ○

Kochi (Cochin) ○

■ **PHNOM PENH**

Ho Chi Minh City ○

South China Sea

Cebu ○

Davao ○

Nicobar Islands (to India)

SRI LANKA

■ **COLOMBO**

■ **SRI JAYEWARDENEPURA KOTTE**

Mindanao

INDIAN OCEAN

■ **MALE**

MALDIVES

■ **BANDAR SERI BEGAWAN**

Medan ○

MALAYSIA

BRUNEI

■ **KUALA LUMPUR**

Manado ○

■ **PUTRAJAYA**

■ **SINGAPORE** **SINGAPORE**

Borneo

Balikpapan ○

Celebes

Sumatra

○ Palembang

Ambon ○

Jayapura ○

INDONESIA

■ **JAKARTA**

Semarang ○

Makassar ○

New Guinea

Malang ○

Java

Flores Sea

■ **DILI**

EAST TIMOR

Timor

AUSTRALASIA & OCEANIA

Timor Sea

○ Dalian

N

▲ **DUBAI** *is the biggest city in the United Arab Emirates (UAE). Most of it has been built in the last 60 years.*

A belt of thousands of islands stretches from southeast Asia to Australia. There are more than 13,500 islands in Indonesia alone.

0 km ─────── 1000

0 miles ─────── 1000

147

Life in Asia

Asia contains just about everything—great wealth and extreme poverty, modern ways and ancient traditions, empty deserts and overcrowded cities, small-scale farming and high-tech industry.

Burj Al Arab Hotel, Dubai

TAKE A PICTURE

These limestone pinnacles near Guilin in China were formed by rainwater, which has gradually worn away all the surrounding rock.

TAKE A PICTURE

Mount Fuji is a volcano near Tokyo in Japan. The Japanese consider it a sacred mountain, and it often appears in Japanese paintings.

TOURISM

Asia's most-visited tourist attractions are the Great Wall of China and the Taj Mahal in India. There are more modern attractions in Dubai, famous for its shops and nightlife, and home to some of the world's tallest buildings.

▼ ANGKOR WAT *in Cambodia is the largest religious monument in the world. Originally built as a Hindu temple, it is now a Buddhist center of worship.*

OIL

About 80 percent of the world's easily accessible oil is in the Middle East, and money from oil has made some of the countries in this region extremely rich.

MANUFACTURING

From clothes to cars, lots of goods sold in Western countries are made in Asia. Many companies have factories there because it is cheaper to employ workers in parts of Asia than in Europe or the U.S.

MUSIC AND DANCE

This girl is performing a classical Indian dance. These are often inspired by traditional Hindu stories and poems. The dancer's moves and hand gestures tell the story.

FOOD

Rice is the staple (main) food for many people in Asia. It is served with many Chinese, Thai, and Indian dishes, such as curry or stir-fried foods.

ANCIENT AND MODERN

There are huge differences in people's lifestyles around the continent. Many Asians live in big modern cities, such as Shanghai, Kuala Lumpur, Manila, and Seoul. But in other areas, people such as the Bedouin live much as their ancestors did hundreds of years ago. Many still live in tents and move from place to place.

In parts of Mongolia, nomadic farmers live in traditional felt tents, called yurts.

In Japan, many people live in modern apartment buildings.

WILDLIFE

Tigers are only found in northern, eastern, and southern Asia. The tiger is now an endangered animal, because large areas of its habitat have been destroyed and it is often hunted for its skin.

TECHNOLOGY

Some of the most innovative tech companies in the world can be found in Asian countries including South Korea, Japan, China, and India. They design and manufacture many kinds of electronic products.

FARMING

China is the world's largest producer of grains, including rice and wheat, while India is the world's largest producer of milk and dairy products.

DID YOU KNOW?

1 The Himalayas contain 14 peaks that are over 26,000 ft (8,000 m) high—there are no other mountains this high elsewhere in the world.

2 Asia was the birthplace of all the world's major religions, including Judaism, Christianity, Islam, Hinduism, and Buddhism.

3 The world's deepest lake is Lake Baikal in Russia, at 5,371 ft (1,637 m). It contains more water than the five North American Great Lakes.

4 Japan is home to 10 percent of all the active volcanoes in the world. It has more than 100 active volcanoes, while many lie dormant.

5 The Indian railway system is one of the world's largest employers, with more than 1.4 million staff members.

Australasia and Oceania

The region known as Australasia includes the countries of Australia, New Zealand, and Papua New Guinea, and some of the islands in between. Australia is so big that it is a continent in its own right. To the east lie thousands of tiny Pacific Islands, known as Oceania.

FACTS ABOUT THE REGION

- **Covers** approximately 6 percent of Earth's land area
- **Number of countries** 14 independent countries and 16 dependencies
- **Biggest country** Australia, which is also a continent
- **Most common languages** English, Mandarin, and Arabic
- **Population of the region** estimated at around 43 million
- **Largest city** 5 million people live in Sydney, Australia
- **Highest point** Mt. Wilhelm in Papua New Guinea is 14,793 ft (4,509 m) high
- **Longest river** The Murray-Darling in Australia is 2,330 miles (3,750 km) long
- **Biggest lake** Lake Eyre in Australia

Population density
People per 0.39 sq miles (sq km)

- below 50
- 50–90
- 100–149
- 150–199
- 200–299
- above 300

How many people?

About 43 million people live in Australasia and Oceania. This is just 0.5 percent of the total world population. The vast majority of people live in Australia, which has a population of 25.7 million.

THE OUTBACK

Away from the coasts, Australia is mostly a hot, dry, desertlike plain, known as the outback. People live in the remote towns, and many run large sheep and cattle farms, also known as stations. Most of the animals found in the outback live only on this continent.

Arafura Sea

Philip
Sea

NGERU
Babele

PA

ASIA

INDIAN
OCEAN

Timor
Sea

Darwin

Broome

Great Sandy Desert

WESTERN AUSTRALIA

AU S

Great Victoria Desert

Geraldton

Kalgoorlie

Perth

Albany

Nullarbor Plain

N

0 km 1000
0 miles 1000

▼ ULURU *is a large outcrop of sandstone rock in the centre of Australia. It is a sacred site to First Nations Australians.*

PACIFIC
OCEAN

Huahine Tahiti,
Polynesia

The Pacific Islands

The thousands of islands scattered across the Pacific are divided into three main groups: Melanesia, Micronesia, and Polynesia. Many of these islands are volcanoes, and many have submerged apart from their fringing coral reefs, called atolls.

MICRONESIA *means "small islands." The islands in this group are coral reefs or atolls.*

FAMOUS PLACES

■ The Great Barrier Reef, off Australia's northeast coast, is the world's largest coral reef (👁 p76). It has built up over the last million years or so.

■ The town of Rotorua on New Zealand's North Island is famous for its geysers and bubbling pools of hot mud, caused by volcanic activity under the ground.

Northern Mariana Islands (to US)

Mariana Islands

Saipan
Micro

HAGÁTÑA (US)

MARSHALL ISLANDS

Bikini Atoll

Caroline Islands

Chuuk

Pohnpei ■ PALIKIR

Kosrae

Ralik Chain

■ MAJURO ATOLL

Ratak Chain

MICRONESIA

KIRIBATI
Kiritimati (Christmas Island)

POLYNESIA *means "many islands"—there are more than 1,000 of them.*

■ TARAWA ATOLL

Tungaru

YAREN ■

NAURU

KIRIBATI

KIRIBATI

Line Islands

Marquesas Islands

Melanesia

APUA NEW GUINEA

Rabaul

New Britain

Madang

Lae

Solomon Islands

Solomon Sea

Strait

■ HONIARA

PORT MORESBY

Guadalcanal

SOLOMON ISLANDS

VANUATU

Banks Islands

TUVALU

FUNAFUTI ATOLL ■

Tokelau (to NZ)

Penrhyn

Northern Cook Islands

Millennium Island (Caroline Island)

Tuamotu Islands

Wallis & Futuna (to France)

SAMOA

APIA ■

American Samoa (to US)

■ PAGO PAGO

Cook Islands (to NZ)

Society Islands

Polynesia

Vanua Levu

PORT-VILA ■

New Caledonia (to France)

Îles Loyauté

Viti Levu

■ SUVA

TONGA

Niue (to NZ)

■ AVARUA

Southern Cook Islands

Rarotonga

■ PAPEETE

Tahiti

French Polynesia (to France)

Pitcairn, Henderson, Ducie, and Oeno Islands (to UK)

NOUMÉA

FIJI

■ NUKU'ALOFA

Îles Gambier

Coral Sea

Cairns

Great Barrier Reef

Townsville

nt Isa

Rockhampton

ENSLAND

IA

Brisbane

PACIFIC OCEAN

▶ FIRST NATIONS AUSTRALIANS *were the first inhabitants of the continent and are the traditional owners. Their cultural beliefs and ceremonies are still practiced today, and so is the sharing of cultural knowledge with others.*

NEW ZEALAND *is about 1,250 miles (2,000 km) away from its nearest neighbor, Australia.*

Great Dividing Range

NEW SOUTH WALES

CANBERRA

AUSTRALIAN CAPITAL TERRITORY

VICTORIA

Geelong Melbourne

Augusta

elaide

ray

Sydney

Newcastle

Tasman Sea

Bass Strait

Tasmania TASMANIA

Hobart

Auckland

Rotorua

Hamilton

North Island

Cook Strait

■ WELLINGTON

South Island

Southern Alps

Christchurch

Dunedin

Stewart Island

NEW ZEALAND

▶ WILDLIFE *Animals on the continent range from New Zealand's native tuatara to Australia's kangaroos, which live in the bush, surviving on grasses. They are most active in the early morning and evening, when it is cooler.*

▶ DINGOES *are wild dogs. They come from domestic dogs that people brought to Australia.*

Life in Australasia and Oceania

▲ KOALA *are marsupials that rarely drink, obtaining moisture from the leaves they eat.*

The First Australian people came to Australia more than 65,000 years ago. The people of the Torres Strait have lived there for 12,000 years. The Māori only arrived in New Zealand around a thousand years ago. An average of 13 people live per sq mile (5 people per sq km) in this continent.

WILDLIFE

The region's unique wildlife includes Australia's marsupials (pouched mammals), such as kangaroos and koalas, and New Zealand's flightless birds, such as emus and kiwis.

Kiwi

TAKE A PICTURE

The Great Barrier Reef is home to more than 1,625 species of fish, including 1,400 species of coral, as well as thousands of plants.

FAMOUS AUSTRALASIANS

- **Ernest Rutherford** (1871–1937) New Zealand scientist and Nobel Prize winner, whose investigations revealed the structure of the atom.
- **Howard Florey** (1898–1968) Australian pharmacologist, who was awarded the Nobel Prize for his work in developing the drug penicillin.
- **Cathy Freeman** (born 1973) Australian sprinter. At the Sydney Olympics in 2000 she became the first of the First Nations Australians to win a gold medal in running.
- **Jonah Lomu** (1975–2015) New Zealand rugby player. Lomu was the all-time top try scorer in the Rugby World Cup, a record he now shares with South African rugby player Bryan Habana.

TAKE A PICTURE

New Zealand's southwest coast is punctured by many long, narrow inlets, known as fjords. The most famous is Milford Sound.

▼ SYDNEY *Australia's biggest city is built around a large harbor. The Harbour Bridge is one of the country's most famous landmarks.*

MUSIC

This First Nations Australian wind instrument, called a didgeridoo, is made from a hollow tree trunk. It makes a droning sound.

▲ DIDGERIDOOS *are traditionally made from Eucalyptus trees.*

SPORTS

The most popular sports in Australia and New Zealand are cricket and rugby. Aussie Rules Soccer is unique to Australia. New Zealand is famous for extreme sports, such as bungee jumping.

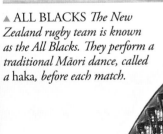

▲ ALL BLACKS *The New Zealand rugby team is known as the All Blacks. They perform a traditional Māori dance, called a haka, before each match.*

TOURISM

Many people visit Australasia to take part in outdoor activities, especially water sports such as snorkeling on the Barrier Reef and surfing and windsurfing off Australia's beaches, and trekking in New Zealand.

FARMING

Sheep farming is important in Australia and New Zealand—in fact, there are about five times as many sheep as people in Australia and New Zealand. Wool and meat are among their biggest exports, but mining is big as well.

World flags

Every country in the world has its own flag. Countries use flags to highlight their identity.

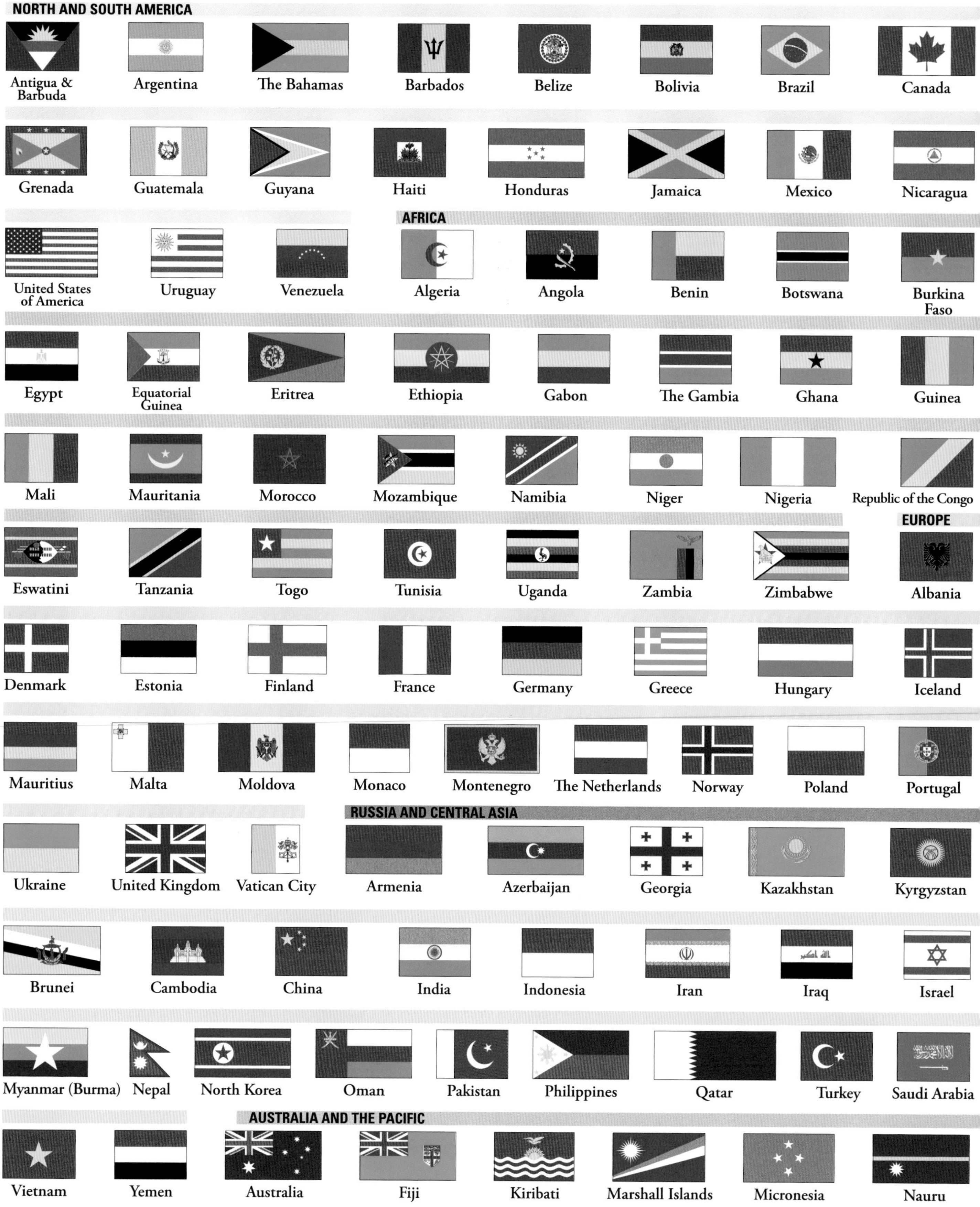
NORTH AND SOUTH AMERICA
Antigua & Barbuda
Argentina
The Bahamas
Barbados
Belize
Bolivia
Brazil
Canada
Grenada
Guatemala
Guyana
Haiti
Honduras
Jamaica
Mexico
Nicaragua
United States of America
Uruguay
Venezuela
AFRICA
Algeria
Angola
Benin
Botswana
Burkina Faso
Egypt
Equatorial Guinea
Eritrea
Ethiopia
Gabon
The Gambia
Ghana
Guinea
Mali
Mauritania
Morocco
Mozambique
Namibia
Niger
Nigeria
Republic of the Congo
Eswatini
Tanzania
Togo
Tunisia
Uganda
Zambia
Zimbabwe
EUROPE
Albania
Denmark
Estonia
Finland
France
Germany
Greece
Hungary
Iceland
Mauritius
Malta
Moldova
Monaco
Montenegro
The Netherlands
Norway
Poland
Portugal
Ukraine
United Kingdom
Vatican City
RUSSIA AND CENTRAL ASIA
Armenia
Azerbaijan
Georgia
Kazakhstan
Kyrgyzstan
Brunei
Cambodia
China
India
Indonesia
Iran
Iraq
Israel
Myanmar (Burma)
Nepal
North Korea
Oman
Pakistan
Philippines
Qatar
Turkey
Saudi Arabia
Vietnam
Yemen
AUSTRALIA AND THE PACIFIC
Australia
Fiji
Kiribati
Marshall Islands
Micronesia
Nauru

■ **Religion:** The flags of many European countries feature the Christian cross; the flags of many Islamic countries are based around the four traditional Arab colors—red, white, green, and black.

■ **Regions:** Some countries that are made up of different regions show this in their flags. The crosses of St. George, St. Patrick, and St. Andrew in the UK flag represent England, Ireland, and Scotland, respectively.

■ **Tricolors:** many flags consist of three colored vertical stripes, known as a tricolor. These flags are inspired by the red, white, and blue French flag, adopted during the French Revolution.

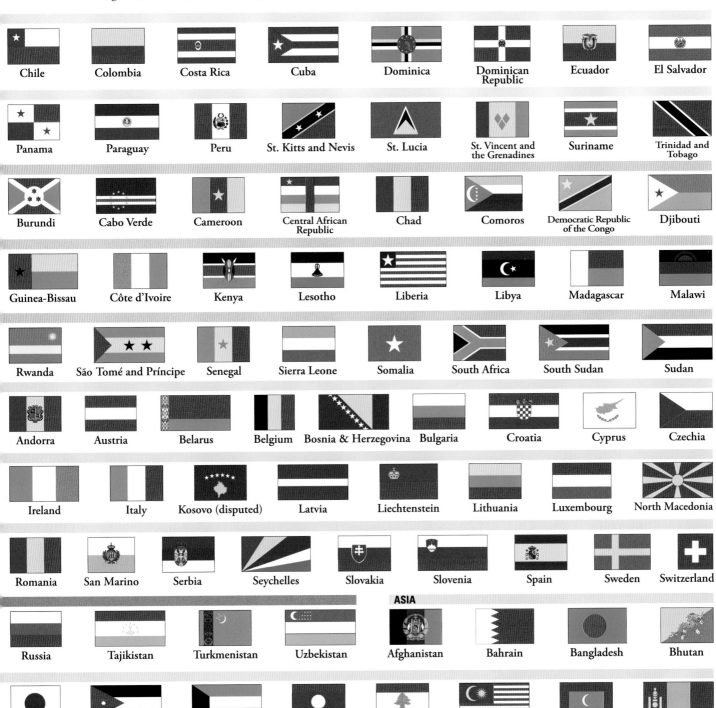

Chile · Colombia · Costa Rica · Cuba · Dominica · Dominican Republic · Ecuador · El Salvador

Panama · Paraguay · Peru · St. Kitts and Nevis · St. Lucia · St. Vincent and the Grenadines · Suriname · Trinidad and Tobago

Burundi · Cabo Verde · Cameroon · Central African Republic · Chad · Comoros · Democratic Republic of the Congo · Djibouti

Guinea-Bissau · Côte d'Ivoire · Kenya · Lesotho · Liberia · Libya · Madagascar · Malawi

Rwanda · São Tomé and Príncipe · Senegal · Sierra Leone · Somalia · South Africa · South Sudan · Sudan

Andorra · Austria · Belarus · Belgium · Bosnia & Herzegovina · Bulgaria · Croatia · Cyprus · Czechia

Ireland · Italy · Kosovo (disputed) · Latvia · Liechtenstein · Lithuania · Luxembourg · North Macedonia

Romania · San Marino · Serbia · Seychelles · Slovakia · Slovenia · Spain · Sweden · Switzerland

ASIA

Russia · Tajikistan · Turkmenistan · Uzbekistan · Afghanistan · Bahrain · Bangladesh · Bhutan

Japan · Jordan · Kuwait · Laos · Lebanon · Malaysia · Maldives · Mongolia

Singapore · South Korea · Sri Lanka · Syria · Taiwan · Thailand · Timor-Leste · United Arab Emirates

New Zealand · Palau · Papua New Guinea · Samoa · Solomon Islands · Tonga · Tuvalu · Vanuatu

CULTURE

What makes one group of people different from another? Whether it's their religious beliefs or the music they listen to, culture reflects the ways in which people live.

World religions

A religion is a set of beliefs that explain where the world came from, what happens after death, and how we should live our lives. Religious people come together to worship and take part in festivals. They believe in an unseen, spiritual world that cannot be explained by science.

TELL ME MORE...

The vast majority of people in the world are members of a religious tradition. Roughly a third of the world's population are Christians, and a fifth are Muslims. About 15 percent of people describe themselves as non-religious.

Abrahamic religions

Judaism, Islam, and Christianity are part of the same "family" of religions, known as the Abrahamic religions. All three consider Abraham as one of the forefathers of their faith. Islam and Christianity have been spread throughout the world by immigrants and missionaries.

▲ THE ABRAHAM ICON *sits in the Church of the Holy Sepulchre, Jerusalem.*

The six religions with the most followers in the world are:

 Christianity **Islam**

JUDAISM

Judaism emerged more than 3,500 years ago in the Middle East, among a tribe called the Israelites. Jews believe that there is only one God, who created the world and continues to care for it.

▶ *MENORAH The candles on this nine-branched holder are lit during* Chanukah, *the Jewish festival of light. The central candle is used to light the eight outer candles—one for each day of* Chanukah.

PASSOVER

Passover is a festival that celebrates the release of the Israelites from Egypt, where they were held in slavery. Jews believe that God sent ten plagues against the Egyptians, the last of which killed all first-born children and animals. The Israelites marked their houses with lamb's blood and God "passed over" without harming them. After this, the Pharaoh released the Israelites.

▲ SEDER
This is a special meal in which symbolic foods are placed on a special platter in the middle of the table, including bitter herbs to signify suffering and an egg to represent rebirth.

▼ THE *KIPPA*
Some Jewish men wear a skullcap—called a kippa—*to show their respect for God.*

▲ THE *TORAH is the sacred text that Jews believe God dictated to Moses on Mount Sinai. It includes the Ten Commandments, which show the Jewish people the right way to live. Together with other sacred texts, it makes up the Tanakh.*

CHRISTIANITY

Christians believe that Jesus Christ, a Jewish holy man born in Bethlehem, around 0 CE, was God in human form. According to Christian tradition he was put to death, but returned to life three days later. The Christian Bible is made up of the Jewish Tanakh—the Old Testament—and a new set of scriptures— the New Testament, a record of the lessons and life of Jesus while he lived on the Earth.

◄ THE CHALICE
Holy Communion is a Christian ritual in which bread is eaten and wine is drunk to remember Jesus's sacrifice. The wine may be served in a chalice.

▲ THE SUPPER AT EMMAUS
This stained glass window shows Jesus, having risen from the dead, sharing a meal with two disciples.

Catholicism There are many different branches of Christianity, the largest of which is Roman Catholicism. The leader of the Roman Catholic Church is the Pope. Catholics believe that Jesus appointed Saint Peter as the first head of the Church, and the Pope is his successor.

▲ THE CROSS
Jesus Christ died on a cross. Christians believe that because of this sacrifice, his followers will have eternal life with God in heaven.

According to the Catholics, **saints** are people who lived especially holy lives. Some saints are linked with specific countries or causes. Saint Andrew is the patron saint of Russia and Scotland.

 **Hinduism** **Buddhism** **Sikhism** **Judaism**

ISLAM

Islam was founded in Arabia in the 7th century CE by the Prophet Muhammad. Muslims believe in one God, Allah, who sent prophets down to Earth, the last one being the Prophet Muhammad. Earlier prophets included Abraham and Jesus.

The *Qur'an* Allah's teachings, as dictated to the Prophet Muhammad, were documented in a book called the *Qur'an*. Muslims try to live by rules set down in the *Qur'an*. The most important duties are known as the Five Pillars:

- proclaiming your beliefs
- praying five times a day
- donating to the needy
- fasting during *Ramadan*
- making a pilgrimage to Mecca

Ramadan is the ninth month of the Islamic calendar, during which the *Qur'an* was revealed to the Prophet Muhammad. Throughout *Ramadan* Muslims neither eat nor drink between dawn and sunset. This helps them to be closer to Allah and to remind them of the suffering of those less fortunate. *Ramadan* ends with *Eid ul-Fitr*, the Fast-Breaking Festival. Believers visit the mosque for *Eid Namaz* (*Eid* prayers) and eat traditional foods with family.

► MECCA, *in Saudi Arabia, is the birthplace of the Prophet Muhammad. Muslims must face Mecca's Khana e Kaaba (central cubic building), the holiest site in Islam, whenever they pray, wherever they are in the world.*

Religions such as Hinduism, Buddhism, and Sikhism have their roots in South and East Asia. However, during the 20th century they spread across the world as a result of migration. While the six religions with the most followers account for nearly 85 percent of all believers, millions more follow other religions and faiths both old and new.

HINDUISM

Hinduism originated in India in about 1500 BCE. Most Hindus believe that souls are born again after death, and that good or bad deeds in this life result in a good or bad rebirth. The greatest goal of Hinduism is to find perfect peace and liberation by escaping the cycle of rebirth.

▲ WORSHIP
Hindus believe in many gods. Ganesha (above left) is linked to wisdom, while the goddess Durga (above right) is associated with female strength. Also important to Hindus are Vishnu (savior of the world) and Shiva (destroyer of the world).

▲ THE SACRED COW
Cows are greatly revered by Hindus. Killing cows is banned in parts of India, and cows are allowed to wander wherever they like.

▲ DIWALI
Diwali is the Hindu festival of lights. It marks the victory of good over evil. Families light oil lamps to invite Lakshmi, the goddess of wealth and purity, into their homes.

SIKHISM

Sikhism was founded in the 15th century by Guru Nanak, in what is now Pakistan. Sikhs believe in one all-powerful God, who is best understood through meditation. The holy book of the Sikhs is the *Guru Granth Sahib*, which is the teachings of the first leaders of the Sikh faith, the ten Gurus.

▶ THE WORD OF GOD
This Indian Sikh man is working on a hand-written version of the Guru Granth Sahib. *This holy book is treated with utmost respect: it is placed on a throne, and a sacred whisk is waved over it as it is read.*

◀ THE GOLDEN TEMPLE
Located in Amritsar, Punjab, India, it is one of the holiest places for Sikhs.

▼ THE FIVE Ks
Most Sikhs outwardly show their devotion by keeping five symbolic objects starting with the Gurmukhi letter ਕ, which corresponds with the English letter K.

- Kesh *(uncut hair). Sikhs do not cut their hair, and Sikh men allow their beards to grow.*
- Kara *(a steel bracelet)*
- Kanga *(a wooden comb)*
- Kaccha *(a cotton undergarment)*
- Kirpan *(a small steel sword)*

BUDDHISM

Buddhism was founded in India about 2,500 years ago. Buddhists do not worship a god, but instead follow the teachings of a *Shakyamuni* (sage) called the Buddha. Like Hindus, Buddhists believe in rebirth. The Buddha showed his followers how to escape rebirth and suffering through good deeds and meditation, which help in achieving Nirvana (enlightenment).

▼ BUDDHA STATUES
Statues of the Buddha often show him meditating in a cross-legged position. The Big Buddha on the island of Koh Samui, Thailand, was built in 1972 and is 49 ft (15 m) tall. It can be seen from several miles away.

▲ PRAYER WHEELS
Tibetan Buddhists use prayer wheels printed with mantras, which are verses that bring about spiritual understanding. As the wheel is turned, the mantra reappears over and over again.

▲ BUDDHIST TEMPLES
Buddhist temples are home to monks and nuns who have chosen to follow a life of good deeds and meditation. The temples are designed to symbolize the elements: earth, air, fire, and water, with wisdom represented by the pinnacle at the top.

SHAMANISM

Shamanism is the ancient, widespread belief that an invisible world of good and evil spirits exists all around us. Specially trained people called shamans can perform rituals which allow them to communicate with the spirit world. The Chukchi people of Eastern Siberia, for example, have shamans in their community who use drums to contact the spirit world.

CONFUCIANISM

Kong Fuzi (Confucius) was a Chinese philosopher (551–479 BCE) who stressed the importance of respecting elders, acting dutifully towards the family and state, and honoring ancestors. His sayings are found in a book called *The Analects*, which is a collection put together after his death.

BELIEFS OF THE FIRST NATIONS PEOPLES

The First Nations peoples of Australia traditionally believe that the land, the sea, animals, and plants were created by ancestor spirits. These spirits, which live in a hidden world called the Dreamtime or the Dreaming, continue to give life to our world. Stories and songs about the Dreamtime have been passed down from generation to generation for thousands of years.

Celebrations

Celebrations are an incredibly important part of religious, public, and family life. They bring people together, give people something to look forward to, and are generally a time for enjoying oneself.

HANUKKAH

- **Where** Jewish people across the world.
- **When** An 8-day festival begins on the 25th day of the month of Kislev (November/December).
- **What happens** Families gather to light candles, make blessings, sing, and eat traditional fried foods such as doughnuts.
- **What it's celebrating** The rededication of the holy Temple, which the Jews regained after a military victory against the Greeks.

TELL ME MORE...

Chinese calendar In the Chinese calendar, each year is named after one of the 12 animals of the Chinese zodiac: rat, ox, tiger, rabbit, dragon, snake, horse, goat, monkey, rooster, dog, or pig.

LENT

- Christians celebrate Lent, a 40-day period of fasting and praying that leads up to Easter. In this period, they remember the 40 days Jesus spent fasting in the desert. Religious parades and processions mark Lent in many countries.

CHINESE NEW YEAR

- **Where** China and Chinese communities across the world.
- **When** It begins with the new moon on the first day of the new year, which falls in January–February, and ends on the full moon 15 days later.
- **What happens** Everyone hangs lanterns in their windows and dragon dances are performed in the streets. Families celebrate with a special meal and honor their ancestors. Red clothes are worn, which represent happiness.
- **What it's celebrating** New beginnings and the sowing of new crops.

DIWALI

- **Where** India, and celebrated by Hindus all over the world.
- **When** Within the months of Asvina and Kartika (October/November).
- **What happens** Diwali is the Festival of Lights. People light *diya* (small lamps) and put them around their houses and gardens. They give each other gifts of sweets and let off fireworks.
- **What it's celebrating** The return of Lord Ram from exile and his crowning as king. According to legend people lit lamps to light his way in the darkness. The lights also show the "inner light" or soul within a person.

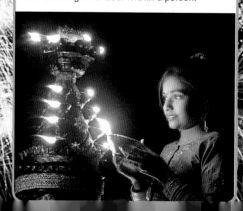

RIO CARNIVAL

- **Where** Rio de Janeiro, Brazil
- **When** Carnival goes on for four nights in February or March, just before Lent.
- **What happens** Everyone takes to the streets in carnival clothes, and they dance or ride on huge floats. The highlights of the carnival are a competition between samba schools and parades of amazing costumes.
- **What it's celebrating** Pre-Lent fun

FASNACHT (CARNIVAL)

- **Where** Austria, Germany, Alsace (France), and parts of Switzerland.
- **When** The day before Ash Wednesday—the Tuesday before Lent begins.
- **What happens** Families gather together for a feast and many areas have processions to welcome in the springtime. Honored members of a town dress up as the carnival prince and peasant. Everyone else dresses up in anything from clown costumes to witches or even fruit!
- **What it's celebrating** It's a time of celebration before the self-denial of Lent. It also goes back to pre-Christian times when it was a way to drive out the evil spirits of winter and encourage spring and good crops.

DÍA DE LOS MUERTOS

- **Where** Mexico
- **When** November 1 and 2
- **What happens** People build altars in their homes covered with photos and possessions of their dead relatives to guide the loved one home.
- **What it's celebrating** Relatives who have died, but still live on in the memory. People believe that on *el Día de los Muertos* (the Day of the Dead) it is easier for souls of the departed to visit the living.

EID UL-FITR

- **Where** Celebrated by Muslims all over the world.
- **When** Every year, Eid takes place on a different date of the Muslim calendar (which is a lunar calendar), at the time of a new moon.
- **What happens** Families and friends get together to pray, give each other cards and gifts, and share special feasts. People go to the mosque for *Eid Namaz* (Eid prayers).
- **What it's celebrating** The end of the month of Ramadan, which is a time for prayer and thinking of others. During Ramadan, Muslims avoid eating between dawn and sunset.

THANKSGIVING

- **Where** U.S.
- **When** 4th Thursday of November
- **What happens** Families gather together for a feast and traditionally eat turkey and gravy, stuffing, and pumpkin pie.
- **What it's celebrating** Thanksgiving Day is a holiday in the U.S. People celebrate the successful harvest early European settlers of the country experienced in 1621. According to legend, the settlers were taught by Indigenous people to share the natural abundance of Earth by caring for crops, hunting, and fishing.

▲ **FIRST THANKSGIVING** *Indigenous people joining in the feast with New England pilgrims.*

CHRISTMAS

- **Where** North America, Europe, Australasia, and by Christians around the world.
- **When** December 25
- **What happens** Families get together to go to church, give each other presents, and eat traditional foods, such as roast turkey and panettone in parts of Europe.
- **What it's celebrating** The birth of Jesus Christ.

Panettone

HALLOWEEN

- **Where** U.S., Canada, and across Europe.
- **When** October 31
- **What happens** Children go "trick or treating" often dressed up as witches or skeletons. People carve faces in pumpkins and light a candle in them.
- **What it's celebrating** The evening before All Saints (or All Hallows) Day, when Christians commemorate the saints. Some Halloween traditions may be based on pagan customs, such as lighting bonfires before winter.

Art

Art tells us an enormous amount about the history and culture of people. We can tell what people did in everyday life and what they wore through their art. We can learn about their religious beliefs, their sports, and their skills.

📷 **TAKE A PICTURE**

First Nations Australian art dates back many thousands of years, and contemporary pieces are popular. Some of the art is connected to the sacred belief in Dreamtime. The painting above is a modern mural on an urban wall.

ANCIENT ART

A huge amount of art has been found in tombs of the Pharaohs that were built in ancient Egypt. They give us an incredible window into how people lived about 5,000 years ago.

The art of the Aztecs

By the 15th century, the Aztecs had created a short-lived empire in modern-day Mexico. It was destroyed soon after the Spanish invasion of 1519. They produced jewelry in gold, jade, and turquoise, as well as ceramics and textiles with angular, geometric patterns.

Cave galleries

A series of famous Paleolithic paintings in the Altamira cave near Santillana del Mar, northern Spain were developed over around 15,000 years, as descendants of the original artists added to them.

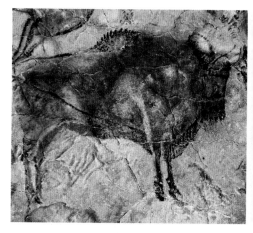

Terra-cotta army

In 1974, one of the most extraordinary pieces of art ever found was discovered by farmers. It was a huge army of Chinese warriors made out of terra-cotta pottery. In time, archaeologists found more than 8,000 life-size statues guarding the tomb of the first emperor of China, Qin Shi Huang, who ruled from 221–210 BCE. Some of the warriors even have horses.

▶ ANCIENT SCULPTURE
Ancient Greek sculpture heavily influenced Roman art. This Roman marble sculpture, The Discus Thrower, *was based on an original Greek bronze sculpture.*

◀ AFRICAN SCULPTURE
The Kingdom of Benin (1440–1897) in southern Nigeria produced some of Africa's most beautiful sculptures. This brass head of Queen Mother Idia shows her with a striking pointed headdress.

Sculpture

Sculpture has been around since prehistoric people carved shapes into rock. While early peoples sculpted religious decorations and icons, the ancient Greeks made lifelike statues.

Art imitating life

The ancient Greeks were interested in ideals—statues that showed a perfect body. The ancient Romans were influenced by Greek art, but they were more interested in portraiture: statues and images of a particular person, such as this portrait of a gladiator. Portraits were important for celebrating the lives and achievements of people's ancestors.

Religious art

Many pieces of art depict religious scenes. They might present religious figures from history, or religious symbols and traditions. The artists often used gold leaf (thin sheets of gold) and rich reds.

RUSSIAN ICONS
Icons are images or representations of a religious figure. They are mainly painted in the symbolic style of Byzantine art.

TIBETAN ART
A thangka *(embroidered banner) and a* mandala *(diagram) are often used for meditation. The details on their patterns convey spiritual ideas.*

COLORS FROM NATURE

In the past, people had to make colors using materials such as crushed rocks, minerals, plants, or insects. To make paint, they mixed their powder or juice with egg yolk or animal fat among other things. Over the centuries, artists found their perfect color in all sorts of strange ways.

White – sourced from chalk
Black – sourced from charcoal
Golden Indian yellow – perhaps made from the urine of cows that had been fed mango leaves
Strong red – sometimes made from the crushed and dried bodies of female scale insects (*Dactylopius coccus*)
Green – made from the juice of parsley flowers
Brown – made from the inner bark of the oak tree (*Quercus tinctoria*)
Dark violet – made from crushed elderberries
Dark brown – created from the ink of a small squidlike creature called a cuttlefish (*Sepia officinalis*)

Modern art

From the late 1800s, artists made bolder works of art, using such media as film, photography, and more. Art could now range from an oil painting to a building wrapped in fabric or people sitting still for hours in a setting. Works by female and Black artists became more prominent globally.

Four Ballerinas on Stage
by French artist Edgar Degas

IMPRESSIONISM

In the 1860s, a group of artists broke away from painting religious or historical subjects and instead painted everyday scenes in a new style. These Impressionists often painted outdoors, aiming to capture the impression of light and create a snapshot of real life. They included Claude Monet, Édouard Manet, Edgar Degas, and Berthe Morisot.

◀ THE TECHNIQUE
Short brushstrokes of pure color produced a sketchy, patchy, spontaneous effect painting that suggests a fleeting moment in time.

POINTILLISM

French artist Georges Seurat invented a technique called pointillism. He used tiny dots of pure color that, when one stands back, seem to merge to make new colors. This is known as optical mixing.

◀ THE TECHNIQUE *From a distance, this lady's hat looks red. But it is actually made up of red, green, yellow, and blue dots.*

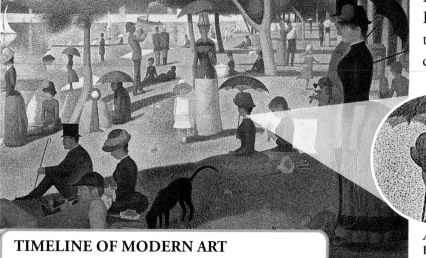

A Sunday on La Grande Jatte—1884
by Georges Seurat

TIMELINE OF MODERN ART

1860s–1890s	1880s–1905	1880s	1880s–1890s	1907–1914
Impressionism developed in France when artists tried to capture a fleeting moment.	Post-Impressionist artists, including Paul Gauguin, Paul Cézanne, and Vincent van Gogh, painted vibrant, bold, and often personal pictures.	Pointillism developed. It is a form of art where paintings are made up of dots of color.	The work of Expressionist artists including Edvard Munch conveyed people's feelings, such as joy or sorrow.	Cubism was created. It is a form of art that shows several different views of an object at once.

CUBISM

Pablo Picasso, one of the most famous modern artists, experimented with space by breaking pictures up into distorted and weird shapes. *Three Musicians* looks like a muddled-up picture, but the instruments the musicians are playing can be seen. This style is called Cubism. It shows a scene from several different points of view all at once.

Three Musicians by Spanish artist Pablo Picasso

SCULPTURES

Zimbabwean sculptor Henry Munyardazi was a key member of a major modern African sculpture movement inspired by the Shona culture of southern Africa. He blended natural shapes influenced by Shona carvings with the striking, simple forms of much modern art.

POP ART

Artists made brightly colored artworks using images based on modern life, such as film stars, comic strips, hamburgers, and soup cans. American artist Andy Warhol made colorful screen-print portraits.

Screen print of Marilyn Monroe by Andy Warhol

ART TODAY

To capture people's lives and emotions, some artists use everyday items, make films on their cell phones, or create textile art. Others are experimenting as much as ever, pushing the boundaries, and finding new techniques and settings for their art.

▲ DIGITAL ART *A Tokyo-based art collective called teamLab has created many interactive landscapes using digital technology.*

▲ INSTALLATIONS *British artist Tracey Emin transported the beach hut where she met her boyfriend to an art gallery.*

1910–1950s	1920s	1950s–1960s	1970s–MODERN DAY
Abstract art distorted the shape and color of subjects. Jackson Pollock made pictures by splashing paint over a canvas on the floor.	Surrealist artists including Salvador Dalí and René Magritte began to paint in a dreamlike style. This is Magritte's 1964 self-portrait *The Son of Man*.	Pop art emerged. It uses ideas and images from popular culture, such as food packaging, comics, or famous people.	Black British artist Lubaina Himid has featured the experiences of Black women, and especially their absence from art, in her ground-breaking works.

Writing and printing

Imagine a life without books, newspapers, comics, magazines, menus, letters, and emails—it would be a very different place. Writing gives us news, entertains us, and more importantly documents history and teaches and spreads ideas. Printing allows one person's ideas to be communicated to millions of people at the same time.

ANCIENT WRITING

The earliest form of writing didn't use letters, but pictograms—symbols that each represent a single word or sound. Some of the earliest writings are from ancient Egypt. Known as hieroglyphs, these pictograms have been traced back over 5,000 years. Nearby, in Mesopotamia (present-day Iraq), people started to keep accounts about taxes and crops using cuneiform script on clay tablets.

▼ *Cuneiform script was carved into wet clay using a blunt reed. Pictograms became simplified into wedge-shaped markings.*

◄ *Hieroglyphs on the Temple of Hathor, Egypt*

Methods of writing
Modern pens are very different to the original methods of writing, such as reeds for carving clay, or a quill (bird feather) dipped in ink for writing on animal hide. The Romans used lead pencils more than 2,000 years ago, but the graphite pencils we use today were invented in England in the 1500s. But some traditions remain: Japanese script is still written with a brush and ink.

WRITTEN LANGUAGES

There are more than 7,000 different languages spoken in the world today and many of them have their own letters or characters when written down. Although there are many localized styles of writing in the world, there are five main types that dominate.

► CYRILLIC *is used by many Slav people (in eastern Europe), such as Russians. It is thought to have evolved from the older Greek script.*

◄ THE ARABIC ALPHABET *just uses consonants. Three letters are also long vowels; short vowels are shown by signs above or below the consonants. Arabic is read from right to left.*

▲ CHINESE *is one of the oldest written texts in the world. It includes pictograms called characters.*

▲ LATIN *writing evolved about 2,600 years ago. It is the most widely used alphabet in the world.*

▲ DEVANĀGARĪ *is an Indian script that is syllabic; instead of letters, it has symbols for consonants and vowels.*

PRINTING

The Chinese first invented printing by blocks in the 7th century. A word or whole page was carved onto a wooden block, which was dipped in ink and printed onto cloth. The block could be dipped and printed again and again, but each print had to be done by hand.

▲ BAD MOVE *Between 1041–1048, Chinese printer Bi Sheng invented movable type. Each block was carved with a character, and blocks could be rearranged to make new pages. But with thousands of characters, it was hard to use.*

◄ THE GUTENBERG PRESS
Four hundred years after Bi Sheng, in c. 1440 Johannes Gutenberg of Germany invented the mechanical printing press, which used metal movable type. For the first time in Europe, books could be mass-produced, with the Christian Bible (1455) being one of the first.

FACT

Every day, millions of newspapers are printed all over the world. Japanese newspaper *Yomiuri Shimbun* has the highest circulation in the world, with an estimated 8 million readers each day.

How do presses work?

Like the earliest hand printing, presses use blocks carved in relief—with reversed, raised letters that print the right way round. Letter blocks, called "type," are set into a frame and covered in ink, and the paper is pressed down on top.

BESTSELLERS

The most popular books in the world are known as bestsellers.

■ The biggest seller of all time is the Christian Bible at an estimated 6 billion copies. It has been translated into more than 700 languages.

■ The *Qur'an* has sold nearly 3 billion copies.

■ Mao Zedong's *Quotations from Chairman Mao* sold some 900 million copies.

■ The seven *Harry Potter* books by J.K. Rowling have sold more than 500 million copies worldwide.

■ *Le Petit Prince (The Little Prince)* by Antoine de Saint-Exupéry has sold more than 140 million copies in 300 languages.

Color printing

How many colors can you see on this page? Technically, there are just four: cyan (C), magenta (M), yellow (Y), and black (K). As the paper runs through the CMYK printing rollers, a certain amount of each colored ink is printed onto the paper. At the end of the run, the layers of ink have built up to produce thousands of different shades.

Cyan

Magenta

Yellow

Black

Final image

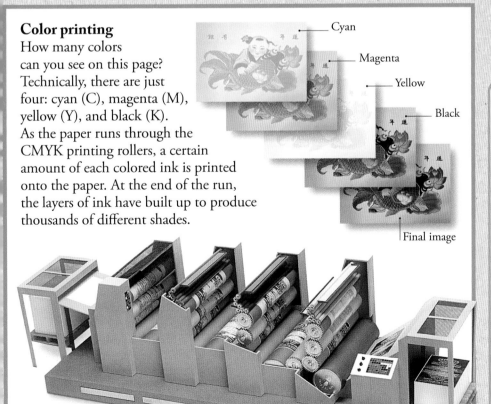

Education

It's an essential part of culture to pass on knowledge to the next generation. In most parts of the world, this knowledge is taught in school. What you learn in the classroom and beyond gives you the skills that you will need for the future. Without reading skills, you would find it hard to read this book.

▲ SCHOOL UNIFORM *Many schools around the world have surprisingly similar uniforms. Some schools have unusual extras as part of their uniform—children who live near the Sakurajima volcano in Japan have to wear hard hats to school because the volcano hurls rocks daily onto the nearby town.*

IN SCHOOL

Children have been going to school for thousands of years. Archaeologists discovered a school building in the ancient city of Ur (in modern-day Iraq)—a city that fell into ruin more than 3,000 years ago. In some ways, school hasn't changed very much since then. Across the world, children still sit together in classes to be taught lessons by a teacher.

TELL ME MORE...

In parts of the world where there are places without schools and qualified teachers, or families who can't afford to pay for schooling, many children can't go to school. The right to education is a basic human right for everyone, as declared by the United Nations (UN) in 1948.

MANY SUBJECTS
Senior school students discuss a topic in a sociology class with their teacher at a school in Western Ghana, Africa. Around the world, older students study a wider range of subjects than younger ones.

What's on the timetable? Right now, on the other side of the world, a child is being taught reading, writing, maths, and sports, just like you. But children from different countries may learn things specific to their culture in their school. For example, some boys in Mongolia attend monastery schools to learn to be Buddhist monks, while also studying medicine and art.

▲ HAKA *Students in New Zealand learn a traditional Māori dance, the* Haka.

Other ways of schooling Lots of children around the world are taught at home by their parents or tutors. Another way of learning is remote schooling, which is useful for children who live very far away from a school. This has become more widespread since 2020, when schools around the world shut down because of the COVID-19 pandemic. Remote schooling means that the students are taught online by teachers. Classes can be viewed through video calls, learning apps, and websites.

▲ LEARNING REMOTELY *In the early years of the COVID-19 pandemic, most students accessed classes remotely.*

Community education is especially important when it comes to passing down cultural traditions, and most of this is done outside of school.

▲ WEAVING *A mother from a Marsh Arab community (in modern-day Iraq) teaches her girls an essential skill.*

▲ REINDEER HERDING *A Nenet boy (in Russia's Far North) spends three months a year at home learning herding.*

Always learning Education isn't just about sums and spelling: you learn many other things in school, possibly without even realizing it. When you play sport, you are learning how to stay healthy, how to be part of a team, and how to compete. When you study history, geography, and religion, you learn about people and the different ways of life around the world. And when you interact with your classmates and teachers, you learn how to develop relationships.

▲ PLAYING SPORT *These children aren't just learning the rules of football but also how to stay fit and healthy.*

EDUCATION FOR ALL

Teaching programs at many schools are adapted for students of all abilities. For students with learning disabilities, teachers undergo special training that enables them to support these students well.

What happens next? Have you ever thought about what you would like to do once you leave school? Some careers, such as architecture or the law, need a degree and professional qualifications. Practical careers, such as mechanics and hairdressing, might offer apprenticeships— "on the job" training where you work with (and so learn from) someone who is already doing that job.

It doesn't stop here! Education may continue beyond the end of school. Although not every student goes to college or university, it may improve their chances of getting a job. Lots of people attend classes to brush up on old skills or learn entirely new ones.

Music

Most people enjoy music in some form, whether they choose to play an instrument, or sing, or simply listen. Music brings people together at all sorts of events.

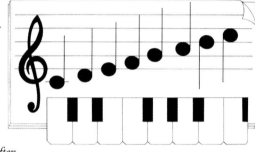

▲ THE FIRST MUSIC *We know that music has been played and enjoyed for thousands of years because ancient drawings have been found showing musical instruments.*

NOTATION

The most common way to write music today is the five-line notation using dots, symbols, and abbreviations. It is based on a system used by Roman Catholic monks in the 10th century. When you learn a musical instrument, you learn to read music at the same time.

Pitch is how high or low a note sounds. Notes are grouped into sets of eight, known as an octave and written on five lines called a stave.

The "clef" shows what notes are on the stave. This is the treble clef.

The "key signature" shows which key the music is in.

The speed of the music, or "tempo," is often written in Italian. "Allegro" means "quickly."

The "rest" shows where the musician should pause.

A line marks the end of the "bar." Each bar contains the same number of beats.

The shape of each note tells the musician how long to play it.

Allegro

The "time signature" shows the musician the number of beats to a bar.

mf — Dynamic markings indicate how loud to play the music. "mf" means moderately loud.

Certain types of notes can be joined together with beams.

National anthem Each country of the world has its own cultural song, called their national anthem. They are often sung at important national occasions, including sporting events.

TELL ME MORE...

Computer programs called DAWs (Digital Audio Workstations) can help musicians write music and compose orchestral pieces without learning traditional notation.

▶ THE SOUTH AFRICAN *national anthem includes five of the eleven official national languages, including Africaans, English, and isiZulu.*

◀ FOLK MUSIC
A country or an Indigenous people often have their own style of music and dance, known as folk music.

▶ RELIGIOUS MUSIC
Music is used a lot in religious worship around the world, whether in song—for example, this Christian choir singer—or using instruments like these Buddhist monks.

SOUND OF THE PEOPLE

A type of music can often be unique to the culture of a nation or people.

■ **The didgeridoo**, a First Nations instrument from Australia, is made from a naturally hollow tree or branch. It is often used in traditional ceremonies.

■ **The sitar**, a stringed instrument, is one of the best-known of all Indian sounds. It has extra strings that lie beneath the main strings that vibrate to give it its shimmery sound.

■ **The djembe drum** is a goblet-shaped wooden drum covered in a skin that is played by hand. The drum

originated in west Africa and is still an important part of the culture in many west African countries. The rhythmic beat is often used in dance.

MUSIC STYLES

■ **Classical music** is a general term for music written to be performed in a concert hall. Often it is composed for an orchestra, for a choir, or for the opera.

■ **R&B** or rhythm and blues was originally performed by Black Americans in the 1940s. It was a mixture of religious gospel music and blues (slow melancholy songs). R&B now includes soul and funk-influenced pop music.

■ **Jazz** originated in the early 20th century in the U.S. It was a blend of music played by enslaved Black people and European instruments. The saxophone, trumpet, and double bass are three of the key sounds in jazz bands.

■ **Rock'n'roll** emerged in the U.S. in the 1940s and 1950s, growing out of gospel, jazz, R&B, and country music. Bands used guitars and drums.

■ **Rock music** emerged during the 1960s and includes lots of different styles from punk rock to heavy metal.

■ **Reggae** originated in Jamaica in the 1960s. It has a slow rhythmic style and is often associated with the Rastafarian religion.

■ **Hip-Hop** started in the 1970s when DJs began to speak rhymes over the music they played at parties. This became rap music, one of the most popular styles of music today.

■ **Country music** is a blend of traditional music, mainly from the southern states of the U.S., and rock'n'roll.

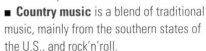

■ **Dance** The dawn of the computer age and highly developed synthesized sound led to a new sound designed to fill dance floors. DJs mixing music using turntables live on the dance floor have become big stars in themselves.

■ **Pop music**, or popular music, is not a particular style of music, but music that is made popular by people buying or streaming it online, watching videos, or paying to see it performed live. Pop stars often also have a large social media presence.

173

The orchestra

An orchestra is a group of musicians who play different instruments which are grouped into strings, woodwind, brass, and percussion. Each instrument plays a different part to make one piece of music.

WOODWIND

■ Woodwind instruments make sound when air blown into them vibrates. Players can alter the sound by covering holes with their fingers, or pushing down on metal "keys" that cover holes the fingers cannot reach. The clarinet is a woodwind instrument and there are more than 12 types of clarinet, though not all are still in use. The one shown here is a bass clarinet, which produces a deep, mellow sound.

PERCUSSION

■ Percussion instruments are struck, scraped, or shaken. When you bang a percussion instrument, such as a drum, its surface vibrates, making the air inside ring with sound. This sound adds movement and momentum to a piece of music. Cymbals also vibrate to produce sound—they are clashed together in a swinging, brushing movement during the climax in orchestral music.

ANTONIO VIVALDI

Antonio Vivaldi (1678–1741) was born and raised in the Republic of Venice. He composed music in the Baroque style. His most well known piece is *The Four Seasons*, in which he tried to capture the atmosphere of each season.

CONDUCTOR

■ A key figure in most orchestras, the conductor directs the musicians using gestures of their hands and arms.

MANY ORCHESTRAS

Many cultures have developed their own types of orchestra. In Indonesia, a gamelan ensemble consists of many percussion instruments, such as gongs or chimes, flutes, and some stringed instruments. The music played is often very spiritual. This orchestra usually performs in religious ceremonies and celebrations.

▶ GAMELAN ORCHESTRA
The ensemble of different instruments produces a complex melody. The drum players who lead the rhythm sit in the middle.

BRASS

■ Brass instruments are long tubes that open into a bell shape at one end. To play them, the musician blows into the mouthpiece. Long tubes, such as that on a trombone, sound deep. Shorter tubes, such as that on a horn, sound higher. As well as air, lots of liquid is blown in. This is let out through the spit valve.

STRINGS

■ String instruments are played by plucking or running a bow across the strings. The double bass shown here is the deepest member of the string family.

Let's perform

Everyone enjoys the spectacle of a show, be it a play, an opera, a film, or a dance. What these performing arts have in common is that they communicate between people, and reflect their time and their culture.

DANCE

Everywhere in the world, people love to dance. A dance can be a performance, part of a religious ritual, or something to do for fun. Most dances happen in time to music or a beat.

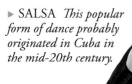

▶ SALSA *This popular form of dance probably originated in Cuba in the mid-20th century.*

Street dance is any dance that people have created for themselves, instead of being formally invented. Types of street dance include break-dancing and tango.

Religious dance *Bharathnatyam* is a Hindu dance performed mostly by women. It is one of the classical dances of India. The steps are incredibly precise. Skilled dancers flow from pose to pose with complex movements of the feet, hands, arms, neck, head, and even the eyes!

Ballet requires great strength, skill, and grace, and it involves very specific and formal positions and movements. Classical ballets, such as *Swan Lake* and *Giselle*, feature only these traditions, while modern ballets (right) are often much freer and more expressive.

Dance is important in many traditional cultures. Dances are usually performed to the rhythm of drums and there are special dances for all kinds of occasion—weddings, funerals, harvests, hunts, religious ceremonies, and even to prepare for war.

THEATER

People have been taking to the stage for thousands of years, performing everything from comic and tragic plays to pantomimes, operas, and musicals. The oldest plays were performed in ancient Greece and included song and dance as well as acting. Some of their outdoor theaters still stand today.

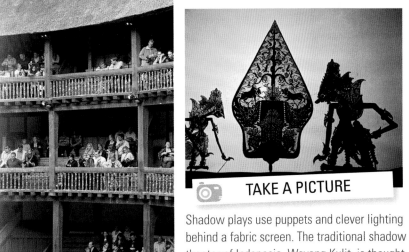

◄ THE LION KING *is a musical play based on the animated feature film by Disney.*

TAKE A PICTURE

Shadow plays use puppets and clever lighting behind a fabric screen. The traditional shadow theater of Indonesia, Wayang Kulit, is thought to be more than 800 years old.

FACT
Most Hollywood feature films are filmed digitally. If they are shot on film, they use 10,000 ft (3,000 m) of tape, wound onto five double reels.

MOVING PICTURES

In 1895, the Lumière brothers astounded audiences with the first "movies," and films have been a popular form of entertainment ever since. Movies are made up of a sequence of still images, which create the impression of movement when they are shown in rapid succession.

HOLLYWOOD is a part of the city of Los Angeles, but the word is often used to mean the whole American film industry. Hollywood movies are watched all over the world, sometimes with subtitles or "dubbed" into other languages.

Asian martial arts movies made the names of stars such as Bruce Lee, Jackie Chan, and Jet Li. They are famous for elaborate stunts and fight scenes, and for special effects.

Bollywood is the name used to describe the Hindi film industry based in Mumbai (Bombay), India. Bollywood films are produced in the Hindi language at a rate of about 1,000 a year. They usually include extravagant musical scenes.

177

Sports

Sports can be good for health. It brings people together, especially in team sports, for competitive fun. Some enjoy just taking part, but others love to win.

BALL GAMES

Soccer is a typical team sport where 11 players try to kick the ball into their opponents' goal.

▲ SOCCER *is arguably the most popular sport in the world. People all over the world play it in schools and parks, on the streets, or wherever they can. Billions of people watch the FIFA World Cups for men and women, which are held every four years. Soccer fans are fiercely loyal to their local or national teams.*

- **Tennis matches** are played either as singles, between two players, or doubles, between four players.
- **Cricket** is played by people in more than 100 countries. The best international teams play in Test matches.
- **Table tennis** or ping-pong became an Olympic sport in 1988. It is popular around the world, with an estimated 30 million competitive players.
- **Football** uses a ball with pointed ends. Players wear protective padding, and are allowed to carry the ball or make passes.
- **Rugby Union** is played with an oval ball between teams of 15 players.

▲ GOLF *is played using a club to knock a small ball into a hole in as few shots as possible.*

▲ VOLLEYBALL *is played between two teams of six players over a net. It was invented in the 1890s.*

CONTACT SPORTS

- **Capoeira** is a martial art from Brazil that combines dance and acrobatics and is performed to music.
- **Wrestling** dates back thousands of years. It is a form of hand-to-hand combat.

◀ BOXING *is a tough sport, demanding huge upper body strength. Boxers wear padded gloves.*

▶ KARATE *is a Japanese martial art. It uses moves such as punching, kicking, and knee and elbow strikes.*

- **Judo** first appeared in Japan in the 1800s but developed from far earlier techniques.
- **Kung Fu Taolu** is China's national sport, where it is known as *wushu*.

▶ SUMO WRESTLING *was once part of the training given to Samurai warriors and is a traditional and ritualistic combat sport of Japan. Each contestant tries to wrestle the other to the ground or out of a 15 ft (4.55 m) diameter circle.*

EXTREME SPORTS

- **Surfing** Surfers ride lightweight boards just ahead of a breaking ocean wave.

- **Ski jumping** involves skiing down a steep ramp, leaping, and landing safely.

- **Hang gliding** features the use of a triangular-shaped wing to glide through the air. Gliders can stay up for many hours by finding rising air columns.

- **Cliff diving** sees people dive off from a coastal cliff to perform acrobatic moves before hitting the water.

◀ EXTREME CLIMBERS *ascend ice and rock faces that appear almost impossible to climb.*

◀ BMX *is bicycle motocross. It involves racing around a dirt track or spectacular jumps and tricks.*

▲ SKYDIVING *Skydivers usually leap from a small plane and free-fall before opening a parachute to enable safe landing. Worldwide, there are hundreds of skydiving drop zones. Instead of a plane, some skydivers have jumped from helicopters or hot-air balloon baskets.*

RACING

- **Drag racing** is the fastest land-based sport. It originated in the U.S. and takes place between two high-powered dragster cars.

- **Speed skaters** can reach speeds of slightly under 40 mph (64 kmph).

- **Horse racing** with powerful thoroughbred horses may be over flat ground or over jumps.

- **Yachts** of all sizes are used for competitive racing.

▲ FORMULA ONE (F1) *Grand Prix races are fast and exciting.*

▶ ROAD CYCLISTS *may cover huge distances in a race such as the Tour de France.*

◀ SPORTS FOR ALL *In athletics, track races range in distance from 60 m and 100 m short sprints to the 10,000 m. Paralympic (or Parallel Olympics) races (left) and other events are held for a range of disabled athletes, after each Olympic Games. The Special Olympics are organized for athletes with disabilities related to learning, thinking, or adapting.*

OLYMPIC GAMES

The Olympic Games is the most important sporting event in the world. Every country is invited to take part—athletes from 205 nations plus a refugees' team took part in the Tokyo Olympics in 2021. Winners receive a gold medal.

The original Olympic Games were first recorded in 776 BCE and were held in Olympia, Greece. The first modern-day Olympics were held in Athens in 1896. As a reminder of its origins, an Olympic torch of fire is carried from Olympia to the Games by a series of relay runners. It's used to light an Olympic flame in the stadium.

▶ BASKETBALL *became a part of the Olympic Games for men in 1936 and for women in 1976.*

Architecture

Architecture is the design of buildings and other structures, such as bridges. An architect's job is to make sure a building is well built, and safe and pleasant to use. It also has to be suitable for its purpose—theaters need room for a stage and dressing rooms, for example. Architects also try to make buildings look interesting and inspiring.

GETTING STARTED

Before designing a building, architects need to know what the building is for, where it is to be built, and how much money can be spent on it. They then work out what the building will be made from, and the position and measurement of every wall, door, and window, which they record in great detail on drawings called plans. Sometimes they make a scale model of the building too.

CHANGES IN STYLE

Every period of history is marked by its own style of architecture. This reflects changes in taste and fashion, and new building techniques and materials. Most cities are a mixture of old and new buildings that show many different styles.

▲ ANTONI GAUDÍ *was a Spanish architect with a distinctive style. His most famous work is the Sagrada Familia, the unfinished basilica in Barcelona.*

▲ STILT HOUSES *Some people who live along coasts and rivers build their houses on stilts to avoid flooding.*

▶ BAMBOO HOUSES *The Gamo people of Ethiopia use bamboo to make thatched houses.*

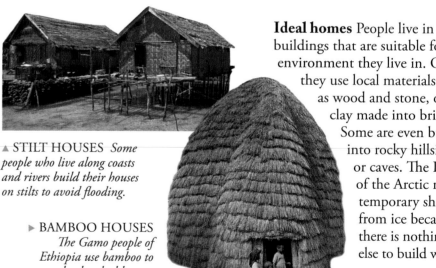

Ideal homes People live in buildings that are suitable for the environment they live in. Often they use local materials, such as wood and stone, or clay made into bricks. Some are even built into rocky hillsides or caves. The Inuit of the Arctic make temporary shelters from ice because there is nothing else to build with.

TIMELINE OF ARCHITECTURE

ANCIENT EGYPT	ANCIENT GREECE	ANCIENT ROME	BYZANTINE	GOTHIC
2590–2500 BCE Pyramids of stone were erected in the Nile valley as tombs for kings.	**700–44 BCE** Ancient Greeks built temples with specific proportions, known as the classical style.	**200 BCE–500 CE** The Romans used concrete to construct many large buildings and structures.	**330–1453** Byzantine buildings were characterized by rounded domes on square bases, and arches supported by columns.	**1100–1500** Grand buildings of the medieval period feature pointed arches and flying buttresses to support high roofs.

LONGHOUSES

Long, narrow dwellings, designed to house an extended family, are one of the oldest types of building in many places, from Asia to North America. They could be built of stone or, most commonly, of wood, like the longhouses of the Iroquois people, which have a wooden frame covered with boards or tree bark. Such dwellings could be made longer if the family expanded.

FAMOUS STRUCTURES

Some structures are instantly recognizable because of their design. Every major city has a number of famous buildings, but each has a different style, according to the period in which it was built.

▲ HŌRYŪ-JI PAGODA
Part of a 7th-century Buddhist temple complex, this building is one of the world's oldest wooden structures.

▲ TAJ MAHAL
This marble building is one of the finest examples of 17th-century Islamic architecture.

▲ NATIONAL GALLERY, CANADA
The gallery is a striking modern structure of glass and granite.

Modern designs Computers enable architects to design buildings that would not have been possible before. They can quickly figure out whether a shape can be built and even allow the architect to walk around a virtual building.

▼ THE DESIGN *of the Guggenheim Museum in the Spanish port of Bilbao is said to resemble a ship.*

‹B›AROQUE
‹16›50–1750
‹T›he very grand, ‹o›rnate style of ‹B›aroque design ‹w›as created in ‹It›aly, France, ‹an›d Spain.

SKYSCRAPERS
1880s
The first skyscrapers were built in Chicago, following the invention of the elevator.

ORGANIC ARCHITECTURE
1900–1950s
Organic architecture, with its curved shapes inspired by nature, was promoted by American architect Frank Lloyd Wright.

Sydney Opera House

BAUHAUS
1919–1933
The German Bauhaus school created designs based on clean lines, cubic shapes, and flat roofs.

ECO-LIVING
1980s onward
Houses were built to be more energy efficient and use environmentally friendly materials.

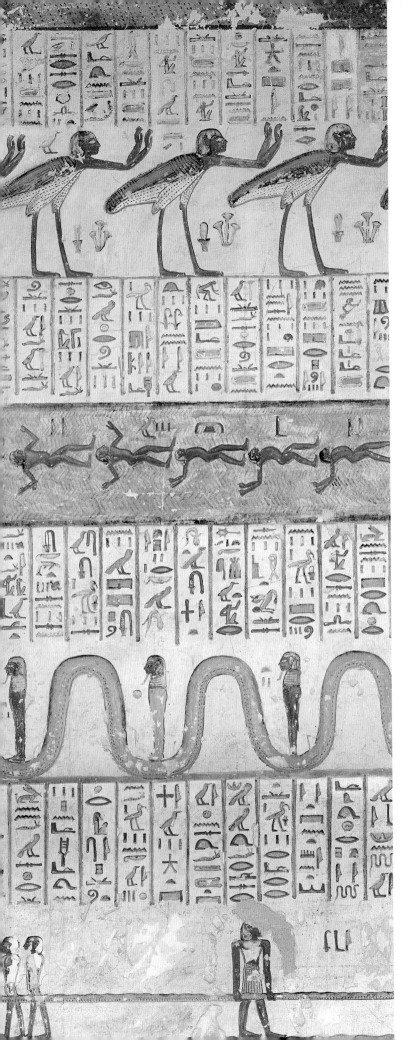

HISTORY AND POLITICS

History and politics is the study of the lives
of people and the activity of governments
and rulers in the past from written records.

Tales from the past

History is the study of things that have happened in the past. This can be anything from the earliest people to events of the last few years. Like detectives searching for clues, historians look at evidence from the past known as primary sources.

Digging for clues The work of archaeologists helps historians to know more about early people. During their excavations of a site, archaeologists uncover and study early buildings and landscapes, identify human and animal remains, and find and examine artefacts—objects made by people from the past.

▼ MAYA RUINS *The Maya civilization of central America flourished between 200 and 900 CE. In Maya ruins, archaeologists have found many steep-sided pyramids with steps leading up to a temple.*

Archaeology site After doing an aerial and surface survey of the area, the archaeologists begin excavating the site, removing the earth layer by layer and recording any discoveries.

STUDYING ARTEFACTS

■ **What is the object made from?**
The artefact shows the materials available and the skills of those who crafted it.

■ **Who would have used the object?**
The artefact may give clues about the status of people in society.

■ **What was the object used for?**
Historians may be able to understand what the people's culture was like from the artefact and whether the materials or the artefact itself has traveled long distances through trade.

Bronze Age pendant

10th-century BCE statue from the Middle East

Ancient Greek vase

Since ancient times, records of births, marriages, and deaths, census results, and tax records have been kept. Eyewitness accounts and inscriptions have recorded important events and the lives of famous people. Other sources are the diaries and personal letters of ordinary people living through extraordinary events.

▲ SOLDIER'S JOURNAL *The diary of a US infantry soldier tells of his life during the American civil war (1861–1865).*

▲ ANNE FRANK'S DIARY *Between 1942 and 1944, a young Dutch-German Jewish girl wrote a diary while in a secret annex, hiding from the German Gestapo.*

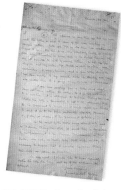

▲ NEHRU'S LETTERS *Jawaharlal Nehru wrote many letters to foreign leaders during India's freedom struggle and his time as the country's first prime minister.*

A group of Koreans in 1890

▼ AT WORK AND PLAY *Photographs show the way of life and the changes in clothing styles and in technology, tools, and machines.*

Caterpillar tractor used in France in the 1920s

Old photographs Since the mid-1800s, photography has become increasingly popular. Photos provide a visual source to historians studying the lives of people. Since recorded sound was developed, historians can also study oral accounts of people talking about their lives and reactions to events.

Early 1900s folding roll-film camera

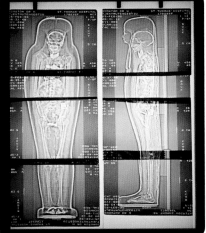

An X-ray of an Egyptian mummy

New technology Advances in technology help historians. Radiocarbon dating, X-rays, and thermal scans can reveal previously unknown details about artefacts, while LiDAR (a form of laser scanning) enables archaeologists to peer inside ruins more closely.

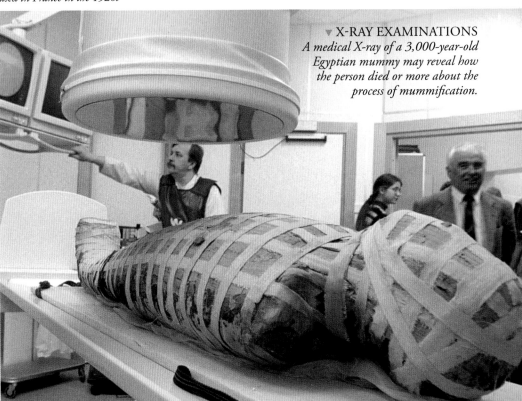

▼ X-RAY EXAMINATIONS *A medical X-ray of a 3,000-year-old Egyptian mummy may reveal how the person died or more about the process of mummification.*

Early people

From the limited fossil records, historians can only make suggestions at the possible origins of humans. There were many different hominins—species related to humans that walked upright—but over five million years, all but one became extinct. Only *Homo sapiens* (or modern humans) survived.

OUT OF THE FORESTS

Many historians think that more than six million years ago (MYA), apelike creatures moved out of the forests of Africa to live on open ground. To survive, they learned to stand and walk upright to see farther and move quickly, leaving their hands free to carry possessions and learn new skills. About one MYA, early people migrated out of Africa and spread out across the continents.

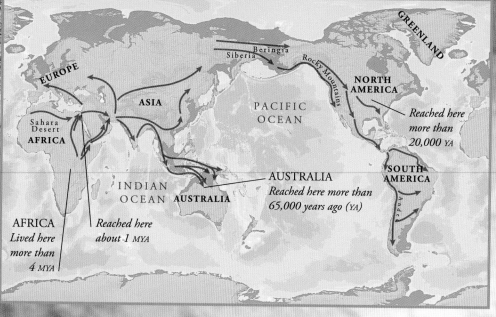

GREENLAND

Siberia Beringia

EUROPE

ASIA

Rocky Mountains

NORTH AMERICA

Reached here more than 20,000 YA

PACIFIC OCEAN

Sahara Desert
AFRICA

INDIAN OCEAN   AUSTRALIA

AUSTRALIA
Reached here more than 65,000 years ago (YA)

SOUTH AMERICA

Andes

AFRICA
Lived here more than 4 MYA

Reached here about 1 MYA

TIMELINE OF HOMININS

AUSTRALOPITHECUS AFARENSIS

Dated: around 4 MYA
Fossils found in Africa with very low forehead and projecting face.

HOMO HABILIS

Dated: 2.4–1.4 MYA
Tools found with fossil remains that had large skulls.

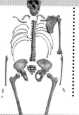

HOMO ERECTUS

Dated: 1.8 MYA–110,000 YA
Fossils in Africa, Europe, and Asia found with long, low skulls and large molar teeth.

WHO'S WHO?

- **Lucy:** A female skeleton found in Ethiopia and estimated to have lived 3.2 MYA. She was about 3 ft 6 in (107 cm) tall.
- **Nutcracker man:** Teeth and skull fragments found in Tanzania of a hominin estimated to have lived about 2 mya. He had the biggest, flattest cheek teeth and thickest teeth enamel of any hominin, and he ate mostly grass.
- **Peking man:** One of 40 individuals found at a site in China and estimated to have lived c. 400,000 YA.
- **Old man:** A 30- to 40-year-old skeleton with severe arthritis found in France. Estimated to have lived 60,000 YA, he would have had a height of 5 ft 6 in (168 cm).

▶ PEKING MAN
Historians have found evidence that the Peking man and his companions would have lived in caves, made tools, and used fire to keep warm and cook food.

TELL ME MORE...

As the early people moved northwards, they had to cope with a colder climate and survive the ice ages. Clothes were first made from animal skins, but later people discovered how to spin and weave wool.

STONE AGE

- **Palaeolithic period:** People moved around following the herds and used clubs and sharpened stones to hunt.
- **Mesolithic period:** Hunters made bows and arrows and the gatherers made baskets for collecting fruits and nuts. People continued to move around.
- **Neolithic period:** People became food producers so were able to have a more settled lifestyle. They made wooden and stone agricultural tools and developed new crafts, such as pottery.

▼ FIRST TOOLS
Pieces of flint were shaped by chipping away flakes, leaving a sharp edge.

Pebble hammer for shaping flint

▶ GATHERERS' TOOLS
Flakes of flint were attached to wooden handles. These tools were used to dig up edible roots and cut wood for fires.

A spark was made by hitting an iron stone against a flint.

Bark for collecting fruits and nuts

Feathers

◀ HUNTERS' TOOLS
The metal tips of the arrows were dipped in poison made from beetle larvae.

▶ CARVINGS
Animal bones were skilfully carved to show pictures and to make small sculptures.

Carving of a mammoth

HOMO NEANDERTHALENSIS

Dated: 400,000–40,000 YA
Fossils found in Europe and Middle East with protruding jaw, receding forehead, and weak chin.

HOMO SAPIENS

Dated: 300,000 YA to present
Found all over the world, these skulls have a rising forehead, prominent chin, and light bone structure, and can fit a large brain.

Ancient Egypt

From about 6,000 years ago, cities began to appear along the banks of large rivers. The civilizations in Egypt and Mesopotamia (now Iraq) were the earliest. Around 3000 BCE, Egypt was unified to become the first large state under the rule of a pharaoh (king).

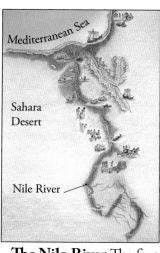

The Nile River The first ancient Egyptians were able to establish farming communities in this otherwise desert landscape all thanks to the Nile River. Annual flooding kept the land alongside the river fertile and watered the crops.

Tombs for the pharaohs Towering tombs were built under the pharaohs for their journey to the afterlife to become a god. Pharaoh Khufu (reign 2589–2566 bce) was placed in the King's Chamber of his pyramid, which is the largest one and took about 20 years to build using over two million limestone blocks.

Inside, passages led to burial chambers where the pharaoh was buried with his belongings.

One of the smaller pyramids was for Khufu's wives.

PYRAMIDS AT GIZA

The pyramids at Giza near Cairo, Egypt, were built more than 4,000 years ago. The Great Pyramid is the only surviving monument of the Seven Wonders of the Ancient World.

EGYPTIAN GODS AND RELIGION

- **Many gods and goddesses:** Ancient Egyptians believed that their deities helped keep Egypt successful.

- **A living god:** The first pharaohs were thought to be a living version of the god Horus—a hawk-headed god of the sky that protected the pharaohs.

- **Making mummies:** Egyptians preserved the dead bodies of important people by wrapping them in linen bandages with sacred symbols and amulets. They believed this helped transport them to the afterlife in one piece.

Anubis | Isis | Osiris

▼ GOLDEN MASK
The preserved body, or mummy, of Tutankhamun was discovered with a magnificent golden face mask on its head.

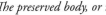

WHO'S WHO?

- **Hatshepsut** (reign 1473–1458 BCE) This successful queen assumed the role of a pharaoh in place of her young stepson.
- **Tutankhamun** (reign 1333–1323 BCE) This boy pharaoh's splendid tomb was discovered in 1922.
- **Rameses II** (reign 1279–1213 BCE) His long reign was a period of peace and prosperity in Egypt.
- **Cleopatra VII** (reign 51–30 BCE) The last pharaoh kept Egypt independent by making alliances with the Roman leaders Julius Caesar and Mark Antony.

Egyptian social pyramid The pharaoh at the top controlled all land, people, and possessions, and the vizier, his most trusted advisor, oversaw all the pharaoh's plans. The peasants at the bottom worked in the fields producing the crops collected as taxes to feed everyone, but during the flood season joined the craftspeople, working on building projects.

Pharaoh
Vizier
Nobles | Priests
Scribes | Soldiers
Craftspeople and merchants
Peasants | Enslaved people

ANCIENT EGYPTIAN ARTEFACTS

Historians have been able to discover much about the lives of ancient Egyptians from the markings, possessions, and records found.

▲ ANKH *Hieroglyphic symbol meaning "life," often shown being held by gods and pharaohs.*

▲ SCARAB DUNG BEETLE *Sacred symbol meaning "rebirth," relating to the god Khepri, who pushed the sun across the sky.*

▲ PAPYRUS *The inner pith of this tall plant that grew along the Nile was used to make paper.*

189

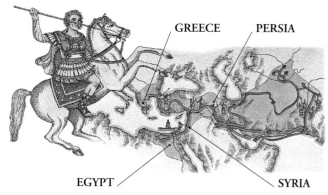

Alexander the Great's empire

Alexander the Great's empire
Alexander III (356–323 BCE), king of Macedon and the Greek city-states from 336 BCE, led a 13-year-long military campaign that created a Greek empire. He conquered the Persian empire, Syria, and Egypt and continued east as far as what is now India.

Greeks *and...*

The ancient Greeks had one of the most advanced civilizations. They made great strides in philosophy and science, and their culture influenced many other nations.

▼ PARTHENON *A temple dedicated to the Greek Goddess Athena, who the city was named for. It was the largest building on the acropolis.*

GREEK POLITICS

- The Greeks formed a collection of independent city-states.
- When a city needed to expand, the Greeks set up a new colony city around the Mediterranean Sea.
- The Greeks invented the democratic system in which people voted for their leader. However, only free men could vote.

ATHENS' ACROPOLIS
The best-known acropolis was built in the city-state of Athens.

The propylaia was the gateway to the acropolis.

AN ACROPOLIS

- **Site:** An acropolis is an area of a city sited on high ground as a home for the city's god.

- **Buildings:** The main public and religious buildings were built on the acropolis.

- **Date:** The buildings seen today on the acropolis in Athens were mostly built in the mid-5th century BCE.

TIMELINE

492–449 BCE	470–399 BCE	431–404 BCE	336–323 BCE
After a 50-year war, the Greek city-states succeeded in defeating an invading Persian army.	Socrates, one of the first great philosophers, lived and taught in Athens.	The Peloponnesian War between the rival city-states of Athens and Sparta and their allies was fought. It involved almost all the Greek world.	Alexander the Great expanded the Greek empire across Persia.

Romans

Starting out as a people from a small town ruled by a king in 753 BCE, the ambitious Romans ended up conquering a vast empire with their army made up of highly trained, efficient legions.

▼ THE ROMAN FORUM *At the center of every Roman city was an open space surrounded by the main temples and public buildings. People gathered here to do business.*

The Roman empire By 117 CE, the Roman empire stretched around the Mediterranean Sea, up through western Europe to Britain and across into Asia. In the 3rd century, the empire was divided between two emperors for better control.

GAUL
Rome ■   ■ Constantinople
GREECE
Mediterranean Sea
EGYPT

TAKE A PICTURE

Aqueducts, such as the Pont du Gard in France, are just one example of the Romans' great engineering feats across their empire.

TELL ME MORE...

The Roman Republic, formed in 509 BCE, was governed by a senate, but senators came from wealthy families, and only male Roman citizens could vote. Women had few legal rights, though they could own property.

148 BCE	58–50 BCE	27 BCE	476 CE
At the end of the fourth Macedonian War, the Roman Republic finally defeated the ancient Greeks.	Julius Caesar, the military leader of the Roman Republic, conquered Gaul in western Europe.	Augustus changed the Roman Republic to an empire and became the first emperor of Rome.	Attacks from Germanic peoples caused the collapse of the Western Roman empire.

Medieval times

The period between the fall of ancient empires and the emergence of new, stronger states in Europe, Asia, the Middle East, and parts of Africa is known as "medieval" (or "the Middle Ages"). It saw intense warfare, struggles about who should hold land and power, the rise of new religions, and exciting artistic developments.

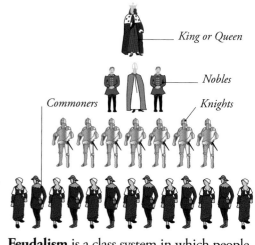

King or Queen

Nobles

Commoners

Knights

Feudalism is a class system in which people hold their land in exchange for service, often military, to those of the next highest class. Common in Europe, types of feudalism also developed in Japan, China, India, and parts of Africa.

📷 TAKE A PICTURE

On Christmas Day, 800 CE, Charlemagne (742–814) was crowned Holy Roman Emperor by Pope Leo III. Charlemagne strengthened central government, encouraged education and the spread of Christianity, and made his kingdom—Francia—into a great power.

Elaborate towers of city's cathedral

▶ FIGHTING FOR POWER
Medieval European rulers were not all-powerful. They had little power to tax and depended on income from their lands. They often had to fight against their own powerful nobles and fought frequent wars against neighboring countries (one between England and France lasted over a century). Fortified castles were important to control the surrounding land, and sieges were more common than pitched battles.

◄ FIRST UNIVERSITY *Founded as a* madrasa, *or religious school, by Fatima al-Fihri in 859* CE, *al-Qarawiyyin (in modern-day Morocco) is the world's oldest continually operating university.*

Islamic learning Scholarship flourished in the Muslim lands of North Africa and the Middle East in the Middle Ages. Centers of learning developed, such as the Bayt al-Hikmah ("House of Wisdom") in Baghdad, Iraq, where Ancient Greek and Roman manuscripts were translated into Arabic, and the first universities were founded. Scholars such as the mathematician al-Khwarizmi (780–850), the surgeon al-Zahrawi (936–1013), and the physician Ibn Sina (970–1037) made great advances.

Medieval Africa In west Africa, the kingdoms of Ghana, Mali, and Songhai grew rich from trading gold and salt across the Sahara Desert. Mansa Musa, a 14th-century Malian king, was reputedly the richest man ever. In east Africa, the kingdom of Aksum (in modern-day Ethiopia) built huge *stelae* (needle-shaped monuments), while in the south, the kingdom of Kongo (in modern-day Angola and the Democratic Republic of the Congo) also prospered from control of trade routes.

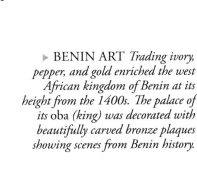

► BENIN ART *Trading ivory, pepper, and gold enriched the west African kingdom of Benin at its height from the 1400s. The palace of its* oba *(king) was decorated with beautifully carved bronze plaques showing scenes from Benin history.*

TIMES OF CHANGE

While warfare shaped the physical boundaries of countries during the Middle Ages, there were many other events that changed the world at that time.

▲ WEAPON OF WAR *The Chinese discovered gunpowder. From the 10th century, it was used in rockets and early guns. Europeans used it later.*

▲ BLACK DEATH *In the 1340s, the Great Plague killed 30–50 percent of Europe's population.*

▲ EXPLORATION *Explorers opened up trade routes to other parts of the world. European colonizers would follow.*

THE REFORMATION

■ During the Middle Ages, the Catholic Church, with the pope at its head, was very powerful throughout Europe.

■ But not everybody was happy with the Church's power and influence. The opponents called themselves Protestants.

■ In 1517, German monk Martin Luther spoke out about corruption of Church officials. Other reformers in Switzerland and France proposed similar ideas to reform the Church.

■ New, Protestant churches were set up in northern Europe, sparking religious wars, but eventually ending the total power of the Catholic Church in Europe.

China's dynasties

CHINA IN 221 BCE *united by the first emperor Qin Shi Huang.*

Dating back at least 4,000 years, China is one of the oldest continuous known civilizations. Since the first city-states along the Huang He river, China expanded (and at times contracted) under the control of a succession of monarchs until 1912. Periods of unity and disunity have shaped the country's politics and history.

▼ WATCH TOWERS *were positioned at intervals along the wall.*

GREAT WALL OF CHINA

The Great Wall of China started as multiple walls built to protect the northern border from invading neighbors. Qin Shi Huang (first emperor) instructed the linking up of already-existing fortifications to construct a Great Wall. However, the central sections of wall seen today were repaired, strengthened, and expanded during the Ming Dynasty. The wall stretches for about 12,427 miles (21,000 km) today.

TIMELINE OF DYNASTIES

DYNASTIES	221–206 BCE QIN	206 BCE–220 CE HAN	618–907 TANG
Much of Chinese history can be split into time periods of the dynasties, or royal families. Each dynasty brought its own changes to the country.	A short-lived dynasty during which the traditional beliefs of Kong Fuzi were suppressed and his books were apparently burned.	The Silk Road—an important trading route—was established from China, and would eventually stretch to the Mediterranean Sea.	Art and culture flourished in China during the Tang period.

Middle kingdom

Zhōngguó (pronounced ung-gwo) means "Middle Kingdom." The name was first used by the rulers of the ancient Western Zhou Dynasty (1046–771 BCE), but referred to the central states around the Huang He river. Throughout China's history, the country was called by the name of the ruling dynasty, such as "Han," "Tang," "Song," "Yuan," "Ming," or "Qing." Only since 1912 has *Zhōngguó* officially been used for the country's name.

COSTLY PROJECT *Over a million soldiers, prisoners, and local people were enlisted to build the Great Wall, and many thousands died during its construction.*

Forbidden City In 1420, the Ming emperor and his household moved to a vast imperial palace in the capital, Beijing. Court officials and members of the imperial family were allowed inside, but only the emperor had unlimited access to all of the buildings.

▲ AROUND 800 BUILDINGS *survive enclosed by a 26 ft (7.9 m) high city wall.*

TAKE A PICTURE

Qin Shi Huang (first emperor) ordered that thousands of life-size clay warriors, horses, and chariots, known as the terra-cotta army, were to be made to guard his tomb and help him rule his empire in his afterlife (👁 p165).

0–1279 SONG	1271–1368 YUAN	1368–1644 MING	1644–1912 QING
ere were advances paper-making d woodblock nting (right). e Movable pe was invented China.	The Mongolian Yuan Dynasty was founded by Kublai Khan, the grandson of the famous Genghis Khan.	Production increased of the very popular blue-and-white porcelain with painted scenes.	The queue was a hairstyle of the Manchu people, who established the Qing Dynasty. All Chinese men were forced to wear this hairstyle.

Islamic golden age

HISTORY AND POLITICS

In the 7th century, Prophet Muhammad established an Islamic state in the Arabian Peninsula. In the centuries after his death, the Islamic empire expanded rapidly, spreading the faith and laws of Islam based on his teachings.

MECCA

Prophet Muhammad was born in Mecca (in what is now Saudi Arabia). After being forced out of the city due to his teachings, he returned eight years later with his followers to take control and establish the city as the center of the faith of Islam.

TELL ME MORE...

In 661, Muslims were divided over who to choose as the next leader. The Shia accepted the descendants of Ali (Prophet Muhammad's son-in-law), known as Imams, while the Sunni chose the descendants of the Umayyad Dynasty, titled caliphs.

◄ PROPHET OF ISLAM
At the age of 40, Prophet Muhammad had the first of many revelations about the word of Allah (God). His teachings were to become intertwined with the politics and social aspects of an Islamic state. His name is shown here in stylized form.

ISLAMIC ARTEFACTS

The Islamic civilization had a distinctive style in art, crafts, and architecture, and made great advances in mathematics, astronomy, and medicines.

▲ ISLAMIC ART
Calligraphy and mosaics of glazed tiles were used to decorate buildings.

▲ ASTROLABE *Muslim astronomers perfected this instrument for calculating a person's position by using the sun and stars.*

▲ OTTOMAN VASE
Flowers and large leaves were widely used as decorative patterns.

TIMELINE OF ISLAMIC EMPIRES

622–632 MUHAMMAD

Prophet Muhammad took control of Mecca and established the Islamic civilization.

661–750 UMAYYAD DYNASTY

The caliphs of the Umayyad family expanded the Islamic empire (shown in green).

EUROPE

Damascus ■ ■ Baghdad

■ Mecca

AFRICA

750–1258 ABBASID DYNASTY

Baghdad was made the Islamic capital and the city became the world's center of trade, learning, and culture.

Silver and copper basin

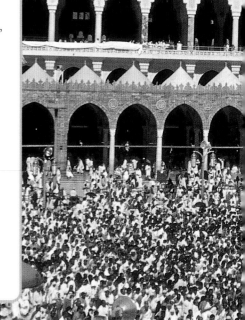

WHO'S WHO?

■ **Prophet Muhammad** (570–632) He was the founder of the Islamic religion and the first Muslim political leader.

■ **Ali ibn Abi Talib** (599–661) He was the son-in-law of Prophet Muhammad, who became the first Imam in 656.

■ **Harun al-Rashid** (766–809) The fifth Abbasid caliph, who was the subject of the stories *The Thousand and One Nights*, also called *The Arabian Nights*.

■ **Fatima al-Fihri** (800–c. 880) She was the founder of the al-Qarawiyyin mosque in Fez, Morocco. It became one of the world's first universities.

■ **Saladin** (1137–1193) A Muslim sultan (governor) of Egypt, Syria, Yemen, and Palestine, who defeated the crusaders and captured Jerusalem in 1187.

Minarets are the highest points in the mosque. Traditionally a muezzin *calls everyone to prayer from the minaret.*

▼ KAABA *According to Islamic tradition, this cube-shaped building in Mecca is said to be the house of Allah. Muslims (followers of Islam) are expected to visit it at least once in their lifetime.*

The Grand Mosque in Mecca

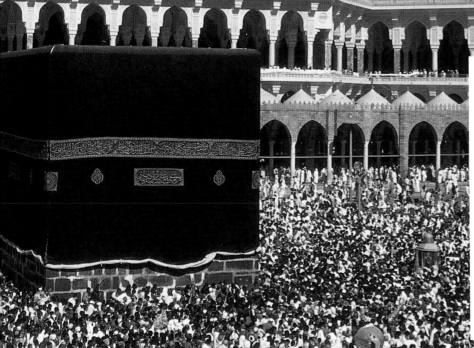

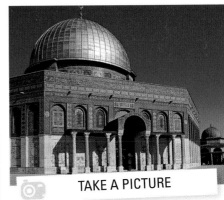

TAKE A PICTURE

The Dome of the Rock shrine in Jerusalem was completed in 691 and is the oldest existing Islamic building in the world.

1258 RISE OF THE SULTANS

Mongol invaders captured Baghdad and converted to Islam, while local rulers, called sultans, governed Egypt, Syria, and Palestine.

1369–1506 TIMURID EMPIRE

Timur, a Turkic-Mongol warrior, conquered the Islamic lands and one of his descendants, Babur, founded the Mughal empire in northern India.

c. 1300–1922 OTTOMAN EMPIRE

The Ottoman Turks ruled over the Islamic state and expanded their empire (shown in green) into eastern Europe.

Aztecs

At the end of the 1100s, a tribe of hunters and gatherers from northern Mexico migrated south and, during the 1200s, settled as farmers on the islands of Lake Texcoco in the central Valley of Mexico.

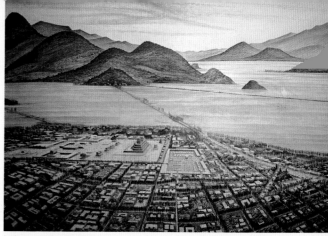

Tenochtitlán

Around 1325, the Aztecs began building their vast capital city, Tenochtitlán, in the center of Lake Texcoco. Several causeways linked the island-city to the mainland. In the center was a complex of religious buildings surrounded by palaces, warrior schools, and a ball court for playing a game called *ulama*.

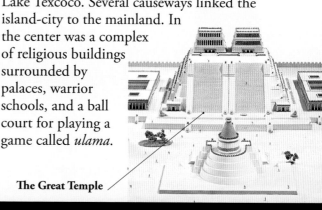

The Great Temple

Map of empires
At the height of their empires, the Aztecs ruled over more than six million people in central and southern Mexico, and the Incas ruled over 12 million people living in the Andes mountains and along the Pacific coast.

Aztecs

Incas

1300s   CULTURES ESTABLISHED
The Aztec and Inca tribes create settlements and increase in population.

Incas

A tribe of farmers led by their king, Manco Cápac, settled in Cuzco in the highlands of Peru during the 1100s. They were later to form a strong and powerful warrior-nation.

FAST FACTS

- Inca kings were called Sapa Inca.
- The Inca language was Quechua and the Aztec language was Nahuatl.
- Both civilizations worshiped many gods and performed human sacrifices.
- The Incas built a system of roads to help trade, and the Aztecs used cacao beans as a means of payment in trade.

▲ MANCO CÁPAC
First ruler of the Incas

Knotted strings

Gold statue

▲ GOLD *Many precious metals, such as gold, were found in South America, and metalworking was an important craft.*

▲ QUIPU *The Incas used ropes with different-sized knots to record information about their expanding empire.*

◀ CACAO *A bitter-tasting chocolate drink was made using the beans of the cacao plant.*

Pod

Beans

RITUAL MASK
Masks, often set with jewels, had a religious purpose.

Mask set with turquoise

WHO'S WHO?

- **Acamapichtli** (reign 1376–1396) A member of the ruling family of a neighboring state, who became the first king of the Aztecs. The name "Acamapichtli" means "handful of reeds."
- **Moctezuma I** (reign 1440–1469) This ambitious king greatly expanded the Aztec empire through trade and conquest.
- **Moctezuma II** (reign 1502–1520) The Aztec empire reached its largest size during his reign before the Spanish conquest began.
- **Hernán Cortés** (1485–1547) This Spanish colonizer overthrew the Aztec empire in 1521 and claimed Mexico as land belonging to the Spanish Crown.

▲ **RITUAL KNIFE**
Prisoners were sacrificed to the god of war by Aztec priests using knives of flint. Rituals for their gods was an important part of Aztec life.

Empire building The Aztecs became rich and powerful under Moctezuma I. As a nation of formidable warriors with a large army, they received tribute in food and other goods from cities in their empire. Merchants could trade goods with distant lands, creating more wealth for the Aztecs.

Moctezuma I (left)

Spanish attack

Spanish conquest
In 1519, the Spanish and their local allies attacked the Aztec capital. After bitter fighting, they killed the last Aztec emperor. The Spanish colonizers took over their lands, ending Aztec civilization.

1400s EMPIRES EXPANDED
The Aztecs and Incas extend their control over other tribes and gain more land.

1500s CIVILIZATIONS DESTROYED
The Aztec and Inca empires are destroyed by the arrival of Spanish colonizers.

◀ **MACHU PICCHU**
Mountain city built by Pachacuti Inca.

Inca conquests
Pachacuti Inca Yupanqui (reign 1438–1471) began the expansion of the Inca empire. A vast network of roads were built to link their territory.

Francisco Pizarro
In search of gold and other precious metals in South America, the Spanish colonizer Pizarro met the Incas. In 1533, he took control of Cuzco and claimed the land for Spain.

TELL ME MORE...

Atahuallpa, the last Inca ruler, was kidnapped following a meeting with the Spanish on 16 November 1532. Pizarro's forces killed him in 1533.

▶ **LLAMAS** *were valued for their wool, their meat, and for carrying goods along the roads.*

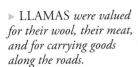

Pizarro (center) meets Atahuallpa (left)

Colonial America

By the early 1600s, many Europeans were sailing across the Atlantic Ocean to eastern North America, where they established colonies, pushing out the Indigenous communities who lived there.

Reconstruction of the *Mayflower*

TELL ME MORE...

In November 1620, a group of Pilgrims arrived from England aboard the *Mayflower*. They had come to the Americas so they could worship freely without persecution. They founded Plymouth in what is now the state of Massachusetts.

▶ POCAHONTAS
She was the daughter of a chief of the Powhatan people. Pocahontas was forced to make peace between the Jamestown settlers and her people. She was captured and held for ransom by the colonists during a conflict in 1613.

Conflict begins

At first the Pilgrims and nearby Indigenous communities of North America traded peacefully, allowing the European settlements to grow. But relations worsened as the settlers took over more Indigenous land to build towns. In 1675, open war broke out between the Wampanoag people and the colonists, the first of many conflicts with European settlers.

TIMELINE OF COLONIAL AMERICA

1607

The Jamestown settlement in Virginia was the first permanent English settlement in North America.

1608

Quebec City was founded by the French along the Saint Lawrence River.

1620

The *Mayflower* Pilgrims established Plymouth colony.

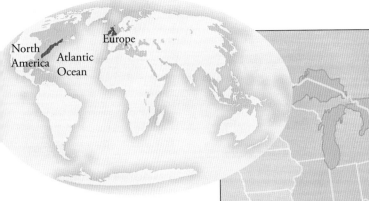

The original 13 colonies

Other British territories

MS	Massachusetts (including Maine)
NH	New Hampshire
RI	Rhode Island
CN	Connecticut
NY	New York
NJ	New Jersey
PA	Pennsylvania
MD	Maryland
DEL	Delaware
VA	Virginia
NC	North Carolina
SC	South Carolina
GA	Georgia

The British colonies By 1733, there were 13 colonies loyal to Britain along the east coast of North America. In 1763, the French surrendered their land to the British. In the 1760s, Britain began to tax the American colonists but their authority over the New World was starting to weaken as the colonists no longer needed their protection.

TAKE A PICTURE

The historic area of Williamsburg, which served as Virginia's capital from 1699 to 1776, has been restored, re-creating colonial times.

▶ DECLARATION *On July 4, 1776, the Congress of the American colonies (below) issued a Declaration of Independence, signed by representatives of all 13 colonies. The united colonies were free, independent states.*

American Revolution In the 1770s, the American colonists began to rebel against British rule and were especially angered by the heavy tax on tea in 1773. Between 1775 and 1783, the colonists fought the British army and won. The British were forced to recognize the newly independent United States of America.

1663	1763	1773	1775–1783
Companies were established to trade goods, such as fur skins, and tobacco, with Europe.	The French surrendered their colonies to Britain, expanding the area the British controlled.	The Boston Tea Party, in December 1773, was a protest by some American colonists angered by high taxes paid to the British.	In the American Revolution, the 13 colonies rebelled against the British and won independence.

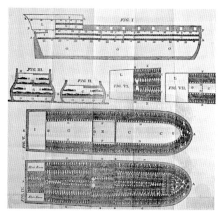

▲ TRANSPORT *This ship was designed to carry around 450 enslaved people, but more than 600 were often packed in, chained together.*

The slave trade

Although slavery existed in many societies, the scale and brutality of the transatlantic slave trade were horrifying. It began with the Portuguese transporting enslaved people from Africa to Madeira in 1470. By the time slavery was abolished in the Americas 400 years later, around 12.5 million enslaved Africans had been forcibly brought there, with about 2 million dying on the way.

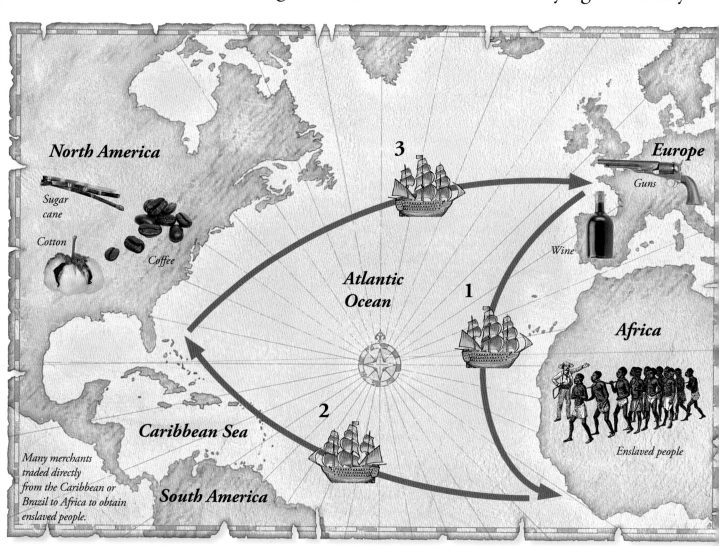

North America

Sugar cane

Cotton

Coffee

3

Atlantic Ocean

1

Africa

Enslaved people

Caribbean Sea

Many merchants traded directly from the Caribbean or Brazil to Africa to obtain enslaved people.

South America

Europe

Guns

Wine

2

THE TRIANGULAR TRADE

The slave trade was all about money. European traders exported goods to Africa, then used the ships to pick up people. Profits made from the sale of goods produced on plantations where enslaved people were forced to work funded the slave trade.

1 EUROPE TO AFRICA *The Europeans traded copper, iron, cloth, wine, glassware, and guns with African landlords for people.*

2 AFRICA TO AMERICAS *People were snatched from villages and fields and marched to the coast to board ships plying the "Middle Passage."*

3 AMERICAS TO EUROPE *Sugar, rice, cotton, coffee, tobacco, and rum from the plantations were brought back to Europe.*

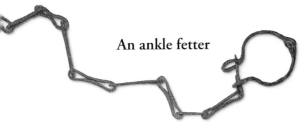

An ankle fetter

NO ESCAPE

From the moment they were first seized in Africa, enslaved people were forced to wear shackles, such as neck collars and ankle fetters. They were chained together so that they could not escape, and those who tried to flee were brutally beaten. They were then shipped off forcibly to the European colonies in the Americas.

▲ FOR SALE *On arrival in the Americas, enslaved people were taken to markets, where they were sold by auction to plantation owners. Men, women, boys, and girls were all put up for sale.*

◀ IN THE FIELDS *Enslaved people were made to pick crops such as cotton.*

Forced labor Enslaved Africans were taken to work on the plantations set up by European settlers. Life was brutal, with long hours, poor food rations, no wages, and frequent abuse. Their children belonged to the plantation owner, who could sell them to other plantations and away from their families.

THE ROAD TO ABOLITION

Confederate general

Union general

■ **The Abolition of Slave Trade Act** was passed in Britain in 1807, outlawing the slave trade, but slavery itself didn't end in the British empire until 1833, in the United States until 1865, and in Brazil until 1882!

■ Abolition was one of the main causes of the **Civil War** (1861–1865), as the Southern Confederate "slave states" did not want to end slavery—but the Northern Union states did.

■ By the mid-1800s, many people were calling slavery illegal and campaigning for it to end. These were the **abolitionists**. Many were Black, and some of them were formerly enslaved. Famous names included Sojourner Truth and Solomon Northup.

▲ HARRIET TUBMAN *led hundreds of enslaved people to their freedom, at great risk to herself. She later became a leading abolitionist (those calling for slavery to be made illegal).*

203

Colonization

Since the 1600s, European countries had taken land and steadily gained influence over countries around the world. From the mid-1800s, they competed against each other to control new trade markets, increasing the size of their empires and becoming wealthy.

USA

North America

Many people from Europe emigrated to the U.S. or Canada to escape bad conditions at home, such as the potato famine in Ireland. The arrival of these new settlers led to even more conflict with Indigenous peoples as settlers moved into remote inland areas across the continent.

TELL ME MORE...

Goyathlay (1829–1909), also known as Geronimo, was a leader of the Bedonkohe Apache (Diné) people in what is now Arizona and New Mexico. He fought for more than 30 years against the U.S. government's seizure of Apache lands, before being captured in 1886.

EMPIRES AND TRADE

European countries imported raw materials from their empires and exported manufactured goods back to their colonies.

North America

Europe

▶ RAILWAYS
A vast network of tracks was laid across countries and continents for the transportation of goods by train.

Africa

Coffee

Gold

Sugar cane

South America

Cocoa

▶ SOUTH AMERICA
During the 1800s, many of the countries in South America became independent. Only the Portuguese, British, French, and Dutch had colonies with big plantations.

▶ SOUTH AFRICA *The discovery of diamonds in the mid-1800s transformed a poor colony into a much desired one for colonists and sparked conflicts in the area.*

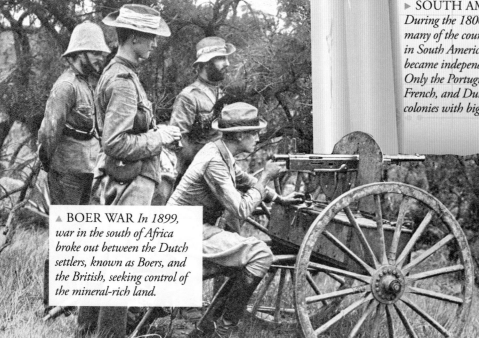

▲ BOER WAR *In 1899, war in the south of Africa broke out between the Dutch settlers, known as Boers, and the British, seeking control of the mineral-rich land.*

Africa

The conquest of Africa began in the 1870s, when European countries competed against each other to gain control of land on this continent. The finding of precious raw material such as gold and diamonds also drew in more Europeans, who used local people to work in mines and plantations.

Russia

China

This map shows the borders and empires in 1900.

Empire-builders

The main European colonial powers were Great Britain, France, the Netherlands, and Portugal. By the end of the 19th century, Great Britain's empire covered one-quarter of Earth's land surface.

- ● Britain
- ● France
- ● Spain
- ● Portugal
- ● Italy
- ● Netherlands
- ● Germany
- ▨ Ottoman empire

INDEPENDENCE

Quit India Movement

In the early 20th century, many colonies started campaigning to become independent countries. In India, leaders of the freedom struggle started many campaigns to demand self-rule from Britain, including the Quit India Movement of 1942. During the 1940s and 1960s, most colonies gained independence from European colonial rule, with India gaining freedom in 1947.

COLONIES

European countries recognized overseas colonies as a source of cheap raw materials for their industries. They often took over land rather than negotiating with local rulers and forced local laborers to work under appalling conditions. The European powers grew richer at the expense of their colonies, which they plundered.

Cotton　**Rubber**

▼ EGYPT
The Suez Canal opened in 1869, allowing an easier and quicker access route to Asia.

Suez Canal　　Tea

India

Ivory

▶ MALAYSIA
The British government set up very profitable tin mines and rubber plantations.

Tin

Coffee

Gold

Australia

▶ INDONESIA
After the success of the Dutch East India trading company in the 17th and 18th century, the Dutch government took control and set up big plantations to grow crops such as coffee and spices.

▲ AUSTRALIA
The discovery of gold in the town of Victoria in the 1850s led to a gold rush. The European population grew very quickly.

India

By 1900, Britain ruled the whole of India. Many British administrators and traders with their families lived there, enjoying the privileged colonial lifestyle. Owners of tea plantations became rich while the local workers lived in poverty.

Australia

The British used convicts to establish their first colonies in Australia. Free settlers began to arrive in 1793. The First Nations Australians were pushed off their land by the new settlers and forced into the Outback—a dry, desertlike area that the settlers did not want.

◀ THE FIRST FLEET *In 1788, British navy ships transported convicts to Botany Bay in Australia.*

▲ FACTORIES *From the 1790s, steam power replaced the previously water-powered machines. Inside the factories, the noise of the machines was deafening. Outside, the towns were dirty and unhealthy places.*

Industrial Revolution

Between 1750 and 1850, the development of power-driven machines transformed the lives of people first in Britain and then other European countries and the United States. This period is known as the Industrial Revolution.

Child labor Children as young as six years old worked in the factories, until 1833 when under-nines were banned in the UK. They worked up to 12 or 14 hours a day with few breaks. Sometimes, they were injured or even killed by the machinery.

TIMELINE OF KEY INVENTIONS

1712

Thomas Newcomen built the first commercially successful steam engine. It was used to pump water out of mines.

1764

James Hargreaves invented the spinning jenny—a mechanized spinning wheel that could spin eight threads at once.

1769

James Watt designed a more efficient steam engine by improving Newcomen's model.

TELL ME MORE...

The Industrial Revolution caused much unrest especially from the skilled textiles workers angered by the introduction of looms that could be used by unskilled workers for low wages, forcing them out of a job. One group, known as the Luddites, destroyed the machines in cotton and wool mills.

WHO'S WHO?

■ **James Watt** (1736–1819) A Scottish engineer who made improvements to the steam engine in 1769 so that machines could be powered without water.

■ **Francis Cabot Lowell** (1775–1817) An American merchant who established the first textile mill in the United States.

■ **George Stephenson** (1781–1848) An English engineer who built the first public railway line in the world.

■ **Isambard Kingdom Brunel** (1806–1859) A British engineer who designed many tunnels, bridges, railway lines, and ships.

■ **Henrietta Vansittart** (1833–1883) A British engineer who improved on her father's designs for screw propellers for ships, including the *Lusitania*.

Cotton gin The U.S. became the world's leading cotton producer thanks to the invention of the cotton gin by Eli Whitney. This machine could quickly separate the cotton fibers from the seeds, which had previously taken ages by hand.

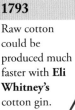
TAKE A PICTURE

Canals were built to transport heavy loads to and from the factories. The boat lifts on the Canal du Centre, Wallonia in Belgium show the amazing engineering feats of this age.

Railway mania In 1803, Richard Trevithick added wheels to his steam engine so that it could run along tracks. Within thirty years, a network of railways for transporting raw materials, goods, and people by steam locomotives was constructed. Traveling around was now much quicker.

1793

Raw cotton could be produced much faster with **Eli Whitney's** cotton gin.

1801

Joseph-Marie Jacquard's loom was the first machine to be controlled by punched cards – an idea later used in computing.

1830

The world's first all-steam passenger railway opened in Britain.

1856

Henry Bessemer invented a process for producing steel more efficiently using a high-temperature furnace.

World War I

At the beginning of the 1900s, military and political tensions existed between some of the countries of Europe. The assassination of the heir to the throne of Austria-Hungary was the spark needed to fire up a war that involved the world.

WHO'S WHO?

- Two main groups battled each other—the Allies, led by the British, French, and Russian armies, and the Central Powers, led by the German, Austria-Hungary, and Turkish armies.
- The British and French armies included many recruits from their colonies and territories around the world.
- In total, over 30 countries were drawn in to take part in the fighting.
- The USA joined the war in 1917.

MILITARY TRANSPORT

- **Aircraft:** Biplanes and triplanes were used to fly over enemy lines to observe their movements and take photographs.
- **Vehicles:** Horse-drawn vehicles were gradually replaced by mechanical ones to transport men and supplies to and from the front line.
- **Tanks:** The first tanks used in 1916 were not very reliable but a year later they were leading the way across to the enemy trenches, shielding the troops.
- **Warships:** Fleets of warships were used to protect supply ships from attacks by the German U-boats.

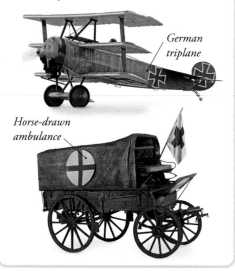

German triplane

Horse-drawn ambulance

Allied powers

Central powers

Neutral nations

X Key battle sites

World at war Although most of the fighting took place in Europe, there was also fighting in the Middle East, in Africa, in China, and on the Pacific Ocean. Many troops from Britain's colonies fought in the British Army, including 1.3 million Indians.

TIMELINE OF WORLD WAR I

1914

The assassination of Archduke Franz Ferdinand on June 28, 1914, caused Austria-Hungary to declare war on Serbia. European countries took sides and by August, the Great War had begun.

1915

Allied forces, including many Australians, invaded the Ottoman empire at Gallipoli but were forced to withdraw after months of fighting.

THE FRONT LINE

By the end of 1914, a network of trenches zigzagged from the Belgian coast to the Swiss border, forming the Western Front. From these positions, the Allied troops tried to push back the advancing German army, but neither side made much progress. Under fire from machine guns, the strip of land between each other's trenches was impossible to cross.

▶ CROSSING NO-MAN'S LAND
Most attempts to advance occurred at dawn or dusk.

Bayonet on rifle

Gas attack
A deadly chlorine gas was used for the first time in the battle for the Belgium town of Ypres in 1915.

TAKE A PICTURE

More than half of the 65 million men who fought in the war were killed or injured, and about 10 million civilians also died.

1916
The naval battle of Jutland was the largest fought in World War I.

1917
The U.S. joined the Allies, angered by the German U-boat attacks on shipping in the Atlantic Ocean.

1918
At 11am on the 11th day of the 11th month (November), an armistice (cease-fire) took place. A peace treaty was later signed.

World War II

The peace treaty signed at the end of World War I (the Treaty of Versailles in 1919) forced Germany to give up much of its land and wealth and restricted the size of its army. Twenty years later, the Nazi Party in Germany had rebuilt the nation, and its leader, Adolf Hitler, was determined to rule Europe.

Adolf Hitler

Adolf Hitler (1889–1945) Born in Austria, Hitler became an influential politician in Germany. After being appointed chancellor in 1933, Hitler created a one-party state and made himself an all-powerful dictator.

FAST FACTS

- Resistance groups of people from German-occupied countries helped the Allies by spying and acts of sabotage.
- British radio operator Noor Inayat Khan was sent to France to help the resistance there. She worked for months, sending messages to and from the resistance.

▲ GAS MASK *Countries feared that gas would be used by the enemy, so many people were issued gas masks. They were never needed.*

Destruction Bombing raids by the Allied and Axis powers caused huge destruction across Europe, the USSR, and east Asia. The raids were intended to target strategic buildings, such as airfields, factories, ports, and railways but often homes were destroyed, killing civilians or forcing them to evacuate (leave the area).

TIMELINE OF WORLD WAR II

1939	1940	1941	1942
On September 1, Germany invaded Poland. Two days later, Britain and France declared war on it.	Between July and October 1940, the German air force battled the British air force in the skies above Britain.	On December 7, Japan attacked the U.S. naval base at Pearl Harbor in Hawaii. The U.S. then entered the war.	In August, the Germans begar the six-month-long battle for Stalingrad in the Soviet Unior

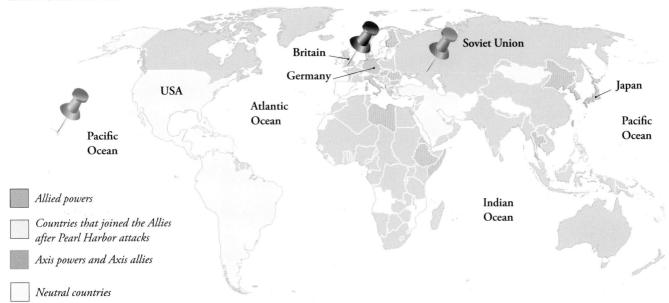

- Allied powers
- Countries that joined the Allies after Pearl Harbor attacks
- Axis powers and Axis allies
- Neutral countries

Main players Until mid-1941, the two sides were the Axis (Germany, Italy, Japan, and some east European countries) and the Allies (Britain, France, and countries in their empires). Nations around the world became involved when Germany invaded the Soviet Union and Japan's attacks began.

BATTLE OF BRITAIN *After conquering France in June 1940, Germany planned to take over Britain. The British air force was targeted first, but the German air force was unable to defeat it.*

STALINGRAD *Germany invaded the Soviet Union in 1941. There was huge loss of life on both sides, especially in the battle for Stalingrad in the south. In 1943, the weakened German army surrendered.*

PEARL HARBOR *The unexpected attack by the Japanese air force on the U.S. naval base in Hawaii damaged or destroyed 19 ships and killed 2,403 people. The U.S. declared war on the Axis powers.*

▼ **CAMPS OF DEATH** *Auschwitz in Poland was one of six main "death" camps set up in the country to kill Jews and other people.*

THE COLD WAR

📷 **TAKE A PICTURE**

After the war, relations between the Soviet Union and the U.S. became very tense. Eastern and Western Europe were separated. The collapse of the Berlin Wall, Germany, in 1989 became a symbolic end to this Cold War.

The Holocaust The Nazi Party was very anti-Semitic (against Jews). They forced Jews to wear badges with a yellow star and from 1942 sent them (and others deemed undesirable) to concentration camps. Millions died from illness, starvation, and in gas chambers.

43

May, the Axis ny in North rica finally rendered the Allies.

1944

On June 6 (D-Day), Allied forces invaded the beaches of Normandy, France, and began to push back the Axis forces.

1945

In May, Germany surrendered. Japan surrendered only after the U.S. dropped atomic bombs on two of its cities—Hiroshima and Nagasaki—in August.

Revolution!

History has been marked by episodes when a sudden uprising of people driven by hardship has overthrown those in power. An alternative political system has been established in the hope for a better life.

REVOLUTIONARY LEADERS

- **Vladimir Lenin** (1870–1924) was leader of the Bolshevik Russian Social Democratic Workers' Party and first head of the Soviet state.
- **Mahatma Gandhi** (1869–1948) was a leading figure in India's freedom movement.
- **Mao Zedong** (1893–1976) was a Chinese communist leader and the founder of the People's Republic of China.
- **Fidel Castro** (1926–2016) became prime minister of Cuba in 1959, was elected president in 1976, and stood down in 2008.

The Year of Revolution

A wave of unrest spread across many European countries in 1848. With many starving and unemployed, the demonstrators wanted more rights and a greater say in how their countries were governed. Although the revolts fizzled out, they were the sparks for later political reforms.

▼ In March, a peaceful demonstration in Vienna, Austria, turned violent.

1789

"LIBERTY, EQUALITY, FRATERNITY!"
Despite France facing severe food and money shortages, King Louis XVI and his wife Queen Marie-Antoinette enjoyed a luxurious lifestyle.

1799

1848

"WORKERS OF ALL LANDS, UNITE!"
In 1848, a German political writer, Karl Marx, published his thoughts on communism.

The storming of the Bastille

On July 14, 1789, the starving people of Paris rioted when they heard rumors that King Louis XVI had ordered the army to suppress the commoners and wanted to raise taxes.

▼ LOUIS XVI
Executed in 1793

▼ Napoleon wrote over 36,000 letters.

The French Revolution

After the death of Louis XVI, the country became a republic but there was a reign of terror with thousands of people executed at the guillotine. In 1799, the army eventually gained control under the dictatorship of its general, Napoleon Bonaparte.

▶ NAPOLEONIC WARS Napoleon crowned himself emperor of the first French empire in 1804 and led successful military campaigns across Europe.

Cuban revolution The revolutionary Fidel Castro led a small band of rebels and peasants in their two-year fight against the large army of the dictator Fulgencio Batista. When Castro took power in February 1959, he made many reforms, improving Cubans' healthcare and education, but he also took political prisoners and suppressed many people.

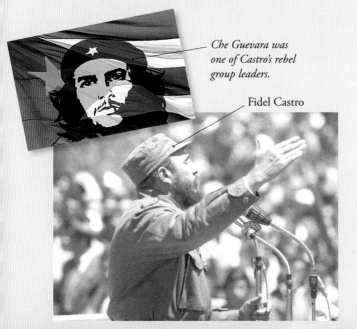

Che Guevara was one of Castro's rebel group leaders.

Fidel Castro

无产阶级文化大革命全面胜利万岁

Chairman Mao reimposed his control

China's cultural revolution In 1966, the leader of the Chinese Communist Party, Mao Zedong, launched a campaign to make China a classless society. Millions of educated and privileged people were forced into manual labor to be "re-educated," and many thousands were killed.

▲ *Everyone had to read and carry around a copy of Mao's "Little Red Book," which was filled with quotes from the leader.*

1917

"I WILL NEVER RETIRE FROM POLITICS, THE REVOLUTION, OR THE IDEAS I HAVE." *Castro ran Cuba for 32 years.*

1956– 1958

1966– 1976

"SMASH THE OLD WORLD, ESTABLISH A NEW WORLD." *Young people in China formed the Red Guards to promote Mao's message.*

2011

Arab Spring In 2011, "Arab Spring" protests broke out in many Arab countries, including Yemen and Bahrain, against governments that ruled harshly, denying basic freedoms. These protests overthrew the Tunisian government, but in Syria and Libya, the uprising led to violence and civil wars. In Egypt, the army took control.

▲ *Striking workers and mutinous soldiers marched on the streets of Petrograd.*

The two revolutions Stirred up by the Bolshevik Party, the starving and war-weary Russians demonstrated against the unpopular Tsar (king) Nicholas II in February 1917, who then abdicated. In October, led by Vladimir Lenin, the Bolsheviks overthrew the government to form the first communist state.

▲ HAMMER AND SICKLE BADGE *In 1922, Russia was renamed the Union of Soviet Socialist Republics (USSR). Their symbol represented the unity of the workers and peasants.*

Protesters in Tahrir Square in Cairo, Egypt

In the news

Every day, history is being made. Events affecting people's lives and altering the politics of nations around the world are reported in the newspapers, or on the radio, television, and the Internet.

CLIMATE CHANGE

In December 2015, almost 200 countries signed a historic agreement in Paris to tackle climate change. The agreement aims to keep the overall increase in global temperatures "well below" 3.6°F (2°C), with a more ambitious target of 2.7°F (1.5°C).

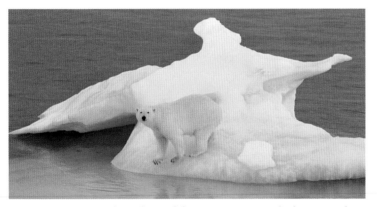

▲ POLAR BEAR *The melting of the Arctic ice caps, which serve as the bear's home and hunting ground, is a serious threat to the species.*

Scientists argued these were the largest increases possible without provoking catastrophic—and irreversible—changes to the world's climate. In a major breakthrough, rich countries agreed to provide poorer nations with "climate finance" to control their CO_2 emissions and switch to renewable energy.

CHINA

▲ HIGH-SPEED RAILWAY *Train crosses a viaduct in southwest China.*

In 2013, Chinese president Xi Jinping unveiled the ambitious "Belt and Road Initiative (BRI)" program, a multi-billion-dollar investment scheme connecting over 60 countries, with a combined population of 4.5 billion. Dubbed a modern-day version of the ancient Silk Road, the plan is to create a network of trade routes and energy hubs centered on roads, railways, and ports, across four continents.

SYRIA

In 2011, pro-democracy demonstrations spread through the Arab World. In Syria, the government used force to crush the opposition, resulting in a civil war which has left nearly 500,000 dead and more than five million refugees. Intervention from Iran, Russia, and the U.S. has complicated the conflict.

◀ WAR RUINS
Children play in the abandoned tanks of forces loyal to Syrian President Bashar al-Assad, amid the rubble of civil war.

TAKE A PICTURE

The Black Lives Matter movement began in the U.S. in 2013 after the killing of a Black teenager. The movement aims to highlight discrimination, inequality, and brutality faced by Black people. It has since spread to many other countries.

MIGRATION

Refugee numbers have peaked globally at over 82 million, with most refugees coming from Syria, Venezuela, Afghanistan, South Sudan, and Myanmar. The largest refugee populations have been taken in by countries such as Turkey, Jordan, Uganda, Pakistan, Lebanon, and Germany. The Russian invasion of Ukraine in 2022 displaced over 14 million people from their homes.

Refugees who have crossed from Turkey by boat land on the Greek island of Lesvos.

◀ PETROCHEMICAL PLANT *Industrial facilities around the world continue to spew polluting greenhouse gases into the environment, despite controls such as the Paris Agreement.*

THE RISE OF POPULISM

After the global economic collapse of 2008, many Western countries experienced a rise in populist movements claiming to represent the interests of ordinary people. Led by individuals who painted a picture of wealthy, corrupt elites, populism capitalized on the feeling of many that they had lost out to globalization as their jobs disappeared and wages stagnated.

Former U.S. President Trump points his finger at the press.

Fake news
The election of Donald Trump as U.S. president in 2016 coincided with growing concerns about the spread of "fake news"—stories on the Internet that were not true. Social media made it easier for these to spread, undermining some people's trust in the media.

What is a government?

A government is a small group of people who make laws and decisions about how their country is run. They raise money from people in taxes and decide how this money is to be spent, such as on retirement pensions and benefits, hospitals, schools, the army, police, and the building of new roads.

ONE-PARTY STATE

In some countries, only one political party is allowed to exist; all others are banned. When there is an election, the one party decides who the candidates will be and the voters only get to approve that choice.

▶ REPUBLIC OF CUBA
The Cuban Communist Party is the only recognized political party.

Fidel Castro (in power 1959–2008)

WHO'S WHO?

- **President** A head of state of a republic with either extensive powers (as in the U.S.) or limited powers (as in Germany).
- **Prime minister** The head of government in a parliamentary democracy.
- **Dictator** A ruler with absolute power.
- **Monarchy** The hereditary rule of a single person, absolute (with unchecked powers) or constitutional (with limited powers).
- **Political party** An organization of people with similar aims.
- **Opposition** The parties that are not in a government or have minority representation and may disagree with the governing party.
- **Senate** The upper house of a legislative assembly (as in the U.S.).
- **Cabinet** A group of ministers or others that advises a head of government.
- **Representative** A person who is elected to represent the public in making laws.

MONARCHY

Many countries, such as the UK, have a king or queen who acts as head of state but does not govern the country. But there are a few countries where the monarch still holds all the power and governs the country. These "absolute monarchs" are not elected, but when they die power passes to their son or daughter.

▲ KINGDOM OF BRUNEI
The Sultan of Brunei (right) has absolute power.

MILITARY RULE

In some countries, if the government is weak or unpopular, the army seizes power and forms a military government. The country is governed by a military junta—a group of senior military officers, often with one particular general in control.

◀ THE UNION OF MYANMAR
Myanmar, also known as Burma, was ruled by military leaders from 1962 to 2011, having overthrown the then government in a coup. They suppressed almost all dissent, including placing the leader of the opposition under house arrest. Though democratic elections finally took place in 2016, the military overthrew the government and took power again in 2021.

NON-DEMOCRATIC

▲ THE CANDIDATES

In an election, candidates run for office representing different political parties. The person who gets the most votes is elected and the party with the most elected candidates holds the majority of power in the government.

SYSTEMS OF GOVERNMENT

A constitution is a written document or unwritten code that establishes the structure and rules of the political organization of a country. Constitutional democracies may take the form of republics as in France and the U.S. or constitutional monarchy as in the UK and Spain. The country may have a presidential system (U.S.), a parliamentary system (UK), or a semi-presidential system (France).

▼ PROTESTS

If people disagree with a bill, they will often organize protests to try to make their government take notice or change it.

VOTING IN ELECTIONS

In a democracy, all adults are allowed to vote. On election day, they choose from a list of candidates, most commonly selecting them by putting a cross or number on a piece of paper next to their preferred candidate's name. This is then placed in a ballot box. In some countries this is done using an electronic voting machine or computer screen. The candidate with the most votes is elected.

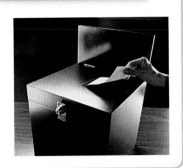

TYPES OF DEMOCRATIC GOVERNMENT:

United Kingdom (UK) constitutional monarchy

Parliament

House of Commons		House of Lords

Governing Party:	Opposition Parties:	Senior bishops	Unelected Lay peers	Senior judges
Prime Minister	Opposition Leaders			
Cabinet	Shadow Cabinets			
Members of Parliament	Opposition MPs			

▲ **UNITED KINGDOM (UK)** *The monarch acts as head of state, but the parliament is responsible for making and changing the laws in the UK, which is done with the majority approval of both the House of Commons and the House of Lords.*

United States of America (U.S.) constitution

Executive Branch	Legislative Branch	Judicial Branch
The White House	The U.S. Capitol	Supreme Court and other law courts
President	Congress	
Vice President	Senate — House of Representatives	
Cabinet	Elected Senators — Elected Representatives	

▲ **UNITED STATES OF AMERICA (USA)** *The U.S. is one of the oldest constitutional republics and has three separate branches of government. The executive branch carries out the instructions of Congress, the legislative branch creates and changes laws, and the judicial branch manages the system of justice.*

DEMOCRATIC

SCIENCE

Science helps us understand the workings of the universe and everything in it. We increase our knowledge by observing, experimenting, and testing theories.

What is science?

Science is the search for knowledge about the world and the way it works. Unlike other ways of explaining how the world works, science is based on experiments that test theories (ideas).

JAPANESE MYTH *says that the gods stirred the ocean to create the first island.*

BEFORE SCIENCE

In the past, people relied on ancient stories to explain such things as how life began, why the Sun appears to cross the sky, what lies beyond the oceans, and so on. These stories often came from religious books or from scholars who dreamed up imaginative ideas without checking them. Because the stories were never tested, there were hundreds of different versions, and every culture had a different version of "the truth."

COPERNICUS'S MODEL

One of the greatest ever scientific theories was put forward by Polish astronomer Nicolaus Copernicus in 1514. His idea was that Earth travels around the sun rather than vice versa. At first, people thought this was foolish because the sun moves across the sky each day, as though it's going round Earth. But Copernicus discovered that this is an illusion caused by Earth spinning round.

▲ COPERNICAN WORLD SYSTEM
Pictures like this showed the sun at the center of the universe for the first time.

How does science work?

Science began when people started to check their ideas about the world. One person to do this was an English doctor named William Gilbert (1544–1603). He carried out many experiments on magnetism and eventually proved that Earth is like a giant magnet.

◄ OLD MARINER'S COMPASS *Gilbert showed that compasses point north because of Earth's magnetism.*

Testing theories

Scientists begin with an idea or "theory." Imagine you have a cold but get better after drinking orange juice. You might form a theory that oranges cure colds. To test this, you could give orange to people with colds. If they get better faster than people who don't drink orange juice, the theory is strengthened.

Orange juice

Proving theories

Although scientists can prove that a bad theory is wrong, they can never prove that a good theory is absolutely right. Even if a theory seems correct, someone could always do a new experiment in the future and prove it wrong. So theories always remain theories.

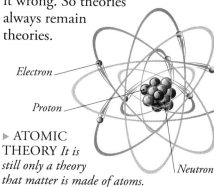

Electron

Proton

▶ ATOMIC THEORY *It is still only a theory that matter is made of atoms.*

Neutron

TIMELINE OF SCIENCE

c.350 BCE	1543	1665	1687	1730–1880
Aristotle is often called the first scientist. His ideas helped lay the foundations of modern sciences such as physics, chemistry, and biology.	**Andreas Vesalius** was a Belgian who wrote a seven-chapter book about the human body.	**Robert Hooke** was an English scientist. He used an early microscope to show that cells are the building blocks of all living things.	**Isaac Newton** was an English scientist. He set out new ideas about motion and gravity.	Many scientists built on one another's work to understand electricity and turn it into a useful source of power.

THE SCIENCES

Since science began more than 2,000 years ago, our knowledge of the world has increased enormously. Science has led to many discoveries that have transformed society, such as cures for diseases. It has also led to amazing new inventions, such as telephones, televisions, space rockets, and computers. These practical spin-offs of science are called technologies.

Medicine

Medicine is the science of healing illnesses. In the past, people believed that diseases were a punishment for bad behavior. Scientists now know that most diseases are caused by microscopic organisms, inherited genes, or faults with a person's immune system.

Chemistry

All substances are made of chemicals, from your hair and teeth to the air around you and the paper in this book. Chemists investigate how atoms join together in different ways to form molecules, or how molecules break apart and recombine to form new substances.

Biology

Biology is the scientific study of living things. Its many branches are devoted to different kinds of life, including botany (the study of plants) and zoology (the study of animals). The most important idea in biology is the theory of evolution by natural selection, which explains how living things came to exist in their current form.

▶ FOSSIL
Preserved remains of living things helped scientists to understand evolution.

Physics

Physicists investigate energy and movement. They study the tiniest particles of matter that make up atoms, and things that aren't made of matter at all, such as time, light, gravity, and space. Physics led to the invention of space rockets and the discovery of radio waves, which gave us cell phones and television.

Geology

Geology is the study of Earth and its interior. Geologists study how rocks form from chemicals called minerals and how they break down or change into other types of rock. Geologists also look at processes that happen deep underground in Earth's interior. These processes cause earthquakes and volcanic eruptions, and continually reshape our planet's surface over long periods of time.

Astronomy

Planet Earth is a tiny speck of matter in a vast Universe of planets, stars, galaxies, and colossal areas of empty space. Astronomy is the study of this gigantic realm beyond our own planet. Thanks to telescopes and rocket technology, astronomers can now study space at first hand.

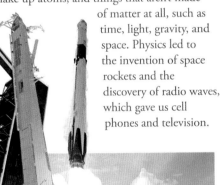

1869	1890–1956	1905–1915	1952–1953	1989
Dmitri Mendeleev was a Russian chemist. He laid the foundations of modern chemistry when he wrote the Periodic Table.	Scientists developed the atomic theory. They worked out how atoms are put together and how they break apart.	**Albert Einstein's** theories of relativity changed physics with new ideas about space, time, light, and gravity.	**Francis Crick, James Watson**, and **Rosalind Franklin** (left) unraveled the structure of DNA, the genetic code inside living things.	**Tim Berners-Lee** invented the World Wide Web, a new way of sharing information.

Mighty atoms

Everything is made up of atoms. These incredibly small particles are the building blocks of all matter, from the rocks that make up our Earth, and the animals, plants, and other creatures that live on it, to the planets and stars in distant galaxies.

INSIDE ATOMS

Atoms may be small, but they contain even smaller particles. Protons and neutrons cluster together in the nucleus at the center of the atom. Electrons move in a cloud that surrounds the nucleus. Strong electrical forces hold these small particles together inside atoms.

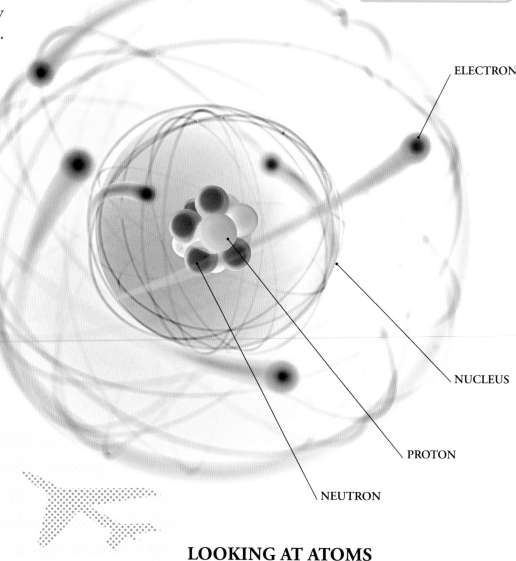

▼ ATOMS *Just as the images on a computer monitor consist of tiny dots of light called pixels, objects in the real world are made of tiny dots of matter called atoms.*

ELECTRON

NUCLEUS

PROTON

NEUTRON

LOOKING AT ATOMS

Atoms are too small to see. In fact they are much smaller than the wavelengths of visible light, so a microscope is not much use either. Instead, scientists "see" atoms by taking pictures of the electric fields around these tiny particles.

Glucose

$C_6H_{12}O_6$

- Also known as dextrose
- First isolated from raisins in 1747 by Andreas Marggraf

Plants make this simple sugar using the energy in sunlight. Animals eat these plants and other animals and then use the glucose in them as a source of energy to stay alive.

Alcohol

C_2H_6O

- Also known as ethanol
- Formed by the action of yeast on natural sugars

The word "alcohol" is the common name for ethanol, which is the type of alcohol found in beer, wine, and spirits. In concentrated form it kills germs. Doctors and nurses use it to clean the skin before an injection.

Water

H_2O

- Covers around 70 percent of Earth's surface
- Essential for life

Without water, life on Earth could not survive. This simple molecule makes up around 60 percent of the human body. Water is the only molecule that exists naturally on Earth in three different forms (or states)—as a solid (ice), a gas (water vapor), and a liquid (water).

Vitamin B$_7$

$C_{10}H_{16}N_2O_3S$

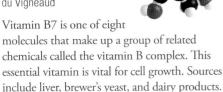

- Also known as biotin or vitamin H
- First isolated in 1940 by Vincent du Vigneaud

Vitamin B7 is one of eight molecules that make up a group of related chemicals called the vitamin B complex. This essential vitamin is vital for cell growth. Sources include liver, brewer's yeast, and dairy products.

Vitamin D

$C_{28}H_{44}O$

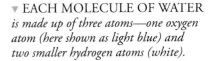

- Also known as ergocalciferol
- First isolated in 1922 by Edward Mellanby

Vitamin D is essential for building strong bones. This molecule is made in the body when the skin is exposed to sunlight. Other sources include fortified cereals and fatty fish.

Diamond

C

- Hardest known substance in nature
- Highly prized as a gemstone for jewelery

Diamond is a rare form of carbon in which each carbon atom bonds with four other carbon atoms to form a tightly packed crystal structure. Diamonds are very hard, so they are used to make the tips of drills.

MOLECULES Atoms stick together to form bigger particles called molecules. The force that holds them together is called a chemical bond. Atoms form chemical bonds by donating or sharing electrons with other atoms.

▼ EACH MOLECULE OF WATER *is made up of three atoms—one oxygen atom (here shown as light blue) and two smaller hydrogen atoms (white).*

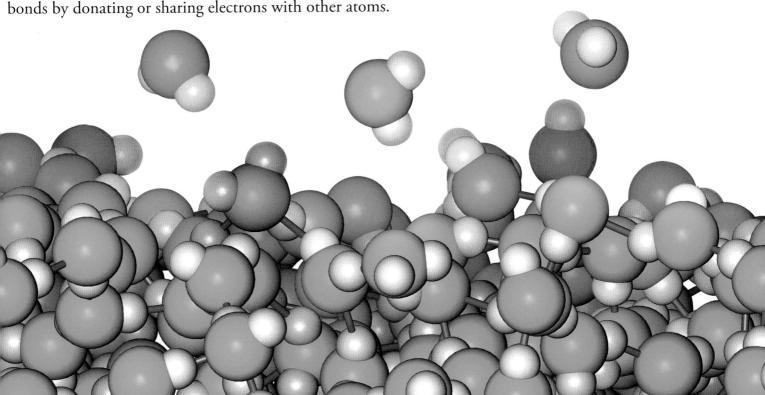

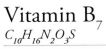

Solid, liquid, or gas?

Almost everything in the world exists in one of three states of matter. Solids keep a fixed shape, liquids have no fixed shape but fill the container in which they are held, and gases float around with no fixed shape or volume.

▲ SOLID *The atoms or molecules in a solid are packed tightly together.*

SOLID STATE

The atoms or molecules in a solid substance are held together by electrical forces. They are arranged in a repeating pattern called a crystal lattice—similar to the way apples or oranges stack together in a grocery store. This makes the solid dense and hard.

▲ LIQUID *The atoms or molecules in a liquid are packed less tightly than those of a solid.*

SOLID TO LIQUID *If you heat up an ice cube to its melting point, the solid ice gradually turns into liquid water. Ice melts at temperatures above 32°F (0°C).*

Melting

Freezing

LIQUID TO SOLID *When the molecules in liquid water lose energy, they freeze and turn into solid ice. Water freezes at 32°F (0°C).*

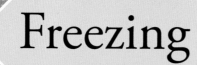

Carbon crystals A diamond is made up of many carbon atoms, which line up to form a crystal. The arrangement is so perfect that the carbon atoms are held very tightly. This makes diamond the hardest substance found in nature.

CHANGING STATES

If you heat a solid enough, the atoms or molecules from which it is made get enough energy to break apart and slide over each other. The solid melts and changes from the solid state into the liquid state. Heat the liquid further, and it boils, changing into the gaseous state.

INTO THIN AIR

- Some substances, such as iodine, can change directly from a solid to a gas without first becoming a liquid. This is called sublimation.
- At room temperature, dry ice (frozen carbon dioxide) sublimes to become carbon dioxide gas.

LIQUID STATE

The atoms or molecules in a liquid substance can slide over each other, so a liquid can be poured into a container. But the electrical forces between the atoms or molecules in a liquid stop them from pulling apart.

▲ GAS *The atoms or molecules in a gas are held so loosely that they can fly away into space.*

GASEOUS STATE

The electrical forces between the atoms and molecules in a gaseous substance have broken down completely, so they will fill the container in which they are held. Gases cannot be poured like liquids, and many, but not all, are invisible.

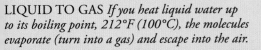

LIQUID TO GAS *If you heat liquid water up to its boiling point, 212°F (100°C), the molecules evaporate (turn into a gas) and escape into the air.*

Evaporation

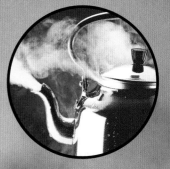

Condensation

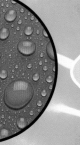

GAS TO LIQUID *When water vapor in the air loses energy, the molecules stick together and become liquid water.*

Liquid metal At room temperature, nearly all metals are solids. But there is one exception—mercury. Mercury has a melting point of –38°F (–39°C), so it stays liquid—even if you put it in a freezer.

Heating up Solid aluminum reacts with liquid bromine to give solid aluminum bromide. The reaction produces a lot of heat, and the excess bromine boils. This produces brown fumes of bromine gas.

Mixing chemicals

A few common substances are made of just one chemical, such as pure water or pure salt. Most of the things that we come across every day, however, are combinations of several chemicals.

COMPOUNDS

Many substances undergo changes when they are mixed together. The chemical bonds that bind the molecules to each other break apart and then recombine to form new substances called compounds.

▲ OIL AND WATER *never combine because their molecules repel each other.*

▲ WASHING LIQUID *is a mixture of soap, water, and other chemicals.*

MIXTURES

Some substances do not react when they are added together because they cannot form chemical bonds. These are called mixtures. Mixtures can easily be separated again because the original substances do not change.

TYPES OF MIXTURE

Mixtures are made of different elements or molecules. During mixing, some of the substances may become harder to see. In coarse mixtures you can usually spot each substance. Suspensions may look like a single liquid, but eventually they separate out. Solutions are the most thoroughly mixed—it is often difficult to tell there is more than one substance.

▲ COARSE MIXTURE *In some mixtures the particles are large enough to be seen and separated easily. Gravel is a coarse mixture.*

▲ SUSPENSION *When small soil particles are mixed with water they form a suspension. Eventually the heavier solids will sink to the bottom.*

▲ COLLOID *These are like suspensions, but the particles do not sink to the bottom. In milk, tiny droplets of fat float in a watery solution.*

▲ SOLUTION *When one substance dissolves in another it is called a solution. Seawater is a solution of salt and water; air is a solution of gases.*

SEPARATING MIXTURES AND COMPOUNDS

It is much easier to separate a mixture than a compound. Mixtures can be separated using physical methods, such as evaporation, filtration, flotation, or distillation. Separating compounds may require several steps before you get the substance you want, including mixing with other chemicals, heating, and filtering.

◀ CHROMATOGRAPHY
This is used to identify colored substances in a mixture. A drop of the mixture is placed onto chromatography paper and solvent is then dripped onto it. As the solvent travels across the paper, the different substances travel across the paper at different speeds. Scientists can then work out what each substance is by the distance it has traveled.

▼ PANNING FOR GOLD
Gold prospectors separate grains of gold from river gravel by swirling the gravel around in a shallow pan. The heavier gold sinks to the bottom and can be picked out.

CHEMICAL REACTIONS

When the atoms of two or more substances rearrange themselves to form a new compound, we say that a chemical reaction has taken place. Most chemical reactions are irreversible— you cannot turn a cake back into eggs and flour. Some reactions can be reversed but may need heat or pressure to change back.

▲ IRON *can be prevented from rusting by coating it with a less reactive metal, such as zinc (left).*

Reversible reaction When iron is exposed to air or water it starts to react. The metal reacts with oxygen, which turns the iron into the reddish brown iron oxides we call rust. However, if you were to heat the iron oxides in a blast furnace they would change back into iron and oxygen.

▲ ALLOY *This is a solid solution in which one metal has dissolved in another. Alloys are often tougher and more durable than the original metals.*

Irreversible reaction Burning wood causes irreversible changes. The carbon atoms in the wood react with oxygen in the air to form ash, smoke, and carbon dioxide. The wood also loses energy as heat and light. Even if you put all these things together in a test tube they would not change back into wood. Another irreversible change happens when food starts to rot. Tiny micro-organisms feed on the food and turn it into new substances. This process is called decomposition.

SCIENCE

227

It's elementary

An element is a pure substance that cannot be broken down into simpler chemicals. An element is made of only one type of atom. So, the element hydrogen is made only of hydrogen atoms, and gold of gold atoms.

WHERE DO ELEMENTS COME FROM?

Most scientists believe that much of the hydrogen and some of the helium in the universe were formed in the "Big Bang" that formed the universe. Hydrogen has the smallest and simplest atoms, and helium has the next smallest.

THE PERIODIC TABLE

Scientists recognize 118 different elements, which have been organized into a chart known as the periodic table. This table was first devised in 1869 by Russian chemist Dmitri Mendeleev, who organized elements with similar properties into groups. The elements are arranged by the size of their atoms.

Every element has a one- or two-letter symbol. For example, Kr is the symbol for the element Krypton. Scientists use these symbols to write down the chemical formulae for molecules and chemical reactions.

Kr — Symbol
KRYPTON — Name
36 — Atomic number

Metals are on the left and center of the table. On the right are gases and non-metal solids.

H HYDROGEN 1																		He HELIUM 2
Li LITHIUM 3	Be BERYLLIUM 4											B BORON 5	C CARBON 6	N NITROGEN 7	O OXYGEN 8	F FLUORINE 9	Ne NEON 10	
Na SODIUM 11	Mg MAGNESIUM 12											Al ALUMINIUM 13	Si SILICON 14	P PHOSPHORUS 15	S SULPHUR 16	Cl CHLORINE 17	Ar ARGON 18	
K POTASSIUM 19	Ca CALCIUM 20	Sc SCANDIUM 21	Ti TITANIUM 22	V VANADIUM 23	Cr CHROMIUM 24	Mn MANGANESE 25	Fe IRON 26	Co COBALT 27	Ni NICKEL 28	Cu COPPER 29	Zn ZINC 30	Ga GALLIUM 31	Ge GERMANIUM 32	As ARSENIC 33	Se SELENIUM 34	Br BROMINE 35	Kr KRYPTON 36	
Rb RUBIDIUM 37	Sr STRONTIUM 38	Y YTTRIUM 39	Zr ZIRCONIUM 40	Nb NIOBIUM 41	Mo MOLYBDENUM 42	Tc TECHNETIUM 43	Ru RUTHENIUM 44	Rh RHODIUM 45	Pd PALLADIUM 46	Ag SILVER 47	Cd CADMIUM 48	In INDIUM 49	Sn TIN 50	Sb ANTIMONY 51	Te TELLURIUM 52	I IODINE 53	Xe XENON 54	
Cs CAESIUM 55	Ba BARIUM 56	LANTHANIDES OR RARE-EARTH METALS 57–71	Hf HAFNIUM 72	Ta TANTALUM 73	W TUNGSTEN 74	Re RHENIUM 75	Os OSMIUM 76	Ir IRIDIUM 77	Pt PLATINUM 78	Au GOLD 79	Hg MERCURY 80	Tl THALLIUM 81	Pb LEAD 82	Bi BISMUTH 83	Po POLONIUM 84	At ASTATINE 85	Rn RADON 86	
Fr FRANCIUM 87	Ra RADIUM 88	ACTINIDES or RARE-EARTH RADIOACTIVE METALS 89–103	Rf RUTHERFORDIUM 104	Db DUBNIUM 105	Sg SEABORGIUM 106	Bh BOHRIUM 107	Hs HASSIUM 108	Mt MEITNERIUM 109	Ds DARMSTADTIUM 110	Rg ROENTGENIUM 111	Cn COPERNICIUM 112	Nh NIHONIUM 113	Fl FLEROVIUM 114	Mc MOSCOVIUM 115	Lv LIVERMORIUM 116	Ts TENNESSINE 117	Og OGANESSON 118	

La LANTHANUM 57	Ce CERIUM 58	Pr PRASEODYMIUM 59	Nd NEODYMIUM 60	Pm PROMETHIUM 61	Sm SAMARIUM 62	Eu EUROPIUM 63	Gd GADOLINIUM 64	Tb TERBIUM 65	Dy DYSPROSIUM 66	Ho HOLMIUM 67	Er ERBIUM 68	Tm THULIUM 69	Yb YTTERBIUM 70	Lu LUTETIUM 71
Ac ACTINIUM 89	Th THORIUM 90	Pa PROTACTINIUM 91	U URANIUM 92	Np NEPTUNIUM 93	Pu PLUTONIUM 94	Am AMERICIUM 95	Cm CURIUM 96	Bk BERKELIUM 97	Cf CALIFORNIUM 98	Es EINSTEINIUM 99	Fm FERMIUM 100	Md MENDELEVIUM 101	No NOBELIUM 102	Lr LAWRENCIUM 103

Compounds

Most chemicals are not pure elements, but compounds. A compound is a chemical made up of two or more elements that are chemically combined.

Water is a compound made of two hydrogen atoms and one oxygen atom.

RADIOACTIVE DECAY

Some elements are made of atoms so large they spontaneously break apart. This is called radioactive decay, and the subatomic particles (smaller than atoms) and energy released by it can be dangerous. Each radioactive element has a half life, the time it takes for half of its atoms to break apart.

Gold
Aurum

- **Group** Transition metals
- **Discovery date** nknown (prehistoric mes)
- **Melting point** ,948°F (1,064°C)
- **Boiling point** 5,137°F (2,836°C)

Gold gets people excited. It has been prized nd valued since prehistoric times, and turned nto many crowns, idols, and crosses over the enturies. Gold never loses its shine and is easy o melt and mold. It is measured in carats— ure gold is 24 carats.

Iron
Ferrum

- **Group** Transition metals
- **Discovery date** Unknown (prehistoric times)
- **Melting point** 2,800°F (1,538°C)
- **Boiling point** 5,182°F (2,861°C)

Iron is a versatile and abundant metal. We use it to build bridges and make machines and cutlery. Iron is vital to your well-being. It gives red blood cells their color, and helps to carry oxygen around your body. The center of Earth is made largely of iron.

Helium
Helium

- **Group** Noble gases
- **Discovery date** 1868
- **Melting point** −458°F (−272°C)
- **Boiling point** −452°F (−269°C)

Helium is the second most abundant element in the universe, after hydrogen. It was discovered in space, before we found it on Earth. It weighs very little and is used to make things such as airships and balloons float in air. It is also used in liquid form as a coolant in big scientific computers.

Mercury
Hydrargyrum

- **Group** ransition metals
- **Discovery date** re-1500 BCE
- **Melting point** −38°F −39°C)
- **Boiling point** 675°F (357°C)

Mercury is poisonous, although in ancient imes it was thought to have healing and ife-giving properties. Early chemists alchemists) once thought it held the secret o making gold. At room temperature nercury is a liquid.

Carbon
Carbon

- **Group** Non-metals
- **Discovery date** Unknown (prehistoric times)
- **Melting point** diamonds 6,917°F (3,852°C) sublimes 8,672°F (4,800°C)

Carbon is vital to all living things and on Earth it is frequently exchanged between the air, living things, and the soil, in a never-ending cycle. Carbon atoms can join together to make coal and diamonds, as well as with other elements to make more than 10 million compounds.

Uranium
Uranium

- **Group** Actinides
- **Discovery date** 1789
- **Melting point** 2,075°F (1,135°C)
- **Boiling point** 7,468°F (4,131°C)

Uranium is a naturally occurring radioactive metal and was named after the planet Uranus. It is refined and used in industry, nuclear power stations, and warfare. In the 1940s, it was used to make the atomic bomb "Little Boy" that was dropped on Hiroshima in 1945.

Calcium
Calcium

- **Group** Alkaline-earth metals
- **Discovery date** Pre-100 CE
- **Melting point** 1,548°F (842°C)
- **Boiling point** 2,703°F (1,484°C)

Calcium is the most abundant metal found in our body and is vital for many cellular reactions. It is also a key component of bones and shells, giving them strength. Calcium is also found in milk, chalk, and seaweeds.

Phosphorus
Phosphorus

- **Group** Non-metals
- **Discovery date** 1669, by German chemist Hennig Brandt
- **Melting point** 111°F (44°C)
- **Boiling point** 537°F (281°C)

This fiery element is very reactive and so isn't found naturally on Earth. Phosphorus is used to make matches, fertilizers, and some weapons. It is also a component of DNA, and it helps make energy in your body.

WHO'S WHO?

- **Robert Boyle** (1627–1691) This British scientist laid the foundation for modern chemistry and proposed the idea of elements.
- **Henry Cavendish** (1731–1810) This scientist was the first to prove water was not an element, but a compound.
- **Joseph Priestley** (1733–1804) He was a clergyman and scientist who discovered several gases including oxygen.
- **Alfred Bernhard Nobel** (1833–1896) He was a scientist who created dynamite and founded the Prize named after him.
- **Marie Curie** (1867–1934) She was famed for her work on radioactivity and discovered polonium and radium.

Energy

Energy is the power behind our world. Although you can't see it, you can't do much without it. Whenever things move, light up, change shape, get hotter or colder, or make noises, energy is involved.

Freewheelin
turns potent
energy into
kinetic energ

STORED ENERGY

You can do two things with energy: store it or use it. It takes lots of energy to ride a bike up a hill, but that energy doesn't disappear. It's stored by your body and by your bike in a form called potential energy. You use this stored energy when you race back down without pedaling. The potential energy you stored is then converted into kinetic energy (movement energy).

TYPES OF ENERC

Energy exists in many different forr
Almost everything we do invol
changing energy from one form ir
another. When we're "using" energy, we
actually converting it into another for.

Kinetic
The energy moving things have. Racing cars have lots of kinetic energy.

Light
A kind of kinetic energy carried by invisible waves of electricity and magnetism.

Electromagnetic
Electromagnetic energy is also carried by radio waves, X-rays, and microwaves.

Heat
Hot things have energy because their atoms or molecules move more quickly than in cold things.

Electrical
Electricity is a convenient form of energy that can be carried along wires.

Nuclear
Atoms can release energy from their nucleus (central core).

Gravitationa
Falling things, s as this waterfall, release potential energy stored using gravity.

CHANGING ENERGY

Heat-sensitive photograph There's a fixed amount of energy in our universe. We can't make any more or use any up. All we can do is change energy to other forms. When a car brakes, its kinetic energy doesn't vanish. It changes to heat in the brakes and wheels (glowing in this heat-sensitive photograph).

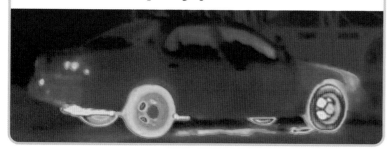

RENEWABLE ENERGY

Earth has limited amounts of fossil fuels, such as oil, coal, and gas. Once we've used them, there will be no more. There are unlimited amounts of renewable energy. This includes energy from the sun, the wind, and the oceans. We can go on using renewable energy forever.

ENERGY SOURCES

Most of the energy people now use (around 83 percent) comes from fossil fuels. The rest comes from renewable energy and nuclear power.

▼ TURBINES *(water wheels) behind these channels generate electricity when water flows past them.*

Hydroelectric power
Energy from moving rivers and seas

- **Percentage of current energy use** 7 percent
- **Reserves left** Unlimited

Rivers flow from mountains and hills down to the sea. This means they release stored potential energy. Hydroelectric power stations capture this energy to make electricity.

Fossil fuels
Energy from coal, gas, and oil

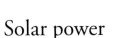

- **Percentage of current energy use** Coal 27 percent, gas 25 percent, oil 31 percent
- **Reserves left** Coal 140 years, gas 50 years, oil 50 years

Although bad for the environment, fossil fuels are still the world's main energy source. Coal is cheap to make electricity, gas is easy to pipe to homes, and oil is convenient for powering vehicles.

SCIENCE

Geothermal power
Energy from Earth's internal heat

- **Percentage of current energy use** Less than 1 percent
- **Reserves left** Unlimited

Deep inside, Earth is hot molten rock. Some of this heat is released when volcanoes erupt. Geothermal energy means using Earth's inner heat to generate hot water and electricity.

Biomass and biofuel
Energy made using living plants and animals

- **Percentage of current energy use** Uncertain
- **Reserves left** Unlimited

Growing plants and animals store energy we can use in the future. We can grow crops to make oil for vehicles, which is called biofuel. We can make electricity by burning wood or animal waste, which is called biomass.

Solar power
Energy made from the Sun's light or heat

- **Percentage of current energy use** About 1 percent
- **Reserves left** Unlimited

Almost all the energy on Earth originally comes from the sun. We can tap the sun's energy directly to make electricity. Solar panels like these turn sunlight into electricity.

Wave power
Energy from seas, oceans, and tides

- **Percentage of current energy use** Less than 1 percent
- **Reserves left** Unlimited

Wind moving over seas and oceans stores energy in waves. Waves have kinetic energy (because they move) and potential energy (because they're above the normal sea surface). We can use the energy in breaking waves and shifting tides to generate electricity.

Nuclear power
Energy made from atomic reactions

- **Percentage of current energy use** About 4 percent
- **Reserves left** Raw uranium, 90 years

Atoms are made of tiny particles held together by energy. Large atoms can release this energy by splitting apart. Small atoms can release energy by joining together. Most nuclear power stations make electricity by splitting apart large uranium atoms.

Wind power
Energy from air currents moving across Earth

- **Percentage of current energy use** About 2 percent
- **Reserves left** Unlimited

Wind turbines work like propellers in reverse. As their rotors spin in the wind, they turn small generators inside and make electricity.

Feel the force

Forces are at work all the time, pulling you down to the ground, stopping you from slipping over, and pushing you one way and then the next. Forces act on everything, from the tiny nuclei inside atoms to the planets and stars that make up the universe.

PULLING AND PUSHING

A force is a push or a pull. For example, your hand applies a pulling or pushing force to open and close a door. Forces act on all objects all of the time. They make them move or change their speed or direction.

Your hand applies a pushing force on a toy car to make it move.

HIDDEN FORCES

Usually you must touch an object to push or pull on it. But some forces act on things without touching them. For example, this magnet pulls on these paperclips with a magnetic force.

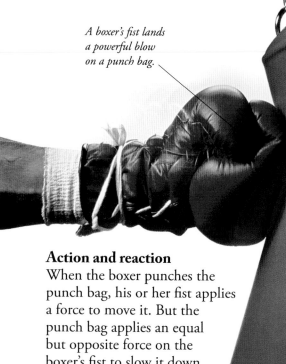

A boxer's fist lands a powerful blow on a punch bag.

Action and reaction
When the boxer punches the punch bag, his or her fist applies a force to move it. But the punch bag applies an equal but opposite force on the boxer's fist to slow it down.

232

FRICTION FORCES

Roll a ball along the ground and eventually it will come to a standstill. Friction acts on the ball to slow it down. Try to push a heavy box along the floor. Friction provides grip, making it hard to get the box moving.

Disc brakes create friction on the brake disc to slow the car.

INERTIA

When there are no forces acting on an object, it will either stay still or keep moving in a straight line at the same speed. This is called "inertia." In practice, friction usually slows down a moving object.

◀ RUNAWAY CART! *When you let go of a grocery cart, it carries on moving under its own inertia.*

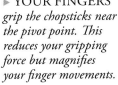

▶ YOUR FINGERS *grip the chopsticks near the pivot point. This reduces your gripping force but magnifies your finger movements.*

Fulcrum

MAGNIFYING FORCES

People use machines to magnify forces. Machines called levers move around a pivot point called a fulcrum. Most levers magnify forces, but they act over a shorter distance than the force you put in. Simple levers include chopsticks, a pair of pliers, and a nutcracker.

Fulcrum

▶ PLIERS *convert the weak force of your hand on one side of the lever into a stronger gripping force on the other side of the lever.*

Fulcrum

▶ A NUTCRACKER *crushes a walnut by turning the weak force of your hand into a stronger force nearer the fulcrum.*

BALANCED FORCES

When two or more forces act on an object, they combine to produce a single "net force." In some cases, the forces combine to make a larger net force. In other cases, the forces work against each other, resulting in a weaker net force. Sometimes the two forces cancel each other out completely.

◀ TUG-OF-WAR *If both teams pull on a rope with the same force, the net force is zero and nobody moves.*

233

Gravity

Gravity is the force of attraction that pulls things together. On Earth, we experience it as the force that pulls us down onto the surface of the planet. In the universe, gravity is the force that pulls planets in orbit around stars.

Weight and mass
Weighing scales measure the pulling force that Earth's gravity exerts on your body. Gravity exerts more pulling force on a body with greater mass, so the scales would register a higher weight for a person with greater mass.

WEAK OR STRONG?
Gravity may seem impressive, but it is actually the weakest known force in the universe. It takes objects the size of planets and stars to produce a noticeable effect. The sun's gravity is strong enough to hold all the planets of the solar system in orbit around it.

GRAVITY AT WORK
Take up skydiving and you will soon feel the full effects of gravity at work. When you jump out of a plane, gravity makes your body accelerate towards the ground. At the same time, air rubs against your body, creating friction, or drag, which works against gravity. Eventually the two forces balance, and you stop accelerating—you have reached "terminal velocity."

According to legend, Galileo dropped balls of different weight from the Leaning Tower of Pisa to show they hit the ground at the same time.

Gravity and Galileo
The first modern scientist to study gravity was an Italian called Galileo Galilei (1564–1642). He did lots of experiments and concluded that in the absence of air resistance all falling objects would accelerate downward at the same rate. It is the air resistance, called drag, that allows some objects to reach the ground more slowly than others.

▲ TERMINAL VELOCITY *The highest velocity reached by skydivers with an unopened parachute is about 125 mph (200 kmph). Opening a parachute slows the skydiver down by increasing drag.*

NEWTON

▼ SCIENCE GENIUS
Sir Isaac Newton was the first person to figure out that the force of gravity keeps the moon trapped in orbit around Earth.

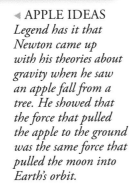

◀ APPLE IDEAS
Legend has it that Newton came up with his theories about gravity when he saw an apple fall from a tree. He showed that the force that pulled the apple to the ground was the same force that pulled the moon into Earth's orbit.

EINSTEIN

▼ WARP FACTOR *Albert Einstein came up with another theory to explain gravity. He suggested that a big mass, such as a planet, warps space and time in the same way as a heavy ball resting on a rubber sheet.*

▼ RELATIVE SUCCESS
Einstein came up with his theory in 1915. A few years later, astronomers confirmed his theory, when light from a distant star was shown to bend as it passed the sun.

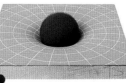

The warping effect creates the force of gravity.

Center of gravity
Gravity pulls down on an object through a point called the center of gravity. An object will tip over if its center of gravity is too high or moves outside the base of the object. All-terrain vehicles have a very low center of gravity so they can drive up and down steep slopes.

Vomit Comet Astronauts appear to float in this reduced-gravity aircraft that is designed for weightlessness training. The plane follows the path that an object in free fall would take. In fact, the astronauts and the aircraft are accelerating at the same rate, but there is no contact between them. The plane is nicknamed the "Vomit Comet" because it makes some astronauts feel sick.

EXPLODING STARS

Stars are powered by nuclear reactions. In the core of the sun, hydrogen atoms combine to form helium, releasing extreme heat. When the sun runs out of hydrogen in its core, the core will collapse. The collapse of the core of a larger star might release enough energy that the star is seen as a supernova. The outer parts of the star are blown into space.

Electricity

Everything in the universe is made up of atoms that we can't see. Each atom has particles that transport an electric charge. Electricity powers items we use every day, from lights to computers. It is carried to our homes by a series of cables and power stations.

Neutron
Proton
Electron

Charge carriers Atoms contain particles that carry electrical charge. Protons are found in the nucleus and carry a positive charge. Neutrons are also found in the nucleus, but are uncharged. Electrons orbit around the nucleus and carry a negative charge.

CHARGED CLOUDS

Lightning strikes when static electricity builds up in a storm cloud. Negative charge collects at the bottom of the cloud, while positive charge builds up near the top. Eventually the negative charge shoots down to the ground in a bolt of lightning.

Static electricity The build-up of static electricity can make your hair stand on end. If you touch the metal dome of a Van de Graaff generator, positive charge transfers to your body, including your hair. The hairs repel each other, making them stand on end.

TELL ME MORE...

Static electricity can be very handy if you are a farmer. Crop spraying delivers pesticide as a spray of fine droplets. The spray can be given an electric charge so that the droplets repel each other and spread out over the crops.

BATTERIES
provide power

PAPER CLIP
acts as a switch

BULBS
light up

Current electricity
Electrons can flow through metals and other conductors. This flow of electrical charge is called current electricity, and it can be used to light up our homes and power electrical devices, such as microwaves and televisions.

NERVES

The nerves inside your body work like electric wires. They carry messages between the brain and different parts of your body in the form of electric signals.

Magnetism

Whenever there is electricity, there is magnetism. This mysterious, invisible force draws some metal objects together or pushes them apart.

WHAT CAUSES MAGNETISM?
The same moving electrons that create electricity also create magnetism. This force acts through an invisible magnetic field. You can see this field of force if you scatter some iron filings around a bar magnet.

The compass aligns with the magnetic field of the bar magnet.

Natural magnet Earth is a giant natural magnet whose magnetic field makes compass needles point towards the magnetic North Pole. Earth's magnetic field extends thousands of miles into space, forming a vast area known as the magnetosphere.

▲ LIKE POLES REPEL
Magnets have north and south poles. If you push the same poles together they repel each other.

▲ UNLIKE POLES ATTRACT
Push opposite poles together and a powerful force of attraction will snap the magnets together.

MAGNETIC NORTH POLE   MAGNETIC SOUTH POLE

Electromagnetism Magnetism and electricity are united by the force of electromagnetism. If you move a magnet next to a wire, electricity flows through the wire. Similarly, whenever electrons flow through a wire, they create a magnetic field around the wire.

◄ ELECTRICITY *flowing through the loops of electric wire inside an electromagnet generate a powerful magnetic field to lift scrap metal.*

A motor turns the blades of a food processor.

Moving motor Electrons flowing through a wire coil can make a magnet move in and out of the coil. Electrical energy changes into kinetic energy. This is how an electric motor works. Electric motors power devices ranging from toys and appliances to huge electric trains.

Science of sound

Sound is a form of energy. It passes through air, water, and solid objects as invisible waves. We can hear sound because the waves make the delicate skin of our eardrums vibrate. The vibrations are converted to nerve signals that travel to the brain.

Good vibrations Objects can give out sound energy when they vibrate. This vibrating guitar string causes molecules of air to bump into each other. The collisions between molecules spread like ripples in a pool, carrying the sound outwards in all directions.

▶ A TUNING FORK *vibrates at a particular frequency, so it always gives out sound at the same pitch.*

FACT

Sound waves travel through air at about 740 mph (1,190 kmph). This is slower than light waves, which is why we hear the sound of a distant jet aircraft or explosion after we see it. Sound travels faster under water, at about 3,125 mph (5,000 kmph), though the exact speed varies with temperature.

▼ PEAKS AND TROUGHS
The height, or "amplitude," of peaks and troughs in a sound wave dictates loudness.

Peak

Trough

SOUND WAVES

We can't see sound waves, but we can get a good idea how they work by watching the way a wave travels along a glowing string. The end of the string is vibrated by a machine called an oscillator.

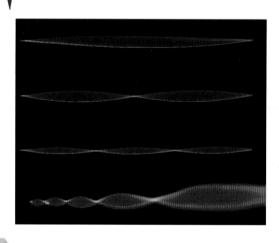

◀ FREQUENCY 0.5 HERTZ (HZ) *The string is vibrating with a long wavelength.*

◀ FREQUENCY 1 HZ *Vibrations in double time give shorter wavelengths.*

◀ FREQUENCY 1.5 HZ *At this higher frequency the wavelength shortens again.*

◀ FREQUENCY 2.5 HZ *High-frequency sound waves make high-pitched sounds.*

DECIBEL SCALE

We measure the loudness of sound using the decibel scale. This is what mathematicians call a "log scale," meaning the quietest sounds measure about 0 dB, a sound twice as loud increases by 10 dB, a sound four times louder by 20 dB, and a sound eight times louder by 30 dB.

▲ 0 dB
The tiny sound of a finger brushing skin.

▲ 15 dB
A whispered conversation.

▲ 60 dB
A normal speaking voice.

▲ 90 dB
The sound of a high-speed train passing by.

Seeing with sound Sound waves bounce off objects in the same way light waves do. Dolphins and bats are able to use these echoes to picture objects around them. With the aid of computer-imaging software that converts sound waves into pictures, we can do the same.

Echolocation
Seeing with sound

◄ FIRST PHOTO
Advanced ultrasound scanners can produce amazingly detailed images such as this unborn baby.

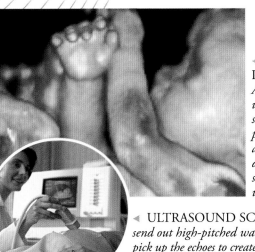

◄ ULTRASOUND SCANNERS
send out high-pitched waves and pick up the echoes to create an image.

Bat calls The echolocation calls produced by bats are loud but so high-pitched that most people cannot hear them at all. Bats have incredibly sharp hearing and use faint echoes from nearby surfaces to pinpoint prey or detect obstacles.

Sonogram
A sound diagram

PITCH AND TONE

The way we hear a sound depends on the shape of the sound waves. The spacing of waves affects the frequency or pitch of the sound. Closely packed waves indicate high pitch, while stretched out waves are low-pitched. A clear-toned sound, such as that made by a bell, creates smooth waves, while harsh tones, such as drumbeats, make jagged-looking waves.

The "sonic shock" caused by a supersonic aircraft causes water in the atmosphere to condense, forming a visible cone, or collar, of vapor.

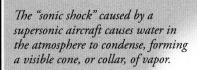

▲ 100 dB
The blast of a car horn.

▲ 110 dB
The sound of a thunderstorm overhead.

▲ 120 dB
The roar of a jet aircraft taking off.

Breaking the sound barrier
When a supersonic aircraft breaks the speed of sound, it overtakes its own sound waves, pushing them closer together to create a "sonic boom." A whipcrack is a type of sonic boom, caused when the whip tip breaks the sound barrier.

Light fantastic

Energy takes many forms. Light is one we are familiar with because our eyes are specially adapted to detect it. However seeing light is one thing—understanding it is more tricky.

HOW DOES LIGHT TRAVEL?

Puzzlingly, light behaves as though it is made of both waves and particles. Like waves, light can be reflected and refracted, and its wavelength can be measured. Other types of wave need something (a "medium"), to ripple through, but light can travel across a vacuum.

LIGHT WAVES

LIGHT PARTICLES

Shadows

Light travels in a straight line, and cannot bend round obstacles. The space behind an obstacle looks dark because the only light reaching it is that reflected from other objects nearby.

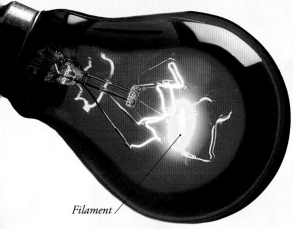

Filament

Where does light come from?

Atoms that are excited by a collision return to their normal state by emitting light energy. The atoms in a heated lightbulb filament shed their excess energy by flinging out tiny packets of light called photons, causing the filament to glow.

THE SPEED OF LIGHT

- Light is the fastest moving thing in the Universe. It travels across empty space at the unimaginable speed of 186,411 miles/second (300,000 km/second).
- One light year is the distance light can travel in one year. This is about 5.9 trillion miles (9.5 trillion km). Light years are used to measure colossal distances across space. The Sun is a mere 499 light seconds away.
- Albert Einstein worked out that if there was a way to travel at close to light speed, time would slow down and you would age more slowly.

▼ ALL A BLUR
Fast-moving objects appear blurred because light travels much faster than our brain takes to interpret what we are seeing.

REFLECTION When light strikes an object, some of it is bounced back or "reflected." The angle of reflection is always the same as the angle at which the light hits the surface, so on a smooth surface we see a perfect reflection, or mirror image. If the surface is curved or uneven, the image is distorted.

The break in the straws is an illusion caused by refraction.

REFRACTION When light crosses the boundary between two media with different densities (such as air and water), it bends, or "refracts." This is why objects standing in water appear distorted at the surface. If you try to touch a coin or pebble in a bucket of water, it will not be exactly where your eyes tell you it is.

Lenses A lens is a transparent object with curved surfaces that refract light in a predictable way. An object close behind a bulging or "convex" lens will appear magnified while one seen through a dished or "concave" lens will appear reduced in size. Telescopes, microscopes, and spectacles all use lenses.

▸ IMPERFECT *eyesight can be corrected with artificial lenses.*

FIREWORKS
The atoms of different materials emit light of different colors or wavelengths. Firework makers use this to create wonderful displays.

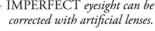

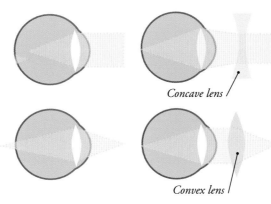

Concave lens

Convex lens

◂ SHORT SIGHT *is when the eye focuses an image too far forward. It is corrected with a concave lens.*

◂ LONG SIGHT *causes the image to focus too far back, so the retina only detects a blur. It is fixed with a convex lens.*

Heat haze
Refraction can happen when light passes through air of mixed density. Cool air over hot ground contains layers of variable density, and light passing through the layers is bent, causing a shimmering heat haze. In extreme cases the effect results in a "mirage"—a watery-looking reflection of the sky.

Spectrum

The universe is full of electro-magnetic radiation, which travels in waves. Our eyes see a small range of these waves as visible light, but we can also detect the effects of other radiation types.

FACT

To remember the colors of the visible spectrum in order, memorize this phrase: "Richard Of York Gave Battle In Vain," for Red, Orange, Yellow, Green, Blue, Indigo, and Violet.

RAINBOWS

We see rainbows when white light is refracted as it passes through different media, such as drops of water or thin layers of oil. Sunlight passing through rain or mist from a fountain creates rainbows, and we see them produced by solid materials such as crystal or Perspex.

Prism

White light contains a mixture of visible wavelengths.

When waves strike the surface of a different medium at an angle, they are bent by an amount that differs slightly for different wavelengths. The bending is known as "refraction."

Because short wavelengths refra[ct] more than long ones, the differen[t] wavelengths of th[e] spectrum are separated by the prism.

THE ELECTROMAGNETIC SPECTRUM

The visible spectrum is a small part of a much larger spectrum of energy waves. We have found technological uses for most types of electromagnetic radiation.

The wavelengths of different types of electromagnetic radiation range from shorter than an atom to millions of miles (kilometers) long.

WAVELENGTH

GAMMA RAYS

Gamma radiation is immensely powerful. In large quantities, it damages our cells and DNA.

X-RAYS

X-rays pass through our bodies. We can use them to take pictures of our insides.

ULTRAVIOLET (UV)

Ultraviolet rays damage our cells. Sunscreen can help filter them out.

VISIBLE RAYS

Visible light waves make the world a colorful place for us to experience and enjoy.

Color vision Objects appear colored to our eyes because their surfaces reflect some wavelengths of light but not others. Plants have chemicals called pigments that color their fruits and flowers, making them attractive to the animals that disperse their pollen and seeds. Most fruit-eating animals see in color.

A tomato absorbs green and blue light and reflects red.

Lemons reflect red and green light, which we see as yellow.

Blackberries absorb all colors of light, reflecting very little.

Green peppers reflect green light and absorb red and blue.

Adding color

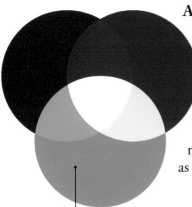

Televisions produce hundreds of colors by mixing red, green, and blue light in different quantities. Blending these three primary wavelengths to create new colors is known as color addition.

A color television picture is made of tiny red, green, and blue dots called pixels.

Subtracting color

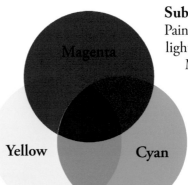

Magenta
Yellow
Cyan

Paints create colors by absorbing light rather than emitting it. Mixing the primary paint colors of magenta, yellow, and cyan creates new colors by reducing the range of wavelengths that are reflected. This is called color subtraction.

Unstoppable waves

Electromagnetic radiation is everywhere. Visible light is bouncing off this page, allowing you to see the words and pictures printed in different colors. But other kinds of electromagnetic wave are passing straight through the pages and through your body without you even noticing.

▲ COLOR PRINTING *The microscopic dots used in color printing come in four colors but blend to create the illusion of thousands more* (👁 *p168–169*).

INFRARED (IR)

Warm objects emit IR radiation. IR cameras see heat as white or red. Cool objects appear blue.

MICROWAVE

Microwaves make certain molecules move very fast and give out lots of heat energy.

RADIO WAVES

Data, sound, and pictures can be transmitted as radio waves. Cell phones,

radio, and TV sets convert longer radio waves back into images and sound for us to see and hear.

Evolution

Over long periods of time, all species of organism slowly change. This gradual change, called evolution, is driven by the process of natural selection. This process allows organisms that are best suited to their environment to survive and reproduce.

The father of evolution
The English naturalist Charles Darwin first proposed the theory of evolution after studying hundreds of different animals, plants, and fossils. He realized that many species were related and had a common ancestor. Modern DNA testing is now proving that his theory was correct.

NATURAL SELECTION

Darwin observed that most animals and plants produce more offspring than survive to become adults. He realized that nature was selecting those with the characteristics best adapted to their surroundings, allowing them to pass on their characteristics to future generations.

▲ SURVIVAL TACTICS
Frogs produce hundreds of eggs, but only a few grow into adult frogs.

ARTIFICIAL SELECTION

In the wild, species evolve by natural selection. However, humans have been helping evolution by choosing animals and plants with desirable characteristics and breeding them to produce sheep with more wool, cows that give more milk, and crops that have better yields. This process is called artificial selection.

Domestic dogs All dogs are descended from wolves. Over time, humans selectively bred them for things such as hunting or herding ability, speed, and size, so that we now have hundreds of breeds.

Broccoli (flowers)

Cauliflower (flowers)

Gray wolf

These dogs have all got a little bit of wolf in them.

Wild cabbage

▶ ADVANTAGE
Having a long neck allows the giraffe to eat leaves that other species cannot reach.

Adaptation Darwin's theory can explain why a giraffe has a long neck. In the search for food, those that could reach a bit higher had an advantage over those with shorter necks. Over time, new generations developed longer and longer necks.

THE FOSSIL RECORD

Fossils show that life on Earth has changed throughout its history. Each major layer of rock may contain species that are slightly different to those below or on top of it. Although it is not easy to find fossils that show every change in a species, this birdlike *Archaeopteryx* (right) is a clear example that birds evolved from feathered dinosaurs.

Family trees Scientists trace evolution by examining fossils and seeing where they fit on the family tree. Many elephant fossils have been found that show how these animals developed tusks and a long trunk, but not all are direct ancestors of modern elephants.

Phiomia

Brussels sprouts (large buds)

Moeritherium

Gomphotherium

Deinotherium

Asian elephant

Red cabbage (leaves)

Green cabbage (leaves)

Cabbages These vegetables may look different, but they are all descended from the wild cabbage. Brussels sprouts, cabbages, cauliflowers, and broccoli have been bred for their leaves, flowers, or buds.

EVOLUTION AND GENES

Organisms use DNA to pass on their characteristics to the next generation. DNA is divided up into sections called genes. A gene may be code for a particular characteristic, such as hair, feathers, skin, or scales.

Woodpecker finch

Medium ground finch

Vegetarian finch

Warbler finch

New species When Darwin visited the Galápagos Islands, he noticed that all the finches looked like a species on the mainland but had different beaks. He realized that all these species had evolved from the same ancestors, but their beaks had changed to suit the food sources on each island.

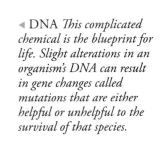

◄ DNA *This complicated chemical is the blueprint for life. Slight alterations in an organism's DNA can result in gene changes called mutations that are either helpful or unhelpful to the survival of that species.*

HOW LIFE BEGAN

It remains a mystery how life began. Earth was so hot that life began in the oceans, perhaps around vents in the ocean floor (right). Simple molecules began to copy themselves, then formed into cells and colonies, and finally, complicated organisms.

Genes *and* DNA

FACT
There are around 20,000 genes in the human genetic code. Some appear just once and others repeat many times. About 99 percent of human genes are identical to chimpanzee genes. Even more amazingly, you share over 80 percent of your genes with a dog!

Unless you are an identical twin, your body is built according to a unique set of biological instructions, your own genetic code. These instructions, or genes, are present in all cells and are passed from parent to offspring.

▶ DNA *is made up of two chains, linked down the middle by molecules called bases, which always pair up the same way. The order of the bases spells out the genetic code.*

DNA FOR DUMMIES
Genes are made of a substance called Deoxyribonucleic Acid, or DNA. DNA is a very long molecule, found packed up tight in the chromosomes in the nucleus of every cell.

Cell membrane

Nucleus

DNA

Chromosomes

▲ CHROMOSOMES *Human beings normally have 46 chromosomes in every cell, except gametes (egg and sperm cells), which have just 23.*

▲ CELL *All living things are made of cells. When cells divide, the nucleus divides too, and the genetic message is duplicated in each new cell.*

IN THE GENES
When a person inherits two different genes from their parents, often one will dominate the other. For example, the gene for brown eyes overrides the one for blue eyes.

+   =

TIMELINE OF MEDICINE

1859	1865	1869	1952–1953
Charles Darwin's book *On the Origin of Species* outlined the importance of inherited traits in evolution.	**Gregor Mendel's** experiments on pea plants proved the existence of genes.	**Friedrich Miescher** extracted DNA from cells. He called it "nuclein."	The research done by **James Watson** and **Francis Crick** (left), and **Rosalind Franklin**, revealed the structure of **DN**

GENETIC CODE

A genome is the entire genetic code inside an organism. The first genetic code to be sequenced in full was that of a virus known as bacteriophage phi X174, in 1977. In 1995, the first bacterial genome was sequenced, and in 1990, scientists began to sequence the human genome. The project took 13 years to complete, with findings published in 2003. They found that the genes were padded out by sequences of "non-coding DNA," which had no obvious function. The human genome contains about three billion base pairs and codes.

▲ THE CHROMOSOMES *in this preparation have been treated to make a particular gene glow green.*

FACT FILE

■ Scientists can "cut and paste" genes from one species into another to create useful characteristics. The genetically altered organism is called "transgenic." Transgenic bacteria help produce useful drugs. Some people still use transgenic mice to research cures for many diseases.

▲ GLOW FOR IT *These mice were given a jellyfish gene to make them glow in the dark.*

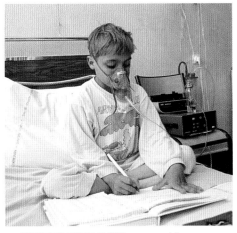

▲ CYSTIC FIBROSIS *is caused by a mutation in a gene controlling the production of sweat and mucus.*

Genetic diseases Some genes contain errors which cause them to malfunction. These faulty genes can cause diseases such as cystic fibrosis and sickle cell anaemia. Most disease genes are "recessive," like the gene for blue eyes, meaning the disease only develops if a child inherits a faulty copy from both parents.

GM crops Genes can be transferred into plants to create transgenic, or "genetically modified" (GM) crops. GM technology has been used to produce rice enriched with vitamins, sweet corn and cabbages, which produce their own insecticides, and soybeans that survive being treated with weed killers that kill all other plants.

▲ CHEMICAL CURE *GM crops have modified the use of synthetic (chemical) pesticides on fields and orchards, leading to a reduction in the use of insecticides but an increase in herbicide use.*

Cloning means using DNA from an organism to create an identical new individual, or clone. Some clones occur naturally—many plants and some simple animals reproduce by cloning, and identical twins are clones. Artificial cloning can be used to grow new organs for transplant patients.

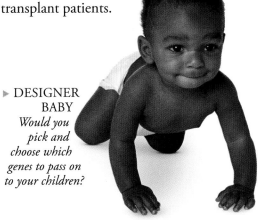

▶ DESIGNER BABY *Would you pick and choose which genes to pass on to your children?*

1961	1970	1990	1996	2003
Marshall Nirenberg deciphered the genetic code hidden in the order of the bases.	**Frederick Sanger** began sequencing DNA.	Doctors used **gene therapy** for the first time, treating a four-year-old girl suffering from an immune disorder.	The first experimentally cloned mammal, **Dolly the sheep**, was born.	The completed sequence of the **human genome** was published.

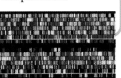

Forensic science

Forensic science helps the police fight crime. Most people think of murder investigations when they talk about forensics, but forensic scientists deal with a range of crimes. Some are computer specialists who trace "cybercriminals" on the internet, for example, while others are art experts who identify forgeries.

CRIME SCENE DO NOT ENTER CRIME SCENE

◄ CRIME SCENE
Forensic scientists seal a body inside a body bag. The corpse will be stored at a mortuary until the postmortem.

Postmortem After any suspicious death, a doctor called a pathologist will do a postmortem. This involves cutting open the body to find out the cause and time of death. If the corpse has been dead for a long time, the time of death can be established by studying the kinds of insects present.

CRIME SCENE

Crime scene investigators collect the evidence at a crime scene. They look for any clues that might secure a conviction, from bloodstains and body fluids to fibres and footprints. Crime scene investigators photograph all the evidence and then take it back to the crime lab for further analysis.

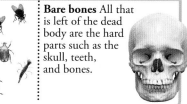

DEAD-BODY TIMELINE

3–36 hours	0+ hours	0–24 hours	50–365 days
Rigor mortis There is a chemical change in the muscles that makes a corpse stiffen up. This starts about three hours after death and lasts about 36 hours.	**Bacterial decay** Bacteria start to break down the body. In warm, moist conditions, the soft, fleshy parts rot very quickly.	**Insect invasion** Insects such as flies lay eggs inside the body. When the larvae hatch, they start to feed on the rotting remains.	**Bare bones** All that is left of the dead body are the hard parts such as the skull, teeth, and bones.

FINGERPRINT FEATURES

If you look at your fingertips, you will notice they are covered in tiny ridges. The ridges form distinct patterns of arches, loops, and whorls. No two people have been found to have the same prints (not even identical twins) so they can be used for identification.

Double loop | Whorl | Arch

DNA fingerprinting
Everyone has a unique DNA sequence (except for identical twins). Forensic scientists can turn a DNA sample into a fingerprint by breaking the DNA into small fragments and then making these spread through a sheet of gel to form a series of bands.

DO NOT ENTER CRIME SCENE DO NOT ENTER

Leaving prints
Criminals leave prints on everything they touch. Prints left in bloodstains show up clearly. Other visible marks can be left on soft materials such as soap. Latent prints are invisible ones made by skin oils. They show up when forensic scientists dust the crime scene.

Dusting brush

▶ DUSTING FOR PRINTS *A forensic scientist dusts a window to reveal a set of prints hidden on the glass.*

Digital data
Long gone are the days of using ink to record fingerprints on paper. Instead, the police use electronic scanners to record the prints digitally. The police store the prints on a database, which can then be used to match the prints found at crimes scenes. Another method is iris scanning, which looks at the colored tissue around the pupil.

▶ FINGER SCAN *A scanner records the pattern of arches, loops, and whorls that make up a fingerprint.*

▼ IRIS SCANS *The scanner records the features of the iris, which is unique to each person.*

RECONSTRUCTING THE FACE

Forensic scientists have studied skeletal remains. They can help forensic artists to build up a 3D image of the face from the skull. Facial reconstruction is extremely important. It has helped the police solve crimes that happened decades ago. It also reveals what people from ancient civilizations looked like.

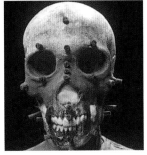

▲ DEPTH MARKERS
The artist makes a cast of the skull. Pegs act as depth markers for skin and muscles.

▲ FACE SCULPTURE
The artist uses a modeling tool to build up the muscle layers with modeling clay.

▲ SKIN DEEP *The artist adds a layer of clay to form the skin. The head is now fully reconstructed.*

Cybercrime
Crime involving computers is on the rise. The crimes often involve people stealing credit-card details and pretending to be someone else. Computer experts are helping the police to track down these cybercriminals.

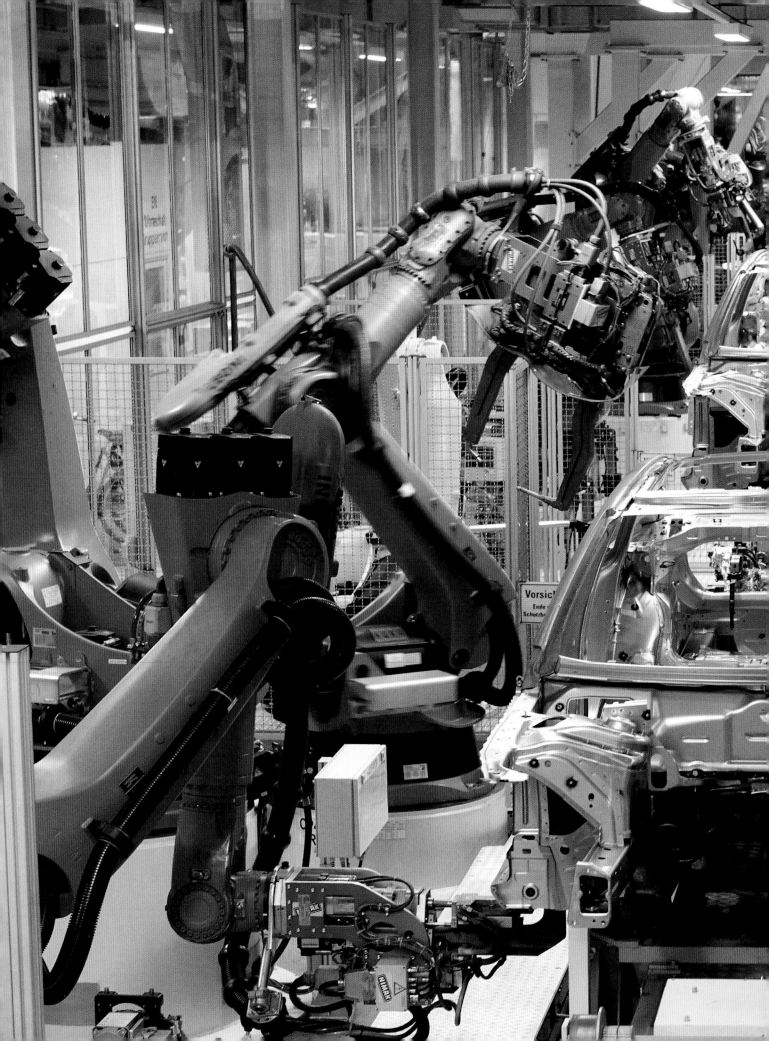

TECHNOLOGY

Technology solves practical problems to make our lives easier. It often uses science to find ways to improve things such as medicines or communications.

Inventions *and* discoveries

Since people began living in simple dwellings, inventions have been a part of technological development. From the first use of stone for tools to the worldwide dependence on computers, people are always finding something new.

▲ 3500 BCE
POTTER'S WHEEL
Originally potters had to mold pots with their bare hands. With the invention of the potter's wheel, pots were a lot easier to make.

▼ 3500 BCE
BRICK
People started making strong, waterproof bricks by baking them in a kiln instead of just letting the mud they were molded from dry in the sun.

▲ 3800 BCE
ROAD *Neolithic peoples crossed marshlands using a timber trackway, now called Sweet Track, in modern-day Somerset, UK. This is one of the oldest known roadways.*

▲ 6000 BCE
DRUM *Drums have been used for thousands of years. The remains of drums as old as 6000 BCE have been found by archaeologists.*

▲ c. 8500 BCE
WHEAT AND BARLEY *have been used to feed people for thousands of years. It is thought that it was first grown in the Middle East.*

---

1 MYA (MILLION YEARS AGO) ⊢————————————————⊣ **5000 BCE**

▲ 1 MYA
FIRE *Although fire has been used for more than a million years, it was only around 1 million years ago that hominins learnt how to control it fully.*

▲ 4000 BCE
SCALES
Early scales were beam balances. A straight length of metal or wood was held from its center, pans were hung from either end, and an object was weighed in one pan against weights in the other pan.

▼ 4000 BCE
MIRROR
Early mirrors were discs of polished bronze or copper. The first glass mirrors came nearly 4,000 years later.

▼ c. 3500 BCE
WHEEL *Without the invention of the wheel we wouldn't be able to do lots of things today. Early wheels were made from planks of wood and were used in Mesopotamia and the Balkans. They were most likely to have been developed by potters who desired to make completely rounded pots.*

▲ 10,000 BCE
WHISTLE *Archaeologists have found whistles dating from 10,000 BCE. The whistle may well have been among the first musical instruments.*

▲ 8000 BCE
CHISEL
About 10,000 years ago, people started to make stone chisels. The chisel gave the user more control when carving soft materials, such as wood.

▲ 5000 BCE
PLOW *Seeds grow better in soil that has been prepared by a plow. Early plows were pushed or pulled by people to prepare the ground.*

ΑΒΓΔΕΖΗΘ
ΙΚΛΜΝΞΟΠ
ΡΣΤΥΦΧΨΩ

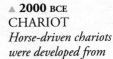

▼ 3000 BCE
RAMP
Around 3000 BCE, people started to use a mechanical aid called a ramp to help with building work. Heavy stone blocks were easier to pull up a ramp than to lift straight up.

▲ 2500 BCE
ARCH
The first arches were built in Mesopotamia (modern-day Iraq). The top of two walls were built until they met each other in the middle to form an arch.

▲ 2500 BCE
INK
Ink was originally made from soot and gum. It came as a dry block, which had to be mixed with water.

▲ 2000 BCE
CHARIOT
Horse-driven chariots were developed from oxcarts. Chariots were faster than carts as they only had two wheels and were much lighter.

▲ c. 900 BCE
ALPHABET WITH VOWELS AND CONSONANTS
The Greeks adapted the ancient Phoenician alphabet (with symbols for vowels) and made their own, which included symbols for vowels and consonants.

▼ 1500 BCE
SHADOW CLOCK
The ancient Egyptians were among the first to develop a clock. The Egyptian shadow clock had to be turned in the opposite direction halfway through the day. It had a straight scale to show hours of the day.

2500 BCE   **2000 BCE**

3200– 3000 BCE
DAM
The earliest known dam was constructed at Jawa in eastern Jordan. Built with slabs of basalt and with rock-filled reinforcements, it protected a walled settlement of around 2,000 people from floods.

▶ 3000 BCE
CANDLE
Candlesticks dating from at least 3000 bce have been found in Egypt and Crete. Candles are made by putting thin cords in liquid wax.

▲ 2500 BCE
WELDING
Welding was first used to join pieces of metal together to make jewelry.

▲ 2000 BCE
LOCK
First developed near Nineveh (in modern-day Iraq), this lock made from a piece of wood and pins was used by the ancient Egyptians. Most of the locks we use today are based on the concept of the original locks.

▲ 1700 BCE
RUNNING WATER
Minoans in Crete were the first to build drains and pipes so they could have running water in the palace of Knossos.

▼ 3000 BCE
COTTON
Cotton fabrics were made in the valley of the River Indus.

◀ 1000 BCE
MAGNET
According to a myth, magnets get their name from a place called Magnesia, which may have been located in Greece.

The golden age of invention and discovery came in the last two hundred years. New scientific theories helped people invent things that changed the world.

**▲ 1268
SPECTACLES**
English scientist Roger Bacon came up with the idea of using a magnifying glass as a reading aid. Around 1290, monks in Italy took it a step further by inventing spectacles.

**▼ 1565
PENCIL**
Conrad Gesner of Switzerland is credited with inventing the pencil but may only have been writing about an existing invention.

**▲ 1700s
INDUSTRIAL REVOLUTION**
Jobs moved from farms into factories, where new machines greatly increased production.

**▼ 1800
ELECTRICITY**
Working separately, the Italian scientists Luigi Galvani and Alessandro Volta invented the first device to give a continuous flow of electricity.

**▼ 1876
TELEPHONE**
Alexander Graham Bell holds the patent for the telephone. He was the first to make it successful, but there is evidence that others, such as Antonio Meucci, invented it first.

**◀ 1878–1879
LIGHT BULB**
Joseph Swan and Thomas Edison came up with the idea of the electric light bulb independently. No need for candles and gas lamps—life would be much easier for everyone.

**1500
CE**

**1800
CE**

**▼ 1455
PRINTING PRESS**
Johannes Gutenberg's invention allowed multiple copies of books to be printed, making them available for everyone to read.

**▲ 1608
TELESCOPE**
Hans Lippershey is generally credited with inventing the telescope, but Galileo was the first person to use it for astronomy.

Movable type using metal letters made printing quick and cheap.

**▲ 1783
HOT-AIR BALLOON**
The French Montgolfier brothers invented the first hot-air balloon that could carry people.

**▼ 1826
MATCHES**
John Walker dipped a wooden stick in a mixture of chemicals, and the first friction match came to light.

▼ 1868 TYPEWRITER
Christopher Sholes and partners patented the typewriter. The American company Remington and Sons took their invention into production in 1873.

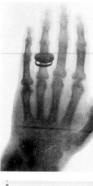

▲ 1895 X-RAY
Wilhelm Röntgen's discovery of X-rays earned him the first Nobel Prize for Physics in 1901.

◀ 1982
CD
The first compact discs hit stores in 1982. They were once a popular way of storing data in digital form.

▶ 2001
MP3 PLAYERS
Apple launched its first portable MP3 player, called the iPod. By 2003, MP3 players were becoming integrated with mobile phones.

▲ 1903
POWERED FLIGHT
The pioneers of powered flight were Orville and Wilbur Wright, who took to the skies in a plane known as the Wright Flyer. Orville's first historic flight over the sands of Kitty Hawk in North Carolina lasted only 12 seconds.

▼ 1973
CELL PHONE
The first cell phone was demonstrated. Available ten years later, the first commercial cell phone was about the same size as a brick. It was developed and launched in Japan.

▲ 1989 WWW
The World Wide Web (WWW) was developed by British computer scientist Tim Berners-Lee. This collection of linked documents accessible by computer was made available to the public in 1991.

▼ 2010 IPAD
The Apple iPad has helped make tablets popular. Three years before, Apple had led the way with its revolutionary iPhone.

▲ 1970s
PERSONAL COMPUTERS
Early home computers such as this one had tiny memories. This one could only store about 1,000 words, or 10 million times less data than a modern computer.

1959
COMPUTER CODING
Grace Hopper developed COBOL, the first major programming (coding) language.

1900
CE

2000
CE

Penicillin mold

▼ 1957
FIRST SPACE SATELLITE
The Soviet Union launched the first artificial satellite, Sputnik 1, on October 4. Within a month, they had launched a dog called Laika into space aboard Sputnik 2.

▲ 2019
QUANTUM COMPUTER
Google built a super-fast atomic computer that could solve problems well beyond the reach of today's ordinary computers.

▲ 1928
ANTIBIOTICS
Sir Alexander Fleming discovered penicillin but left it to others to turn it into a practical treatment that has saved millions of lives.

▲ 1982
ARTIFICIAL HEART IN A HUMAN
American doctor Robert Jarvik developed an artificial heart from plastic and Velcro that pumped blood using compressed air.

Q System One, a quantum computer built by IBM.

◀ 1938
BALLPOINT PEN
A Hungarian named László Bíró came up with a design for the ballpoint pen, but World War II delayed production until 1943.

1965
KEVLAR
American chemist Stephanie Kwolek invented Kevlar, a material five times stronger than steel. Kevlar is used to make tires, fireproof clothing, bulletproof vests, and spacesuits.

FAST FACTS

■ TV images were first sent across the Atlantic Ocean between London and Hartsdale, New York, in 1928, by Scottish engineer John Logie Baird.

■ In 1978, Japanese engineers at Sony made recorded music truly portable when they developed the Sony Walkman.

■ Black American doctor Patricia Bath invented a laser device for treating an eye condition called a cataract. This helped millions see better.

SLICE OF SURGERY

Surgeons use all kinds of modern materials and technology. Remote-controlled robots even allow doctors in one place to carry out routine surgical operations on patients in another country.

▲ THROUGH THE KEYHOLE
Surgeons use an endoscope to look inside a patient's body.

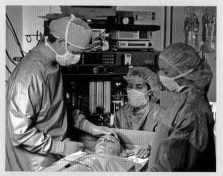

▲ PLASTIC FANTASTIC *Skin grafting is one of the most common procedures in plastic surgery.*

▲ HEART SURGERY *is now routine thanks to advances in technology.*

Modern medicine

Medicine has come a long way since the Greek philosopher Hippocrates laid the foundations for modern medicine nearly 2,500 years ago. Advances in all areas of medicine are now helping us live longer, healthier, and happier lives.

MEDICINE IN MINIATURE

Making things smaller allows doctors to see and do more. In the future, nanotechnology could revolutionize medicine with developments such as nanorobots.

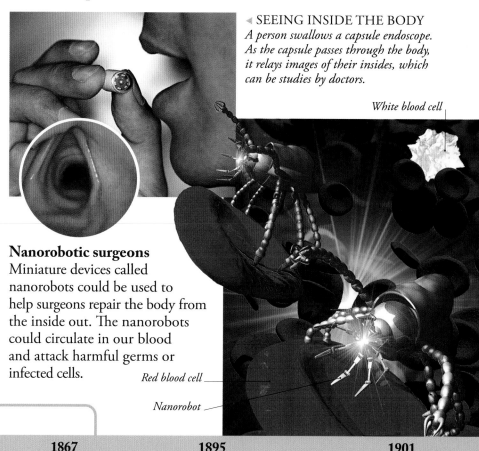

◀ SEEING INSIDE THE BODY
A person swallows a capsule endoscope. As the capsule passes through the body, it relays images of their insides, which can be studies by doctors.

White blood cell

Nanorobotic surgeons
Miniature devices called nanorobots could be used to help surgeons repair the body from the inside out. The nanorobots could circulate in our blood and attack harmful germs or infected cells.

Red blood cell

Nanorobot

MEDICINE THROUGH TIME

6,500 BCE	1590 CE	1867	1895	1901
Trepanation was a form of primitive surgery that involved drilling holes in the skull to release "evil spirits."	Dutch father and son Hans and Zacharius Jannsen invented the first microscope, opening up the invisible world of the cell.	Sterilization practices were pioneered by Joseph Lister.	X-rays were discovered by Wilhelm Röntgen and inspired chemist Marie Curie's work on radioactivity. X-rays are used to look inside the body without the need for invasive surgery.	Karl Landsteiner discovered the ABO human blood group system.

STEM CELLS

It is now possible to grow new tissues and organs from stem cells rather than wait for transplants. Stem cells are primitive cells that can divide and produce any type of cell in the body. The body will not reject tissues and organs grown from stem cells because they come from the patient's own body.

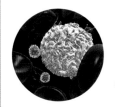

◄ STEM CELL
Doctors use stem cells taken from the body.

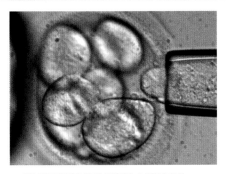

▲ EMBRYONIC STEM CELLS
In the laboratory, scientists isolate the stem cells from a developing embryo.

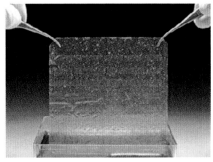

▲ SKIN FROM STEM CELLS
These stem cells are used to generate new skin for use in transplant surgery.

BODY REBUILDING

When the body cannot repair itself, doctors use technology to rebuild it. Advances include miniature retinal implants that can restore sight and prosthetic limbs under direct control of the brain.

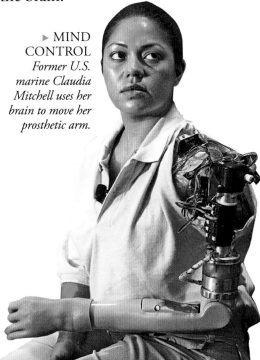

► MIND CONTROL
Former U.S. marine Claudia Mitchell uses her brain to move her prosthetic arm.

▲ SPRINT CHAMP
Blake Leeper, Team USA, is a sprinting champion with spring-loaded legs.

WHO'S WHO?

■ **Hippocrates** (c. 460–c. 375 BCE) suggested that disease has natural causes rather than being a punishment from the gods. More than 500 years later, a female Greek doctor named Metrodora wrote a book called *On the Diseases and Cures of Women.*

■ **William Harvey** (1578–1657) studied the circulatory system and showed how the heart pumps blood around the body.

■ **Elizabeth Blackwell** (1821–1910) became the first woman to graduate with a medical degree from Geneva College in New York in 1849.

■ **Marie Curie** (1867–1934) discovered radium in 1898, which lead to important treatments for cancer.

■ **Sir Alexander Fleming** (1881–1955) discovered penicillin.

■ **Charles Drew** (1904–1950), a Black American doctor, invented the blood bank in 1940.

■ **Christiaan Barnard** (1922–2001), a South African surgeon, performed the first successful heart transplant in 1967.

■ **Tu Youyou** (1930–), a Chinese chemist, discovered a treatment for malaria.

950	1957	1985	1996	2007	2016
urgeons from Chicago erformed the first successful rgan transplant—giving a idney to a woman named uth Tucker.	The first practical transistorized pacemaker was made by Earl Bakken.	For the first time, surgeons used a robotic assistant called PUMA 560 to help take a tissue sample from the brain.	Scientists cloned the first mammal—Dolly the Sheep (died 2003).	Doctors made huge strides in stem cell research.	U.S. scientists created body parts using 3-D printing.

Human ear

Electric cars

Most cars use gasoline, made from oil, which causes pollution and adds to global warming. Oil supplies are running out, too. That's why car designers are turning to electric motors, which can use energy from cleaner sources.

▲ *Open the hood of an electric car, and you won't find a gas engine. Instead, there's an electric motor (shown below in a cutaway).*

HONDA CLARITY FUEL CELL

Although this might look like an ordinary car, it's powered in what could be a much cleaner way. In a normal car, the engine burns gas, releases energy, and makes pollution. But in this car, the fuel tank is replaced by a kind of battery called a hydrogen fuel cell. This takes hydrogen from a tank and oxygen from the air, causes them to react, and produces electricity. The only waste product is steam, so if the hydrogen comes from a clean source, there is no pollution at all.

Copper coils of motor

Electric motor

Gears make the car's wheels turn at the right speed

Drive shaft turns axles

Axle drives left wheel

Stationary part of motor

Axle drives right wheel

Turning part of motor

HYDROGEN CAR

1 The **hydrogen tank** stores enough fuel to power the car for up to 400 miles (650 km).
2 Hydrogen from the tank and oxygen from the air chemically react inside the **fuel cell** to make electricity.
3 The **rechargeable battery** stores energy released when the car brakes and helps the fuel cell power the car.
4 The **power drive unit** works like a transmission. It makes electricity flow from the battery to the motor.
5 The **electric motor** is light and compact and turns the front wheels to drive the car along.

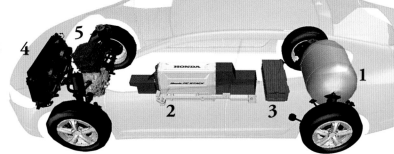

ElectraMeccanica Solo EV
Three-wheeled, one-person car

- **Top speed** 80 mph (129 kmph)
- **Range** 100 miles (161 km)
- **Made in** China/USA

Cars often carry just one person, so why not have one-person cars? This one looks like a car from the front and a motorbike from the back. It's small and easy to park but still has lots of cargo space.

Microcab
Useful for short journeys

- **Top speed** 40 mph (64 kmph)
- **Range** 50–100 miles (80–160 km)
- **Made in** UK

Fuel cell cars are being used as taxis in Birmingham, England. They are incredibly light and can travel for 100 miles (160 km) before they need to stop and refuel.

NIO EP9
High-speed record breaker

- **Top speed** 195 mph (313 kmph)
- **Range** 265 miles (426.5 km)
- **Made in** China

This speedster has broken lap records at famous race circuits. It features four electric motors, one for each wheel, and can race from 0 to 62 mph (0–100 kmph) in just 2.7 seconds and to 124 mph (200 kmph) in 7.1 seconds.

Venturi Astrolab
High-performance car powered by sunlight

- **Top speed** 75 mph (120 kmph)
- **Range** 68 miles (110 km) on battery
- **Made in** France

This solar car has no engine or fuel cell. Instead, it's covered in solar panels with lenses on top. These capture sunlight, turn it into electricity, and store it in batteries.

FACT

Few electric cars are 100 percent eco-friendly, because their batteries have to be charged using electricity. Most electricity still comes from power stations burning fossil fuels. These cause pollution and add to global warming.

Tesla Model X
State of the art seven-seater

- **Top speed** 155 mph (248 kmph)
- **Range** 348 miles (560 km)
- **Made in** USA

This 16½ ft (5 m) long sports utility vehicle (SUV) holds seven people in three rows of seating. Falcon-wing doors lift up and over the car roof to allow passengers in and out of the car.

Falcon-wing doors

► SAFETY FEATURES
The front storage area will crumple to absorb impact in a collision.

Anti-collision safety sensors

TESLA MODEL X

- 100 percent electric.
- Powered by 8,256 battery cells.
- Supercharger can recharge batteries from 0 to 50 percent in 15 minutes.
- Burns no gasoline or oil.
- Can accelerate from 0 to 60 mph (0–96 kmph) in just 3.8 seconds.

Through a lens

Cameras are everywhere. Cell phones often include one, and they are used in security systems, space exploration, medical equipment, and speed cameras. Cameras are devices that capture still or moving images.

▶ MEMORY CARDS *can store thousands of digital images.*

GOING DIGITAL

Digital cameras store pictures in digital (number) form on a memory card. Their lenses focus the image onto an electronic sensor (CCD or CMOS) that converts the light into electrical charges. The charges are measured to give digital values. Computer chips process the data to construct the image, which is then stored on a memory card.

The digital screen lets the user check and review images.

A control dial allows the photographer to have control over settings.

An built-in flash provides light when it is too dark to take a photo.

A circuit board processes information from the sensor into a digital format.

Autofocus system makes sure an image is clear.

THE DIGITAL SENSOR

A digital camera requires a sensor in order to work. A shutter allows light to pass through the lens to a sensor. The sensor is a grid of millions of pixels.

Each pixel measures the amount of light that hits it through a green, blue, or red filter.

The measurements are changed into digital information, which is used to make the final digital image.

TIMELINE OF CAMERAS

1500s–1800s
Artists used more developed camera obscuras to trace images of scenes onto paper. The invention of the camera obscura led to the development of modern-day cameras.

1840s
Simple photographic cameras were in use by the 1840s and were little more than a wooden box with a hole cut to hold a lens. Images were recorded on a glass or metal plate.

1880s
Photographic film was made in the 1880s. It was made from a strip of plastic coated with crystals of a silver compound. Cameras were developed to include an automatic shutter mechanism allowing the right amount of light in the lens.

1920s
Small cameras with interchangeable lenses were developed in the 1920s. This allowed photographers to take a wider range of photographs.

Movie cameras are similar to still-image cameras except that they take pictures continually. Each separate picture ("frame") captures a slightly different image so that when the frames are run back through a projector, you get the illusion of continuous movement. Movie cameras can also record sound at the same time.

Professional studio cameras are used in television. They split the light into red, green, and blue and detect each color separately, which gives a better quality image. The pictures are sent to a separate recorder. Most studio cameras are mounted on special trolleys, but they can also be attached to moving vehicles.

Video cameras
The first video cameras used tape to record and store images. Now, they use optical discs or memory cards. Over the years, they have become smaller and lighter and can be carried in one hand or even fitted to helmets to take action video footage.

Helmet-mounted GoPro HERO5

▼ INSTANT PRINTS
Polaroid cameras take pictures that develop themselves, producing a photo a minute or so after it has been taken.

TECHNOLOGY

Lenses *can be changed over to obtain a required effect. Wide angle lenses, as the name suggests, are used to take wide shots.*

Filters *control the light coming through the lens.*

FACT
The first CCTV (closed-circuit television) camera was installed in the UK in 1949. It was put in Guy's Hospital, London. There are roughly one billion surveillance cameras in use worldwide.

Light *needs to travel through the lens in order to capture an image.*

1970s
Cameras were made with automatic exposure and electronic autofocus in the 1970s.

1990s
The technology for digital cameras was invented in the 1970s, and it was developed in the 1980s, but it wasn't until the 1990s that digital cameras came into popular use.

2010s
Smartphones were fitted with tiny but powerful digital cameras, enabling users to take high-resolution pictures easily. These are often shared on social media.

Global village

Technology is helping to bring our planet together. People on the other side of the world may live up to 12,500 miles (20,000 km) away, but you can email or phone them in seconds. Billions of computers, smartphones, and other devices are now connected by a giant network called the Internet.

INTERNET

The Internet is a network of computer systems all using the same rules to link the world's computers. In theory, every computer in the world can be indirectly connected to every other one. There is no central control system for the Internet. This means it can survive major failures.

ELECTRONIC MAIL

Electronic mail (email) is a way of sending written messages between computers. Invented in 1971, it has now become one of the world's favorite forms of communication—especially for work. No one really knows, but it's thought somewhere between 100 and 500 billion emails are sent worldwide each day.

FACT

The World Wide Web is like a huge library you can use over the Internet. It has billions of websites containing well over 30 billion web pages, which may feature images, pieces of music, and sound files.

CELL PHONES

The bases of ordinary phones are attached in place because they have to be connected with wires. Cell phones can go anywhere because they send signals with radio waves. Smartphones are cell phone computers that allow people to make voice calls and also run programs called apps, take photos and videos, view websites, and send emails.

NEWS

When letters were the fastest way to communicate, it could take months for news to go round the world. Now, with satellite and Internet technology, you can watch events happening live. Using a website, you can even set up your own journal called a blog.

BRINGING PEOPLE TOGETHER

The Internet has created new ways for people to connect. Social networking sites, such as TikTok, Instagram, YouTube, Twitter, and Facebook, allow people to make friends and share interests. Facebook has around 2 billion members who use it every day. If it were a country, it would be the biggest on Earth.

Is this real?

Virtual reality (VR) uses computers to create the illusion of being in a completely different environment. VR stimulates the senses with artificial sights and sounds, tricking the brain into thinking the experience is real.

FACT
Augmented reality (AR) is a way of adding computer-generated information to real-world images. One popular example of AR involves pointing your phone camera at famous buildings to see useful facts and figures about them.

◄ INTERAC
*A woman wea
an Oculus Rift
headset to play
VR games and
interact with
virtual worlds.*

 VR GAMES
Virtual reality re-creates the sensation of snowboarding.

HAVING FUN WITH VR

In most VR systems, headsets or glasses project the image of the virtual world in front of the user's eyes. People interact with the virtual world using devices such as joysticks, tracking balls, control wands, voice-recognition software, data gloves, and treadmills.

VIRTUSPHERE

The "VirtuSphere" is a ball that moves on rollers, so the user can walk on an unlimited amount of space. The user wears a wireless headset to track movement and create a picture of the virtual world.

INDUSTRIAL DESIGN

Architects, manufacturers, and designers use VR to test new products or building designs. Testing in the virtual world eliminates any problems before actual work is carried out.

◄ USING VR *The VirtuSphere has many uses, ranging from military training to virtual tours of museums.*

► WALK IN THE PARK
An architect uses VR to look at a proposed design for a new park.

TRAINING DOCTORS AND SOLDIERS

The military uses virtual reality to simulate dangerous battle scenes without putting the lives of any soldiers at risk. And in hospitals, trainee surgeons practice virtual surgery on computer screens without harming live patients.

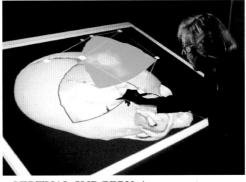

▲ VIRTUAL SURGERY *A surgeon views a VR image of a patient's head prior to surgery.*

▲ WAR GAMES *A soldier fights on a virtual battlefield to train for real combat.*

FLIGHT SIMULATION

Pilots train in flight simulators—one of the earliest forms of virtual reality. The pilot sits inside a life-size replica of a cockpit and views computer-generated images of the outside world. The controls of the simulator respond in the same way as those of a real aircraft.

◀ FLIGHT SIMULATOR
Using VR, a pilot can learn to fly without putting lives in danger.

SPACE EXPLORATION

The space agency NASA used virtual reality to help with the design of its Mars rover vehicles before it sent them to the surface of Mars. Astronauts also use VR to prepare for space missions.

◀ MARS ROVER *An engineer uses virtual reality to help understand the problems of navigation on the rocky surface of the Red Planet.*

Robotics

Robots are machines that can do the sort of jobs that people do but never get tired or bored. Some robots work in dangerous places. Others have artificial intelligence, making them clever enough to solve problems and learn from experience.

ROBOTIC SURGERY

Surgeons use robots to do operations that would be too difficult for human control. They study the operation site on a TV screen and guide the robot by remote control.

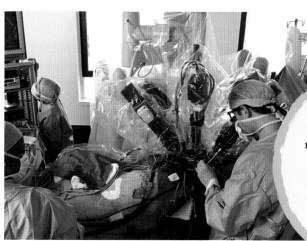

◄ DA VINCI *is a surgical robot used to perform complex surgical procedures.*

FACT

In 2001, surgeons used robotic surgery to remove a patient's gallbladder. The surgeons were based in the U.S., but the robot and patient were in France.

FACIAL EXPRESSIONS

Engineers at the Massachusetts Institute of Technology developed a robot called Kismet. The robot copies human expressions by moving parts of its "face" and can learn by talking and interacting with people.

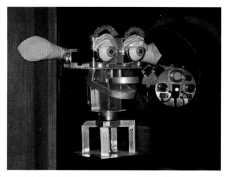

▲ HAPPY *Kismet can simulate human emotions, such as happiness, by copying the smiles of people it talks to.*

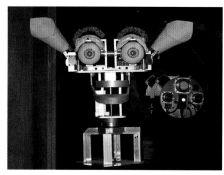

▲ SURPRISE *The robot can learn from experience but will appear "surprised" in unusual situations.*

Space exploration

■ **Name** Perseverance
■ **Cost** $2.75 billion

In 2021, NASA's mobile robot, *Perseverance*, reached Mars, 348 million miles (560 million km) away. The robot rover has begun studying the Martian soil for signs of ancient life.

Spy plane

■ **Name** MQ-1 Predator Drone
■ **Cost** $20 million for four (2009)

The Predator Drone is an unpiloted aerial vehicle used for surveillance. It is controlled, via a satellite link, by a pilot on the ground and is equipped with two Hellfire missiles.

Bomb disposal

■ **Name** Flir PackBot
■ **Cost** $100,000–$200,000

This portable robotic bomb disposal unit is equipped with a color camera and a telescopic arm and pincer to disarm explosive devices, such as land mines, without risking lives.

UNDERWATER ROBOTS

Robots can be built to explore the ocean depths to seek out shipwrecks, recover lost items, help lay underwater cables, and monitor marine life. Most underwater robots are shaped like small torpedoes or submarines but OceanOne looks like a human diver. Eight small thrusters drive it through the water, the robot's stereo cameras give it 3-D vision, while grippers on each of its arms can adjust how much force they use to handle objects the robot finds underwater.

Industrial robots

- **First used** 1960s
- **Cost** Varies according to use

Industrial robots such as those used in car assembly lines are computer-controlled machines that do the same jobs over and over again. They are fast and accurate and do not get tired like human workers do.

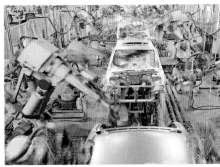

Personal robots

- **Name** Pepper
- **Cost** $1,800

Pepper was designed as a social robot. It listens to voice commands and questions using its four microphones and can detect if someone is happy, sad, or angry using its 3-D camera system. It can work as an assistant.

▲ ROBOT VACUUM CLEANER
The Roomba robotic vacuum cleaner senses objects and avoids them. More than 30 million Roomba robots have been sold so far.

267

Nanotechnology

The word *nanotechnology* describes the development of devices on the scale of atoms. Scientists hope to use this new technology to produce some amazing inventions, from nanorobots used in surgery to nanomaterials that could take people to the moon.

This nanocar is the size of a single molecule and is powered by electrons. It was designed by Bernard Feringa, one of three scientists who jointly won the 2016 Nobel Prize for Chemistry for their work in creating nanomachines.

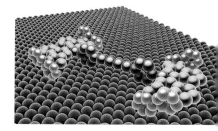

WHAT'S IN A NAME?

The word *nano* means one-billionth. So there are one billion nanometers in 3 ft (1 m). Nanotechnology is the study of devices that are billionths of a meter in size. To give you an idea of exactly how small that is, one nanometer would be 100,000 times smaller than the width of a human hair.

▶ ROTATING PARTS
Individual carbon and hydrogen atoms arranged in a circle could form the bearings for rotating parts in a nanomachine.

FACT FILE

■ By weight, carbon nanotubes are more expensive than diamond or gold.

■ In the future, nanotechnology may be used to assemble individual molecules into the parts for electronic devices such as smartphones and tablets.

■ Other electronic devices using nanosized parts include flexible digital screens and sensors that may detect chemicals in the air.

■ Scientists hope to build nanosensors to weigh molecules as small and as light as a strand of deoxyribonucleic acid (DNA).

■ Nanotechnology is being used to make "smart drugs" that target individual cancer cells and kill specific germs.

Carbon nanotube

Nanomaterials Scientists are getting very excited about structures called carbon nanotubes. These tiny tubes of carbon atoms are stronger than diamond and extremely long compared with their width. They are better conductors of electricity than metal, which makes them ideal for future electronics.

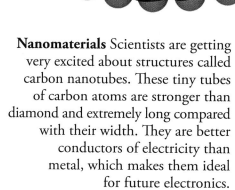

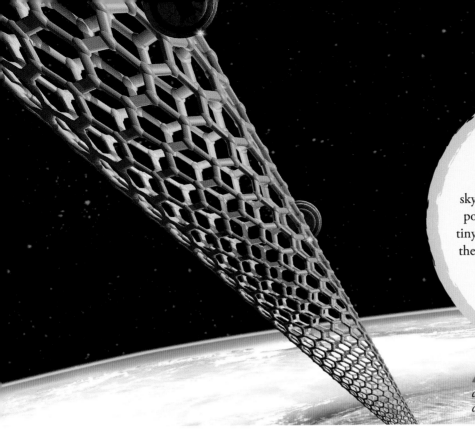

FACT
Scientists are looking at the possibility of using **strong nanomaterials** to build very tall skyscrapers. Carbon nanotubes are one possibility. The carbon atoms in these tiny tubes form hexagon shapes, making them extremely strong and lightweight. Engineers could use the carbon nanotubes as the supporting structures for the skyscrapers.

▲ ONE IDEA *that's out of this world is to use carbon nanotubes to build a space elevator that could transport people on Earth to the moon.*

NANOTECHNOLOGY IN ACTION

Scientists have already made tiny electric motors, gears, and springs that are just a few hundred nanometers across. In the future, they hope to connect these miniature parts to make nanomachines and nanorobots. These devices could be used to help surgeons repair the human body from the inside or they could circulate in our blood and attack harmful germs.

▶ A ROBOT FLY *is similar in size to a real fly, but the electronic components inside the robot fly are nanometers across.*

Common fly **Robotic fly**

Robotic ants Scientists are using micro-robotic ants to study the behavior of real ants. Nanotechnology helps in the manufacture of the tiny electronic circuits that control the movement of the robots.

Everyday nanotechnology While the future uses of nanotechnology may lie with hi-tech industries, such as electronics and robotics, this emerging technology has already found uses in many everyday items, ranging from clothing and paints to cosmetics and health-care products.

◀ NANOPARTICLES *in sunscreen ensure even coverage and do not leave white marks on the skin.*

◀ A WATER-REPELLENT *fabric is covered with a layer of nanoparticles. The water forms a near-perfect sphere as it touches the waterproof layer and rolls away from the fabric. The droplets collect dirt as they roll over the surface, and so they clean the fabric, too.*

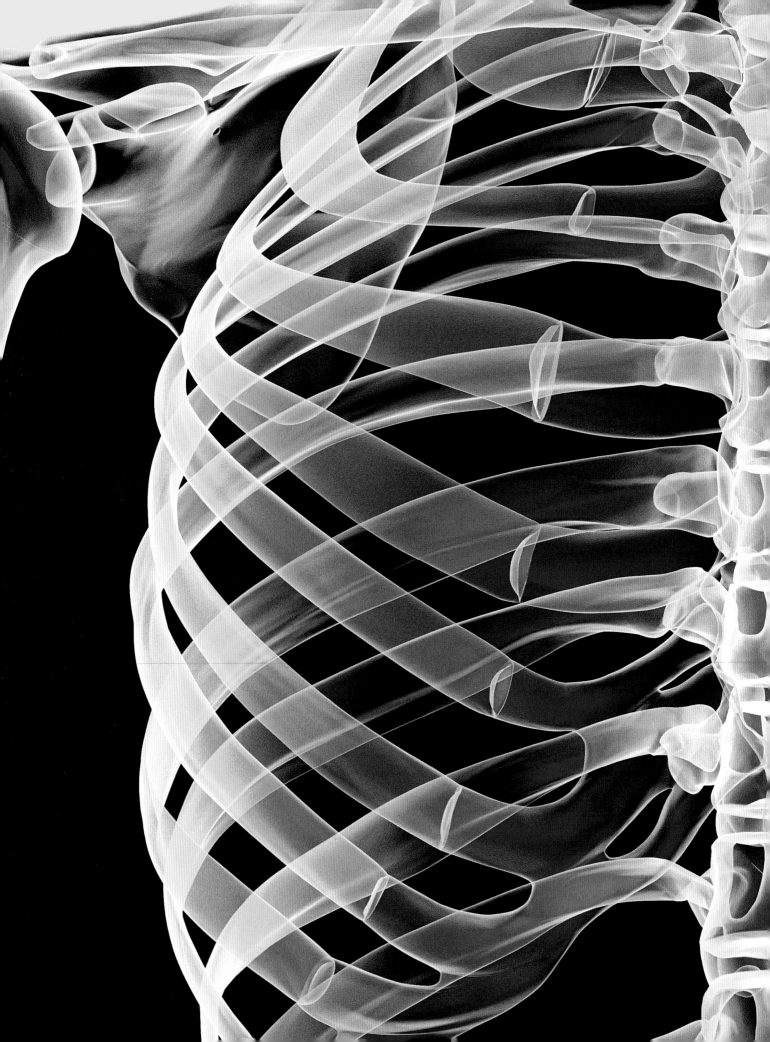

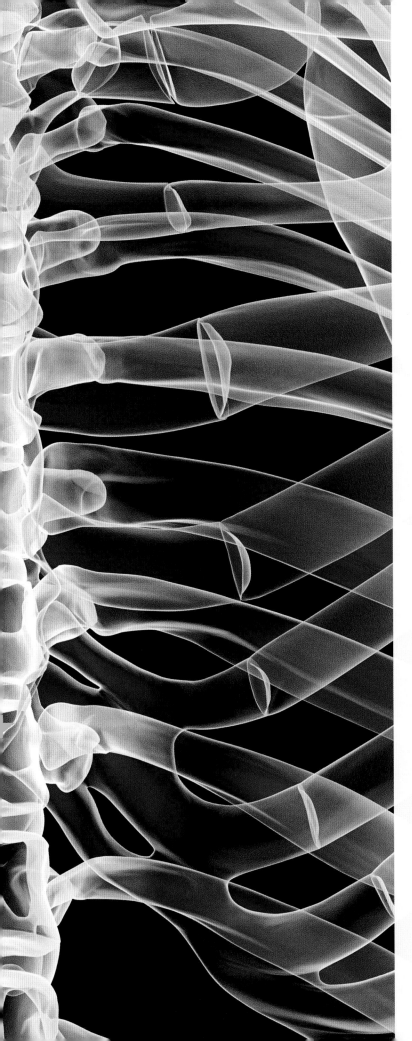

THE HUMAN BODY

The human body is an amazing machine.
Humans are mammals who breathe air and
eat plants and animals to nourish their bodies
and provide energy.

Your body

Nearly 8 billion human beings share planet Earth. Each is unique. But we all share certain characteristics—notably, our basic body systems, from our circulatory to our respiratory system. Body systems are made up of groups of tissues and organs that work together.

The nervous system is composed of the brain, the spinal cord, nerves, and sense organs. This is what controls everything the body does, much of it automatically.

The respiratory tract draws air into the lungs, extracts oxygen required for life, then expels waste carbon dioxide. The system also enables people to speak.

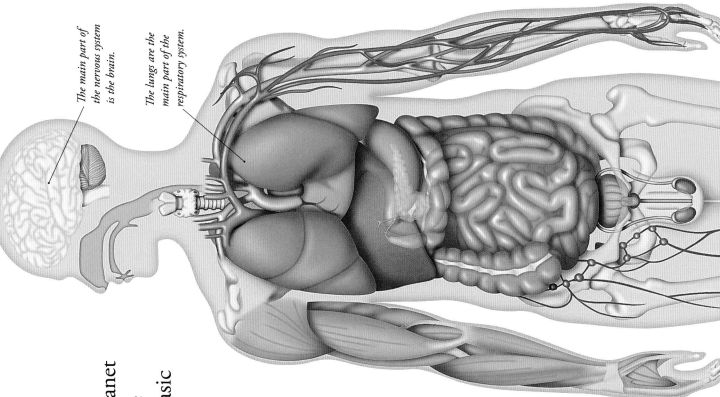

The main part of the nervous system is the brain.

The lungs are the main part of the respiratory system.

SKIN, HAIR, AND NAILS

Our skin, hair, and nails form a protective covering and together form a body system called the integumentary system. Your hair and nails grow through your skin, which is the body's largest organ. Dead skin cells are constantly shed from the surface of the skin.

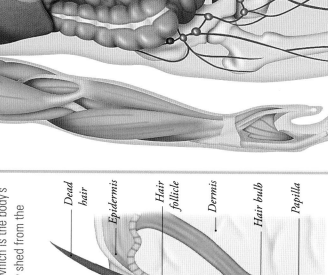

Dead hair
Epidermis
Hair follicle
Dermis
Hair bulb
Papilla

FAST FACTS

■ Human hair will grow between ¼ in (6 mm) and ⅓ in (8 mm) every four weeks.

■ On average, a person sheds about 1 lb (0.5 kg) of dead skin cells each year.

■ An adult human's skin weighs approximately 11 lb (5 kg).

■ Skin is waterproof.

■ Fingernails grow over two times faster than toenails.

The skeletal system is the moveable skeleton that provides a frame for your body and protects your internal organs. An adult has 206 bones.

There are about 10 body systems, but it's difficult to state an exact figure, as the muscular system and skeletal system are sometimes combined and referred to as one system.

Skin covers your body. It contains hair follicles, nerve endings, sweat glands, and tiny blood vessels called capillaries.

Each of the body's systems has its own job to do. If all are functioning properly, they will work together to ensure the body's overall health.

The digestive system processes the food you eat, taking out the nutrients your tissues need and getting rid of the waste. It is basically a long tube.

The heart is at the center of the circulatory system.

The cardiovascular or circulatory system pumps blood around your body. Blood transports oxygen and other vital substances to your organs and tissues and then removes waste products.

The muscular system is made up of muscles attached to bones by tendons, smooth muscles in your organs, and heart muscle. Muscles need a regular blood supply to bring them the oxygen and energy they require to work efficiently.

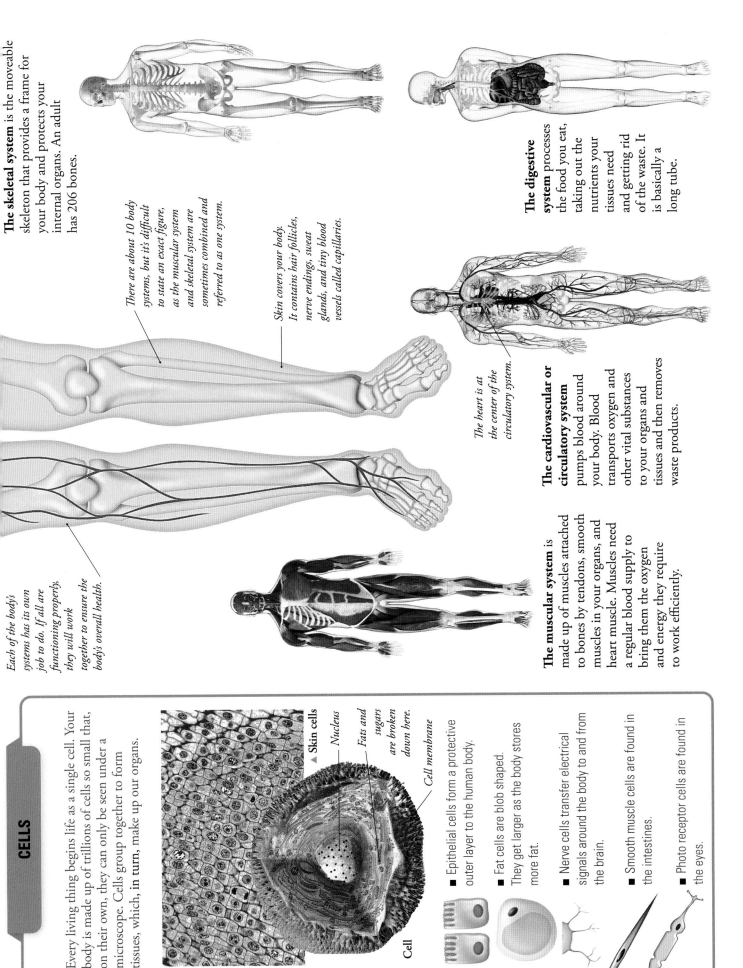

CELLS

Every living thing begins life as a single cell. Your body is made up of trillions of cells so small that, on their own, they can only be seen under a microscope. Cells group together to form tissues, which, in turn, make up our organs.

▲ **Skin cells**

Nucleus

Fats and sugars are broken down here.

Cell membrane

Cell

- Epithelial cells form a protective outer layer to the human body.

- Fat cells are blob shaped. They get larger as the body stores more fat.

- Nerve cells transfer electrical signals around the body to and from the brain.

- Smooth muscle cells are found in the intestines.

- Photo receptor cells are found in the eyes.

Bones

Your bones form a framework for your body called a skeleton. If you did not have a skeleton, your body would flop all over the place. Bones also protect your soft internal organs (such as your heart) and work with muscles to make you move.

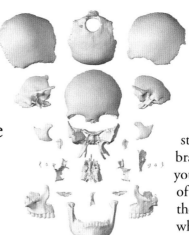

Pieces of the skull

Your skull is made up not of one bone but of a large number of bones. The pieces of the upper skull lock together to form an incredibly strong casing for your brain, while 14 bones form your facial bones. The shape of your facial bones and their muscles determines what you look like.

FAST FACTS

- There are 206 bones in the human body.
- Compared to a steel bar of the same weight, bone is six times stronger.
- Your largest bone is your femur. Your smallest bone is the stirrup bone, which is in your ear. It's no larger than a grain of rice.
- About eighty bones make up the human skull, backbone, and ribs.
- You need calcium in your diet to make your bones hard.
- You have the same number of neck bones as a giraffe: seven.
- A baby's skeleton is largely formed of cartilage (the stuff that makes your nose bendy).
- The thigh bone (femur) is the longest bone in your body. It is about a quarter of your height.
- More than a quarter of your bones are in your hands.

▼ INSIDE A JOINT
The ends of your bones (in blue below) are covered by smooth cartilage and separated by fluid, so the bones easily slide over each other.

The kneecap (patella) protects the front of the knee.

The thigh bone (femur) is the largest bone in the body.

The pelvic (hip) girdle supports abdominal organs and anchors the legs.

An inner layer of spongy bone is light in weight but also strong.

Arteries (red) supply nutrients and oxygen to the bone's cells.

Blood cells are made in the bone marrow.

The heel (calcaneus) is a short bone.

Inside a bone

Bones are made up of layers, with hard, compact bone on the outside and spongy bone beneath. The spaces in some bones are filled with jellylike bone marrow. Bone marrow stores fat and also produces new blood cells.

BONES AND JOINTS

Bones are living tissue that contain blood vessels, nerves, and cells. They are strong but light, and if they get broken, they can heal themselves. You can bend and move your body because you have lots of joints. These are where two bones meet and move over each other.

Ulna

Radius

Upper arm bone (humerus)

Breastbone (sternum)

Ribs help you breathe. They also protect the heart and lungs.

Collar bone (clavicle)

Shoulder blade (scapula)

Spine or backbone (vertebral column) is the body's central support.

FACT

There are four main types of bone: long (such as the thigh bones), short (such as the heel bones), flat (shoulder bones), and irregular (such as your vertebrae). There are also small, round bones with a funny name: sesamoid (such as the kneecap).

X-RAYS

If you have a broken bone, an X-ray allows your doctor to see what is happening beneath the skin.

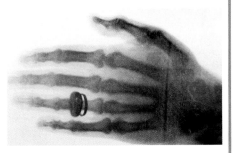

THE FIRST X-RAY *was taken in 1895 by German physicist Wilhelm Röntgen. He took an X-ray of his wife's hand that clearly showed the shadows of the bones and the lighter shadowing caused by the soft tissues.*

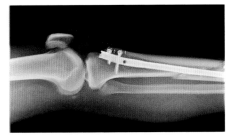

FIXING A BONE *A bone can heal itself if broken, but after an especially bad break, a surgeon may put a metal plate along the bone to hold it rigid while it heals. A fracture can take up to eight weeks to heal.*

TYPES OF JOINT

Some joints (such as your elbows) allow you to bend in one direction. Others (such as your shoulders) allow circular movement.
■ Saddle joints are found at the base of your thumbs.
■ Ball-and-socket joints are found in your shoulder.

■ Hinge joints are found in your knees.
■ There's a pivot joint at the top of your spine.
■ Gliding joints are found in the ankles and wrists.

| Saddle joint | Ball-and-socket joint | Hinge joint | Pivot joint | Gliding or plane joint |

Mighty muscles

Muscles are tissues that move parts of the body by contracting, or getting shorter. You have around 650 skeletal muscles layered over your skeleton, and these make up about half of your weight. They are attached to bones by stringy tendons.

TYPES OF MUSCLE

There are three types of muscle: skeletal muscles move bones when you want them to. Most muscle is skeletal muscle. Cardiac muscle keeps the heart beating. Smooth muscle is found inside hollow organs, such as the digestive tract. You can't control the actions of smooth muscle—they are automatic.

HOW MUSCLES WORK

Skeletal muscles get shorter and fatter when working—they stretch when relaxed. They work because your brain tells them to. If you want to reach out to grab something, your brain tells your arm muscles to work. The muscles shorten, pulling the arm bones. Muscles work in pairs, because they work by pulling. So in your arm, your biceps works to bend your arm and your triceps straightens it.

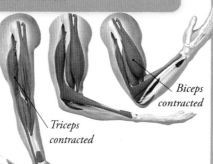

Biceps contracted

Triceps contracted

This large, powerful muscle, the gluteus maximus, straightens the hip when you walk, run, stand up, or climb a hill.

Muscles cover the skeleton and give the body its shape.

The extensor digitorum longus straightens your toes and helps lift the foot up when you walk.

The calf muscle (gastrocnemius) bends your foot downward when you point your toes.

FACT

Muscles need oxygen to make energy. If starved of oxygen, perhaps during a burst of activity, they produce energy without it, and a waste product called lactic acid builds up in the muscle cells. This can cause painful muscle cramps.

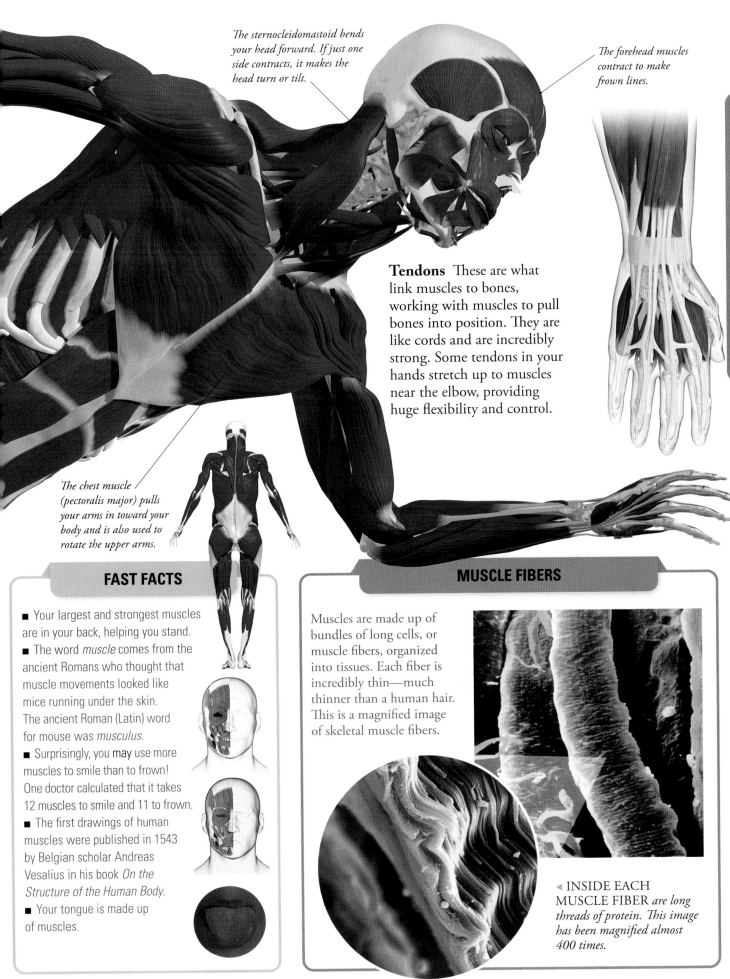

The sternocleidomastoid bends your head forward. If just one side contracts, it makes the head turn or tilt.

The forehead muscles contract to make frown lines.

Tendons These are what link muscles to bones, working with muscles to pull bones into position. They are like cords and are incredibly strong. Some tendons in your hands stretch up to muscles near the elbow, providing huge flexibility and control.

The chest muscle (pectoralis major) pulls your arms in toward your body and is also used to rotate the upper arms.

FAST FACTS

■ Your largest and strongest muscles are in your back, helping you stand.

■ The word *muscle* comes from the ancient Romans who thought that muscle movements looked like mice running under the skin. The ancient Roman (Latin) word for mouse was *musculus*.

■ Surprisingly, you **may** use more muscles to smile than to frown! One doctor calculated that it takes 12 muscles to smile and 11 to frown.

■ The first drawings of human muscles were published in 1543 by Belgian scholar Andreas Vesalius in his book *On the Structure of the Human Body*.

■ Your tongue is made up of muscles.

MUSCLE FIBERS

Muscles are made up of bundles of long cells, or muscle fibers, organized into tissues. Each fiber is incredibly thin—much thinner than a human hair. This is a magnified image of skeletal muscle fibers.

◄ INSIDE EACH MUSCLE FIBER *are long threads of protein. This image has been magnified almost 400 times.*

277

Blood flow

Think of your arteries and veins as a road network for your body. Blood flows through this network, just as trucks move along roads, carrying and delivering the essentials that your cells need and removing waste products. Your arteries and veins are your body's transportation, or circulatory, system.

WHAT BLOOD DOES

Blood delivers oxygen, water, and nutrients to your body's organs and takes away waste carbon dioxide. It also takes white blood cells to where they are needed, to fight infection, and clots to stop bleeding and form a seal to repair damage if you cut yourself. There's more? Yes! It allows you to maintain a steady body temperature.

BLOOD GROUPS

There are four different blood groups or types, and each one is given a letter. You might be type A, B, AB, or O. AB is the rarest. A patient receiving a blood transfusion has to get the same blood group or type O, which can be given to anyone.

It takes a blood cell about one minute to circulate your body.

The heart pumps blood along a network of blood vessels.

The femoral artery supplies blood to the leg.

An adult body contains about 10½ pt (5 liters) of blood.

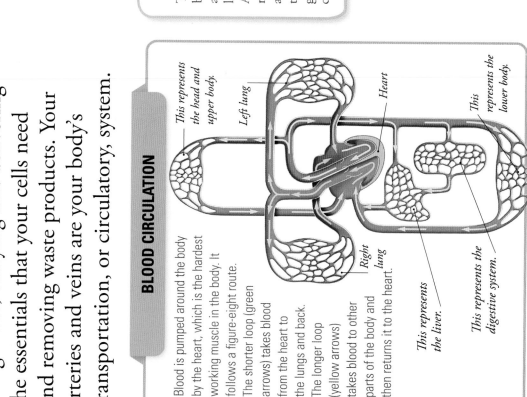

BLOOD CIRCULATION

Blood is pumped around the body by the heart, which is the hardest working muscle in the body. It follows a figure-eight route. The shorter loop (green arrows) takes blood from the heart to the lungs and back. The longer loop (yellow arrows) takes blood to other parts of the body and then returns it to the heart.

This represents the head and upper body.

Left lung

Heart

Right lung

This represents the liver.

This represents the lower body.

This represents the digestive system.

Your heart
and how it works

- **Beats per day** Approx 100,000
- **Average weight** Male: 10½ oz (300 g) Female: 7 oz (200 g)
- **Length** 5 in (12 cm)
- **Width** 3½ in (9 cm)

The muscular human heart is about the size of a fist. It pumps blood around your body, which takes oxygen to the cells, and removes waste. A heart has four chambers, two lower ventricles, and two upper atria. If your heart stops, no other part of your body can work.

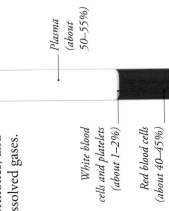

Pulmonary valve

Superior vena cava

Aorta

Pulmonary artery

Right atrium

Right ventricle

Thick cardiac muscle

What goes into blood?
Blood is made up of red blood cells, white blood cells, platelets, and plasma. Plasma is mostly water but also carries proteins, glucose, minerals, hormones, and dissolved gases.

Plasma (about 50–55%)

White blood cells and platelets (about 1–2%)

Red blood cells (about 40–45%)

This is the body's longest vein. Blood flows through it from the foot and lower leg on its journey back to the heart.

▶BODY CIRCULATION
Stretched out, your blood vessels would reach 93,000 miles (150,000 km). That's about four times around Earth.

Blood clots
If you fall over and cut your knee, the cut area scabs over and heals. This happens in a series of steps, as shown below.

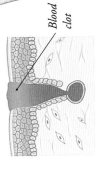

Injury site

Severed vessel

1 INJURY *When skin is cut, it bleeds because of damage to the blood vessels.*

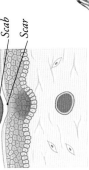

Blood clot

2 CLOTTING *Platelets stick together and a blood clot begins to form.*

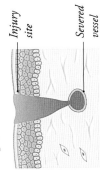

Plug of tissue

3 PLUGGING *The clot forms a plug that stops blood leaking out.*

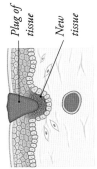

Scab

Scar

New tissue

4 SCABBING *The plug hardens to form a protective scab, which eventually falls off.*

BLOOD VESSELS

There are three types of blood vessel: arteries, veins, and capillaries. Blood begins its journey around the body in a large artery, called the aorta. Arteries have thicker walls than other vessels because the blood flow is at higher pressure.

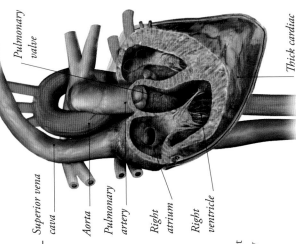

▲ **ARTERIES** *carry blood away from your heart. They have thicker walls than veins or capillaries.*

▲ **VEINS** *carry blood to your heart. Many veins have valves to stop the blood running backwards.*

▲ **CAPILLARIES** *are microscopic, with walls just one cell thick. They link your arteries to your veins.*

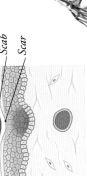

Think! Act!

Your brain is a complex organ. It's a bit like a big computer but more adaptable. It controls all you do. It makes you think. It allows you to learn. It stores your memories. It makes you who you are.

WHAT IS YOUR BRAIN?

Your brain is a collection of about a hundred billion nerve cells called neurons. These are linked to each other, and they share and pass information all day and all night throughout your life.

Message transfer Messages constantly arrive in your brain from your body, sent in the form of electrical signals along nerves. Your brain processes those messages and sends out instructions telling your body what to do.

FACT
Your brain has a joke center, which allows you to understand why a joke is funny. This means that some people with damage to the front of their brains (particularly on the right-hand side) just don't find jokes funny. Given a joke with a choice of different punchlines, they can't tell which is the funny one.

CENTRAL NERVOUS SYSTEM (CNS)

A bundle of nerves called the spinal cord runs from the brain down your back, protected inside a column of bones, the backbone. The brain and spinal cord form your central nervous system.

Cross-section of spinal cord

Spinal nerve _____

▶ THE SPINAL CORD
The cord transports information from the brain to the rest of the body and back via pairs of spinal nerves.

The central nervous system allows you to make voluntary actions such as eating, reading, and walking, as well as controlling many actions itself. For example, you aren't aware of the muscles working in your stomach—they work automatically.

▶ FITTING TOGETHER
This model shows how the brain, spinal cord, and eyes link up.

The spinal cord is as thick as your little finger.

Neurons are thin cells that carry electrical signals called nerve impulses. A neuron has a cell body, with short, spreading projections called dendrites. An axon connects to other neurons.

The axon, a nerve fiber, takes electrical impulses away from the cell body to other neurons.

The nucleus of the cell controls the cell's activity.

Cell body

Dendrites pick up nerve signals.

BRAIN CELL OR NEURON

The nervous system is made up of the CNS and the peripheral nervous system, which consists of nerves that branch to the rest of your body. It's hard working and fast; a nerve impulse travels from the big toe to the spinal cord in one hundredth of a second.

▶ HARD HAT
The human brain is soft and squishy, so it is protected in a bony case called the skull.

The **thalamus** *passes messages between the brain and spinal cord.*

The heavily folded **cerebrum** *is the largest part of your brain.*

The **cerebral cortex** *is the surface of the cerebrum.*

Parts of the brain
The main regions of the brain are the cerebellum, the brain stem, and the cerebrum. The cerebrum is responsible for many complex everyday activities, from eating to speaking.

The **cerebellum** *deals with movement.*

The **hypothalamus** *plays a part in thirst, hunger, and temperature control.*

The **brain stem** *works at the same level when you're asleep and awake.*

YOUR BRAIN

Sight, hearing, speaking, and thinking are controlled in different areas of the cerebrum. Hearing uses an area linked to the ears' nerves. Sight involves a small area linked to the eyes' nerves. Thinking and speaking use large areas of the brain. Heat scans show the different areas.

SIGHT

HEARING

SPEAKING

THINKING

281

Sensing the world

Humans have five senses: sight, hearing, touch, smell, and taste. Your senses tell you about the world around you. They work because billions of nerve cells flash messages to your brain, which interprets the messages and tells you what you are sensing, whether good or bad.

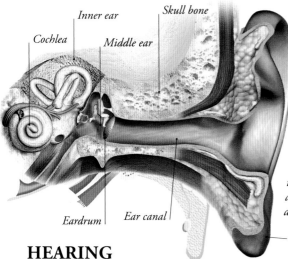

Inner ear
Skull bone
Cochlea
Middle ear
Eardrum
Ear canal
Outer ear

◄ INSIDE THE EAR
Your ear is made up of three main parts— the ear (auditory) canal, the middle ear, and the inner ear.

BALANCE TOO!
Your ear helps you to balance. Hair cells in the inner ear tell your brain about your body's position and movements.

HEARING
Sounds are made up of vibrations, which are funneled inside the ear by the outer ear. Sound waves first travel down the ear canal and vibrate the eardrum. These vibrations reach the cochlea. From here, messages pass to the brain, which interprets the vibrations as sounds we recognize.

Merkel's disc
Meissner's corpuscle
Pacinian corpuscle
Dermis
Free nerve ending

TOUCH
You have about three million pain sensors, and most of these are in your skin. Your fingertips are particularly sensitive. You also have touch receptors that detect light touch, pressure, vibration, heat, and cold.

◄ TOUCH SENSATIONS *Skin layers are full of touch receptors. Some receptors are contained in a capsule, while others are free nerve endings.*

SIGHT
The eye works like a camera. Light from an image passes through the cornea, is adjusted by the lens behind it, and forms an upside-down image on the retina at the back of the eye. This is translated by the brain.

SIGHT

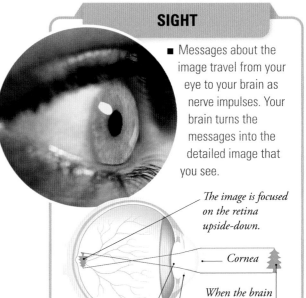

■ Messages about the image travel from your eye to your brain as nerve impulses. Your brain turns the messages into the detailed image that you see.

The image is focused on the retina upside-down.

Cornea

When the brain gets messages from the retina, it turns the image the right way up.

Retina
Lens
Iris

IRIS

Your eye will react differently, depending on how bright light shining into it is. How it reacts is controlled by the iris, a ring of muscle.

Iris
Pupil

▶ IRIS AND PUPIL
The colored part of your eye, called the iris, has a hole in the middle called the pupil. In bright light, the pupil shrinks to prevent too much light from getting into your eye. In dim light, the pupil expands to allow more light into your eye.

Dim light

Bright light

SMELL

Your nose can recognize up to a trillion different smells. Receptors high up in the nasal cavity pick up smell molecules in the air that you breathe in and send signals to your brain. If your brain hasn't come across the smell before, it will remember it so that you recognize it next time.

TELL ME MORE...

■ Smell and taste work together. The flavor of food depends more on smell than taste. This is why it's difficult to taste food if you have a blocked nose.

■ Your senses of smell and taste protect you. If you smell smoke, it warns you of fire. You can smell if food has spoiled. Poisonous food often tastes bitter to make sure you spit it out.

TASTE

It is now thought to be a myth that you can taste particular flavors at different places on your tongue. We have five basic tastes: sweet, sour, salty, bitter, and umami (a savory taste), and these can usually be picked up all over your tongue.

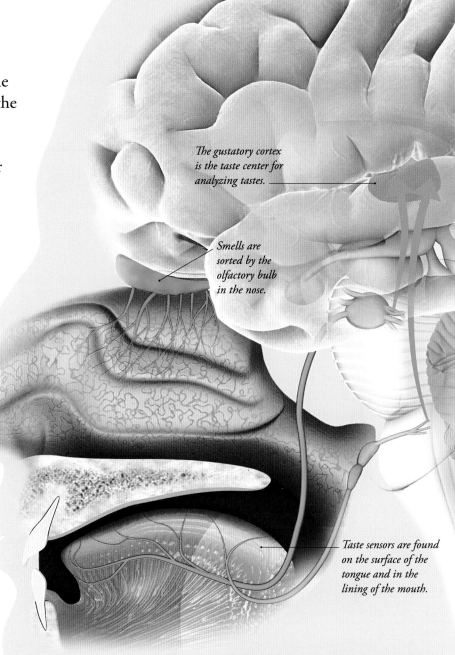

The gustatory cortex is the taste center for analyzing tastes.

Smells are sorted by the olfactory bulb in the nose.

Taste sensors are found on the surface of the tongue and in the lining of the mouth.

▲ SENSE ORGANS *This view inside the head shows the position of the smell and taste organs. They send nerve messages to the brain.*

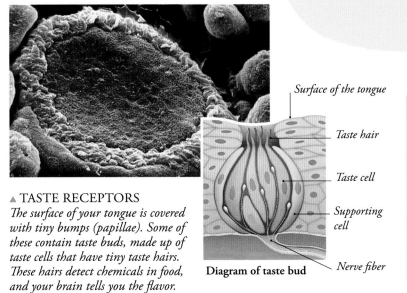

▲ TASTE RECEPTORS
The surface of your tongue is covered with tiny bumps (papillae). Some of these contain taste buds, made up of taste cells that have tiny taste hairs. These hairs detect chemicals in food, and your brain tells you the flavor.

Surface of the tongue

Taste hair

Taste cell

Supporting cell

Nerve fiber

Diagram of taste bud

FAST FACTS

■ Children have around 10,000 taste buds, but the number of taste buds declines with age.
■ People who can't smell are called "anosmic."
■ If you only had one eye from birth, the world would look two-dimensional.
■ There is a tiny blind spot at the back of each eye that can't detect light.
■ There are 3,000 touch receptors in each of your fingertips.
■ Girls usually have more taste buds than boys.

Take a breath

You need to breathe constantly to take in oxygen. You do this by breathing in air, which is taken down your windpipe and into your lungs, where some oxygen is removed and enters the blood. At the same time, carbon dioxide passes into the lungs.

BREATHE IN, BREATHE OUT

Diaphragm moves down, so we inhale.

Diaphragm moves up, so we exhale.

You breathe in when your diaphragm—a dome-shaped muscle at the bottom of your chest—contracts and flattens. This increases the size of your chest cavity so air enters your lungs. Breathing in is helped by your ribs moving up and out.

What happens inside your lungs?
Inside each lung, air tubes called bronchi get smaller and smaller, finally becoming bronchioles. Each bronchiole ends in clusters of small, stretchy air sacs called alveoli. This is known as the bronchial tree, because it resembles an upside-down tree.

Windpipe (trachea)

Left bronchus

Each of the branching networks ends in a bronchiole, which leads into groups of alveoli.

Terminal bronchiole

Capillary

Diagram shows groups of alveoli.

▲ ALVEOLI *Oxygen passes through the walls of the alveoli into capillaries, thin-walled blood vessels (👁 p279).*

▲ BRONCHIOLE *This greatly magnified image shows the end of a bronchiole (in blue) surrounded by a group of alveoli. There are more than 300 million alveoli in each lung.*

CHEST SECTION

Your left lung is smaller than your right lung to allow room for the heart, which is positioned toward the left side of the chest cavity. The heart's position can be seen in a scanned cross-section of the chest, taken from above.

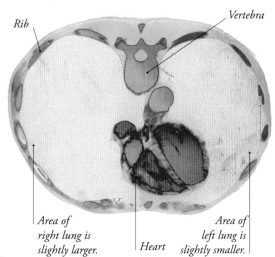

Rib

Vertebra

Area of right lung is slightly larger.

Heart

Area of left lung is slightly smaller.

FAST FACTS

- Flattened out, a pair of lungs would cover a tennis court.
- An average person takes about 12–15 breaths a minute when at rest. After physical activity, they take in about 60 breaths a minute.
- The trachea is about 4 in (11 cm) in length.
- Your lungs act like giant sponges. They take in air instead of water.
- Each minute around 1⅓–1½ gal (5–6 liters) of air pass into and out of your lungs.

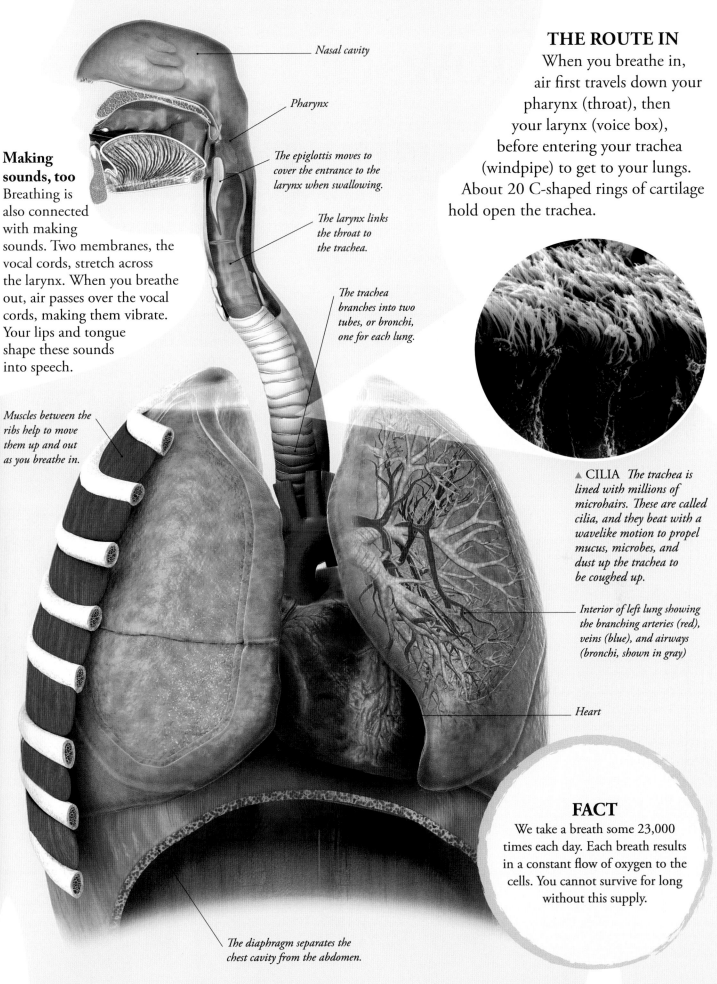

Nasal cavity

Pharynx

THE ROUTE IN
When you breathe in, air first travels down your pharynx (throat), then your larynx (voice box), before entering your trachea (windpipe) to get to your lungs. About 20 C-shaped rings of cartilage hold open the trachea.

The epiglottis moves to cover the entrance to the larynx when swallowing.

The larynx links the throat to the trachea.

Making sounds, too
Breathing is also connected with making sounds. Two membranes, the vocal cords, stretch across the larynx. When you breathe out, air passes over the vocal cords, making them vibrate. Your lips and tongue shape these sounds into speech.

The trachea branches into two tubes, or bronchi, one for each lung.

Muscles between the ribs help to move them up and out as you breathe in.

▲ CILIA *The trachea is lined with millions of microhairs. These are called cilia, and they beat with a wavelike motion to propel mucus, microbes, and dust up the trachea to be coughed up.*

Interior of left lung showing the branching arteries (red), veins (blue), and airways (bronchi, shown in gray)

Heart

FACT
We take a breath some 23,000 times each day. Each breath results in a constant flow of oxygen to the cells. You cannot survive for long without this supply.

The diaphragm separates the chest cavity from the abdomen.

Food flow

We eat to refuel our bodies. We need fuel from food to provide energy, as well as for growth and repair. Digestion is the process by which the food we eat is broken down to extract the nutrients we need. Waste matter is then passed out of the body.

Salivary glands
Saliva is produced by glands in the mouth. It makes food slippery and begins the process of digestion. About 3¼ pt (1.5 liters) of saliva is secreted into the mouth each day.

TAKE A MOUTHFUL

Digestion begins with ingestion when you take in and chew food, mixing it with saliva to make it easier to swallow. Swallowing moves the food into the esophagus, from where it goes into the stomach.

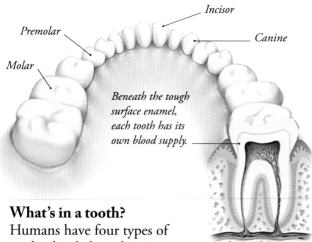

Incisor

Premolar

Canine

Molar

Beneath the tough surface enamel, each tooth has its own blood supply.

What's in a tooth?
Humans have four types of teeth: chisel-shaped incisors cut, while pointed canines tear. The flatter premolars and molars crush and grind. These are the largest teeth.

THE STOMACH AND HOW IT WORKS

Three muscle layers enable the stomach to twist into different shapes.

When food arrives your stomach stretches to store it.

Acid and food are churned together.

Oblique

Longitudinal / Circular

Churned food is passed into the small intestine.

■ **Inside the stomach** Food enters your stomach about eight seconds after you swallow. It is mixed with acids (called gastric juice) and churned into a semi-liquid. Up to 6¼ pt (3 liters) of gastric juices are made in the stomach every day.

▲ A GOOD CHURNING
A meal spends up to four hours in your stomach before being passed slowly on into the small intestine.

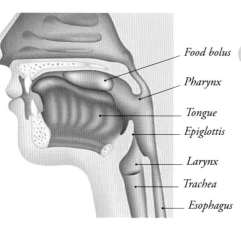

Food bolus

Pharynx

Tongue

Epiglottis

Larynx

Trachea

Esophagus

Down it goes
Once food has been chewed, it is swallowed as a ball called a bolus. It is prevented from entering the larynx and trachea by the epiglottis, a flap of cartilage.

▲ CHEWING FOOD *The bolus of food is about to be swallowed. The epiglottis is in its usual position.*

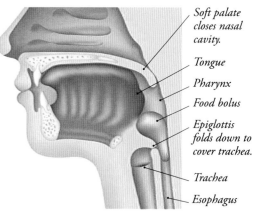

Soft palate closes nasal cavity.

Tongue

Pharynx

Food bolus

Epiglottis folds down to cover trachea.

Trachea

Esophagus

▲ SWALLOWING FOOD *On swallowing, the epiglottis moves down to close entry to the trachea.*

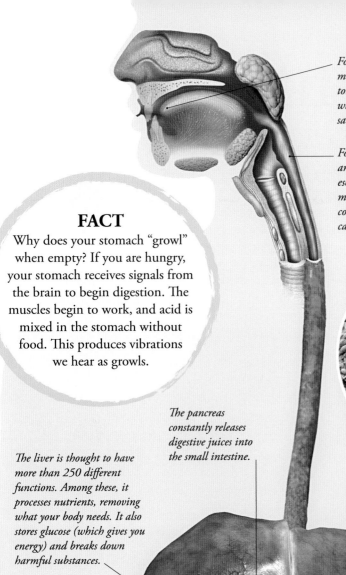

Food enters the mouth, where the tongue assesses whether it is sweet, savory, hot, or cold.

Food is swallowed and passes into the esophagus. It is moved by muscle contractions called peristalsis.

BEYOND THE STOMACH

After leaving the stomach, food enters the small intestine. This is where nutrients are absorbed from the food for use by your body. Material that isn't digested passes into the large intestine where it's turned into feces.

FACT

Why does your stomach "growl" when empty? If you are hungry, your stomach receives signals from the brain to begin digestion. The muscles begin to work, and acid is mixed in the stomach without food. This produces vibrations we hear as growls.

Inbuilt protection
The stomach wall is deeply folded and pitted. Mucus is constantly secreted to prevent the stomach's acids from digesting itself.

Gastric pit

Mucus

The large intestine is where the last nutrients are extracted together with water. Undigested material is combined with other waste products and moved on to the rectum before passing out of the body.

The pancreas constantly releases digestive juices into the small intestine.

The liver is thought to have more than 250 different functions. Among these, it processes nutrients, removing what your body needs. It also stores glucose (which gives you energy) and breaks down harmful substances.

The gallbladder stores bile, a digestive juice. Bile is used to break down fats.

The large intestine is wider than the small intestine.

The small intestine is a long folded tube that produces many different enzymes to digest food. The tube is covered inside with tiny, fingerlike projections called villi. These increase the intestine's surface area for the absorption of nutrients.

FAST FACTS

- The stomach can store about 3¼ pt (1.5 liters) of food.
- A meal takes 18–30 hours to pass through the human body.
- The small intestine is about 17 ft (5 m) in length.
- The large intestine is about 5 ft (1.5 m) in length.
- The liver, the body's largest internal organ, produces about 2 pt (1 liter) of bile a day.
- The large intestine contains billions of bacteria.

SOLID OR LIQUID
Solid food takes longer to break down, which means that a meal stays in the stomach for much longer than a drink, which may pass through in minutes.

The start of life

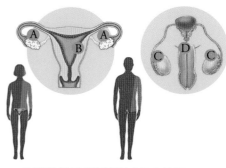

After a sperm fertilizes an egg, it develops in the uterus (the womb). A fertilized human egg takes about nine months to grow into a baby ready for birth. In the uterus, the fetus depends on the placenta (the tissue that links the blood of the mother and fetus) for all its needs.

▲ REPRODUCTIVE ORGANS
Women have two ovaries (A), where eggs, or ova, are stored, and a uterus (B), where a baby is nourished and grows until birth. Men have two testes (C), where sperm are made. They also have a penis (D) through which the sperm travel to get to the eggs.

FERTILIZATION

Millions of sperm swim toward the egg, propelled forward by flexible tails, but usually only one will fertilize it. On contact, the sperm and egg merge to create a single cell—the fertilized egg. The cell then begins to divide.

Each sperm has a rounded head and a long tail.

After an egg is fertilized, it begins to form a barrier to other sperm.

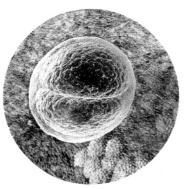

1 WITHIN 36 HOURS *the fertilized egg has divided into two cells. Twelve hours later, it has divided into four cells, and so on.*

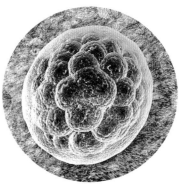

2 THREE TO FOUR DAYS *after fertilization, there is a cluster of 16 to 32 cells. The cluster enters the uterus.*

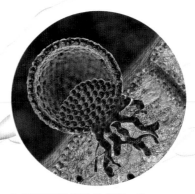

3 ABOUT SIX DAYS *after fertilization, the cell cluster forms a hollow cavity. It attaches itself to the lining of the uterus with rootlike growths.*

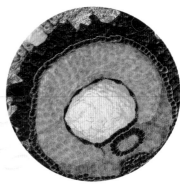

4 ABOUT EIGHT DAYS *after fertilization, an embryo begins to form. New cells will form tissues and organs as a baby develops.*

ULTRASOUND SCAN

■ This is a scan of a fetus inside the womb, taken between four and six months into pregnancy. It was produced using sound waves to form a picture, which was then turned into a three-dimensional (3-D) image. 3-D scans first appeared in the late 1980s.

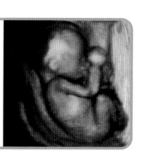

GROWING EMBRYO

Cells continue to divide as the embryo develops. They become specialized, with the head, brain, body, and heart taking shape first, followed by the arms (initially as buds) and lastly the legs. From eight weeks after fertilization, the baby is known as a fetus.

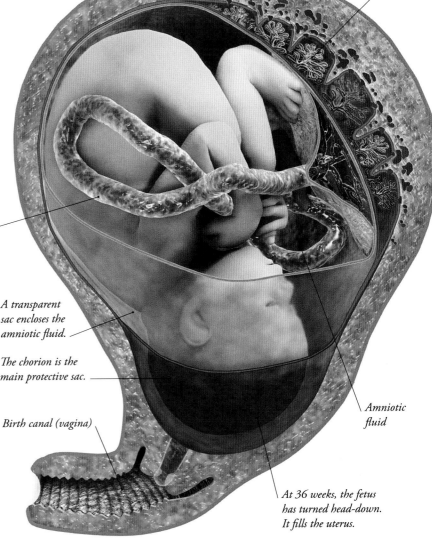

Placenta

The umbilical cord connects the fetus to the placenta.

A transparent sac encloses the amniotic fluid.

The chorion is the main protective sac.

Birth canal (vagina)

Amniotic fluid

At 36 weeks, the fetus has turned head-down. It fills the uterus.

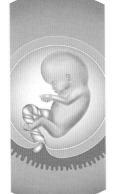

Heart

Developing ear

Developing eye

Umbilical cord

At 3 weeks the embryo is 4/50–2/50 in (2–3 mm) long.

At 4 weeks the embryo is 1/5 in (4–5 mm) long.

Growing embryo Three weeks after fertilization, the embryo is smaller than a pea and looks a bit like a tadpole. At eight weeks, the embryo looks more human but is only the size of a strawberry. The fetus is fully developed at 24 weeks. The last stage of development is growth.

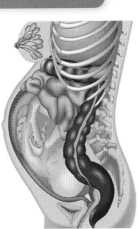

▲ At 8 weeks, the embryo starts to move and is 1–1⅕ in (25–30 mm) long.

PREGNANCY

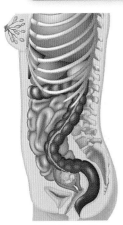

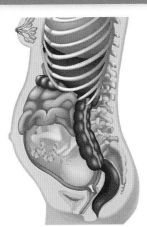

▲ DURING the first three months of pregnancy, called the first trimester, the mother's breasts become larger. Many pregnant women feel sick around this time.

▲ DURING the second trimester, the mother's breasts continue to enlarge, her heart rate increases, and her enlarging womb shows as the fetus grows inside.

▲ DURING the third trimester, the mother's intestines and organs are pushed up. She may feel tired, have back pain, and get breathless when walking about.

Newborn babies adapt quickly to life in the outside world. The umbilical cord, by which it was attached to its mother during pregnancy, is cut. The baby takes its first breaths, forcing its circulation to adapt to breathing air.

TELL ME MORE...

Run and jump, eat a varied diet, and drink lots of water. All these things will help your body to stay as healthy as it can.

Stay healthy

You have just one body for life, so it makes sense to look after it. Giving your body the best chance you can means it will work better for you. That begins with a healthy, mixed diet.

EAT A RAINBOW

Foods can be divided into groups, such as grains and cereals and meat and fish. It is good to eat a range of foods every day, and choose from all the major food groups, eating more of some and less of others (for example, you should eat more vegetables than meat or fish). Thinking of food groups as a rainbow of colors can help separate foods into these groups.

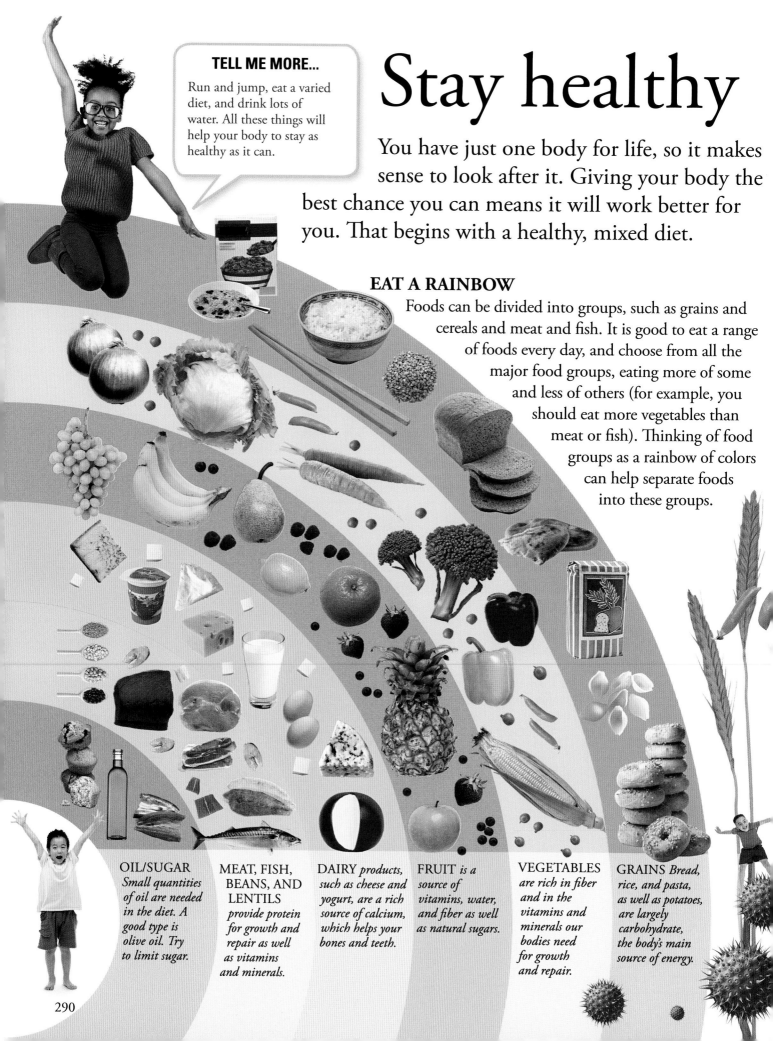

OIL/SUGAR *Small quantities of oil are needed in the diet. A good type is olive oil. Try to limit sugar.*

MEAT, FISH, BEANS, AND LENTILS *provide protein for growth and repair as well as vitamins and minerals.*

DAIRY *products, such as cheese and yogurt, are a rich source of calcium, which helps your bones and teeth.*

FRUIT *is a source of vitamins, water, and fiber as well as natural sugars.*

VEGETABLES *are rich in fiber and in the vitamins and minerals our bodies need for growth and repair.*

GRAINS *Bread, rice, and pasta, as well as potatoes, are largely carbohydrate, the body's main source of energy.*

HEALTH PROBLEMS

It's not always easy for somebody to stay well. There may not be access to clean drinking water, or food may be restricted. Malnutrition is a serious problem in some parts of the world, which is when somebody doesn't have enough of one or more of the food groups. But if your immune system is working well, it will act to protect your body from illness, fighting off the viruses and bacteria that may cause you harm.

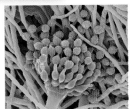

WHAT MAKES US SICK?

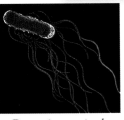 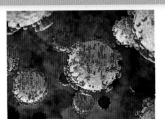

■ **Bacteria** are single-celled organisms. Most are harmless, but certain bacteria invade our bodies to cause illness. Tuberculosis is caused by bacteria.

■ **Viruses** are far smaller than bacteria. They attack our cells from the inside, taking them over. Colds and flus are the result of a viral infection.

■ **Fungi** usually cause infection on the skin's surface, such as athlete's foot, but other fungi can cause serious illness inside the body by damaging the cells.

KIDNEYS

■ Your two kidneys are at the back of your abdomen.

■ The kidneys control the amount of fluid in the body and filter liquid waste from your blood.

■ Filtered waste is removed to the bladder and then expelled as urine.

White blood cells These cells fight bacteria and viruses that might make you sick. Some produce antibodies that work to kill germs. Babies are born with antibodies they inherit from their mother, but they begin to develop their own as they grow.

Red blood cell

White blood cell

Allergies Sometimes the immune system doesn't work properly, identifying things as a threat and attacking them when they aren't. This can cause an allergic reaction. A person might begin sneezing, for example, when in contact with pollen or dust.

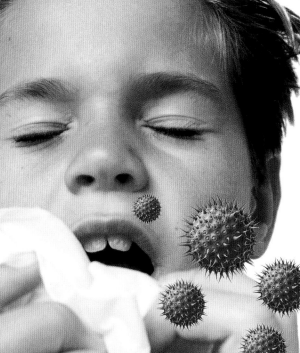

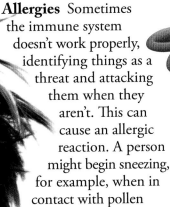

◀ HAY FEVER
Increasing numbers of people around the world are suffering from allergies, such as hay fever. Hay fever is an allergic response to plant pollen. This can be worse at particular times of year, when the pollen count is high.

HOW TO STAY HEALTHY

■ Vitamins and minerals are found in many foods and are essential to general body health.

■ Exercise helps strengthen the heart, lungs, and muscles. It also helps keep the body supple.

■ Water is needed for all the body's processes to function properly. Dehydrated cells will not perform at their best.

■ Good hygiene helps keep germs away. Brushing teeth helps combat tooth decay by cleaning teeth of the bacteria that cause it.

Glossary

Altitude Height as measured above a surface, normally taken as sea level.

Alveoli Tiny sacs in the lungs through which oxygen and carbon dioxide pass to and from the blood.

Amphibian A group of cold-blooded vertebrates, most of which have water-living tadpole larvae, such as frogs.

Apprenticeship Working under a skilled craftsperson to learn a trade.

Arteries Blood vessels that carry blood from the heart to the body.

Artifact An object made by human workmanship.

Artificial intelligence A branch of science that aims to create intelligent machines.

Astrolabe An ancient instrument used to calculate the position of stars in the sky and for navigation.

Atmosphere The gas surrounding a planet or a star.

Atoll An island made of coral reef that is often circular with a central lagoon.

Bacteria Single-celled micro-organisms that can be helpful or harmful to us.

Big Bang The cosmic explosion that created the universe billions of years ago.

Biodiversity A measure of all the different kinds of organisms living in a particular area.

Biofuel Any fuel made from biological matter, such as plants or animal waste.

Biome Any of Earth's major ecosystems with a particular climate and vegetation.

Black hole An object in space with gravity so strong that not even light can escape its pull.

Calligraphy The art of decorative writing.

Camouflage A color or pattern on an organism's body that allows it to blend in with its surroundings.

Canopy The uppermost leafy layer of a tree or forest.

Canyon A narrow valley with steep sides eroded into Earth's surface either on land or under the sea.

Capillaries Tiny blood vessels that connect arteries to veins.

Carnivore An animal that eats meat.

Cells The tiny blocks of living material that form most organisms.

Ceramic A clay material hardened by heat and formed into an object.

Chlorophyll The green pigment in plants that helps them absorb sunlight for photosynthesis.

Chromosomes Packages of DNA found inside the nucleus of most cells.

Climate The average weather conditions over a long period in a particular area.

Cloning The process of producing genetically identical animals or plants.

Colloid A suspension of fine particles dispersed in a liquid or gas.

Colony A group of organisms that live together.

Communism A political theory based on the common ownership of property.

Condensation The change of state from a gas to a liquid.

Continent One of Earth's large landmasses and its surrounding continental shelf.

Crystal A solid in which the atoms or molecules from which it is made are lined up in a regular pattern.

Cubism A style of art that shows a scene from several different points of view all at once.

Deities Gods and goddesses.

Democracy A system of government in which people elect their leaders.

Diaphragm A sheet of muscle that separates the chest from the abdomen internally.

Dictator A ruler who has absolute power.

Distillation Purifying a liquid by boiling it and then collecting the vapor.

DNA Deoxyribonucleic acid, the molecule that contains the blueprint for life.

Echolocation A way of finding objects by bouncing sound waves off them and detecting the "echo"—reflection.

Ecosystem The community of organisms living in a particular area.

Elytra The hard forewings of beetles, earwigs, and some bugs.

Embryo An organism in the earliest stage of its development.

Epiphyte A plant that grows on another plant without damaging it.

Evaporate To turn a liquid to a gas by heat.

Evolution The process by which species change and develop over time.

Exoskeleton An external skeleton that supports and protects an animal's body.

Extinct No longer existing on Earth.

Famine A severe shortage of food, causing widespread hunger.

Fertilization When male and female sex cells unite to form an embryo.

Fetus The developing young of an animal before it is born.

Filtration The process of separating liquids from solids using a filter.

Fossil fuels Fuels containing carbon formed from the remains of ancient organisms.

Friction The force that opposes movement when things rub together.

Fuel cell A device like a battery that generates electricity from hydrogen fuel and oxygen.

Fungi One of the major groups of organisms, including yeasts, molds, and mushrooms, that feed off dissolved organic molecules in the environment.

Galaxies A family of billions of stars, usually with clouds of gas and dust too.

Genes Stretches of DNA that contain the code needed to build a particular protein.

Genome The entire genetic makeup of an organism.

Gills Feathery structures on the bodies of a wide variety of animals, such as some worms, amphibians, and fish, through which oxygen is absorbed from the water.

Gourd A large, fleshy fruit with a hard skin.

Gravity A weak but universal force of attraction between all forms of matter.

Greenhouse gases Gases in the atmosphere that trap heat radiating from Earth's surface and warm the planet.

Habitat The place in which an animal or plant lives in nature.

Herbivore An animal that eats only plants.

Hominins The family of primates to which the great apes and humans belong.

Impressionism A 19th-century style of art characterized by highly finished pieces of art that reflected the artist's response to what they saw.

Inertia The tendency of an object to remain at rest or in constant motion unless a force is applied to it.

Invertebrate A large group including all animals without a backbone.

Joints The meeting point of bones.

Keratin Tough protein found in animals' hair, nails, claws, hooves, horns, feathers, and scales.

Lagoon A shallow body of water separated from a larger one by a narrow land barrier or reef.

Lava Molten rock that has erupted onto the land surface from below the ground.

Magma Molten rock formed below Earth's surface that forms igneous rocks.

Mammals Warm-blooded, furry animals that feed their young with milk.

Mantle The thick mineral layer forming the bulk of Earth between the crust and the core.

Marsupial A mammal that feeds its immature young on a nipple within a pouch of skin.

Matter Anything that has mass and takes up space.

Meditation The process of emptying the mind of thoughts, allowing the body to relax.

Metamorphosis A change in body form shown in animals such as insects and amphibians as they grow into adults.

Microchip The part of a computer made from silicon on which electronic circuits are etched.

Migration Moving from one place to another according to the seasons, usually to find food or to breed.

Mineral A solid material with an orderly crystal structure.

Mirage An optical illusion in which hot air distorts the reflection of an object.

Monarchy A ruling system in which a king or queen is the head of a country but does not necessarily govern it.

Mosaic An image created by using small pieces of colored glass or stone.

Nanotubes A sheet of carbon atoms rolled up into a tube with a diameter of 1 or 2 nanometers.

National anthem The official song sung in celebration of a particular country.

Nebula A cloud in space made of gas or gas and dust.

Neurons Nerve cells.

Nutrients Substances an organism needs for growth and development.

Omnivore An animal that eats all kinds of food, both plants and meat.

Opera A dramatic work set to music.

Orchestra A group of musicians playing different types of instruments, from string and brass to woodwind and percussion.

Organism An individual member of a species.

Ozone An atmospheric oxygen gas, with molecules that have three instead of two oxygen atoms, that forms a protective layer against harmful ultraviolet radiation.

Parasite An organism that lives on another organism and feeds off it.

Peat An organic-rich soil formed from decaying plant remains.

Periodic table A table that organizes all the known elements in order of increasing atomic number.

Peristalsis The wavelike muscle contractions in the digestive tract that move food from the esophagus to the anus.

Persecution The harassment of an individual or group by another individual or group.

Pharaoh The title given to the ancient rulers of Egypt.

Photosynthesis A chemical reaction used by plants to convert light energy into chemical energy for food.

Phylum The biggest division within a kingdom of living things. A phylum is further divided into classes, orders, families, genera, and species.

Phytoplankton Tiny algae and bacteria that drift in the ocean and form a source of food for larger marine animals.

Pigment A substance that colors other materials.

Pilgrim Someone who travels to a sacred place as an act of religious devotion.

Pixel A tiny, colored dot or square. Pixels make up an image on a screen.

Pointillism A painting style that uses small dots of color.

Pollinators Animals that carry pollen from one flower to another.

Pollutants Any substance that contaminates the environment.

Post mortem The medical examination of a dead body to establish the cause of death.

Poverty Not having enough money to take care of basic needs, such as food and clothing.

Predator An animal that hunts other animals.

Prey An animal that is hunted by other animals.

Prophet A person who receives divinely inspired revelations.

Prosthetics The branch of medicine that deals with the manufacture of artificial body parts.

Pupating A stage in an insect's life cycle when the larva breaks down inside a pupa and transforms into an adult.

Reflection When light bounces off a surface and then travels in a different direction.

Refraction When light bends as it travels from one substance to another.

Refugee A person who flees their own country to escape danger.

Reptiles Cold-blooded, air-breathing vertebrates, such as snakes and lizards, with scaly skin.

Reservoir A space above or below ground where liquids or gases are stored.

Rodents Mammals with large and continuously growing incisor teeth.

Ruminate To regurgitate food and chew it again, sometimes called "chewing the cud."

Savanna Tropical grassland and open woodland with wet and dry seasons.

Scavengers Animals that feed on the remains of dead animals.

Shaman A religious leader in some tribes who is thought to have the power to heal people.

Species A group of similar organisms that can breed and produce fertile offspring.

Spores The reproductive structures of some plants and fungi.

Stem cell A type of cell that can multiply and develop into different types of cells.

Sublimation When a solid changes directly into a gas without first becoming a liquid.

Succulent A plant, such as a cactus, that has fleshy tissue that stores water.

Sultan The ruler of a Muslim country.

Supernova A massive star that suddenly gets very bright when it explodes.

Tendons The strips of fibrous tissue that connect muscles to bones.

Textiles Cloth or fabric produced by weaving or knitting.

Tissues Collections of cells that work together to do the same job.

Transgenic A genetically modified organism that contains a gene from another species.

Transpiration The loss of water by evaporation from plant leaves and stems.

Tricolor A flag with three colored stripes.

Tsunami Waves generated by the underwater displacement of the seafloor by an earthquake, slump, or volcano.

Veins Blood vessels that carry blood back to the heart.

Velocity Speed in a given direction.

Venom A poisonous liquid produced by some animals, such as snakes and spiders.

Vertebrate An animal with a backbone.

Viruses Tiny particles that take over cells and reproduce inside them.

Viscosity The "thickness" of a fluid.

Vizier A high-ranking official in a Muslim government.

Index

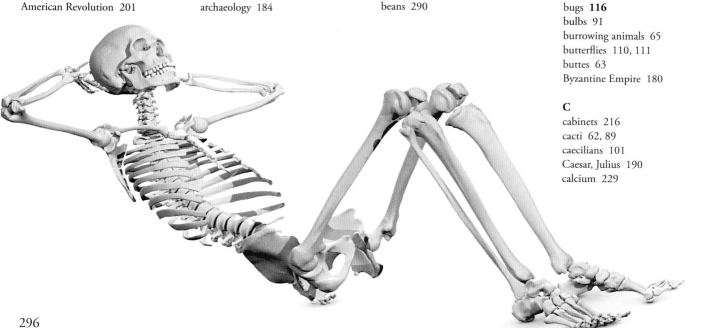

INDEX

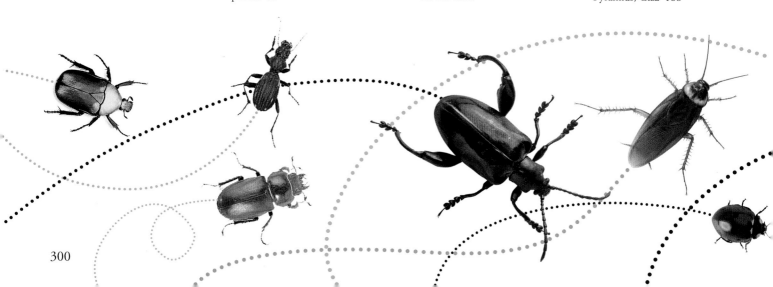

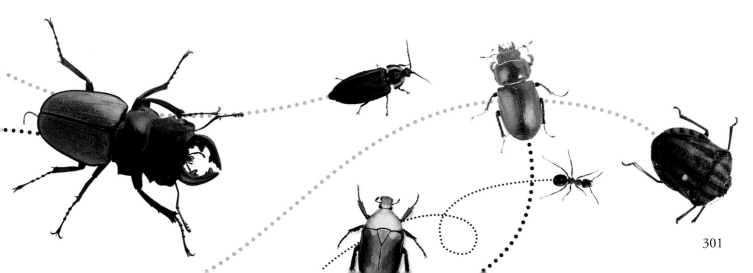

Acknowledgments

The publisher would like to thank the following people for their help with making the book:
Penny Arlon, Kathakali Banerjee, Richard Beatty, Dr. Amy-Jane Beer, Alex Cox, Upamanyu Das, Leon Gray, Sue Malyan, Neha Ruth Samuel, Penny Smith, and Chris Woodford for editorial assistance; Revati Anand, Natalie Godwin, Emma Forge, Tom Forge, Poppy Joslin, Katie Newman, Anna Plucinska, Laura Roberts-Jensen, Pamela Shiels, and Sarah Williams for design assistance; Subhashree Bharati, Suresh Kumar, and Simon Mumford for cartographic assistance; Jaypal Chauhan and Mrinmoy Mazumdar for DTP assistance; Nityanand Kumar and Neeraj Bhatia for hi-res color work; Vagisha Pushp for picture research assistance; Andrea Mills and Saloni Singh for the jacket; Dr. Nemata A. Blyden, Gareth Dawson, Clive Gifford, Ann Kay, Dr. Gabriella Ramos, Dr. Leon Rocha, and Philip Wilkinson for consulting; Bharti Bedi, Lisa Jane Gillespie, Rupa Rao, Nishwan Rasool, Olivia Win-Ricketts, Anirban Saha, Fleur Star, Shelley Ware, and Kevin Anderson & Associates for authenticity checks; Caroline Bingham for proofreading; and Elizabeth Wise for the index.

Smithsonian Enterprises:
Kealy Gordon, Product Development Manager
Jill Corcoran, Director, Licensed Publishing
Brigid Ferraro, Vice President, Business Development and Licensing
Carol LeBlanc, President

The publisher would like to thank the following for their kind permission to reproduce their photographs:

(Key: a-above; b-below/bottom; c-center; f-far; l-left; r-right; t-top)

123RF.com: leonello calvetti 125bl; vasin leenanuruksa / iPhone is a trademark of Apple Inc., registered in the U.S. and other countries 243bc; georgejmclittle 243br; suesamrit 265cl; **akg-images:** 210tl, 253crb; RIA Nowosti 213bl; **Alamy Stock Photo:** 615 collection 266br; 149tl, 171tr; Mark Andrews 259cra; Arco Images 91ca, 99tc; ARCO Images GmbH 51br, 142bl, 151br; Arco Images GmbH / Wittek, R. 93fbr; Asar Studios 266cra; Olivier Asselin 170cb; Gerhard Koertner / Avalon.red 116br; avatra images 112cla; B.A.E. Inc 52cr; Bill Bachmann 151cr, 171bl; Stephen Barnes / Religion 159cb; Stephen Bisgrove 145cl; Blickwinkel 32t, 98bc, 115br, 115cla, 117cl; Steve Bloom Images 94l; Blue Origin 25crb; Oote Boe Photography 185c; BrazilPhotos.com 134cb; Scott Camazine 91cl; Steve Cavalier 108cl; © chrisstockphoto 175cr; Chris Cheadle 45bl, 132tl; David Coleman 181bc; CPA Media Pte Ltd / Pictures From History 194br, 195br; Derek Croucher 37tc; David Noble Photography 145cr, 148tc; David R. Frazier Photolibrary, Inc. 87br; David Dent 29bl, 44b; Dinodia Photos RM 160cl, 205tr; dpa picture alliance 179bl; Redmond Durrell 109bc; Adam Eastland 193cr; Chad Ehlers 29tc, 31tr, 52cra; Elvele Images Ltd 107cr, 107cra; Everett Collection Inc 255cb; Eye Ubiquitous 63c; David Fleetham 109br; Free Agents Limited 177tr; Robert Fried 167tc; Tim Gainey 91tl; Geophoto / Natalia Chervyakova / Imagebroker 119bl; Mike Goldwater 149tc; Tim Graham 133tc; Sally & Richard Greenhill 171br; GRANGER, NYC-Historical Picture Archive 206br, 208br; Greenshoots Communications / GS International 170b; George Henton 213br; Robert Harding Picture Library 3ca, 38clb, 38tr, 136b; Martin Harvey 141tr; Heritage Image Partnership Ltd / Index 199cla; Shaun Higson 165tl; The History Emporium 207br; Bert Hoferichter 181tr; Holmes Garden Photos 193tc; Michael Honegger 215clb; Horizon International Images Limited 25fbl, 38t, 52tr; Peter Horree 175tr, 180cl; Chris Howes / Wild Places Photography 140tr; IanDagnall Computing 190bc, 195bc (Kublai Khan); IGG Digital Graphic Productions GmbH 176bc; Image Register 052 235cr; Image Source Pink 176cl; Imagebroker / Arco Images / Reinhard, H. 150-151bl; imageBROKER / Josef Beck 148b, Stephan Goerlich / imageBROKER 250-251; imagebroker 196cl; Images and Stories 180c, 193tl; Images of Africa Photobank 29tr, 39tr, 140b, Images of Africa Photobank / David Keith Jones 141cla; Interfoto Pressbildagentur 134b, 137ca, 196t, 196-197; Interfoto Pressebildagentur 168-169 (background); J L Images 132-133b; John James 214-215b; Jon Arnold Images Ltd 186; Huw Jones 167cl; Juniors Bildarchiv 113tc; Juniors Bildarchiv / F349 93crb; Jupiterimages 39cr, 52ftr; Anthony Kay / Flight 52crb; Steven J. Kazlowski 96bl; Georgios Kollidas 253br; Karl Kost 149cr; H Lansdown 121cr; Leslie Garland Picture Library 45bc; Ben Lewis 137cl; Mark Lewis 151t; Tony Lilley 145br; The London Art Archive 145bc; Suzanne Long 164tr; Lou-Foto 168fcra; Oleksiy Maksymenko / imageBROKER 259bc; Dirk V Mallinckrodt 91c; Mary Evans Picture Libray 207c, 207crb; Medical-on-line 256cb; Mettafoto 260t; Mira 49bl; Mirrorpix 171tl; NASA 49tl; NASA / digitaleye / J Marshall - Tribaleye Images 221clb; NASA / Pictorial Press Ltd 21tr; Natural History Museum, London 31br; Nature Picture Library 173cl; Niday Picture Library 133cr; Ron Niebrugge 97tl; North Wind Picture Archives 192-193b, 199br, 199ca, 200br, 201bc, 206t, 244t; Michael Patrick O'Neill 134cr; Edward Parker 113c; pbpgalleries 173tl; PCN Photography / PCN Black 179br; David Pearson 149br; Photos 12 261tl; PhotoAlto / Frederic Cirou 171clb; PHOTOTAKE Inc 266tl; Pictures Colour Library 173bl; Pictorial Press Ltd 204cla; The Picture Art Collection 193bl, 195bl; Print Collector 197bl, 199cra, 208bl, 209bl; The Print Collector / Ann Ronan Picture Library / Heritage-Images 200crb; Pump Park Vintage Photography 185cl; Rolf Richardson 177t; Jeff Rotman 112cra; Allen Russell 133c; Friedrich Saurer 124clb; Alex Segre 145tr; Waldemar Sikora 167br; Stefan Sollfors 113bl; SOPA Images Limited 160br; Norbert Speicher 268c; John Sundlof 217bl; Liba Taylor 289br; Tristan3D 15ca, 16br; Travelshots.com 46fclb; Universal Art Archive 198bc; Martyn Vickery 193tl; View Stock 253ca; Visual & Written SL 72r; Visual&Written SL 112br; Visum Foto GmbH 144b; David Wall 208cl; John Warburton-Lee Photography 180crb; Richard Wareham Fotografie 1ftr, 3c, 133cl; Wasabi 177cb; WidStock 43cr; World History Archive 221br; Worldspec / NASA 126-127; Vedat Xhymshiti 215cla; Xinhua 214ca; Zoonar / Wavebreak Media LTD 264ca; Zuma Press, Inc. 259cla; **Ancient Art & Architecture Collection:** C M Dixon 187tl; **Anglo Australian Observatory:** 7tr, 13bc, 13br; **Ardea:** Steve Downer 96tl; Kenneth W. Fink 97cr; **The Bridgeman Art Library:** 190br; Capitol Collection, Washington, USA 201c; Look and Learn 191t, 207t, 252clb; Museum of Fine Arts, Boston, Massachusetts, USA, William Sturgis Bigelow Collection 220tl; Private Collection 188cl; Private Collection / © Michael Graham-Stewart 202tl; **Bridgeman Images:** Peter Newark American Pictures 203tr; **Bryan and Cherry Alexander Photography:** 161cl; **Carnegie Observatories - Giant Magellan Telescope :** Giant Magellan Telescope 21br; **Corbis:** 174cla, 211bl, 211cl; Alinari Archives 165bl; Theo Allofs 49, 63br; © 2022 The Andy Warhol Foundation for the Visual Arts, Inc. / Licensed by DACS, London 167cr; ANSA / ANSA 257tr; Art on File 79br; The Art Archive 191bc, 192tl, 212t; Anthony Bannister / Gallo Images 108bl; Dave Bartruff 213crb; Bettmann 2cr, 3br, 24bc, 34c, 163bl, 169cla, 193bc, 203bl, 203cl, 204bl, 206c, 207bc, 209t, 210bc, 210br, 213tl, 221bl, 246bl, 254cl, 254crb, 257bl, 275cr; Stefano Bianchetti 220tr; Jonathan Blair 19b; Gary Braasch 81bc; Tom Brakefield 84cl, 85cb, 98t; Brand X / Southern Stock 269bl; Brand X / Triolo Productions / Burke 117crb; Andrew Brookes 228-229; Brunei Information / epa 216cb; Burstein Collection 253cb; Angelo Cavalli / Zefa 160c (background); CDC / PHIL 93br; Ron Chapple 52ca; Christie's Images 3ftr, 212br; Christie's Images / © ADAGP, Paris and DACS, London 2022 167bc; Ralph A. Clevenger 109tr; W. Cody 167bl; Construction Photography 42b; Gianni Dagli Orti 165c, 189bc; Fridmar Damm 71tr, 89bc, 145bl; Tim Davis / Davis Lynn Wildlife 97tc; Deborah Betz Collection 221bc; P. Deliss/Godong 294-295; DLILLC 120b; DLILLC / Davis Lynn Wildlife 4-5, 97cra; Doc-stock 111 (Leech); Edifice 253clb; EPA 1fbl, 54br, 55cr, 162br, 162ca, 162cr, 185br; Frederic Soltan 37t; Stephen Frink 111 (Clams), 121br, 122-123t; Jose Fuste Raga 148tl, 180bl, 181c; The Gallery Collection 166bl, 166cl, 166t, 191br, 212clb; David Gard / Star Ledger 172-173; John Gillmoure 162-163; **Courtesy of Gopro:** 261cra; Frank Greenaway 120tl; Martin Harvey 119tc, 120-121ca; Lindsay Herbberd 163cl; Historical Picture Archive 164c; Jack Hollingsworth 129t; Julie Houck 122bl; Carol Hughes 11br; Hulton Collection 211cb; Richard Hutchings 170bl; Image 100 241tr; Image Source 233cl; JJamArt 164bl; Sylwia Kapuscinski 176bl; Kevin Schafer 1bl, 3 (Parthenon), 73cl, 105cl, 121t, 190clb; Matthias Kulka 290-291b, 291tc; Frans Lanting 2br, 59ftr, 66-67t, 73br, 81clb, 81tr, 84ca, 84cra; Danny Lehman 58bc, 163tc; Charles & Josette Lenars 198tr; James Leynse 249crb; Massimo Listri 168fbr; Gerd Ludwig 85bc; Alen MacWeeney 165crb; David Madison 179c; Lawrence Manning 232c; James Marshall 136c; Robert Matheson 292-293; Buddy Mays 97tr; Mary Ann McDonald 94cr; Momatluk-Eastcott 82-83; Moodboard 163clb, 249fbr; Arthur Morris 3ftl, 106t, 107tr; Kevin R. Morris 162cl; David A. Northcott 101cl; Richard T Nowitz 163cr, 200bl, 201cl; Paul A. Souders 3tr, 57tc, 64t, 73bc, 173clb, 236cl; Douglas Pearson 181tc; Philadelphia Museum of Art/© Succession Picasso/ DACS, London 2022 167cla; Michael Pole 87; Radius Images 163br; Enzo & Paolo Ragazzini 184b; Roger Ressmeyer 21cl, 24crb, 158br, 170tr, 221cl, 265b; Reuters 5tc, 25c, 44t, 209cr, 239fbr, 253tl; Reuters / Rafael Perez 216ca; Neil C. Robinson 224clb; Roger Ressmeyer / NASA 26cl; Jenny E. Ross 4tr, 95bl; Pete Saloutos 256cl; Jacques Sarrat / Sygma 174-175; Alan Schein 239bl; Phil Schermeister 61cl; Herb Schmitz 120-121; Denis Scott 18; Denis Scott / Comet 92bl; Smithsonian Institution 198c; Joseph Sohm / Visions of America 201cra; Ted Soqui 255ca; Stapleton Collection 252cr; George Steinmetz 264br; STScI/ NASA 6-7; Jim Sugar 45c; Sygma 84cla, 134clb, 173cra, 255cb; Sygma / (c) Tracey Emin, courtesy White Cube (London) 167crb; Paul Thompson / Ecoscene 161br; Penny Tweedie 3bl, 161cr, 171tc; Underwood & Underwood 181bl, 205cr; Visuals Unlimited 284cr, 291ca, 291tl; Werner Forman 198cr, 199tl; Michele Westmorland 121cl; Nick Wheeler 163tr; Ralph White 245br; Steve Wilkings 4tl, 50; Douglas P. Wilson / Frank Lane Picture Agency 123bc; Keith Wood 43bl; Lawson Wood 110fcl (Sponges); Michael S Yashamita 35c; Zefa 84bl, 224bc, 242t; Jim Zuckerman 273bl; **Depositphotos Inc:** SeventyFour 163cb; **F. Deschandol & Ph. Sabine:** 117bc, 117br; **DK Images:** Roby Braun / Gary Ombler 125c; Roger Bridgman 260cl; British Library 212bc; British Library Board 168fbl; British Museum 172t, 184cr, 184crb, 184tr, 199tr; Geoff Dann / Jeremy Hunt - modelmaker 280br, 281cl; Courtesy of the Egyptian Museum, Cairo 189cl; ESA - ESTEC 25fbr; Rowan Greenwood 5tl, 161cla; Imperial War Museum 210c; Simon James 191bl; Jamie Marshall 63tr, 161ca, 213tc; Judith Miller / Ancient Art 168tc; Judith Miller / Wallis and Wallis 195fbr; Courtesy of The Museum of London 187cr; Museum of the Order of St John, London 168bl; NASA 25tc; National Maritime Museum, London 196cb; National Museum of Kenya 186br; Courtesy of the Natural History Museum, London 39bc, 40 (Limestone), 40 (Pegmatite), 40 (Siltstone), 40 (Tillite), 41, 41 (Agate), 41 (Calcite), 41 (Lapis lazuli), 41 (Magnetite), 41 (Quartz), 41 (Sulfur), 68br, 69c, 104cr, 116cr, 186bc, 186fbl, 187tc, 224br, 245, 245 (Gomphotherium), 245 (Moeritherium); Stephen Oliver 47br; Oxford University Museum of Natural History 40 (Peridotite); Courtesy of Sam Tree of Keygrove Marketing Ltd 249cla; Courtesy of The Science Museum, London 38c, 40 (Obsidian), 40 (Pumice), 169fcra, 220bl; St Mungo, Glasgow Museums 159fcr; Courtesy of the U.S. Army Heritage and Education Center - Military History Institute 185tl, 202cra; Courtesy of The American Museum of Natural History 187c; Courtesy of the University Museum of Archaeology and Anthropology, Cambridge 187crb; Wilberforce House Museum, Hull City Council 203tl; Jerry Young 61cr, 102c, 117ftr, 138c; **Dorling Kindersley:** James Kuether 125clb; Oxford University Museum of Natural History 40fbr; Whipple Museum of History of Science, Cambridge 196cb; **David Doubilet:** 74c; **Dreamstime.com:** Alphaspirit 262-263; Antonella865 141clb; Svetlana Day 79crb; Iakov Filimonov 136tr; Paul Hakimata / iPad is a trademark of Apple Inc., registered in the U.S. and other

ACKNOWLEDGMENTS

countries 255cr; Handmademedia 291tc; Martin Holverda 15cla, 16ca; Chris Kelleher 200tr; Luminis 47tl; Martiapunts 79cra; Carolyn Morrison 214cl; Luciano Mortula 181tr; Rafael Ben-ari / Lucidwaters 162tr; Sean Pavone 195tr; Planetfelicity 26cb; Andrey Popov 255bl; Nataliia Prokofyeva 261br; William Roberts 221tr; Dmitry Rukhlenko 160c; Sam74100 290tl; Sdecoret 291ca; Sfrecords Music 172bl; Mark Turner 125ca; Wirestock 137cra; Swee Ming Young 116bc; **ESO:** E. Slawik 19tl; **FLPA:** Ingo Arndt / Minden Pictures 116tl; Nigel Cattlin 116bl, 116crb; R. Dirscherl 103cra; Michael & Patricia Fogden / Minden 79bl; Mitsuaki Iwago / Minden Pictures 95ca; Heidi & Hans-Juergen Koch 102cr; Gerard Lacz 99tl; Chris Newbert / Minden 109cr; Norbert Wu / Minden Pictures 106cl, 302-303; Pete Oxford 102cl; Schauhuber/Imagebroker 117fbr; Mark Sisson 113br; Jan Vermeer / Minden Pictures 106br; Tom Vezo / Minden Pictures 112cl; Albert Visage 120c; Tony Wharton 121bl; Shin Yoshino 84clb; **R Gendler:** 1ftl, 11bl; **Getty Images:** 55br, 115c, 136bl, 180tl, 247bc, 257cr, 257cl; Peter Adams 137br; AFP 159fbr, 173bc, 173tr, 211cr, 247c, 251tc; AFP Photo / Jamie Mcdonald / Pool 179cb; AFP / Odd Andersen 172br; Chandan Khanna / AFP 25fbr; Doug Allan 108br; William Albert Allard 149tr; Theo Allofs 65cl, 151bc; Altrendo 62c; Anadolu Agency 215tr; Tito Atchaa 238bc; Rob Atkins 230 (skyline sunset); Aurora / Ian Shive 110cr (coral); Aurora / Jurgen Freund 92tr; Aurora / Sean Davey 103bc; Paul Avis 239bc; Daryl Balfour 140tc, 244bl; Jim Ballard 12; John W Banagan 2cra, 45r, 238fbr; Anthony Bannister 65tc; Tancredi J Bavosi 234bl; Walter Bibikow 231bl; Bloomberg 258c, 267cr; Steve Bly 49tr; Steve Bonini 67tr; Philippe Bourseiller 77fbr; John Bracegirdle 67cr; Per Breiehagen 130b; The Bridgeman Art Library 133cr, 165tr, 189br, 193br, 196br, 196cr, 212bl, 252crb; The Bridgeman Art Library / Anton Agelo Bonifazi 159tr; The Bridgeman Art Library / German School 3cb, 159ftr, 169tc; The Bridgeman Art Library / Italian School 158b (background); Jan Bruggeman 240-241; Frank & Joyce Burek 75bc; JH Pete Carmichael 110cr (Tarantula); Luis Castaneda Inc 111bc; Angelo Cavalli 63tc, 137bl; Paul Chesley 81cla; China Span / Keren Su 169cb; John Coletti 69br; Jeffrey Coolidge 80bl, 230 (plugs), 232t; Gary Cornhouse 262tr; Livia Corona 137tr; Daniel J. Cox 59fbl, 69cr; DEA / G. Cozzi Cozzi 140tl; Derek Croucher 101tc; Mark Daffey 73bl; Stefano Dal Pozzolo - Vatican Pool 159fcla; Geoff Dann 165cl; Peter David 75br; De Agostini Picture Library 3fbl, 39cra, 182-183c, 189tr, 190c; Digital Vision 52-53, 59bc, 59bl, 60cr, 200cl, 204cr, 205cb, 217tr, 230 (radio), 238br, 240r, 242bl; Digital Vision / Rob Melnychuk 158bl; DigitalGlobe 35br, 35crb; Reinhard Dirscherl 1tr, 109cl; Domino 231bl; Rob Elsdale 110b; Grant Faint 230 (racing car); Tim Fitzharris 56-57; Tim Flach 79cl; David Fleetham 110cl (Octopus); Robert Fournier 77br; FPG / Keystone 235tl; David R Frazier 55tr; James French 159ca; Robert Frerck 164br; Roger Garwood & Trish Ainslie 59-59s; Ezio Geneletti 225cra; Georgette Douwma 60br, 77cr, 83tc, 92fcr; Daisy Gilardini 65clb, 70bl, 70-71b; Tim Graham 4ftr, 136tl; George Grall 74br, 100br, 111 (Beetle); Jorg Greuel 60tr, 68bl; Jan Greune 68-69; Christopher Groenhout 124bl; Jeffrey Hamilton 229c; Robert Harding World Imagery 78cla; GK Hart / Vikki Hart 243br; Gavin Hellier 146br, 148tr, 149bl, 225cr; Hindustan Times 185tr; Masanobu Hirose 51; Bruno De Hogues 176br; Ross M Horowitz 83ftr; Simeone Huber 147; Hulton Archive 173crb, 199cla, 205br, 206br, 209bc, 210cr, 210-211, 235tr; Daniel Hurst 231tr; Ichiro 238bl; Image Source 176c, 251bl, 264t;

The Image Bank / Bob Stefko 93tc; The Image Bank / Frans Lemmens 92cr; The Image Bank / Tim Graham 161t (background); Imagewerks Japan 258; Alexander Joe / Afp 178crb; Steven Kaziowski 70c; Ken King 110cl (Ants); Ted Kinsman 1bc, 243fbl; Jonathan Kitchen 231bc; Tim Kiusalaas 230t; Frank Krahmer 138cl; Cameron Lawson 224cl; Lester Lefkowitz 94br; Frans Lemmens 63bc; Darryl Leniuk 234br; Ron Levine 267tr; Look / Jan Greune 57tl; Ken Lucas 72bc; Zac Macaulay 77bc; Macduff Everton 38cr, 163c; Spike Mafford 65cr; Roine Magnusson 58br; Maskot 232cl; Ray Massey 232b; Kent Mathews 233bc; Khin Maung Win / AFP 216bc; Ian McAllister 65cb; Dennis McColeman 254cb; Joe McDonald 120cr; Walter B McKenzie 116cl; Kendall McMinimy 111 (Jellyfish); Medioimages / Photodisc 161ftr; Buda Mendes / STF 257clb; A. Messerschmidt 261tc; Roberto Mettifogo 234-235c; Ethan Miller 259crb; Donald Miralle 178fbl; Alan R Moller 55bl; Laurence Monneret 81cr; Moment / a.v.Photography 156-157; Filippo Monteforte / AFP 159cla; Bruno Morandi 3tl, 144t; Bryan Mullennix 111cr; Darlyne A. Murawski 113tr, 122cl; Narinder Nanu / AFP 160bc; NASA 25cra, 265tl; National Geographic 28-29, 53br, 59tc, 59tr, 107tl, 111 (Starfish), 111tr, 184tl, 230 (saucepan), 231br; National Geographic / Alison Wright 160t; National Geographic / Frans Lanting 92fcl; National Geographic / Michael S. Quinton 71fbr; National Geographic / Paul Nicklen 57tl, 71cl, 71cr; National Geographic / Roy Toft 96cl; Marvin E. Newman 73c; Kyle Newton 239br; Paul Nicklen 76bl; Laurie Noble 137cr; Thomas Northcut 68clb; Michael Ochs Archives 173ca; Stan Osolinski 73br; Panoramic Images 2crb, 56bl, 64b, 66-67c, 76-77, 83tr, 110fcr (Butterfly), 304; Grove Pashley 229br; Danilo Pavone 91fcr; Jose Luis Pelaez 79fcr, 242bc; Per Magnus Persson 227cr; Photodisc 49c, 81tl, 256clb; Photodisc / InterNetwork Media 35tl; Photodisc / Sami Sarkis 60bl; Photographer's Choice / Derek Croucher 92 (ladybird); Photographer's Choice / Harald Sund 71tl; Photographer's Choice / Kevin Schafer 103tr; Photographer's Choice RR / Harald Sund 93tl; Photonica / Theo Allofs 71br; Picture It Now / Handout 178-1179t; Paul Piebinga 72tc; Christopher Pillitz 78b; Popperfoto 211bc; Terje Rakke 75cb; Gary Randall 149cl; James Randklev 66-67b; Rapsodia 142b; Redferns / Helen Boast 173crb; Dan Regan 179cra; Rich Reid 62bl; Gabrielle Revere 291bl; Curtis W Richter 69tr; Riser / John & Lisa Merrill 112tr; Michael Blann 174ca; Patrick Riviere 92br; Robert Harding World Imagery / Steve & Ann Toon 93bl; Robert Harding World Imagery / Thorsten Milse 93tr; Lew Robertson 205cl; Marc Romanelli 231bl; Michael Rosenfeld 145t; Martin Ruegner 231cr; Andy Sacks 236c; Dave Saunders 42t; Kevin Schafer 61tr; Gregor Schuster 263tl; Louis Schwartzberg 95cr; Zen Shui / Laurence Mouton 231c; Gail Shumway 83tl, 101bl; Alan Smith 132cr; Philip & Karen Smith 37cr, 230 (dam); Paul Souders 65crb; Bob Stefko 65br; Stockbyte 60cra, 65tr, 264-265; Stocktrek Images 24-25; Stone / Frank Krahmer 71bl; Stone / Freudenthal Verhagen 92cl; Stone / Jody Dole 60-61 (insects); Stone / Theo Allofs 2fbr, 93ca; STR / AFP / Jiji Press 178; Studio Paggy 162tl; Keren Su 99cr, 195cr; Jim Sugar / Science Faction 1tl, 29tl, 34; Harald Sund 59br; Taxi / Ken Reid 46fbl; Tetra images / Erik Isakson 178tl; Ron & Patty Thomas 4tc, 53cr, 62cb; David Tipling 59tl; Travel Ink 72tr; Travelpix Ltd 68cl, 261br; Yoshikazu Tsuno 3crb; Pete Turner 52b, 241b; Shiva Twin 80-81; Universal Images Group / Education Images 132clb; Joseph Van Os 53crb, 68c; Gandee Vasan 54bc; Visuals Unlimited 229cr; Visuals Unlimited /

Joe McDonald 92c; Ami Vitale 160cr; Zelda Wahl 141c; Andrew H. Walker 177tl; Jeremy Walker 60bc; Caroline Warren 1tc, 60tl; The Washington Post 267br; Bridget Webber 230 (cooling towers); Westend61 49br; Stuart Westmorland 77bl; Ralph Wetmore 236cr; Andy Whale 229cl; Darwin Wiggett 133crb; Win-Initiative 135; WireImage 173br, 173c, 173fbr; Arte Wolfe 58bl; Ted Wood 63cr; World Perspectives 54-55s, 130bl, 146bl; David Wrobel 75bl; Norbert Wu 60crb, 73r, 141br; Zap Art 262-263 (Background); Andy Zito 263ftr (Global Village4); **Getty Images / iStock:** E+ / vm 179cra; Thomas Northcut / Photodisc 234ca; **Polly Greathouse:** 266bc, 266bl; **Honda (UK):** Honda.com 258tr, 258tca, 258br; **Imagestate:** AGE Fotostock 187; Jose Fuste Raga 195tr; **iRobot Corporation:** 267br; **iStockphoto.com:** 262cb, 263clb, 263tr; Terry J Alcorn 197cr; Aldra 110tc; Kimberly Deprey 132c; Alf Ertsland 205c; Arthur Carlo Franco 105tr; Bradley Gallup 201br; Boris Hajdarevic 204-205c; Eric Hood 282crb; Gertjan Hooijer 91tr; Scott Kochsiek 30crb; Richard Laurence 93c; Shaun Lowe 9r; Eileen Morris 189bl; Pete Muller 105tc; Kevin Panizza 119tr; Jan Rysavy 29br, 53cra; Dennis Sabo 111 (Sponges); sgame 291cr; Baris Simsek 218-219; Stephen Sweet 202c; Stefanie Timmermann 254bc; Joan Vicent Cantó Roig 119c; Andrey Volodin 262br; Duncan Walker 197br; Dane Wirtzfeld 178cra; Dan Wood 17b; x-drew 191cr; Serdar Yagci 190fbr; Tomasz Zachariasz 110tr; **The Kobal Collection:** Different Tree Same Wood 177br; Golden Harvest 177bc; **Stefan Kröpelin, University of Cologne:** 138br; **Mary Evans Picture Library:** 187clb; **NASA:** 2ftr, 2tr, 7tc, 10ftr, 12bl, 22cb, 22t, 23bc, 235clb; ESA and The Hubble Heritage Team (STScI / AURA) 10cra; ESA and The Hubble Heritage Team (STSCI/AURA) / J. Blakeslee (Washington State University) 10cra; ESA and The Hubble Heritage Team (STSCI/AURA) / P. Knezek (WIYN) 10tr; ESA, HEIC, and The Hubble Heritage Team (STScI/AURA) 13bl; ESA/J. Hester and A. Loll (Arizona State University) 235bl; ESA / JPL 13cra; ESA/S. Beckwith (STScI) and the HUDF Team 10b; Andrew Fruchter and the ERO Team [Sylvia Baggett (STScI), Richard Hook (ST-ECF), Zoltan Levay (STScI)] 11bc; Hubble Heritage Team (AURA/ STScI) 20br; JHUAPL / SwRI 18clb; Johnson Space Center 23bl, 23clb, 23tr; JPL-Caltech 14cra (Venus), 16cla, 27cr, 27cb; JPL-Caltech / University of Arizona 26bc, 266cra; naturepl.com: Ingo Arndt 113cr; Eric Baccega 99br; Peter Blackwell 103tl; Jurgen Freund 91cr; David Hall 119cl; Tony Heald 104b; Michael D. Kern 112cr; Kim Taylor 116clb; Luiz Claudio Marigo 105br; Rolf Nussbaumer 89; Andrew Parkinson 98bl; Philippe Clement 89bl, 89tl; Premaphotos 111bl, 116bc; Jeff Rotman 118bl; Anup Shah 103c; David Shale 118br; Charlie Sobeck 21cb; David Tipling 106cr; Dave Watts 95t; **naturepl.com:** Bryan & Cherry Alexander 161bl; Matthias Breiter 91tc; **NHPA / Photoshot:** James Carmichael Jnr 113bc; James Carmichael Jr. 85cr; Stephen Dalton 121cla, 121cra; Daniel Heuclin 117tl; Cede Prudente 120tr; James Warwick 84tl; **NOIRLab:** NSF / CTIO / AURA / D.Munizaga 8br; **PA Photos:** AP Photo 257tc, 259c, 262l, 266cr; Carl Bento / AP 92cb; US Army 265tr; **Laurie Hatch Photography:** 20; **Photolibrary:** 173tc; Michael Fogden / Oxford Scientific (OSF) 101cr; Image100 171c, 171cr; North Wind Pictures 202br; Oxford Scientific (OSF) 108bc; Alain Pol 280; Lew Robertson 165bc; **PrairieHill Photography USA:** 115bc; **Rex Shutterstock:** Zuma / Shutterstock 215crb; **Science & Society Picture Library:** 252c, 252cra; **Science Photo Library:** 256bc, 256br; AJ Photo 256tl; ALIX

247cl; Charles Angelo 119br; A. Barrington Brown 246br; John Bavosi 246cr; Andrew Brookes / National Physical Laboratory 249cr; Carolyn Brown 188bl; BSIP, Cavallini James 284bl; Dr Jeremy Burgess 87tr, 88tc, 115clb; Claude Nuridsany & Marie Perennou 121clb; Russell Croman 31bc, 31bl, 31cl, 31cr, 31cra, 31tc (moon phases), 31tl, 53tr; Andy Crump 256cc; Christian Darkin 257br, 269cra; Michael Donne, University of Manchester 249bc, 249br; John Durham 87l; Eye of Science 277bc; Peter Faulkner 85cl; Dante Fenolio 49clb; Mauro Fermariello 248tr; Clive Freeman / Biosym Technologies 223b, 298-299; Mark Garlick 15bc; GE Medical Systems 239tl; Steve Gschmeissner 85cra; Pascal Goetgheluck 269cr; Johnny Greig 261bl; Neal Grundy 238-239c; Steve Gschmeissner 85ca, 285tr, 286tr; Gusto Images 257bc, 275br; Tony & Daphne Hallas 19cra; David A. Hardy 228t; David Hardy 11br; Roger Harris 237t; George Holton 186t; The International Astronomical Union 14-15cr; Makoto Iwafuji 247tr; Adam Jones 38br; James King-Holmes 247br, 247tl; Edward Kinsman 90c, 221tc, 238c, 238cb; Ted Kinsman 230bl; K.H. Kjeldsen 123br; Mehau Kulyk 281tr; Andrew Lambert Photography 225tr, 238t; Volker Springel / Max Planck Institute For Astrophysics 9cb; Martin Land 36cl; Lawrence Lawry 88br; Dr Najeeb Layyous 288br; Leonard Lessin 79cr; David Mack 288l; Dr. P. Marazzi 248bc; Richard Marpole 88tr; Tom Mchugh 109bl, 121crb; Medical RF.com 257tl, 279c; Prof. P. Motta / Dept. of Anatomy / University 'La Sapienza', Rome 277br; NASA 3cr, 23, 26br; NASA / ESA / B Whitmore / STScI-AURA 11t; NASA's Goddard Space Flight Center 52bl; NASA / JPL 234t; NASA / JPL-Caltech / STScI 12c; National Library of Medicine 247bl; National Museum, Denmark 256bl; NREL / US Department of Energy 43tr; David Nunuk 21bl; Claude Nuridsany and Marie Perenou 115bl, 115cl, 115fbl; Gregory Ochocki 51bl; Omikron 283bl; David Parker 282tr; Alfred Pasieka 268cra; Nancy Pierce 249bl; Philippe Plailly 14bl; Doug Plummer 46-47; Detlev Van Ravenswaay 25br; Paul Rapson 237bl, 249cl; John Reader 186bl; John Sanford 17tr; Chris Sattlberger 241tl; Friedrich Saurer 23crb; Science Pictures Ltd 123cr; Teddy Seguin: Osada / Seguin / DRASSM 251cla, 267l; Seymour 242br; Sinclair Stammers 189br; George Steinmetz 194-195; W.T Sullivan III 128tr; Mark Sykes 225bl; Andrew Syred 90b, 123bl, 246c; David Taylor 39br; TEK Image 240l; Geoff Tompkinson 5tr, 274c; US Air Force 269br; US Department of Energy 211br; US Geological Survey 26-27ca; Jim Varney 248cl; Jeremy Walker 88tl; Wellcome Dept. of Cognitive Neurology 281br; Dr Keith Wheeler 123cra, 123tc, 123tr; Dirk Wiersma 38tl; Charles D. Winters 225bc, 226t; Dr Torsten Wittmann 236br; Drs A. Yazdanil & D.J. Hornbaker 268br; Victor Habbick Visions 251tr, 256cr, 269t; **SeaPics.com:** 109tc, 112crb, 118t, 121bc; Gary Bell 93bc; Rudie Kuiter 108clb; **Shutterstock.com:** Ross D Franklin / AP 255crb; Hans Kim 290bl; SciePro 14cra (mercury), 16tl, SF photo 181cla; Chine Nouvelle / SIPA 27br; **SKA Observatory:** 21bc; **Still Pictures:** Randy Brandon 43tl; **Swissdent Cosmetics AG (www.swissdent.com):** 269bc; **teamLab:** 167cb; **Tesla Motors:** 1br; **TopFoto.co.uk:** 252ca; The Granger Collection 254bl; **University of Dundee Archive Services:** Michael Peto Collection: 93l; **Virtusphere, Inc.:** 264bl; **Wellcome Library, London:** Kate Whitley 282br; **Wikipedia, The Free Encyclopedia:** 23br

All other images © Dorling Kindersley
For further information see:
www.dkimages.com